Developments in the
Histories of Sexualities

TRANSITS:
LITERATURE, THOUGHT & CULTURE

Series Editor
Greg Clingham
Bucknell University

Transits is the next horizon. The series of books, essays, and monographs aims to extend recent achievements in eighteenth-century studies and to publish work on any aspects of the literature, thought, and culture of the years 1650–1850. Without ideological or methodological restrictions, *Transits* seeks to provide transformative readings of the literary, cultural, and historical interconnections between Britain, Europe, the Far East, Oceania, and the Americas in the long eighteenth century, and as they extend down to present time. In addition to literature and history, such "global" perspectives might entail considerations of time, space, nature, economics, politics, environment, and material culture, and might necessitate the development of new modes of critical imagination, which we welcome. But the series does not thereby repudiate the local and the national for original new work on particular writers and readers in particular places in time continues to be the bedrock of the discipline.

Titles in the Series

For a complete list of titles in this series, please visit
http://www.bucknell.edu/universitypress

TRANSITS

Developments in the
Histories of Sexualities

IN SEARCH OF THE
NORMAL, 1600–1800

EDITED BY CHRIS MOUNSEY

LEWISBURG
BUCKNELL UNIVERSITY PRESS

Published by Bucknell University Press
Co-published with The Rowman & Littlefield Publishing Group, Inc.
4501 Forbes Boulevard, Suite 200, Lanham, Maryland 20706
www.rowman.com

10 Thornbury Road, Plymouth PL6 7PP, United Kingdom

British Library Cataloguing in Publication Information Available

Library of Congress Cataloging-in-Publication Data
Developments in the histories of sexualities : in search of the normal, 1600-1800 /
edited by Chris Mounsey.
    pages cm. — (Transits: Literature, Thought & Culture)
  Includes bibliographical references and index.
  ISBN 978-1-61148-500-4 (cloth : alk. paper) — ISBN 978-1-61148-501-1
(electronic)
1. English literature—18th century—History and criticism. 2. English
literature—Early modern, 1500-1700—History and criticism. 3. Homosexuality
and literature—Great Britain. 4. Gender identity in literature—Great Britain.
5. Homosexuality—Great Britain—History—18th century. 6. Homosexuality—
Great Britain—History—17th century. I. Mounsey, Chris, 1959- editor of
compilation.

  PR448.H65D48 2013
  820.9'353—dc22   2012049964
  ISBN 978-1-6114-8688-9 (pbk : alk. paper)

C AROLINE GONDA AND I met in August 2000 at the annual conference of the British Society for Eighteenth-Century Studies, held at Aberdeen University. Our first conversation was marked by our sadness at what we felt was the exclusion of the lives of people like us—or at least of our same-sex loving foremothers and forefathers—from the history of sexuality that was then at its height in the dominant theoretical approach, Queer Theory. The Foucauldian constructionist analysis which then dominated (and is still in the ascendant), for both of us, failed to pin down anything like the sexuality that we experienced in our own lives, in the search for its history. Sexuality, we believed, was the desire for and physical expression of sex acts by people for other people, and was only partially modified by the social and political world of those who desire in their historical context. The urgency of desire, we considered, exploded forth towards the object of desire, and, if recognized, reciprocated and acted upon, might lead to mutual physical enjoyment, and possibly love over the long term, whether between woman and man, woman and woman, or man and man. Following this belief in the working of sexuality, our personal experiences suggested to us that people in history must have felt the same way, that all of us, historical and modern people must have felt something of the same on our journeys to becoming homosexual subjects. The outcome of the journey for an historical person may have been set against a different context, and led to a somewhat different sense of being a sexual subject, but fundamental to the journey was the body and its desires, which, we believed, could be recuperated. Our conviction was so strong that we decided to hold a conference on eighteenth-century homosexuality to see whether we were wrong, and Foucault was right after all.

As we saw it, the problem with the Foucauldian analysis was that it ignored the glaringly obvious in its fear of essentialism. Based in poststructuralist methodology, Michel Foucault's *The History of Sexuality: An Introduction* employed the dictum "sodomy that utterly confused category"[1] to tread lightly around the problem of reference to the body since reference to things in the world has always been the heart of the philosophical conundrum that led to poststructuralism.[2] How does the mind know that the body is in contact with the world through its mental perceptions? The Foucauldian answer was to ignore reference to the body and to study only mental concepts, such as the social and political, and to ignore the body. Foucault's move was consonant with the methodology of the language-based poststructuralist project in which he was engaged. Originally a product of the French academy, poststructuralism derives its caution about the existence of the body and of other bodies in particular from Descartes' dualism, which influenced Edmund Husserl's *Cartesian Meditations*,[3] which were so hugely influential in many forms of poststructuralist analysis. David Jalal Hyder makes clear the particular link between Husserl and Foucault in "Foucault, Cavailles, and Husserl on the Historical Epistemology of the Sciences," where he writes about Foucault's key term "archaeology:"

> the notion of "archaeology" itself, a form of historical investigation of knowledge that is distinguished from the mere history of ideas in part by its unearthing what Foucault calls "historical a prioris". . . [is] derived from Husserlian phenomenology.[4]

But rather than working in the linguistic to theorize sexuality, Caroline and I believed that sexuality itself might bridge the gap between the mind and body by placing emphasis on sexual perceptions, desires and capabilities which might work in a different way from language.

Even though the subjects in a sexual relationship may be classified by their political and social condition, that set of values does not mask the basic desires, or the response of the body to those desires. If a king commands his footman to sodomize him, the footman might be personally inclined to do so or he might not, but he will try to do what the king commands because of his subordinate role. However, the king cannot command the footman to desire him, or to maintain an erection out of desire for him. At the heart of this example is the irrefutable logic of the body and its mind's desires. The king may crave the footman's physical attention, but all his political power cannot answer the blank stare of unreciprocated desire. Even if the footman is able to use his own fantasy to bring himself to the point where he can fulfil the king's wishes, the act so consummated is not the same as a consensual and mutually desired act.

But this is not to equate and confuse the consensual and mutually desired act with modern homosexuality. The morganatic relationship between king and footman (Edward II and Piers Gaveston?) may have been as fulfilling as that between two modern men who have been politically and economically joined in a civil partnership. Likewise, the apparently equal civil partnership between a modern millionaire and a penniless partner may be fraught by the power dynamic of money and ownership. But while the physical is one level of a relationship and the social and political another, fundamental to it being a relationship at all has to be the physical response to the desire which links the mind and body.

This is not to say that the modern civil partnership is necessarily a perfect physical and mental union. The power dynamic of money and ownership might enslave the penniless partner in return for financial stability. It might mean that the penniless partner only entered into the civil partnership for money. But these possible analyses—and there are many more—all exist as real versions of the ideal physical and mental union, and the compromises of the real relationship are the stuff of life and literature. They ensure that understanding of the queerness of people is local and particular, for as Tolstoy says every family is unhappy in its own way.

The "logic of the body" suggests that Caroline and I might be arguing an underlying similarity that draws together the couple, which might be conceived of in terms of essentialism, the typical binary opposite used to argue against constructionism. As Diana Fuss has argued in *Essentially Speaking: Feminism, Nature & Difference*, essentialism and construction are in play with each other in everyday language,[5] so much so that at times it is hard to understand why essentialism has been cast as the enemy. I have always been fascinated by Luce Irigaray's poetic, complex and beautiful analyses, particularly after I translated *Amante Marine: De Friedrich Nietzsche* as part of my Master of Arts in Continental Philosophy. What is so wonderful about Irigaray's work is that it does not reduce essentialism to the bland idea that we are all alike, and that if we have an essence it will express itself willy-nilly. If we can classify Irigaray as an essentialist the category applies because she offered in her earliest work, 'This sex which is not one' as a counter metaphor to Lacan's phallus in order to close the distance between language and meaning inherent in patriarchal discourse. An oft quoted passage from *This Sex* gives an account of écriture feminine derived from the sexual anatomy of women:

> Thus, for example, woman's autoeroticism is very different from man's. In order to touch himself, man needs an instrument: his hand, a woman's body, language . . . And this self-caressing requires at least a minimum of activity.

> As for woman, she touches herself in and of herself without any need for mediation, and before there is any way to distinguish activity from passivity. Woman 'touches herself' all the time, and moreover no one can forbid her to do so, for her genitals are formed of two lips in continuous contact. Thus, within herself, she is already two but not divisible into one(s)-that caress each other.[6]

The metaphor (if it can be called a metaphor, since believing Irigaray means that no meaning need be carried across) uses the constant touching of the lip(s) of the vagina to close the gap between word and meaning (signifier and signified) that Lacan's phallus explores in "The Mirror Stage."[7] In Irigaray's metaphor words are in constant contact with their meaning(s) like the lip(s) of the vagina, and meanings change and alternate between multiple senses like waves of the sea: there is no need for Lacan's fortress and rubbish heap since no sense is excluded. Thus her essentialist metaphor leads us to the poetic in language, écriture feminine, which disrupts masculine goal directedness: straight talk. And in this way it is queer in a similar sense to Foucault's "utterly confused category."

However, Irigaray's metaphor is problematic as it begins from autoeroticism. Where Lacan's erotic metaphor of the phallus might be completed with the circle of the man's own hand, as Irigaray notes, it may also be completed by an "instrument . . . a woman's body, language:" that is, by communication with another. Irigaray's autoeroticism is in-turned and communicates only with itself. The endless productivity of her language is only to be understood by herself. Or, as part of the feminist movement, understood by another woman who could realize the metaphor of the vagina.

A development of her own ideas and Lacan's, Irigaray's later book *Amante Marine* offers a new metaphor (that word again) which retains something of the Mirror Stage but in a doubled sense that goes some way to encapsulate meaning beyond the self-understanding of auto-eroticism. The book describes her philosophical position with regard to the philosophy of Nietzsche in something more than dialogue or dialectic with the (male) person of Nietzsche, in a mix of écriture feminine and straight talk. If we look at any section we can see that the words do not make grammatically pure sentences, and thus the meaning(s) are multiple and supple, but there is a theme (a goal-directedness?): a critique of Nietzsche, who is addressed in the title and Derrida, who is addressed as "Tympan" on the first page of the book. I have chosen a section in which there is one of the most clear expressions of a double mirroring between the narrator and her interlocutor:

Corps différents, cela sans doute fait la semblance. Car, en l'autre, comment se retrouver sinon en y jetant aussi son même? Et, entre toi et moi, n'y aura-t-il toujours cette pellicule qui nous sépare?

Que tu te mires en moi, si en toi aussi je puis me refléter, ces rêves illimitent nos lieux. Mais si je garde tes images et que tu te dérobes à me rendre les miennes, c'est prison que ton même. Paralysie l'amour de toi. L'univers mouvant de nos mirages entrelacés devenant cerne miroitant de ton monde. La nuée de nos ébats, nuage qui masque le soleil, ou qui ferme l'horizon.[8]

[Different bodies, that no doubt makes the likeness. For, in the other, how is one to find oneself except by also throwing one's self-same (son même) there? And between you and me, will there not always be this film that keeps us apart?

If you were to gaze on yourself in me, and if in you also I could find my reflection, then those dreams would unlimit our spaces. But if I keep your images and you refuse to give me back mine, your self-same (ton-même) is but a prison. Love of you but a paralysis. The moving universe of our entwining mirages becomes the mirroring outline of your world. The mists rising from our encounters become a cloud blotting out the sun, blocking off the horizon.]

I do not want to repeat my own attempts at translating the book here.[9] Nevertheless, to begin with the second paragraph, we read that in order to describe communication between male and female, Irigaray has expanded her metaphor of the vagina's lip(s) into "L'univers mouvant de nos mirages entrelacés" [The moving universe of our interlaced mirages]. In the masculine world of Nietzsche, this becomes "cerne miroitant" [bruising mirroring], from which act of "love" each takes to themselves a view of the other that is not really the other, it is one's own version of the other (ton-même rather than son-même). We mistake what we think of as mirrored of ourselves in the other, for the other. If the other does not fit with what we expect of it we punch it in our anger—we knock it into shape.

All this derives from the fact that she, like Foucault, holds the other suspect, which Irigaray suggests in the first sentence of the first paragraph of the quote: "Corps différents, cela sans doute fait la semblance." "Semblance" does not suggest a resemblance or likeness, but as in the English phrase "a semblance of order" there is a suggestion of untruthfulness or unreality behind an appearance. Therefore, in order to find [retrouver] the other across the "pellicule qui nous sépare" [the film that separates us] one casts oneself in the role of the other: "y jetant aussi son même."

Typical of écriture féminine, Irigaray's choice of words does not lead to a simple (straight talking) understanding, but a series of partially interlocking dynamics. Thus, finding the other is given the word "retrouver" which literally means to rediscover, but the rediscovery is not simply a "finding again." A second complex dynamic between "son-meme" [his ownmost self] and "ton-meme" [your ownmost self], also exists, where in the search for "him" "he" is lost as "he" becomes "yours" in the process of finding. However, at the same time, the knowledge that "he" might have an "ownmost self" is itself an act of mirroring, a "rediscovery": a belief that "he" is like you. These dynamics, I would argue, are what is contained in the idea "L'univers mouvant de nos mirages entrelacés."

In her essentialism, Irigaray would seem to suggest the logic of the body, but these dynamics demonstrate that her acceptance of its existence is *not quite*. Thus, we would argue that Irigaray, like Foucault, is still bound up in the problematic of reference to the world, which derives from a Cartesian questioning of the existence of the other. In turn this leads both to theorize sexuality in complex ways, in ways that do not rely on a simple acceptance of physical existence: the logic of the body.

And if modern sexuality is so complex, diverse and varied, researching into historical sexuality might seem necessarily to be the more difficult because so much of the evidence is muted by a diffidence about directly addressing sexuality in language. Even when an early manual of sexual technique such as *Aristotle's Masterpiece* discusses which meats, herbs and drinks help a man maintain an erection, and mentions the desire that leads "naturally to copulation", there is no other explanation or discussion of sexuality and sexual technique than the bald statement that "it is Natural in young people to desire those mutual Embraces proper to the Marriage Bed."[10] Researching into deviant sexuality would therefore seem the more difficult still because much of the evidence derives from the failure to disguise deviance from those who might censure it: from court cases and horrified newspaper reports of evidence presented in court, probably more salacious than the bare facts. So, for example, much of the information we have about molly culture of the early eighteenth century comes to us from Ned Ward's breathless and indignant account of the Mollies' Club in his *The Secret History of Clubs* (1709), with all the usual exaggerations of sensationalist reportage. Ward's discomfiture when writing about molly culture is palpable. Either it does not fit with his feeling about how people ought to behave, or he is trying to hide his actual participation in its practices behind pretended disgust. Germane to the present argument is that

Ward's language about molly behaviour is complex because of the equivocal way he presents what they did, which appears to be most concerned about whether he will be open to public censure of what he has written. But when we read him we can nevertheless recuperate the bodies that acted and how they acted because he is writing in the empirical tradition of Newton and Locke where things (and bodies) stand behind the words, rather than in Descartes' dualist scepticism of the other and how it may be captured in language.

In the complexities of Ward's language, whether he believed he was writing in the language of regulation or acceptance, he balances accusations of the supposed vileness of molly practices with an intimate knowledge of the physical details of the practices of molly houses. We shall never know what he intended, but the tone of his prose should make us wary of believing his accusations because he seems to know so much about the various roles of the mollies, that he would seem to have actively participated in their Festivals. After descriptions of the men dressed as women acting as though they were women at a childbirth, Ward denounces them: "[T]hey . . . enter upon those Beastly Obscenities, and to take those infamous Liberties with one another, that no Man, who is not sunk into a State of Devilism, can think on without Blushing."[11] Nevertheless, we should not dismiss Ward as a shocked and outraged observer. Since no-one openly engaging in molly culture described it, we might read Ward's evidence carefully in order to get as close as possible to describing a night at the molly house, because one thing we can be certain of is that something was happening. Between the language of regulation and acceptance of molly culture may lie an accurate description of what Ward had seen or participated in. And in order to unpick the text to find out, we can ground our reading in the irrefutable logic of the body. So the essays in this collection will define what *reading carefully* between the languages of regulation and acceptance might be: that is, reading texts against what is identifiable as something that might be possible or likely to have happened, but toward which the text merely gestures.

A careful reading of Ward's description of a night at the Mollies' Club might suggest a description of the use of dildos and possibly fisting, practices which are common enough nowadays, and which happen regularly at sex clubs. First Ward describes the passive partner:

> Not long since, upon one of their Festival Nights, they had cushion'd up the belly of one of their Sodomitical Brethren, or rather Sisters, as they commonly call'd themselves, disguising him in a Woman's Night gown, Sarsnet Hood and Nightrale, who when the Company were met, was to

> mimick the wry face of a groaning Woman, to be deliver'd of a jointed
> Babie they had provided for the Purpose, and to undergo all the Formali-
> ties of a lying in. The wooden offspring to be afterwards Christen'd . . . [12]

While the modern practice of the communal use of dildos and fisting is usually
associated with leather and rubber fetish subcultures, this early coupling of it with
male to female cross dressing might be argued to fit with the similarity between
the anal insertion of a large dildo or a fist and giving birth, both of which mix
pleasure with extreme pain. Furthermore, the anal orgasm derived from a dildo
or fist might be associated with the vaginal orgasm, in a clear parallel between
male and female sexual pleasure at a time when the single sex theory was still a
commonplace. Mollies were men being women at a very basic level—they shared
non-ejaculatory orgasms—and so might dress as women since they felt as though
they were more like women than men.

That molly practice might be understood to be dildo play or fisting will require a little more evidence, but I would argue it is there in Ward's text. Describing
the other mollies' action with the passive man, Ward writes:

> One in a high Crown'd Hat, and an old Beldam's Pinner representing
> a Country Midwife, another busy Ape, dizn'd up in a Hussife's Coif,
> taking upon himself the Duty of a very officious Nurse, and the rest as
> Gossips, apply'd themselves to the Travelling Woman, according to the
> Midwife's Direction, all being as intent upon the Business at hand, as if
> they had been Women, the Occasion real and their Attendance neces-
> sary. [13]

The bevy of "women" "applying" themselves to the "travelling Woman," or woman
in labour, are all being schooled by the Midwife, who directs what happens, and
by the Nurse, who makes sure nothing goes wrong in the group's excitement. The
parallels between the group of men surrounding a sling fisting session in a sex club
and the mollies around the "travelling Woman" seem clear, where an experienced
fister (maybe the "Midwife") directs operations and the fistee's partner (maybe the
"Hussife" or housewife) makes sure his friend is not hurt. One may read of all
this in Gayle Rubin's essay "The Catacombs: A Temple to the Butthole", [14] where
Steve McEachern seems to play the role of midwife, and Cynthia Slater or Fred
Heramb the "Hussife", and of the "Bridal Suite" and the "Back Room," and even
the bar-room that stood at the front of the club which suggested the public bar in
which the mollies met.

But the question remains, of what is meant in Ward's text, by "birthing." It might seem fanciful to draw the parallel between dildos or fisting in a Leather club, and the Molly Festival: the men might just as well be buggering the passive man. But the final evidence of the use of the "jointed wooden babie" becomes clear in the doggerel verse which concludes Ward's account. Here Ward writes of the Mollies Club:

So That, at first, a T[urd] and They
Were born the very self same Way,
From whence they draw this cursed Itch
Not to the Belly, but the Breech;[15]

These lines suggest a founding myth that all Mollies are born through the anus rather than the vagina, which is the reason they derive their desire for pleasure ("Itch") from the buttocks ("Breech") rather than the vagina ("Belly"). The concatenation of the mollies' birth from the anus, and the idea of their re-enacting that birth would seem conclusively to demonstrate what is going on at the club Festival Nights. They re-enact their own births from an anus, by inserting the "jointed wooden babie" into one of their number's anus, and his groaning during the *delivery* is the anal orgasm they crave, and a mark of their own births as mollies. The ceremony is concluded with the Christening of the wooden doll in mockery of the social demand for heterosexuality that they have rejected, and which rejects them.

If it be argued that this description is too much based on the parallel with modern practice (and I have even heard it suggested that fisting was invented in San Francisco in the 1960s) or that it is too far-fetched, I would counter by pointing out that it is highly unlikely that the mollies met every evening to pull a wooden doll out of a cushion stuffed up one of their friends' shirts. Nor does Ward's text suggest it. Mollies prefer the *Breech to the Belly*. The myth of their birth from the anus made this the source of their pleasure, so the "Gossips" surrounding the "travelling Woman" would seem to be "Applying themselves" to the site of their pleasure. Since Ward makes no mention of penises in any of the many and varied terms that are used for that organ, there is no evidence that it be group buggery, and following the irrefutable logic of the body, the "Gossips" can only be "Applying" the "Babie" or their hands. Thus, I would suggest that my reading is not an anachronism derived from Gayle Rubin's description of current practice, though it was suggested by it, albeit what actually happened in the Mollies' Club will always be clouded in a degree of uncertainty. This is only one reading of the text. But nor can readings of molly practices be infinite or ultimately indefinite as poststructuralism suggests. The body has only a few members, and fewer orifices. If someone can convince me that Ward is writing about penises entering the "travelling Woman's" anus then I am happy to countenance it, but there cannot be many more interpretations since the logic of the body does not allow for them.

What my reading demonstrates is how we might recuperate the actions of a group of people at one moment in history and how they might have understood themselves as sexual subjects deviant from the heteronorm. Since they were out of the spotlight it is hard to give a final interpretation following the utmost academic rigour because of the nature of the evidence. But the evidence was read as it presented itself in the text, and shows that there was historical deviant sexuality, and my reading merely makes sense of it in terms of possible bodily actions. If even an eighteenth-century sex manual cannot describe the act of heterosexual copulation, what evidence of deviant sexuality there might be is unlikely to be very direct. However, if one follows the merest suggestion of deviant sexuality when reading historical texts, one opens oneself to being accused of reading oneself into history, or of skewing the evidence and reading it as more positive than it is. On the other hand, the illegality of (particularly male) same-sex practices in the eighteenth century would and did make homosexuals wary of letting others know about what they were writing about, which would either mean that sex was encoded in texts to be read by those who could understand the argot, or that it would be absent.

This analysis and rejection of the Foucauldian and Irigarayan methodologies in favour of the logic of the body, which I have just encapsulated, was several years in the making, and on the way there have been six Queer People conferences which have helped develop it. Three publications that derived from this series of conferences have marked steps on the way to it. Friendship and Same-Sex Love,[16] a special number of the *British Journal for Eighteenth-Century Studies*[17] and *Queer People: Negotiations and Expressions of Homosexuality 1700-1800.*[18] The first of these collections explored reasons for the shift away from the Foucauldian analysis of sexuality and constructionism, but without falling into essentialism or historicism. The second expanded upon these ideas, while the third featured two sections in which the theoretical constructionist and the essentialist methodologies were demonstrated to have always been dependent at some level upon one another.

The present collection explores the interplay between the political and personal in the light of the logic of the body. It finds that, as in the Ward text, in oppositions created by the official exclusion of banned sexual practices there is often a widespread acceptance of those outlawed practices at an interpersonal level. At different times and in different places, state legislation is seen to set up a "normal" by rejecting a particular practice or group of practices, a "normal" that is derogated by popular practice since the very banned acts themselves are thought at grass-roots level to be acceptable expressions of bodily desires, or at least acts which may be described. At the same time, as some of the essays demonstrate, the language of regulation also appears in popular cultural products doing the work of the legislature. But as all the essays show, it is language that speaks of the functioning of the body and its desires. In interrogating what has hitherto been seen as a theoretical position historically, the essays lend themselves further to an understanding of how the political and the personal can be recovered from historical evidence without the modern analyst imposing his or her own viewpoint on them, following the logic of the body.

George Haggerty argues in his essay: "Carefully thought out and brilliantly argued theoretical moves are not the window dressing on a disembodied literary criticism; instead, they offer the lifelines that can get us beyond the limits of our own historical imaginations."[19] Thus, writing in opposition to David Halperin he recommends reading strategies for texts by which to discover, in the proper sense, historical facts. Haggerty cites Valerie Traub's idea of "'cycles of salience' which resist the teleological accounts that often culminate in twentieth-century sexological recognition. These cycles do not necessarily follow development models or other attempts to make simple sense of a long and complex history of female-female relationships. They suggest episodic historical resonance."[20] Thus, Haggerty suggests that there is no possibility that accounts of female-female sexual relations in the past might lead to, or be examples of what we know now as the modern lesbian. Rather, incidences of women writing about their attraction to other women are seen as evanescent experiences, "explosively volatile"[21] moments that come into existence and then cease to exist, leaving hardly a trace. But the repeated recognition of minute traces points to their reality in the past.

Haggerty argues that reading history is as though we are seeing ghosts, a thought captured in a rigorous way by Carla Freccero, in the term *Spectrality*, the haunting relation between past and present. What Freccero means, Haggerty argues, is that when you look at history you see it as though it is a ghost, not as though it is the image of something you recognize in your daily experience. And you cannot be sure whether a ghost exists as an object of study, or whether it is a reflection of your own melancholy. As Haggerty writes: "That identification that is also a mark of difference—a ghostly recognition of sameness—is just what has been missing from sexuality studies."[22] Using these two powerful reading strategies Haggerty is able to understand the famous scene of sodomy from *Fanny Hill* in a remarkably untheoretical way.[23] It is no longer a simple interaction of hierarchy between the penetrated and the penetrator, but may be understood as an encounter intended for pleasure, and even possibly between two lovers. *Fanny's* (John Cleland's) sensational discourse can be picked apart and the bodies of the men glimpsed at in coitus through a crack in the wall seen to be moving in harmony in history.

In the same way, David Orvis argues that although Foucauldians have denied the possibility of same-sex coupledom as constitutive of self-awareness or a life-style option before the construction of modern homosexual consciousness, same-sex marriage can be clearly seen on the early modern stage in two forms; of the actors, men and boys; and in terms of the lack of future of the marriages portrayed (they terminate when the plays finished so are un[re]productive).[24] What is important for the present collection is the visibility of the same sex couples, and their recognition by the audience, which Orvis argues, asked real questions about real heterosexual marriages. These questions are most clear when playwrights turn to metatheatricals, and Orvis turns to *The Taming of the Shrew* to make his point. In the Induction, Christopher Sly is openly married to a cross-dressed page so the audience can laugh at its queerness, but then they see the real marriages between Katherine and Petruccio, Bianca and Lucentio, and the widow and Hortensio are equally queer.

Christopher Nagle's essay also addresses the possibility of being able to say truthful things about what was queer in history.[25] We might be better served, he argues, by attending to historically specific cultural manifestations on their own terms—and not simply to be dutifully historicist in our work, but also to shed light on "the peculiar sexual limitations of the present." Perhaps in this way we might continue moving beyond the residual traces of the essentialist versus constructionist debate as well as the equally pervasive—if less commonly explicit—assumptions about "anachronism" and "alterity," and thus about what counts as legitimate literary and cultural history.

Nagle's account of Ann Batten Cristall's poetry explores its queerness, not merely by searching for the lesbian gaze, but also from the poems' "randomness and irregularity", the strangeness of the names of the protagonists and the gothic subject matter with its special interest in decay, what Nagle calls Cristall's 'decompositional aesthetic.' Ultimately, Nagle argues that Cristall's poetry acts as a challenge to conventional historicism, with its heterosexual expectations. In particular, the construction of new narratives about gender and sexuality within histories of affective relations that refuse to reconsolidate familiar binaries (difference/sameness, repression/liberation, past/present, art/science) shifts the critical landscape away from what Goldberg and Menon call "the compulsive heterotemporality of historicism," but in a different direction from Goldberg and Menon. To a place where the body is alive and self-sustaining until it dies and decays.

Where the lesbian is for Nagle one of a number of queer elements that define an acceptable space for the non-standard body, in Marianne Legault's analysis of Ovid's overtly lesbian story of Iphis and Ianthe, when adapted for the French stage by Benserade, the story is read as ultimately reappropriating the lesbian embodiment as a masturbatory fantasy for the hetero-male. Iphis recounts the first erotically charged moments of her wedding night to her mother:

> J'oubliais quelque temps que j'étais une fille,
> Je ne reçus jamais tant de contentements,
> Je me laissais aller à mes ravissements,
> D'un baiser j'apaisais mon amoureuse fièvre,
> Et mon âme venait jusqu'au bord de mes lèvres,
> Dans le doux sentiment de ces biens superflus
> J'oubliais celui même où j'aspirais le plus,
> J'embrassais ce beau corps, dont la blancheur extrême
> M'excitait à lui faire une place en moi même,
> Je touchais, je baisais, j'avais le cœur content.
>
> [I forgot for a time that I was a young girl,
> I have never received so much contentment,
> I let myself go to my ravishment,
> With a kiss I appeased my feverish love,
> And my soul rose up to the brim of my lips,
> In the sweet sensation of these excessive goods
> I forgot even that, to which I aspired most,
> I kissed this beautiful body, whose extreme whiteness
> Excited me to open myself to it,
> I touched, I kissed, I had a contented heart.][26]

What we see here is an unusual representation of lesbian love for the period, one that seems to accept the physical union of two women. However, far from admitting a possibility that Ovid had so vehemently denied, that is, the female homoerotic, Legault argues that Benserade renders this lesbian erotic representation only to better emphasize what the play portrays incessantly: its ridiculousness. Benserade even comments: "And to make theaters speak of us / Such an encounter is worthy of being staged" ["Et pour faire parler les théâtres de nous /Une telle rencontre est digne qu'on la joue"] (act 5, scene 1). The lesbian, this odd being, must thus be placed on the comic stage, her "buffoon love" ["amour bouffon"], as defined by Ergaste, is to be witnessed in order that it can be mocked.

The lesbian heroine in Benserade's comedy, though at first glance promising, is in the end brutalized by the language of regulation in representations of the female body having sex with another seen as grotesque and the ridiculous, a textual assault that finally culminates in the collectively celebrated exile of the undesired lesbian body. In the author's vision, Legault argues, the lesbian body has no place in society. The play must rather succumb to the heteronormal and re-create Iphis in a "normal" role. And this from a Libertine writer is queer indeed.

Clorinda Donato's essay on Alessandro Verri's novel *The Adventures of Saffo* (1783), makes a more positive claim, but along similar lines as Legault, about the language of regulation of homosexual roles and practices in popular Italian fiction. Donato notes that Margaret Reynolds and Joan De Jean argue that Verri's novel, which draws Sappho as a heterosexual rather than a homosexual, is a negative representation of women. On the contrary, Donato reads the unqueering of Sappho as a positive step, and necessary, since it is part of a tradition of reading women's cultural agency as important and commonplace. She argues that neither Reynolds nor De Jean considered the Italian literary context of Verri's *Sappho*, which praised the intellect of the woman poet. Verri's novel, in fact, restores a positive connotation to the term Sapphic as the descriptor of the woman who writes poetry. This reappropriation of the term, Donato notes, served Madame de Staël, for whom Verri's work became the model for her novel Corinne, ou l'Italie. And Staël's highly autobiographical account of being a writer, embodied in the poet, Corinne, was fashioned on the biography of Maria Maddalena Morelli, or Corilla Olimpica, her name in Arcadia. But the term "Sapphic" which these women could now use of themselves as indications of their female excellence would still hold in them the possibility of homosexuality.

Developing the idea of crisis in the language of regulation is Chris Roulston's essay on the Woods Pirie trial. In this most complex case, where a mixed race schoolgirl accuses her teachers of being in an active lesbian relationship, the Scottish courts were perplexed by the fact that they could not come to a decision because no crime had been committed: lesbianism has never been a crime in England or Scotland. What did it mean, then, to be accused of an act and to come before the law, on the basis of a 'crime' that the law did not recognize? While the judges on both sides were unanimously repelled by this "disgusting subject", it nevertheless eluded the epistemological frame of the law itself. The task of the judges, therefore, was to rule on the truth or falsehood of the accusation of deviant female sexuality while simultaneously confirming that its non-representation within the law was the logical reflection of its non-existence. Roulston argues that what happens is an endless cycling through the available regulating discourses of race, class, and colonialism, none of which can latch onto the evidently knowable thing (lesbianism), because it has no legal status. What is interesting too is the endless recycling of the plot of the trial, into essay, play and two filmed versions. The essay demonstrates the fact that our desire to see and to understand outweighs our initial shock at being confronted by something new and undefined, because, though excluded from (the) language (of the law) it could be understood in relation to the logic of the body and its desires.

Sally O'Driscoll's essay explores the language of regulation and acceptance in an account of two apparently similar types of bodies well known in the eighteenth century: the fop and the molly. Each is a form of effeminate masculinity, the former acceptable, and the latter not. This is because, O'Driscoll argues, that "following on the heels of rake and fop, the molly supposedly combines sodomy with effeminacy, providing modern readers with a recognizable figure—one who is familiar because the language of sexuality and the language of gender presentation come to seem inseparable by the twentieth century." It is this cross historical recognition which is important here, for O'Driscoll is not making an identification of an essential transhistorical self, but rather attempting to understand the distinction between foppish effeminacy and molly transvestism as an analogy to the modern tension between transgender and transsexual identities, a tension that can be summed up as an opposition between a postmodern, transgender, queer celebration of the dissolution of sex and gender binaries, and a transsexual reclamation of precisely those binary identities.

Thus, O'Driscoll brings us a careful study of two different kinds of effeminate masculinity: that which is associated with fops, and that which is associated with mollies. Her work in the archives of pamphlets brings new light to the opposition, pointing out how the eighteenth-century mind could distinguish between the effeminacy that led to sodomy, and that, which did not. And in so doing, the paper explores the popular image of the difference between two types of body that look the same, effeminate and male, but which are distinguished by the object of desire: desire for men and desire for women. Using the opposition between fops and mollies, O'Driscoll gives us an eighteenth-century version of the essentialism/construction debate, pointing out how in the fop, "habit can lead to effeminacy,

and thence toward sodomy," (construction) but concomitantly, this does not im-
bue the fop as necessarily sodomitical—which the (essentially criminal) molly *is*.
For, as O'Driscoll argues, the cross-dressed male molly does not attempt to pass as
female, because his cross dressing is not to show off his sexual proclivity—as the
passive partner in a sodomitical sex act, but to show that the molly is not ashamed
of his sexual preference. The molly created a social scene, and inhabited it joyously,
rather than cruising randomly in the hope of finding a partner.

Beginning from a similar starting point, Katharine Kittredge demonstrates
how the same failures in the twentieth-century distinction between transsexual
and transgender are visible in descriptions of eighteenth-century masculine
women. Where the terms transsexual and transgender attempted to trace a stable
sexual binary that could explain the different experiences of two types of people
whose feelings of sex and gender did not conform to the heteronorm, Kittredge
finds only a myriad of possibilities of different experiences. And it is the same for
eighteenth-century female to male cross dressers. Once again, their cross dressing is less an attempt to pass as the other sex, but rather both eighteenth-century
"breeches parts" and twentieth-century drag performances focus on the dual nature of the image presented—the heightened tensions created by the gender/sex
disparity that is clear to see.

Thus, Kittredge reads the celebrated female to male cross dressing actress,
Charlotte Charke as ultimately, chaotic and contradictory. Descriptions of her
that try not to define her as one thing or another, she argues "may be the best way
to understand ambiguous but clearly transgressive 'gender outlaws' like Charke.
Although such descriptions are not academically comfortable or intellectually satisfying, tolerating the co-existence of seemingly contradictory interpretations may
be the only way to retain some semblance of a true portrait of Charke," just as it is
in the twentieth-century attempt to define transsexual and transgender.

Thomas A. King discusses the meaning of language itself, in his essay "The
Sound of Men in Love." Taking as his starting point the fact that spoken language
is an embodied act, he explores the sounds of words to discern the loving from the
unloving between men in the comeliness of their language. In particular, the words
"I" and "you" are explored, pointing out, King argues, that friends wish to be able
to use the other pronoun for themselves. He explains that in humanistic discourse
friendship was a mode of yearning, in language, for a mutuality of placement, the
obligation to constitute oneself and one's friend as subjects of the same speech act,
to locate one and an other within the enunciative field of classical rhetoric. It is only
in the moment when language is spoken that it is possible to bring about this swap-

ping of subject positions which is, according to King, love itself: "recorporealization of self and other as "I" and "thou/you," called "love," was, and is, if illusively, specific to the speech situation, a consequence of those deictic acts through which the "empty signs" of "I" and "you" became "full," embodied by a specific addresser and a specific addressee; deixis offers the (illusory) promise that one can become "I" by addressing a particular "you" in a specific time and space." Thus, King reinterprets the page to stage argument in Shakespeare's *Tempest* using Castiglione's *Book of the Courtier* as a guide to humanistic language between same-sex friends.

Bringing the collection to a conclusion, Caroline Gonda's essay explores the crossover in the languages of acceptance and regulation of the body in the cases of two successful nineteenth-century transvestites, James Allen (a woman who lived as a man and was married to a woman) and Lavinia Edwards (a man who lived as a woman with another woman). During the life of each couple, they appear to have been accepted and to have passed successfully respectively as a heterosexual couple and as sisters; if anyone knew the truth, it did not attract comment. The language of regulation comes into play, however, in the form of the autopsy reports, which recorded James Allen as a 'perfect woman' and Lavinia Edwards as a 'perfect man'. Reports in the Times record how neighbours were shocked by the revelations, considering Allen to be a hermaphrodite or quarter man, speculating that Allen's 'wife' might herself be a man in disguise, and suggesting that Edwards must be the father of his 'sister's' child, which was born several months after his death. Extensive coverage of both cases in newspapers and other publications, including works of medical jurisprudence, struggled and failed to make sense of these two "freaks of nature" and their cross-dressed lives. Though the logic of the body informs both cases, the body's desires escape knowledge or definition; and Gonda concludes that neither the authorized nor the unauthorized discourses available are able to regulate the irrepressible queerness of these extraordinary subjects.

What all these essays have in common is their various ways of circumventing the nullity of the Foucauldian analysis. I have tried here to draw out their common analyses of language, corporeality and desire, but this is to miss out on the individuality of each analysis, to which I shall leave each author to speak for themselves through their own words.

Notes

1. For example, both the signifier and signified derived from Saussure are mental concepts. Neither element of language is regarded as a thing in the world, in Michel Foucault's *The History of Sexuality: An Introduction*, trans. Robert Hurley, vol. 1 (New York: Vintage Books, 1978), 101.

2. For example, both the signifier and signified derived from Saussure are mental concepts. Neither element of language is regarded as a thing in the world, in Foucault's *The History of Sexuality*.

3. Edmund Husserl, *Cartesian Meditations: An Introduction to Phenomenology*, trans. Dorion Cairns, 12th ed. (Dordrecht: Kluwer Academic Publishers, 1999).

4. David Jalal Hyder, "Foucault, Cavailles, and Husserl on the Historical Epistemology of the Sciences," *Perspectives on Science* 11, no 1 (2003): 107.

5. Diana Fuss, *Essentially Speaking: Feminism, Nature & Difference* (New York: Routledge, 1989). I have discussed this in more detail in the "Introduction," *Queer People: Negotiations and Expressions of Homosexuality, 1700-1800*, eds. Caroline Gonda and Chris Mounsey (Lewisburg, PA: Bucknell, 2007).

6. Luce Irigaray, *This Sex Which is Not One*, trans. Catherine Porter with Carolyn Burke (Ithaca, NY: Columbia University Press: New York, 1985), 24.

7. Jacques Lacan, "The Mirror Stage as Formative of the Function of the I as revealed in Psychoanalytic Experience," in *Écrits: A Selection*, trans. Alan Sheridan (London: Tavistock, 1977), 1-7.

8. Luce Irigaray, *Amante Marine: De Friedrich Nietzsche* (Paris: Minuit, 1980), 20-21. The official translation by Christine Gill, from *Marine Lover of Friedrich Nietzsche*, (New York: Columbia University Press, 1991) which follows the French, does scant justice to Irigaray's complexity.

9. I was in contact with Luce Irigaray in 1989 about a translation, but did not pursue the project to completion as I believed it to be impossible since—more than usual in wrestling the source into the target language—the French words do not correspond adequately in all their multiple meanings with English equivalents.

10. Anonymous, *Aristotle's master-piece completed in two parts: the first containing the secrets of generation, in all the parts thereof. Treating, of the benefit of marriage, and the prejudice of unequal matches, signs of insufficiency in men or women; of the infusion of the soul; of the likeness of children to parents; of monstrous births; the cause and cure of the green-sickness: a discourse of virginity. Directions and cautions for mid-wives. Of the organs of generation in women, and the fabrick of the womb. The use and action of the genitals. Signs of conception, and whether of a male or female. With a word of advice to both sexes in the act of copulation. And the pictures of several monstrous births, &c. The second part, being a private looking-glass for the female sex. Treating of the various maladies of the womb; and of all other distempers incident to women of all ages, with proper remedies for the cure of each. The whole being more correct, than any thing of this kind hitherto published.* (London: printed by B. H[arris]. and are to be sold by most booksellers, 1697), 1-2.

11. Edward [Ned] Ward, *The Secret History of Clubs: Particularly the Kit-Cat, Beef-Stake, Vertuosos, Quacks, Knights of the Golden-Fleece, Florists, Beaus, &c. with their original* (London: 1709), 287.

12. Ward, *The Secret History*, 285.

13. Ibid., 285-6.

14. In Mark Thompson, ed., *Leatherfolk: Radical Sex, People, Politics & Practice* (Los Angeles: Alyson Books, 1991), 106-18.

15. Ward, *The Secret History*, 299.

16. Caroline Gonda and Chris Mounsey, eds. "Friendship and Same-Sex Love," in *Studies in English Literature* 46, no. 3 (2006).

17. *British Journal for Eighteenth-Century Studies*, 29, no. 2, (2006).

18. Gonda and Mounsey, *Queer People*.

19. Chapter 1 below, 6.

20. Chapter 1 below, 3.

21. Chapter 1 below, 3.

22. Chapter 1 below, 7.

23. John Cleland, *Memoirs of a Woman of Pleasure* 2 vols., (London: 1749), vol. 2, 175.

24. Chapter 2 below, 19.

25. Chapter 3 below, 50–51.

26. Isaac de Benserade, *Iphis et Iante (1634)* (Paris: Lampsaque, 2000), act 5 scene 4.

THE HISTORY OF HOMOSEXUALITY RECONSIDERED

George E. Haggerty

IN THIS ESSAY, I want to talk about some of the issues facing those of us concerned with the histories of homosexuality. Some time ago, David M. Halperin and I engaged in a debate over the erotics of friendship—that's a debate I will return to today—and in print we have registered vastly different opinions about the usefulness of the thoughtful categorizations Halperin offers in his own work in this field.[1]

Why Do I Disagree with David Halperin?

In *How to Do the History of Homosexuality*, Halperin lays out a very clear outline of historical possibilities, and he develops a series of categories that emerge from his analysis of classical and medieval models. In addition to separating sodomy and friendship as categories that rarely overlap, Halperin also distinguishes "effeminacy," which is a different category from either and with which it rarely coincides, from "inversion." All these categories are distinguished from the twentieth-century "homosexuality," which is many things, including, at times, everything listed in the earlier categories.

After distinguishing "homosexuality" from the other four categories, Halperin notes:

> All of the final four traditional, post-classical, or long-standing categories ("effeminacy," "paederasty/sodomy," "friendship/love," "passivity/inversion") depend critically on notions of gender. This is obvious in the case of effeminacy and passivity/inversion, but it is also true of paederasty/sodomy and friendship/love, since they are defined by the male subject's

embodiment and performance of traditionally masculine and masculin-
izing norms, just as effeminacy and passivity/inversion are defined by the
male subject's violation of them. In these traditional systems of sex and
gender, the notion of "sexuality" is dispensable because the regulation of
conduct and social status is accomplished by the gender system alone.[2]

This is a fascinating proposition, and I am happy to imagine its usefulness in discussing classical and medieval works and even early modern ones. But when I try
to apply these categories to the eighteenth century, I find them frustrating. I have
argued against Halperin's insistence that expressions of love between men, such
as those in heroic drama or in personal letters, cannot be erotic.[3] Halperin argues
that erotic pleasure is excluded from friendships and that the love expressed there
is to be distinguished from what he calls "sexual love." "Sex is a hierarchy," he says
in describing the fifteenth-century Florentine arrests, "not mutuality, sex is something done to someone by someone else, not a common search for shared pleasure
or a purely personal, private experience in which the larger social identities based
on age or social status are submerged or lost."[4]

When I confront English culture, society, and literature in the eighteenth
century, I feel that it is worth arguing for a different model of how male-male
desire was expressed and understood. In the past I have tried to "complicate our
understanding of male-male erotic pleasure" by looking at specific eighteenth
century examples. "Until we understand that emotional bonds can be as erotic as
much of what qualifies as 'sodomy' (or often more erotic)," I have argued, "we will
fail to see the full range of male relations in eighteenth century England."[5]

It seems to me that the argument here is more than one of semantics. As
his comments above suggest, Halperin sees gender as the organizing principle in
sexual encounters between men. This certainly allows for men to have sex with
one another without compromising their own masculinity, much the way the poor
immigrant boys in George Chauncey's *Gay New York* can use sex as a means of survival without compromising their own "straight" status.[6] I see nothing wrong with
this argument, but I do think that in its very rigor it might blind us to examples of
same sex desire that defy the tenets of gendered socialization. The eighteenth century offers examples that defy these categorizations, to be sure; but I am not sure
what that means. I don't think that we can claim the beginnings of the modern
homosexuality in the Restoration playhouse or in the novels and personal writings
of the eighteenth century. It is more complicated than that. I am trying to explain
why certain examples don't fit these categories and how we can best describe what
they do represent. This is really a question about our relation to the past.

What Other Models for the History of Sexuality are Available?

While many of us have been trying to make sense of the history of male homosexuality, other historians of sexuality, not perhaps as hamstrung by Foucault's pronouncements, have made very different cases about the implications of same-sex desire in the past. I want to talk briefly about the work of two such historians, whose essays are included in *The Blackwell Companion to Lesbian, Gay, Bisexual, Transgender, and Queer Studies*, which I edited with Molly McGarry.[7] The first is Valerie Traub, whose essay, "The Present Future of Lesbian Historiography," articulates an historical notion that has not been previously articulated:

> I . . . want to register a shift in my own thinking toward an engagement with the following tripartite hypothesis: 1) There exist certain recurrent explanatory meta-logics which accord to the history of lesbianism over a vast temporal expanse a sense of consistency and, at times, uncanny familiarity. 2) These explanatory meta-logics draw their specific content from perennial axes of social definition, which become particularly resonant or acute at different historical moments. 3) The recurring moments in which these meta-logics are manifested might profitably be understood as cycles of salience.[8]

These "cycles of salience" resist the teleological accounts that often culminate in twentieth-century sexological recognition. They do not necessarily follow development models or other attempts to make simple sense of a long and complex history of female-female relationships. They suggest episodic historical resonance and occasional conflation of forces to produce a different kind of visibility. Traub explains her concept this way:

> Such cycles of salience indicate symptomatic preoccupations about the meanings of women's bodies and bonds. . . . These cycles [are not], precisely, continuity—if by that we mean an unbroken line connecting the past to the present. It is less that there exist transhistorical categories that comprise and subsume historical variation than that certain perennial logics and definitions remain useful, across time, for conceptualizing the meaning of female bodies and bonds. Emerging at certain moments, silently disappearing from view, and then re-emerging as particularly relevant (or explosively volatile), these recurrent explanatory logics seem to underlie the organization, and reorganization, of women's erotic life.[9]

This strikes me as a profoundly important observation, and I have to wonder how far-fetched it would be to imagine that male relations could function similarly. Male friendship may not be as mystifying as female friendship, in part because it does not lie outside the realm of discourse, as, in a masculinist culture, female friendship often does. Still, I think male friendship harbors as many sites for erotic attachment. Those of us studying the literature of male affection might be especially sensitive to the kinds of salience that Traub describes. If we notice 16th-, 17th-, and 18th-century episodes of male-male relations—in the plays and letters of the Elizabethan Age; in and around the cultural activities of James I, or in the letters of Thomas Gray and his contemporaries, for instance—we don't necessarily need to string them together in continuative or trans-historical relation.[10] Rather than insisting, that is, on discriminating sodomy and friendship, or effeminacy or inversion, as separate categories, we might imagine whether the history of male sexuality does not also deserve this kind of attention to the "organization, and reorganization, of [men's] erotic life." Traub goes on to explain her position in these terms:

> The methodological reassessment I am offering is made possible by a steady publication of studies over the past decade. Thanks to social and cultural history, as well as to an even larger body of work by literary critics analyzing cultural representations, we now possess a densely textured picture of what it might have meant for women to love, desire, and have sex with each other at various times in specific locales.[11]

Can it be true that these materials are more widely available for those doing the history of female relations than they could be for those interested in male relations? I don't really think so. But what makes the male sources harder to determine is the very use of friendship rhetoric to mask erotic relations. Men talk openly about their love for one another, and they often place this love at the pinnacle for male-male interaction. It is hard to imagine that erotics could be involved in these public celebrations of male relations; but at times, I am convinced, that is exactly what they do: in heroic drama, in elegiac verse, and in personal letters throughout the eighteenth century.

Key to this complexity is the rhetoric of friendship that Western culture articulates, most vividly, perhaps, in the writings of Michel de Montaigne. His essay "On Affectional Relations" articulates the concept of loving-friendship between men, which Montaigne sees as a "perfect union and congruity." He says: "In the friendship which I am talking about, souls are mingled and confounded in so universal a blending that they efface the seam which joins them together so that it cannot be found. If you press me to say why I loved him, I feel that it cannot be expressed except by replying: 'Because it was him: because it was me.'" Although Montaigne distinguishes this model of loving-friendship from the pederasty of the Greeks, he connects it to marriage: "For the perfect friendship I am talking about is indivisible: each gives himself so entirely to his friend that he has nothing left to share with another. . . . [I]n this friendship love takes possession of the soul and reigns there with full sovereign sway."[12]

Does this articulation render the affectional relations either more or less erotic? Can a marriage be more erotic than inter-generational sexual aggression? I would argue that it could and that the kinds of relationships that Montaigne describes are a sign that male intimacy often defies the category of "friendship" that Halperin and others have articulated.[13]

It remains for those of us doing the history of sexuality to look at those sources and consider once again how it might be possible to talk about love that means more than the non-erotic bond that these historians insist upon. I sometimes think the erotic is so central to friendship that the burden of proof should be on the other side. After all, who is to say that sexual attraction depends on hierarchy and/or that men who see themselves as equal cannot be motivated by an emotional bond that is also erotic? I think there are cycles of salience in the male English tradition as well. There are times when friendships seem tantamount to love affairs, and there are other times when they do not. That does not mean that friendship excludes the sexual; doesn't it rather suggest that friendship may exclude erotics at times and include it at others?

Another exciting essay in *The Blackwell Companion* is Carla Freccero's "Queer Spectrality: Haunting the Past." This essay develops a theory of historicism that can cause scholars of sexuality to rethink the kinds of connections they have been making to the past. Freccero quotes Jonathan Goldberg's study of Eduardo Galeano's *Memory of Fire*, which appeared in *Premodern Sexualities*, which she edited with Louise Fradenberg.[14] After considering Goldberg's essay, which, she says, "combines a desire to un-write the retrospection of historical accounts of the conquest with a deconstruction of the implicit heteronormativity of historical continuity," Freccero develops a notion of a haunting relation between past and present:[15]

> Like Goldberg, I wish to explore the ways a queering of history and of historiography itself reworks teleological narratives of reproductive

futurity that locate in a culminating endpoint the "truth" of the past and the present and thus may open up spaces of foreclosed possibility. At the same time, I want to think about the question of haunting—a mode of "precarious life"—as an alternative model for how queer history might proceed.[16] . . . Spectrality counters the teleological drive of hetero-reproductive futurity on the level of form . . . and proposes an alternative mode of nonlinear temporality that queries the melancholic attachments of some counternarratives of queer, on the one hand, and the illusion of a choice between "life" and "death," on the other.[17]

Spectrality enables us to break through the impasses that have made doing the history of sexuality so fraught with accusation and mutual suspicion. In meditating on Freccero's essay, I find myself wanting to say that theory of this kind—the best queer theory, that is—can only help us. Carefully thought out and brilliantly argued theoretical moves are not the window dressing on a disembodied literary criticism; instead, they offer the lifelines that can get us beyond the limits of our own historical imaginations.

For Freccero,

Spectrality invokes collectivity, a collectivity of unknown or known, "uncanny" (both familiar and yet not) strangers who arrive to frequent us. To speak of ghosts is to speak of the social.[18] Spectrality also acknowledges fantasy's constitutive relation to experience. It suggests that fantasy is the mode of our experiential existence, that it mediates how we live our desire in the world.[19]

Freccero uses the model of spectrality as a way of resisting the two powerful alternatives besetting historiography. The first is melancholy, in which the past is buried and then replaced with the language of lament. Freccero balances this historical distortion with another which she calls colonialism, which is the need to master and control the past.[20] In discussing Anne Cheng's *The Melancholy of Race*, Freccero explores the ways in which spectrality can replace the melancholic relation to the past and reveal the very things that heteronormative history has made invisible. Cheng asks: "what happens if the [lost, mourned] object were to return?" And she answers that "since Freud has posited melancholia as a constitutive element of the ego, the return of the object demanding to be a person of its own would surely now be devastating."[21]

Freccero expands Cheng's answer and pushes in a direction of her own:

"The return of the object demanding to be a person of its own" is one way to think about haunting, the object's return and its demand being what might be said to emerge when one is willing to be haunted, to be inhabited by ghosts. Further, the mutual recognition, entanglement, and disentanglement entailed by this event suggest a more complex relationship between difference and resemblance, alterity and identity (or "sameness"), than (heteronormative) discourses of identity normally allow. For, in order to enable the melancholic object-other to emerge and to demand from "within" the self, there must be identification, if not identity, between the subject and object. And yet, at the same time, for that object to demand, to become (a ghost), somehow to materialize, it must have a subjectivity of its own; it must, therefore, be other/different.[22]

While Freccero is talking mostly about colonial encounters and the impossibility of reading through "historical" accounts, she is also demonstrating ways to queer history. This project has exciting implications for the history of sexuality as well. The very notion of a spectral relation to the past, and the eerily suggestive account of sameness and difference that Freccero offers: this is the challenge to those of us doing the history of sexuality. Of course for the "melancholic object-other to emerge . . . there must be identification . . . between subject and object. And yet . . . for that object to demand . . . it must . . . be other/different." That identification that is also a mark of difference—a ghostly recognition of sameness—is just what has been missing from sexuality studies.

Tentative Musings

If I take my inspiration from Traub and Freccero; if, that is, I look for cycles of salience and approach the past in a spirit of spectral rather than an identitarian engagement, then how would the eighteenth century look? I have my favorite moments, as we all do, and for the purposes of this discussion, I have selected three with which I hope most people are familiar. These examples emphasize love and friendship, but they also introduce and perforce confuse other categories that are offered to explain male homosexual behavior. Let's see whether these new terms will help me to come to terms with them.

My first example comes from Restoration Tragedy. Halperin and I have disagreed[23] about how to read the character of Dolabella in John Dryden's *All For*

Love. At the first appearance of Dolabella in act 3 of the play, he is described as one "whom Caesar loves beyond the love of women," and he uses this lovability to seduce the wavering hero from the pleasures of Alexandria. Antony becomes wistful when Dolabella's name is mentioned in this context:

> He loved me too:
> I was his soul, he lived not but in me.
> We were so closed within each other's breasts,
> The rivets were not found that joined us first.
> That does not reach us yet: we were so mixed
> As meeting streams, both to ourselves were lost;
> We were one mass; we could not give or take
> But from the same, for he was I, I he. (3. 1. 90-97)[24]

Halperin's argument is that the identification these men share makes an erotic/sexual bond impossible, or at least unlikely. But as I pointed out at the time, Dolabella is a strange figure on which to hang this argument. Dolabella is coded as the hyper-sexual love object of both Caesar and Marc Antony, whom Cleopatra can easily enflame and use in her plot to keep Antony from deserting her. Surely Dryden did not choose this character to represent a kind of friendship that was "distanced" from the world of sexual love. More likely, he was trying to show how erotic passions function in the context of imperial power. As in Nathaniel Lee's depiction of Alexander and Hephestion in *The Rival Queens*, moreover, the love expressed here is a bond that adds grandeur to the characters it depicts.[25] Unlike Danny Glover and Mel Gibson in *Lethal Weapon*,[26] whom Halperin cites as exemplary non-erotic friends, Antony and Dolabella do not tease each other and the audience with the naughty possibility of same-sex erotic play. Rather, they express it openly, not as a sordid crime to be snickered about, but as a grand and ennobling sentiment that helps to measure their tragic greatness. Halperin wants to deny the possibility of love between friends in any situation in which this love might seem normative or celebratory. But when Restoration and eighteenth-century audiences encountered these classical models of friendship, surely they saw in them something exotic and exhilarating, something unlike what they saw in the world around them. If at the same time they could be inspired to see the possibility of a friendship imbued with eroticism, then that could have, if not a normative, then an idealizing force all its own.

My second example concerns a pair sometimes called the first gay couple in English literature. Of course I am talking about Captain Whiffle and his surgeon, Simper, from Tobias Smollett's *The Adventures of Roderick Random 1748*.[27] In discussing this foppish sea-captain, G. S. Rousseau says that the "portrait of Whiffle-the-sodomite, powdered, perfumed, and dressed in clothing so stereotypic that it must have been archetypal in the 1740s, is well worth deciphering since it may represent the first authentic description of the enduring male homosexual stereotype in modern culture."[28] Whiffle's dress is described in detail, and his "sensibility" is mocked. When Random enters his chamber to "bleed" him, he "found him lolling on the couch with a languishing air, his head supported by his valet de chambre, who from time to time applied a smelling-bottle to his nose."[29] Later, his regular surgeon Simper enters: "a young man, gayly dressed, of a very delicate complexion, with a kind of languid smile on his face, which seemed to have been rendered habitual, by a long course of affectation".[30] Smollett is of course satirizing Whiffle for "maintaining a correspondence with his surgeon, not fit to be named.[31] I have said elsewhere that whatever is true about this pair, whatever categories we might want to fit them into, we are looking at two men in love.[32]

But now I think it is possible to say even more. Smollett's experience in the navy and his long years on shipboard may have accustomed him to scenes such as the one he describes. The mid-eighteenth century obsession with versions of masculinity, as evidenced in the novels of Fielding, Sterne and Burney; as well as the notorious possibilities of shipboard romance that tales of piracy and other sea adventures make available; all these things make Whiffle and Simper both salient and hauntingly familiar.[33] It is not necessary to prove a sexual identity here. All we need to do is recognize these characters as the familiar prototypes that they are. Surely effeminacy is a short-hand for same sex desire in this case, and the friendship itself, as mired as it is in "affectation," has a spectral familiarity nonetheless. Contemporary materials suggest a cycle of salience in this case too, and, indeed, the phobic representation of two men with an enduring attachment to each other of course suggests that this couple would be recognized by those reading the novel, in the eighteenth century as they are today.

And finally, I would like to consider a case of outright sodomy, that between the two young men who make love in an inn, while Fanny Hill peers through a tear in the wallpaper, in John Cleland's *Memoirs of a Woman of Pleasure*.[34] Toward the end of *Memoirs*, Fanny tells of a short stay in a public house—an axle on her carriage had broken and she was waiting for repairs. From the window, she sees "two young gentlemen" come into the inn and take up the room next to hers. "I could just hear that they shut and fasten'd the door on the inside," she tells the reader, and then, after the search for a peep-hole, she finds a paper-patch, through which she can force her bodkin. She now "commanded the room perfectly, and could see my two young sparks romping, and pulling one another about, entirely to my imagination, in frolic, and innocent play."[35]

Fanny chooses to expose dark mysteries of this scene, and her narrative is structured so as to suggest that this encounter is for her (and for heteronormative culture?) a kind of primal scene.[36] Her account luxuriates in the eroticism the men share:

> The eldest might be, on my nearest guess, towards nineteen, a tall comely young man, in a white fustian frock, with a green velvet cape, and a cut bob-wig.
>
> The youngest could not be above seventeen, fair, ruddy, compleatly well made, and to say the truth, a sweet pretty stripling: He was, I fancy too, a country lad, by his dress, which was a green plush frock, and breeches of the same, white waistcoat and stockings, a jockey cap, with his yellowish hair long, and loose, in natural curls.[37]

Fanny's "sparks" are both in their teens, but she marks one as older and manly, and the other is coded as effeminate, countrified, very young. In so describing the boys, Fanny attempts to gender them, and it will come as no surprise to most readers that the elder boy is the active and the younger boy the passive participant in the sexual engagement that follows. She may use the pederastic language of older man and younger boy as a way of placing this encounter in a tradition she understands.[38] In any case, Fanny's description defies the pederasty model even as she uses it to shape her narrative.

As the account proceeds, the quality of erotic fascination (and horror) is deeply suggestive. Indeed, I would insist that the two years' difference in age (or less) makes it likely that these two boys are friends. The sexual encounter does not seem like an assault. These boys are so close in age, and so alike, that what the scene more actively suggests is a playful friendship that includes the sexual encounter that Fanny describes.

> Slipping then aside the young lad's shirt, and tucking it up under his cloaths behind, he shew'd to the open air, those globular, fleshy eminences that compose the mount-pleasants of Rome, and which now, with all the narrow vale that intersects them, stood display'd, and exposed to his attack: nor could I, without a shudder, behold the dispositions he made for it.

Fanny gives a more detailed account than was otherwise available at the time—in trial records or pornography—and she is seemingly less horrified at the implications of what she describes. In order to read what is going on, she uses the gender terms to which she has access, but surely Cleland insists that the reader see things more clearly than even his narrator does.

> First then, moistening well with spittle his instrument, obviously to render it glib, he pointed, he introduc'd it, as I could plainly discern, not only from its direction, and my losing sight of it; but by the writhing, twisting, and soft murmur'd complaints of the young sufferer; but at length, the first streights of entrance being pretty well got through, every thing seem'd to move, and go pretty currently on, as in a carpet-road, without much rub, or resistance: and now passing one hand round his minion's hips, he got hold of his red-topt ivory toy, that stood perfectly stiff, and shewed, that if he was like his mother behind, he was like his father before; this he diverted himself with, whilst with the other, he wanton'd with his hair, and leaning forward over his back, drew his face, from which the boy shook the loose curls that fell over it, in the posture he stood him in, and brought him towards his, so as to receive a long-breath'd kiss, after which, renew-ing his driving, and thus continuing to harass his rear, the height of the fit came on with its usual symptoms, and dismiss'd the action.

This scene of sodomy that also seems close to pederasty includes friendship and effeminacy as well. Halperin's categories are conflated here because a scene like this one displays all the complications of experience itself. The kiss that the older boy offers to the younger suggests a different kind of intimacy than any of the categories offer. The interaction is not simply one of hierarchy. These boys, so nearly equal in age, take equal pleasure from the encounter. The erotic play between them—the love-making, as it were—cannot be codified or gendered or identified in twenty- or twenty-first-century terms. The scene is moving precisely to the degree that it cannot be categorized in this way. That is why, in the end, the power of this scene is simply too much for Fanny to bear.

> All this, so criminal a scene, I had the patience to see to an end, purely that I might gather more facts, and certainty against them in my full design to do their deserts instant justice, and accordingly, when they had readjusted themselves, and were preparing to go out, burning as I was with rage, and indignation, I jump'd down from my chair, in order to raise the house upon them, with such an unlucky impetuosity, that some nail or ruggedness on the floor caught my foot, and flung me on face with such violence, that I fell senseless on the ground. . . .[39]

Fanny's unconsciousness brings this scene to a fitting conclusion because the "unconscious" is precisely where this visionary encounter image most probably resides. It is a cultural fantasy that both tantalizes and torments. In another essay I have cited Kaja Silverman, who discusses Freud's concept of fantasy, which she calls the "relation of daydreams and their unconscious counterparts." Silverman reminds us that "unconscious desire generally assumes the form of a visual tableau or narrateme" that is often "repressed" to the point that it becomes "fantasmatic": it "underlies a subject's dreams, symptoms, repetitive behavior, and daydreams."[40] In *Memoirs*, a case could easily be made that this "primal" encounter underlies Fanny's "symptoms," whose erotic life is shaped by her attraction to and repulsion at this scene.

The scene functions, that is, like a haunting. What fascinates me here is the degree to which it haunts the reader, as well, in a way that makes it always shocking and always new. Freccero told us that "spectrality counters the teleological drive of heteroreproductive futurity on the level of form." Is it possible to approach this scene in the terms that Freccero suggests?

I think so. I think we can look at this scene and understand it without pushing an identitarian agenda. I think we can let it work on us without trying to master it or colonize, or even categorize it in any way. I am tempted to call it, simply, a love scene, one of the few love scenes between two men that the eighteenth century offers. Freccero said that for the "melancholic object-other to emerge . . . there must be identification . . . between subject and object. And yet . . . for that object to demand . . . it must . . . be other/different."[41] What we encounter here is so recognizable as to encourage identification, as least for some of us, and at the same time, it is profoundly "other/different." Of course this scene is haunting, and the clearest relation we can establish is a spectral one. To make it anything else is to try to fit into categories that we have created. What sense would there be in that?

These approaches to the history of homosexuality by Traub and Freccero offer useful supplements to Halperin's work. They allow us to imagine the past and to see it differently. We can recognize connections to our own world and see them as such, but we can also mark as strange and unfamiliar those encounters we most want to claim. Fanny Hill falls unconscious after seeing two men make love because it is too much for her, and for her culture, to bear. The love these men share, if I can see love in their kiss, marks them as a threat to the culture of which they are a part. For one man to force his affections on a lower-status woman, boy, or slave: that is a question of gender, as Halperin argues. For two boys the same age to take equal pleasure in one another: that is sexuality.

Notes

1. This disagreement is given considerable play in *Love, Sex, Intimacy, and Friendship between Men, 1550-1800*, eds. Katherine O'Donnell and Michael O'Rourke (Basingstoke and London: Palgrave, 2003); see in this book my "Male Love and Friendship in the Eighteenth Century," 70-81; and also, David M. Halperin, "Introduction: Among Men—History, Sexuality, and the Return to Affect," 1-11, esp. 8n9.

2. David M. Halperin, *How to Do the History of Homosexuality* (Chicago: University of Chicago Press, 2002), 134-35.

3. Haggerty, "Male Love and Friendship," 72.

4. Halperin, *How to Do the History of Homosexuality*, 115.

5. Haggerty, "Male Love and Friendship," 73.

6. See George Chauncey, *Gay New York: Gender, Urban Culture, and the Making of the Gay Male World, 1890-1940* (New York: Basic Books, 1994).

7. George E. Haggerty and Molly McGarry, eds., *The Blackwell Companion to Lesbian, Gay, Bisexual, Transgender and Queer Studies* (New York: Blackwell, 2007).

8. Valerie Traub, "The Present Future of Lesbian Historiography," in *The Blackwell Companion to Lesbian, Gay, Bisexual, Transgender and Queer Studies*, Haggerty and McGarry, eds., 125-26.

9. Ibid., 126.

10. See Mario DiGangi, "How Queer was the Renaissance?" in *Love, Sex, Intimacy, and Friendship between Men, 1550-1800*, eds. O'Donnell and O'Rourke, 128-47.

11. Haggerty and McGarry, eds., *Blackwell Companion*, 126. Traub cites studies by herself, Harriett Andreatis, Terry Castle, Carolyn Dinshaw, Emma Donoghue, Lilian Faderman, Judith Halberstam, Susan S. Lanser, Lisa Moore, Valerie Rohy, Martha Vicinius, and Elizabeth Wahl.

12. Michel de Montaigne, "On Affectionate Relationships [On Friendship]," In *The Complete Essays*, trans. and ed. M. A. Screech (London: Penguin, 2003), 211-12, 215. See also Peter Nardi, "Friendship," In *Gay Histories and Cultures: An Encyclopedia*, eds. George E. Haggerty, John Beynon, and Douglas Eisner, vol. 2 (New York: Garland, 2000), 356.

13. For a similar discussion of this material, see George E. Haggerty, *Horace Walpole's Letters: Masculinity and Friendship in the Eighteenth Century* (Lewisburg, PA: Bucknell University Press, 2011), 6, 22.

14. Jonathan Goldberg, "The History that Will Be," in *Premodern Sexualities*, eds. Louise Fradenburg and Carla Freccero (New York: Routledge, 1996), 3-21.

15. Carla Freccero, "Queer Spectrality: Haunting the Past," in *The Blackwell Companion to Lesbian, Gay, Bisexual, Transgender and Queer Studies*, eds. Haggerty and McGarry, 195.

16. Freccero cites Judith Butler, *Precarious Life: The Powers of Mourning and Violence* (London and New York: Verso, 2004).

17. Haggerty and McGarry, eds., *Blackwell Companion*, 192.

18. Freccero's footnote: For an extended discussion of the ways spectrality differs from liberal individualist notions of 'private' haunting, including those that would read Hamlet as a narrative

of social disruption in favor of individual 'alienation' from the social, see my extended readings of Brown, Derrida, and Gordon in *Queer/Early/Modern* (Durham, NC: Duke University Press, 2005), chap. 5.

19. Haggerty and McGarry, eds., *Blackwell Companion*, 196.

20. Freccero discusses Brandon Teena in these terms and shows how both these impulses work in the queer appropriation of Brandon Teena:

"Both gestures—the melancholic and the colonizing—have worked to foreclose how he [Brandon Teena], as ghost, recurs in ways that are not so clear, and demands of us not a definition, but the creation of spaces where categorical definitions so dependent on gender and desire might prove affirmingly impossible. Using spectrality as our hypothesis, then, we might wonder what we would see and hear were we to resist identitarian foreclosures and remain open to ghostly returns." (Haggerty and McGarry, eds., *Blackwell Companion*, 197)

21. Anne Anlin Cheng, *The Melancholy of Race, Psychoanalysis, Assimilation, and Hidden Grief* (New York: Oxford University Press, 2001), 200n22.

22. Haggerty and McGarry, eds., *Blackwell Companion*, 205. Freccero's note:

"Psychoanalytic theories of subjectivity argue that subjectivity—the experience of thinking feeling embodiment—is, first and foremost, intersubjectivity, a relation to an other. In "Mourning and Melancholia," the essay that most vividly evokes the figure of "the other inside," Freud describes melancholia—the continued and ambivalent attachment to an object perceived to be lost—as a kind of incorporation, the taking in of the lost object so that it persists within the self and is preserved. See "Mourning and Melancholia (1917)," in *General Psychological Theory: Papers on Metapsychology*, trans. Joan Riviere, ed. Philip Rieff (New York: Simon and Schuster, 1991, repr. 1997), 164-79. Later, in *The Ego and the Id*, Freud extends the melancholic model to suggest that the ego itself is the "precipitate" of all the attachments to objects loved and then lost, and that it sublimates its attachment to—and contains the history of—lost others, who are then taken up as identifications. Further, for Freud the ego is always a bodily ego; there is a relay of sensation, felt to emanate both from without and from within. This relay maps a kind of psychic body that usually corresponds to the surface of the skin. See Sigmund Freud, *The Ego and the Id*, in *The Standard edition of the complete psychological works of Sigmund Freud (1920-1922), Beyond the pleasure principle, Group psychology and other works*. trans. James Strachey (London: Hogarth Press, 1955), esp. vol. 20, 212n17."

23. O'Donnell and O'Rourke, eds. *Love, Sex, Intimacy and Friendship*, 8-10, 11n9, 72-76.

24. John Dryden, *All For Love*, ed. David M. Vieth (Lincoln: University of Nebraska Press, 1972).

25. Nathaniel Lee, *The rival queens, or, The death of Alexander the Great acted at the Theater-Royal by their majesties servants* (London : Printed for James Magnes and Richard Bentley, 1677).

26. *Lethal Weapon*, directed by Richard Donner (1987; Burbank, CA: Warner Home Video, 1997), DVD.

27. Tobias Smollett, *The Adventures of Roderick Random, 1748*, ed. Paul-Gabriel Boucé (Oxford: Oxford University Press, 1979).

28. G. S. Rousseau, "The Pursuit of Homosexuality in the Eighteenth Century: 'Utterly Confused Category and/or Rich Repository?" *Eighteenth-Century Life* 9 (May 1985): 147; see also Cameron

McFarlane, *The Sodomite in Fiction and Satire, 1660-1750* (New York: Columbia University Press, 1997), 133-36.

29. Smollett, *Roderick Random*, 197.

30. Ibid., 198.

31. Ibid., 199.

32. George E. Haggerty, *Men in Love: Masculinity and Sexuality in the Eighteenth Century* (New York: Columbia University Press, 1999), 74.

33. Hans Turley, *Rum, Sodomy, and the Lash: Piracy, Sexuality, and Masculine Identity* (New York: New York University Press, 2001).

34. John Cleland, *Memoirs of a Woman of Pleasure* 2 vols., (London: 1749). This scene is one of the more frequently cited in discussions of sodomy in the eighteenth-century. In addition to McFarlane's analysis in *Sodomite in Fiction and Satire* (166-73), in which various critical commentaries on Fanny Hill are discussed, recent studies include: Lee Edelman, *Homographesis: Essays in Gay Literary and Cultural Theory* (New York: Routledge, 1994), 183-84; Kevin Kopelson, "Seeing Sodomy: Fanny Hill's Blinding Vision," *Journal of Homosexuality* 23, nos. 1-2 (1992): 173-84; Roy Roussel, *The Conversation of the Sexes: Seduction and Equality in Selected Seventeenth- and Eighteenth-Century Texts* (Oxford and New York: Oxford University Press, 1986). McFarlane claims that John Cleland's *Memoirs of a Woman of Pleasure (1749)*, ed. Peter Sabor. (Oxford: Oxford University Press, 1985), "is a sodomitical fantasy and, as such does not so much confound the novel's representational structures as lay them bare," (160).

35. Cleland, *Memoirs of a Woman of Pleasure*, 157.

36. In examining the spectacle of this scene, Cameron McFarlane notes that "Fanny's penetration into the scene of sodomy constitutes an interesting variant on what Kaja Silverman has called 'sodomitical identification.'" McFarlane, *Sodomite in Fiction and Satire*, 169.

37. Cleland, *Memoirs of a Woman of Pleasure*, 158.

38. For a discussion of the pæderastic tradition in the eighteenth century, see Haggerty, *Men in Love*, chap. 5; see also, George E. Haggerty, "Beckford's Pæderasty," in *Illicit Sex: Identity Politics in Early Modern Culture*, eds. Thomas Di Piero and Pat Gill (Athens: University of Georgia Press, 1997), 123-42.

39. Cleland, *Memoirs of a Woman of Pleasure*, 159.

40. Kaja Silverman, *Male Subjectivity at the Margins* (New York: Routledge, 1992), 160-61.

41. Haggerty and McGarry, eds., *Blackwell Companion*, 205.

QUEER RENAISSANCE DRAMATURGY,
SHAKESPEARE'S *SHREW*, AND THE
DECONSTRUCTION OF MARRIAGE

David L. Orvis

G IVEN THE WEALTH OF SCHOLARSHIP on the transvestite theater, it might seem cliché to take as my starting point the observation that on the Renaissance stage boy actors played the roles of female characters.[1] Indeed, over the past twenty-five years or so, studies of cross-dressing in English Renaissance drama have deliberated at length the cultural significances of compulsory cross-gender casting and of the profusion of cross-gender disguise plots.[2] In her landmark essay on the subject, "Androgyny, Mimesis, and the Marriage of the Boy Heroine on the English Renaissance Stage," Phyllis Rackin argued that the boy heroine was a contested site of signification, at first representing an androgyne, "a symbol of prelapsarian or mystical perfection," and then, as the period went on, becoming "a satirical portrait of the hermaphrodite, a medical monstrosity or social misfit, an image of perversion or abnormality."[3] Building upon Rackin's foundational work, feminist and queer scholars have continued to interrogate the precarious relationship between bodies and clothes. For example, in *Renaissance Clothing and the Materials of Memory*, Ann Rosalind Jones and Peter Stallybrass have suggested that Renaissance plays invited audiences to "speculat[e] on the boy actor" beneath the drag, a spectacle producing "contradictory fixations articulated through fetishistic attention to particular items of clothing, particular parts of the body of an imagined woman, particular parts of an actual boy actor."[4] Will Fisher extended this mode of inquiry in *Materializing Gender in Early Modern English Literature and Culture* to include what he calls "prostheses"—which "can be removed from the body [but which] also shape or materialize the body and self in important ways."[5] Of course, if sex and gender are malleable, then so too is identity. As Laura Levine has shown in *Men in Women's Clothing*, critics of the theater believed that cross-dressing on the Renaissance stage posed a serious threat to masculine identity in particular, as it showed "men are only men in the performance of their masculinity."[6] From this vantage, plays can be seen waxing philosophical, asking playgoers to ponder, in the words of Catherine Belsey, that vexing ontological question, "Who is speaking?"[7] In its original context, this question was asked of characters in Shakespeare's comedies, but as the robust scholarship on Renaissance theatrical practice has amply demonstrated, it could apply to virtually any character in any play as well as to any playgoer who may have accepted the perhaps irresistible invitation to speculate.[8]

I begin with this précis of scholarship on the transvestite theater because for all of its insights, it has overlooked what I want to argue is a salient aspect of Renaissance dramaturgy—the institutionalization of queer marriage. Indeed, although marriage scenes pervade the period's drama, the queerness of these marriages and the dramaturgic practices that enabled them have largely been ignored.[9] And yet, with the exception of foreign troupes employing female actors, plays performed in London's public and private theaters were put on by companies comprising men and boys, and so the vast majority of marriages staged for the theatergoing public excluded women players.[10] Oftentimes, of course, these marital arrangements were performed under the guise of mixed-sex marriages, with boy actors cross-dressing to play the roles of wives and wives-to-be. However, this did not efface the body of the boy underneath the drag. Rather, the "play-boy" (to use Lady Mary Wroth's term) and the character he portrayed sustained, only to exploit, what Michael Shapiro has called the "dual consciousness" of spectators.[11] As adduced by Shakespeare's fondness for female pages—among them, *Two Gentleman's* Julia; *Merchant's* Portia, Nerissa, and Jessica; *As You Like It's* Rosalind; and *Twelfth Night's* Viola—gender-play on the Renaissance stage was often a confounding experience for playgoers: "At any given moment, a performance of a disguised heroine-play could have emphasized any one of the three elements in the boy/girl/boy configuration without necessarily obliterating awareness of the other two. Because all existed within the spectators' consciousness, any one could have been played or merely flashed on the stage at a given moment."[12] Hence, even the most seemingly conventional of Shakespearean marriages (if such a thing exists) was ineluctably queer(ed), as playgoers remained keenly aware of both the mixed-sex marriages pursued in the plays and the man-boy marriages onto which they were superimposed.

The queer relationship between these marriages is what I propose to examine in this essay. In performance, they were both bound up in one another, the dramaturgic marriage enabling the plot-driven one, and distinct, as various metatheatrical gestures revealed, if only momentarily, the gender identities of the players. The queerness here, I would argue, is one of both gender and temporality. The prohibition of women from English troupes meant that boys (and occasionally men, as might have been the case with Lady Macbeth and Cleopatra) played the roles of wives, a theatrical convention that encouraged the dual consciousness Shapiro describes.[13] However, it is not as simple as saying a mixed-sex marriage is contingent upon a same-sex marriage. According to Fisher, "masculinity was not only constructed in contrast to femininity, but in contrast to boyhood; as a result, we can say that men and boys were quite literally two distinct genders."[14] Following this analysis, we have at least three genders involved in the staging of marriage. Matters are further complicated by audience perception, which, obviously, is never uniform. The distinction Fisher makes between men and boys is a case in point. As with all intellectual histories, it is hard to ascertain how widely known or accepted a concept was during a given historical period.[15] And even if we do assume that all or most playgoers recognized the boy as a distinct gender, his development as both a person and an actor, often signaled by his taking adult male roles in theatrical productions, invited conjecture about his gender identity. To put it another way, if boys often became men, and if play-boys often became adult male actors, then spectators may have pondered an actor's gender identity, which may have fallen anywhere along the gender continuum. In speaking about a queer Renaissance dramaturgy, then, I am aiming to open up, rather than dismiss or cordon off, possibilities for gender-play in the staging of marriage, and my readings of particular passages are intended to be suggestive rather than prescriptive.

The same is true for my approach to the queer temporality of staged marriages. As we shall see, this temporality is manifest in and by the coexistence and interdependency of dramatized or dramatic (that is, plot-related) and dramaturgic nuptials. While critics have rightly noted the many ways in which Shakespeare's plays undermine the very spousals they propose—one thinks of Isabella's silence following the Duke's proposal in *Measure for Measure* or the deferral of marriage the Queen announces in *Love's Labour's Lost*—the multivalent temporality of these plays simultaneously allows and forecloses marital futurity.[16] In *The Merchant of Venice*, for example, Bassanio and Portia marry. And yet, while the play may posit a marriage that continues beyond play's end, this future is always-already forestalled, if only because at some point the production must end. All at once, then, the marriage does and does not have a future. This applies to reproductive futurity as well. In *All's Well That Ends Well*, Helena may or may not be pregnant, and Bertram may or may not be obliged to marry her, but pregnancy never comes to term, no matter how many times the play (as Shakespeare wrote it) is performed.[17] In this sense, Shakespeare's marriages succumb to a kind of death drive, repeating compulsively while having no future, to borrow Lee Edelman's by-now familiar phrase.[18] This queer temporality is accentuated by dramaturgic marriage, also performed to a predetermined end, also restricted to the "two hours' traffic of the stage."[19] The actors participating in these marital arrangements re-performed them each time the plays were staged, and the repertory system required actors to wed multiple people in the same theatrical season—even in the same day. What is more, none of these unions were capable of producing children, and so dramaturgic nuptials defied the reproductive futurity alluded to in dramatized marriages. Staging marriage, then, both required and performed a queer temporality, as dramatized unions relied upon, at the same time that they were distinguished from and undermined by, non-procreative unions that had no future.

In examining the precarious relationship between the two kinds of marriage, I want to show not only that the English Renaissance stage queered all marriages—indeed, produced only queer marriages—but also that this deconstructive project exposed all marriages, even those performed offstage, as utterly performative in the Butlerian sense. According to Butler, "The replication of heterosexual constructs in non-heterosexual frames brings into relief the utterly constructed status of the so-called heterosexual original. Thus, gay is to straight *not* as copy is to original, but, rather, as copy is to copy. The parodic repetition of 'the original,' . . . reveals the original to be nothing other than a parody of the *idea* of the natural and the original."[20] Though the period I am interested in perhaps antedates the invention of heterosexuality and the rise to dominance of heteronormativity, Butler's argument about copies belying the authenticity of the original helps explain at least one of the ways in which dramaturgic marriage demystified the mixed-sex marriages permeating Renaissance drama.[21] I would add, however, that in this instance the act of deconstruction was also generative: at the same time that mixed-sex marriage was revealed to be a performance, new marriages, specifically those employed in the deconstructive projects, were put forth as viable marital configurations. In other words, the dramaturgic marriage, which critics often assume was invisible or meaningless, that is, not a marriage *as such*, either because it was a convention common to all troupes or because gay marriage as we understand it today was outside the period's discourse, was no less (but also no more) a marriage than those it facilitated.

This queer Renaissance dramaturgy is perhaps most obvious in plays that deploy metatheatrical conventions such as plays-within-the-plays and in theatrical polemics that debate the vices and virtues of playing and playgoing. John Rainoldes's *Th'overthrow of stage-playes . . .* (1599) and Stephen Gosson's *Playes confuted in fiue actions . . .* (1582) are particularly illuminating examples of the latter, as both fulminate about the dangers of staging marriage.[22] Rainoldes laments the theater's instructing boys how to woo men in marriage; Gosson warns about the mimetic power of staged marriage. As for Shakespeare's contribution to the discourse, one might look at the players in *A Midsummer Night's Dream* and *Hamlet* or the boy brides in *The Merry Wives of Windsor*, but I have chosen to focus primarily on *The Taming of the Shrew*, in part because it represents one of the playwright's earliest reflections on the staging of queer marriage, but also because it both deliberates and enacts the deconstructive project I have been describing.[23] *Shrew* opens with an Induction that explains and then exemplifies queer marriage as a dramaturgic commonplace. As the play's framing narrative, the Induction casts the action proper as the play-within-the-play: having been tricked into believing not only that he is a lord but also that he is married to a lady, Christopher Sly beckons his wife (a cross-dressed page named Bartholomew) to join him as they watch "a pleasant comedy" (Ind.2.125).[24] That comedy, performed by a troupe of men and boys, is the aptly titled *Taming of the Shrew*. Though Sly's marriage to the boy bride is intended as a practical joke, one orchestrated by a lord hoping to make light of the tinker's credulity and shore up class distinctions, its planning and execution attune spectators to the queer dramaturgy that enables the supposedly mixed-sex nuptials of Katherine and Petruccio, Bianca and Lucentio, and the widow and Hortensio. This, I believe, is managed in two ways. First, the Sly plot imports into the play's imagined world the dramaturgic practice of cross-dressing, where it is then used to perform a marriage that is, like all staged marriages, multivalent in its genderplay and temporality. And second, the plot reframes *Shrew* as the play-within-the-play that employs the same practices used to deceive Sly, the ostensible audience of the production. In these ways, the Induction fashions a metatheatrical framework that queers all of the play's marriages.

I want to argue, moreover, that the play's Induction raises the stakes by implicating all marriages in its deconstructive program. This is registered in the Induction's conspicuous setting: scene one takes place in a tavern, scene two in a bedroom. In transforming these spaces into makeshift theaters wherein marital plots are played out—creating, in effect, a theater-within-the-theater—the play collapses distinctions between reality and performance, intimating that even those marriages that happen offstage, in the so-called real world, are performative. That the Induction moves from the tavern to the bedroom is itself notable in that it mirrors anti-theatrical polemicists' concerns about the mimetic power of theater. The relationship is triangulated: the taverns lubricate audiences, making them susceptible to sinful acts, while the playhouses simulate abominations that are then performed in taverns and bedrooms. In dramatizing this relationship for playgoers, the Induction stages its own effects, folding reality into performance. Thus, at the same time that *Shrew*'s Induction deconstructs its own marriages, it revels in its exposing all marriages as utterly performative. In the process, distinctions between dramatic and dramaturgic marriage become increasingly troubled, and new possibilities for marital performance are put into discourse.

Although the primary focus of this essay is the Induction's deconstruction of marriage as a union and a cultural institution, I shall turn, finally, to the play-within-the-play's complicity in this project, evinced through a series of jokes that invoke, to adapt Foucault's phrase, the anus and its pleasures.[25] Abrupt though this might seem, anality in *Shrew* comes to signify the queerness not only of the eroticized bodies of characters and the actors who play them, but also of cultural institutions such as marriage that aim to organize and discipline those bodies. In particular, the jokes I examine conflate the vagina and the anus as undifferentiated sites of pleasure, a conflation that displaces penile-vaginal sex, a potentially procreative kind of sex, as the aim and/or end of courtship and marital consummation. The anus, then, embodies the reconstitution of courtship and marriage through non-procreative forms of intimacy. In exploring anality as simultaneously generative and degenerate, pleasurable and horrific, I am following the germinal work of Jonathan Goldberg, Jeffrey Masten, and Will Stockton, all of whom have shown that in Renaissance discourse, the anus was not, necessarily, a grave.[26] On the contrary, as *Shrew* shows, anal eroticism deconstructs marriage, but it also reimagines marital-erotic configurations as potentially sodomitical.[27]

My approach to *Shrew* is in part a response to a critical tradition that has taken for granted the gender dynamics of marital arrangements and focused instead on the perennial question of whether or not Katherine's submission to Petruccio is genuine or a ruse.[28] This question remains central for readers, audiences, scholars, and directors, but it assumes that the marriages represented in the play conform unequivocally and unproblematically to a husband/wife dichotomy. Interestingly, many of the same critics who identify the Induction as a deconstructive force that destabilizes gender norms and marital roles stop short of suggesting that the gendering and temporality of the institution itself might be under scrutiny. Karen Newman, for instance, has argued that "in the induction . . . relationships of power and gender, which in Elizabethan treatises, sermons, homilies, and behavioral handbooks were figured as natural and divinely ordained, are subverted by the metatheatrical foregrounding of such roles and relations as socially constructed."[29] This "metatheatrical foregrounding" does no less than "subver[t] the play's patriarchal master narrative by exposing it as neither natural nor divinely ordained."[30] For Newman, the Induction's role-play brings to the fore the constructedness of the roles and obligations prescribed to husbands and wives, but it leaves intact the husband/wife dichotomy of marriage. That Sly's union with a cross-dressed page might also call into question the gendering or temporal scope of marriage is never considered. Similar arguments have been made by Michael Shapiro, who argues that the Induction "underscore[s] the use of male actors in female roles," which served to delegitimize common stereotypes about women, and Amy L. Smith, who claims that the play's couching Katherine and Petruccio's marriage in a play-within-the-play "enacts a series of negotiations for power" that permit us to "read Kate's agency through her reiteration of the role of wife—a reiteration that stresses her reshaping of Petruccio and their marriage."[31] Like Newman, Shapiro and Smith see Bartholomew and the play's other female impersonators as undercutting the dominant culture's belief about what it means to be a wife, but not about what it means to use cross-dressed actors to stage wife-hood. In a sense, these critics exercise oscillating thresholds of visibility: when it comes to uncovering gender constructs, the boy actor is visible in tandem with the female character he is playing; when it comes to marriage, the boy actor disappears beneath the drag, and discussions of roles and power differentials between men and women, husbands and wives, can resume.[32]

Critics may not see queer marriage as a possibility for Renaissance drama, but antitheatrical polemicists of the period were in fact quite distressed by its pervasiveness. In *Th'overthrow of stage-playes . . .* (1599), John Rainoldes bemoans the deleterious effects simulated vows have had on boy actors: "I haue thought it a thing vnbeseeming a youth of tender years to be inured, and taught, how hee may by amorous speeches, lookes, and gestures, wooe for a husband, or a wife."[33] There are at least two ways to interpret Rainoldes's concerns. On the one hand, "wooe for a husband, or a wife" could mean "wooe *as* a husband, or a wife," in which case Rainoldes is inveighing against the dramaturgic practice that teaches boy players how to impersonate women and men in courtship. On the other hand, he could be saying that boys are learning how to procure husbands and wives for themselves. Although Fisher's analysis of boys as a third gender would suggest that none of these configurations necessarily would have been perceived as same-sex, at least not in the same way that affective bonds between men or between women were, I submit that Rainoldes's use of the masculine pronoun "hee" to refer to the "youth of tender years" indicates that the polemicist saw in the dramaturgic coupling of men and boys a homoerotic and/or pederastic threat to the conventional mixed-sex gendering of marriage. In other words, for Rainoldes, Renaissance dramaturgy proved unsettling because it taught, and in so doing promoted, the staging of marriages that were *not* between men and women.

Implicit in Rainoldes's complaints is the belief that staged marriage is a transgressive enterprise that has the power to metamorphose those who participate in it. In his *Plays confuted in fiue actions* . . . (1582), Stephen Gosson articulates a similar concern for spectators who witness staged marriage, warning them that the mimetic power of Renaissance plays could induce them to commit acts against their will. Retelling the Xenophon story of the play *Bacchus and Ariadne*, Gosson explains that among these acts, it turns out, is marriage:

> When *Bacchus* rose vp, tenderly listing *Ariadne* from her seat, no small store of curtesie passing betwene them, the beholders rose vp, euery man stoode on tippe toe, and seemed to houer ouer the praye, when they sware, the company sware, when they departed to bedde; the company presently was set on fire, they that were married posted home to theire wiues; they that were single, vowed very solemly, to be wedded.[34]

While critics have tended to concentrate on Philip Stubbes's more salacious claim that "goodly pageants being done, euery mate sorts to his mate, euery one bringes another homeward of their way verye fréendly, and in their secret conclaues (couertly) they play the *Sodomits,* or worse," Gosson's anecdote suggests that plays also have the power to compel single people to enter into binding social contracts.[35] Thus while sodomy, "that utterly confused category," remains the privileged trope for signifying a wide range of transgressions, Gosson's comments demonstrate that beyond provoking playgoers to engage in abhorrent behaviors, the theater can have a longer-term and larger-scale impact on early modern social structures.[36] In fact, if one wants to follow Gosson's logic, the offstage marriage is, to adapt Butler's term, a "copy" of the onstage marriage. And if this is the case, then what kind of union does the transvestite theater inspire? If observing a man and a cross-dressed boy marry enflames playgoers, then what might this say about the foundation and constitution of the ensuing marriages? In conferring this kind of agency upon dramatic performance, Gosson insinuates, perhaps unwittingly, that staged marriage and so-called real marriage possess the same ontological status. Moreover, staged marriage is, or at least is always threatening to become, the formative marriage. Or to return to the idea of "copies," real-life marriages are copies of staged marriages, which are in turn copies of earlier performances, which are in turn copies of still earlier performances, and so on. This endless chain shows that marriage is not essentially one thing—or anything, for that matter. Widespread acknowledgment of this is precisely what worried moralizers such as Rainoldes and Gosson.

If antitheatrical treatises of the period betray cultural anxieties about marriage's performativity, Shakespeare's *Shrew* plays upon these anxieties, often to comedic effect, in what I have described as a deconstructive project that aims to expose the queerness of all marriages. Though Sly's marriage to the cross-dressed page Bartholomew does not take place until the second scene of *Shrew*'s Induction, the play's investment in unveiling and foregrounding the dramaturgic apparatus that makes its queer marriages visible is evident from the outset. The play begins in a tavern, a drunken Sly arguing with the Hostess. Refusing either to pay for damages he has caused or to leave the tavern, Sly says to the Hostess, "I'll not budge an inch, boy" (Ind.1.10-11). While editors tend to gloss "boy" as "a contemptuous form of address to a servant or inferior" or "a term of abuse applicable to either sex," these uses were exceedingly rare.[37] Hence, Juliet Dusinberre has argued that the term "boy" obscures already tenuous distinctions between characters and actors:

> The Hostess must, in Shakespeare's theatre, have been played by a boy actor. But if Sly addresses her as a boy, then a new dimension is added to the interchange. In his drunkenness he seems momentarily to refuse to enter the play: to be, not a drunken beggar, but a drunken actor, who forgets that his dialogue is with a Hostess, and thinks that the boy actor is getting above himself. In other words, the theatrical illusion seems to be tested before it is even under way.[38]

From the play's beginning, then, Sly's identity is undermined, and playgoers are encouraged to ask, in Dusinberre's words, "Is Sly a beggar, or is he an actor who must play a beggar?"[39] This confusion was likely amplified by the fact that there was an actor named William Sly in Shakespeare's troupe, and so here, at the start of *Shrew*, the actor and/or character identified as Sly signals, in his refusing to play his part, that he is, in fact, playing a part—or supposed to be anyway.[40] The crucial point is that Sly and the Hostess are revealed to be boy actors playing roles: the former, an actor named Sly playing a character named Sly who is an actor refusing to perform the role he has been assigned; the latter, a boy actor playing the Hostess to Sly's tavern dweller. Shapiro is right, then, to claim that Sly's term of address for the Hostess "may also, like Cleopatra's 'boy my greatness,' have reminded some if not all spectators what they 'always knew'—that the female character was in fact played by a boy."[41] What remains unclear, however, is where, exactly, the role-playing ends, if indeed it ever does. As the Induction progresses, one never really knows which gender is being performed or how long the performance will last; differences in gender and temporality, especially as they pertain to the actors and the characters they portray, become increasingly indecipherable.

If we add the Hostess to the list of female roles played by boy actors, we see that there are no female characters in *Shrew*, only, to use Shapiro's phrase, "female impersonators."[42] In Renaissance productions, this would have been the case both in the play's imagined world, where Sly's wife and the Hostess are revealed to be cross-dressed boys and the play proper (also the play-within-the-play) is performed by a troupe that excludes women, and in the extratextual world, where the entire production was staged by Shakespeare's company of male and boy actors. The play's insistence upon confounding the worlds, erasing the boundaries between them, is borne out in the Induction's incorporating different kinds of performances, professional as well as amateur, in spaces that are simultaneously theatrical and non-theatrical: theatrical, in the sense that all scenes, regardless of setting, are performed on the stage; non-theatrical in the sense that scenes one and two of the Induction take place in a tavern and a bedroom, respectively. As a framing narrative, then, the Induction highlights the pervasiveness of female impersonation to deconstruct the very conceptualizations of gender and marital temporality upon which the play's main plots, not least the shrew-taming plot, hinge.

The remainder of the tavern scene centers on the Lord's coordinating two kinds of theatrical contrivances: the ploy to have Sly "forget himself" (Ind.1.37) and the play-within-the-play. Both contrivances feature staged marriages, and both use boys to impersonate wives who in effect call into question the naturalization of female brides. As the Lord details his designs, distinctions between role-play and so-called reality begin to break down, and it becomes abundantly clear that marriage is merely another form of dramatic entertainment. In developing this comparison, the Induction demonstrates that spousal roles are themselves performative, bereft of any essential or natural genders or timelines, and a boy is as apt a wife, for however the union might last, as any woman. This perspective on marital performance is advanced as the Induction distinguishes among, at the same time that it renders indistinguishable, at least four concomitant marriages: the dramaturgic marriage between the actors in Shakespeare's company;

the dramaturgic marriages between the actors who inhabit the play-world of the Induction; the dramatic marriages between the characters of Sly's fantasies; and the dramatic marriages between the characters of Shakespeare's *Shrew*. While each of these marriages involves different gender dynamics and temporalities that are further vexed by the very different perspectives afforded certain characters over others, not to mention spectators surrounding the stage, the seemingly distinct marital arrangements are mutually dependent.

The setting for Sly's marriage, which also serves as the impromptu theater for the play-within-the-play, is a richly furnished bedroom, an accommodation that defies the consigning of performance, whether marital or otherwise, to any culturally sanctioned theatrical space. The Lord's choice is significant: on the one hand, the bed and the room that contains it function as metonyms for marital relations; on the other, their use in the manipulation of Sly undermines the naturalized institution for which they often stand.[43] To his fellow huntsmen, the Lord commands, "Take [Sly] up, and manage well the jest. / Carry him gently to my fairest chamber, / And hang it round with all my wanton pictures" (Ind.1.41-43). Unfortunately, the Lord does not specify which kinds of "wanton pictures"—heteroerotic, homoerotic, or pederastic—will be placed around the room, but it is clear that the first step in tricking Sly into believing he is married is to accouter him with finer things. To make sense of these new surroundings to Sly, the Lord needs players:

> Persuade him that he hath been a lunatic,
> And when he says he is, say that he dreams,
> For he is nothing but a mighty lord.
> This do, and do it kindly, gentle sirs.
> It will be pastime passing excellent,
> If it will be husbanded with modesty. (Ind.1.59-64)

Acting as servants, the huntsmen will convince Sly that what he thought was his reality was merely a dream and what he thinks is a delusion is very real. Not coincidentally, the Lord uses the term "husband" to describe how the staged marriage must be performed. Throughout the Renaissance, this word carried multiple significations, and its use as a verb in this context exploits this polysemy. In one sense, the term referred to methodology, meaning "to manage with thrift and prudence."[44] At the same time, however, the word was used as a verb to mean "to provide or match with a husband" and "to act the part of a husband to; to become the husband of, to marry."[45] Drawing upon these definitions, the Lord declares rather cryptically that a husband shall be provided, and this process of husbanding presupposes role-play: in the latter definition, "to become the husband of" or "to marry" follows "act[ing] the part." I would suggest, as well, that the ambiguity created by the passive voice—"it will be husbanded"—reinforces the deconstructive project I have been outlining. Although Bartholomew may be playing the role of the wife in the dramatic marriage, it is unclear who plays the husband, that is, the administrator or manager, in the dramaturgic marriage. It could be Bartholomew, the boy bride charged with persuading Sly he is married; it might also be the Lord himself, the man behind the ruse. Either way, the Lord's diction underscores the multi-facetedness of Sly's staged marriage: it is both dramatic and dramaturgic, it involves multiple husbands and wives, and these husbands and wives negotiate vastly different settings, temporalities, and audiences that are nonetheless inextricably linked in the staging of marriage.

The entrance of the professional players—in fact the third set of players to take the stage, after Sly and the Hostess and the Lord and his huntsmen—only confuses matters further. Requesting a private production for Sly, the Lord remembers a previous play put on by the troupe:

> This fellow I remember
> Since once he played a farmer's eldest son.
> 'Twas where you wooed the gentlewoman so well.
> I have forgot your name, but sure that part
> Was aptly fitted and naturally performed. (Ind.1.79-83)

The Lord's use of the second-person pronoun "you" allows for a slip between character and actor, the kind Rainoldes frets over in *Th'overthrow of stage-plays*. Was it the actor who "wooed the gentlewoman so well," or the character he was portraying? As for the gentlewoman, the Lord remembers that the "part / Was aptly fitted and naturally performed," a compliment that attests not only to the boy actor's proficiency but also to the appropriateness of a boy's playing a female role. Of course, if the play-boy is equipped to play the "wooed . . . gentlewoman," he is also adept at performing the role of the wife.

As it happens, although the marriage of Sly is not a professional theatrical production, and so a play-boy need not be solicited for the part of Sly's wife, enlisting the help of a woman is never mentioned. Rather, the decision is made, without any deliberation, to dress the Lord's page in women's clothes. Beyond providing additional comedic fodder for the Lord and his friends, this choice would have reminded Renaissance audiences that, in accordance with contemporary dramaturgical practices, all the play's wives were boys in drag. In effect, what begins as a jest at Sly's expense becomes a running joke throughout *Shrew* and indeed throughout Renaissance drama. Hence, Renaissance spectators who were duped into believing Katherine and Bianca are female brides were not less gullible than the eminently gullible Sly.

The comparison is not subtle, as the Lord takes the time to explain how Sly's wife, and hence all the play's wives, should play the role so as to be convincing. This includes "dress[ing] in all suits like a lady"; "bear[ing] himself with honourable action / Such as he hath observed in noble ladies / Unto their lords by them accomplishèd"; speaking with "soft low tongue and lowly courtesy"; giving Sly "kind embracements, tempting kisses"; and "rain[ing] a shower of commanded tears" at his lord's recovery (Ind.1.101-125). As feminist critics have rightly noted, the scripting of Sly's wife belies the fixity of gender roles, "teach[ing] that there is no such thing as a discrete sexed or classed identity."[46] But this performative-deconstructive act works at least in part because the boy beneath the women's clothes remains visible to spectators. For the Lord, the interplay between dramaturgic queerness and dramatic heteroeroticism is the pièce de résistance of the play in which Sly unknowingly participates:

> I know the boy will well usurp the grace,
> Voice, gait, and action of a gentlewoman.
> I long to hear him call the drunkard husband,
> And how my men will stay themselves from laughter
> When they do homage to this simple peasant. (Ind.1.127-31)

This passage clarifies what excites the Lord about the performance that will both conclude the Induction and introduce the action proper. While the Lord looks forward to seeing "the boy . . . usurp the grace, / Voice, gait, and action of a gentlewoman," he also "long[s] to hear *him*"—that is, the boy *as a boy*—"call the drunkard husband." For the Lord, the humor arises from Bartholomew's precarious status as Sly's boy bride, a role, the Lord has already told us, that can be "aptly fitted and naturally performed" by a competent play-boy. In this instance, then, the hilarity, and also the titillation, derives from the idea that Sly's wife and the Lord's page are simultaneously discrete and indistinguishable persons. Apparently, play-boys made good wives—perhaps even better wives than women—but to forget or not know that one had married a play-boy was risible.

The coexistence of the boy and the bride in the Induction and throughout the play challenges the stability of gender identity, as various scholars have argued, but it also disrupts the typical gendering of social structures such as marriage that organize and normalize mixed-sex relationships. I largely concur, therefore, with Smith's assessment of *Shrew*'s parading its performativity:

> Indeed the lord's trick in the Induction is not simply about the ability of characters to switch gendered or classed identities but rather about their ability to create those identities *through performance*. Thinking of the Induction as an opportunity to watch the creation of new gendered and classed identities emphasizes the instability of those identities—identities dependent upon performance.[47]

In *Shrew*, the radical potential of performance extends beyond individual gendered and classed identities to include the larger structuring principles that govern them. As Smith points out, Petruccio and Katherine's courtship does not conform to the patriarchal configuration often imputed to it, and "it is better seen as part of a series of more fluid negotiations of power."[48] I shall return to this negotiation as it transpires within a metadramatic production preoccupied with marital performance. For now, I want to say that at the same time that Petruccio and Katherine's courtship and marriage undermines patriarchal mixed-sex marriage, the synchronous unions of two sets of players—those of the troupe hired by the Lord and those of Shakespeare's company—erode the very definition of marriage as between one man and one woman. This cultural work begins in the tavern, with the plotting of Sly's marriage, and continues in the bedroom, when the union is performed.

Before following Sly and everyone else in the bedroom decorated with "wanton pictures," however, I want to address the aptness of the location, especially as it pertains to the play's originary milieu. Shakespeare's choice in bifurcating the Induction, dividing it into a tavern scene, where the scheming happens, and the bedroom scene, where the action is, mirrors the concerns of Renaissance antitheatrical polemicists. Though the anecdotes differ, the causal link forged among the three spaces is consistent across the anti-theatrical oeuvre: participating in and/or witnessing nefarious deeds, particularly when alcohol is involved, leads one to engage in those same deeds in more private spaces. Routinely grouped together because of their Dionysian etiology and their location mostly in the Liberties just outside London, the playhouses and taverns are complicit in promoting pagan activities.[49] In his germinal study of anti-theatrical prejudice, Jonas Barish notes that correlating drinking and playing, both signal activities of the "cult of Dionysus," was "one of the most persistent charges against the stage."[50] According to Gosson, "Playes were consecrated vnto *Bacchus* for the first finding out of wine," which makes players "daunsing Chaplines of *Bacchus*."[51] In his *Refutation for the Apology of actors . . .* (1615), John Greene describes plays as the "fruits of vintage and drunkennesse, consisting of sundry impieties, comprehending euill and damnable things, wherein is taught how in our liues and manners wee may follow all kind of vice with Art."[52] Though Prynne pinpoints the theater as the evil that leads to other vices, a triangulated relationship among drinking, playing, and fornicating is obvious enough:

> In the Play-houses at London, it is the fashion of Youthes to goe first into the Yard, and to carry their eye thorow every Gallery, then like unto Ravens, where they spy the Carrion thither they fly, and presse as neere to the fairest as they can. In stead of Pome-granats they give them Pippins, they dally with their Garments to passe the time, they minister talke upon all occasions, & either bring them home to their houses on small acquaintance, or slip into Tavernes when the Playes are done.[53]

Prynne's word choice—"slip[ping]"; "spy[ing]"; "dally[ing]"—bespeaks an easy transition from public to private, from one depraved act to another. For antitheatrical polemicists, the theaters and the taverns were both the causes and the effects of social disorder and moral decay.

As the closing of the theaters in the 1640s demonstrates, policing public places where drinking and playing happened was not an insurmountable task. Surveilling what people do in private is much more difficult, and the inability ever to know for sure perpetuates tantalizing fantasies that percolate anti-theatrical works. Stubbes's claim about the "secret conclaues [where] (couertly) they [spectators] play the *Sodomits*, or worse," is reiterated by Prynne in *Histriomastix*, with some pertinent amplification:

> M. *Stubs*, his *Anatomy of Abuses p.* 105. . . . affirmes, *that Players and Play-haunters in their secret conclaves play the Sodomites:* together with *some moderne examples of such, who have beene desperately enamored with Players Boyes thus clad in womans apparell, so farre as to sollicit them by words, by Letters, even actually to abuse them.* All which give dolefull testimony to this experimental reason, which should make this very putting on of womans apparell on Boyes, to act a Play, for ever execrable to all chast Christian hearts.[54]

For Prynne, as for Stubbes, the danger inheres in mimetic art, which prompts its viewers to reenact what they have seen. "The growth of desire through the experience of theatre," writes Stephen Orgel, "is a sinister progression: the play excites the spectator, and sends him home to 'perform' himself; the result is sexual abandon with one's wife, or more often with any available woman (all women at the playhouse being considered available), worst of all, the spectator begins by lusting after a female character, but ends by having sex with the 'man' she really is."[55] Orgel's point about the allure of what Prynne calls "Boyes thus clad in womans apparel" captures the anxieties surrounding the transvestite stage. In addition to being monstrosities that contradict deuteronomic code and sumptuary laws that prohibit cross-dressing, boy brides and female pages enticed if not compelled Renaissance playgoers to commit similar acts in private.[56]

Thus, when *Shrew*'s Induction moves from the tavern to the bedroom, the play, much to the dismay of the theater's most vociferous critics, stages its own effects. Audiences watch as Sly follows what Stubbes and his ilk identify as the trajectory of the typical spectator, travelling from the tavern, where he passes out from excessive drinking, to the bedroom, where he dallies with his boy bride. Both locations, of course, are theatrical performances situated on the stage, and so in the space of the Induction Sly manages to visit all three sites typically singled out for censure in anti-theatrical treatises. This might be Shakespeare's way of burlesquing anti-theatrical hysteria, but in the course of mocking and/or celebrating the theater's purported mimetic power, the Induction draws a series of rather unmistakable parallels between theatrical performance and lived experience, closing the culturally constructed gap that separates them.

Whereas the tavern scene sets up the deconstructive project, the bedroom enacts the breaking point where theatricality and reality are folded into one another, realizing all social arrangements, regardless of occasion, as performative. When Sly awakens from his drunken stupor, he finds himself in an unfamiliar room, attended upon by men he has never met. Unbeknownst to the tinker, the bedroom is a mise-en-scène, and he, like everyone around him, is both an actor and a spectator of the drama. Having offered Sly expensive wine, candied fruits, and a diverse wardrobe and art collection to choose from, the servingmen succeed, finally, in convincing him that he is a lord married to a stunning lady:

> Am I a lord, and have I such a lady?
> Or do I dream? Or have I dreamed till now?
> I do not sleep. I see, I hear, I speak.
> I smell sweet savours, and I feel soft things.
> Upon my life, I am a lord indeed,
> And not a tinker, nor Christopher Sly.

Well, bring our lady hither to our sight,
And once again a pot o'th' smallest ale. (Ind.2.66-73)

This passage, Sly's first in verse, marks a metamorphosis—one, however, contingent upon the duration of the Lord's performance. Its success, Newman has stated, relies chiefly on Sly's believing he is married: "Significantly, Sly is only convinced of his lordly identity when he is told of his 'wife.'"[57] In setting off "wife" with quotation marks, Newman means to stress its artificiality: not only is Sly's wife not really his wife, she is also not really a woman. But who or what she "really is" is a matter of perspective. In the 1594 Quarto adjudged to be an imitation or reconstruction of Shakespeare's play, the stage directions refer to Sly's wife as a boy when she enters: "Enter the boy in Womans attire." Both times the boy appears—first dressed as a page, then as Sly's wife—the prefix "boy" is attached to his speeches.[58] In the 1623 Folio, the cue for her entrance reads, "Enter the Lady with Attendants," and the prefix for all her lines is "Lady" or the abbreviated "La."[59] Though pulled from different versions, the latter usually presumed more authoritative than the former, both sets of stage directions and prefixes are equally true, as they offer different, but not mutually exclusive, perspectives on the same event. According to Jones and Stallybrass, in the Folio's version "we are . . . presented with a wild oscillation between contradictory positions: the plot of the Induction demands that we remain aware of Bartholomew *as* Bartholomew, while the language of the text simply cuts Bartholomew, replacing him with "'lady.'"[60] It bears remembering, however, that early modern spectators would not have had access to the playtext—not unless they had purchased a copy of the 1623 Folio, long after the play's first performance. But even if they had seen it on the page, the "wild oscillation" Jones and Stallybrass describe has more to do with the complex arrangement of performances and perspectives than with the text's "simply cut[ting]" anyone. Indeed, playgoers might find themselves laughing at Sly's perceiving his wife to be a lady, but precisely the same joke is being played with the play-within-the-play that tells the stories of Katherine, Bianca, and the Widow. In the same way that Sly is duped, playgoers who find *Shrew* compelling, even after they have been made privy to the Lord's machinations, are deceived by exactly the same marital performance.

Sly's interactions with his wife just before the start of *Shrew* rehearse precisely the kind of queer marriages that will be replayed in the action proper. In particular, Sly's staged marriage foregrounds the multivalency and performativity of the gender dynamics and temporalities that will structure the play's various dramaturgic and dramatic marital arrangements. The performance of these arrangements, in turn, exposes all marriages as fundamentally queer, as fundamentally performative. This is evident from the moment Bartholomew, now a boy bride, greets his/ her husband:

> Bartholomew: How fares my noble lord?
> Sly: Marry, I fare well,
> For here is cheer enough. Where is my wife?
> Bartholomew: Here, noble lord. What is thy will with her?
> Sly: Are you my wife, and will not call me husband?
> My men should call me lord. I am your goodman.
> Bartholomew: My husband and my lord, my lord and husband;
> I am your wife in all obedience.
> Sly: I know it well. (Ind.2.98-104)

The gendering of this marriage is confounded in the Lady/Bartholomew's leading question: "What is thy will with her?" Is the Lady asking this to be coy, or is Bartholomew asking it to mock Sly's gullibility? Surely it is both. As for the Lord, he gets his wish and more in Bartholomew's chiastic reply to Sly's request to call him husband: "My husband and my lord, my lord and husband." The homoerotics of this exchange are hard to miss, Sly implying he already "know[s] . . . well" his wife's "obedience," even though this is hardly the case. However, the queering of time during this exchange is not Sly's invention; rather, it is a form of interpellation managed by the servingman who apprises Sly that he has "these fifteen years . . . been in a dream" (Ind.2.74). When Sly repeats this to his wife just a few lines later (Ind.2.104-5), the implication is that his marriage is at least as old. The very passage of time, then, is itself a performance. Nevertheless, it does not take long for Sly to command his wife to join him in bed:

> Bartholomew: Ay, and the time seems thirty unto me,
> Being all this time abandoned from your bed.
> Sly: 'Tis much. Servants, leave me and her alone.
> [*Exeunt* LORD *and attendants*]
> Madam, undress you and come now to bed. (Ind.2.110-13)

Though the Lady/Bartholomew is able finally to dissuade Sly from (re)consummating their vows right away, the erotically charged exchange gestures toward the possibility of intimacy onstage. Shapiro argues this may have been averted because of cultural anxieties regarding the staging of intimacy: "In Shakespeare's day, the enactment of some sexual intimacy in the world of the play and the possibility of still more to come may have raised some mild anxieties about the prospect of homoerotic contact between two male characters and two male actors. If so, then the audience was probably relieved when the page extricated himself from the problem."[61] And yet, while Sly's wife prevents any private/public displays of affection from happening, the play-within-the-play, employing the same dramaturgical practices used to trick the tinker-turned-noble, is not so modest. A close call, in other words, merely prepares audiences to see Katherine and Petruccio's courtship, especially their kisses in Act 5, as perhaps fulfilling the Induction's deflected queer erotics.[62]

Productions of *Shrew* have handled this fulfillment in two ways: in keeping the Induction onstage for the play's duration, and in doubling the parts. Because the latter tends to preclude the former, companies often choose one or the other, but in many present-day productions, as in Shakespeare's playtext, Sly and his wife remain onstage for the entire play. According to the stage directions in the 1623 Folio, the married couple is "aloft" for all of 1.1. In fact, they interrupt the play at the end of the first scene when Sly begins to nod off (1.1.242-46). Although these are the last lines Sly and his wife speak in the Folio, the playtext indicates they do not exit at the end of 1.1; rather, "they sit and mark" (1.1.247). In the 1594 Quarto, characters from the Induction not only interject throughout the play but also return at its end to comment on the action proper, which Sly describes as "the best dreame / That euer [he] had in [his] life."[63] More importantly, Sly informs spectators he plans to apply what he has learned from the dream in his handling of his own wife: "Ile to my / Wife presently and tame her too / And if she anger me."[64] The couple have no more lines after 1.1 in the 1623 Folio, but nothing in the playtext suggests they exit after this dialogue. Further, the absence of the framing narrative at play's end leaves open the possibility that Sly's marriage outlasts those depicted in the play-within-the-play, if only by a few moments. In more modern productions, companies often use a conflated text, taking the concluding framing narrative from the Quarto and adding it to the Florio. This trend suggests that for many directors and dramaturgs, the ending of the Quarto makes explicit what the Folio implies.[65] This presence of the Induction serves to queer the genders and temporalities of all the play's marriages. It also makes distinguishing among the different marital performances all but impossible. Sly's marriage, for instance, is at once mix-sexed, pederastic, and homoerotic, and it occupies diverse spaces and times. At the same time that *Shrew*'s ending annihilates the dramaturgic marriage between actors that has never had any future, the dramaturgic marriage between the tinker and the page, which is simultaneously a marriage between a noble and his bride, persist in their own fictive times and spaces and in the cultural imaginary that persists, though only to be obliterated in each production, through performance and, yes, literary and performance criticism.

Unsurprisingly, the most common form of doubling is that of Sly/Petruccio and Sly's wife/Katherine. While this convention may in some respects normalize what in Renaissance productions was a more complex layering of genders and temporalities, as the actor who plays Sly's wife and Katherine is typically neither a play-boy nor a Lord's page but rather a female actor playing the Hostess, the frequency with which Sly and Sly's wife take up the roles of Petruccio and Katherine speaks to the play's insistence upon parading its marital performativity. Anticipating Sly's comments in the concluding framing narrative of the 1594 Quarto, these productions often literalize the play-within-a-play as the tinker's dream. Writing about a 1988 production of *Shrew* in Stratford, Ontario, Elizabeth Shafer recounts of the Sly plot:

> Richard Monette [the director] had a Sly who was young, good-looking, and out on the town. Sly was so drunk he couldn't light a cigarette on his own, and his dream began as he collapsed, mouthing some lines from the Induction, without any prompting from a Lord or travelling players. Colm Feore as Sly became Petruchio, while Goldie Semple, the Hostess, became Katharina; at the end, an outbreak of romantic waltzing and music on the crowded stage covered Feore's quick change back to Sly, still unsteady with drink, speechless, dazed, confused and suddenly revealed as the crowd parted.[66]

This particular production dispensed with Sly's queer marriage, but it retained the metadramatic frame and incorporated doubling so as to couch the play's marital performances as the stuff of fantasy. As in *A Midsummer Night's Dream*, however, the dream motif is not so easily dismissed as a containment mechanism.[67] Rather, it has become yet another way in which directors have reimagined the queer work the play performs. In a 1995 Royal Shakespeare Company production, for example, Sly's awakening from the dream-within-the-play was both literal and symbolic, as the tinker began to realize how poorly he had been treating Mrs. Sly.[68] Hence, as in productions that deploy a full framing narrative, seeming differences in gender dynamics, spatiality, and temporality are erected only to be traversed, confounded, and ultimately collapsed.

In myriad ways, therefore, the Induction works to make itself omnipresent in *Shrew*, but the play-within-the-play is at least complicit, if not fully engaged, in this deconstructive program. In the play's first few scenes (one of which Sly will interrupt), in conversations that recall the "husbanding" of Sly's marriage, various characters obsess over the prospect of procuring husbands and wives. Upon his arrival in Padua, Petruccio explains to Hortensio, "I have thrust myself into this maze, / Happily to wive and thrive as best I may" (1.2.52-53). A few lines later, Petruccio reiterates his plan "to wive it wealthily in Padua" (1.2.72). On its face, Petruccio's turn of phrase looks back—or askance, if Sly and his wife are still on stage—to the Lord's scheme, establishing a parallel between them. But it also points to the interdependence of dramatic and dramaturgic husbanding and wiving. In a sense, Petruccio's success depends upon the Lord's, as the play-within-the-play continues only if Sly, the onstage audience, remains convinced that he is watching a play with his wife. Both marriages involve characters being husbanded and wived, and both the wives are, even in the play's imagined realm, cross-dressed boy players. It is ironic, but also to the point, that what Sly knows about *Shrew*'s marriages is precisely what he does not know about his own marriage: he recognizes the play-within-the-play's unions as performances while remaining totally oblivious to his own marriage's performativity.

The play also flaunts its marital queerness through a series of bawdy jokes that invoke the anus and its manifold pleasures. In addition to troubling perceived corporeal differences between characters and the actors who play them, the anal erotics articulated through *Shrew*'s bawdy jokes queers conjugal sexuality, associating it with, and reconstituting it through, non-procreative sex acts. Anality, then, pertains not just to eroticized bodies but to the cultural imperatives and social structures that mediate those bodies. In 1.1, for instance, Hortensio and Gremio discuss the need for Katherine to be wed:

> Hortensio: [W]e may yet again have access to our fair mistress and be
> happy rivals in Bianca's love, to labor and effect one thing specially.
> Gremio: What's that, I pray?
> Hortensio: Marry, sir, to get a husband for her sister.
> Gremio: A husband? A devil.
> Hortensio: I say a husband.
> Gremio: I say a devil. Think'st thou, Hortensio, though her father be
> very rich, any man is so very a fool to be married to hell? (1.1.114-23)

The critical tendency has been to see "hell" as referring to female genitalia, as it does, supposedly, in Shakespeare's Sonnet 144, where the speaker "guess[es] one angel in another's hell" (ln. 12).[69] And yet, while the misogynistic slur may point to Katherine's vagina as the source and sign of her "forwardness," her dual identity as a boy player begs the question of where one might find "hell" on *his* body.[70] One possibility that the play entertains is the anus. Of course, anuses are not endemic to boys, and so here, in the invective against Katherine, the anality of "hell" accommodates the eroticized bodies of both the female character and the boy actors impersonating her. As Stockton writes, this anality "conflates and confuses the anus and the vagina, female and male bodies, and threatens sexual difference." It also "queer[s] opposite-sex relations predicated on genital and orificial clarity, thereby exacerbating a crisis in contemporary understandings of heterosexuality that were not yet formed in the early modern period."[71] "To be married to hell," then, bespeaks an anal eroticism that contributes to, at the same time that it is symptomatic of, the marital queerness *Shrew* is staging, a queerness that is not unique to *Shrew*, but rather common to all marriages.

Petruccio and Katherine are no less aware of the anal erotics that percolate their courtship and eventual marriage. During their very first interaction, they trade a series of barbs that slip between penile-vaginal and penile-anal erotics. The stichomythic banter, which culminates in Katherine striking Petruccio, begins with Katherine's proclaiming Petruccio's indecisiveness:

> Katherine: I knew you at the first
>   You were a movable.
> Petruccio: Why, what's a movable?
> Katherine: A joint-stool.
> Petruccio: Thou has hit it. Come, sit on me.
> Katherine: Asses are made to bear, and so are you.
> Petruccio: Women are made to bear, and so are you.
> Katherine: No such jade as you, if me you mean.
> Petruccio: Alas, good Kate, I will not burden thee,
>   For knowing thee to be but young and light.
> Katherine: Too light for such a swain as you to catch,
> And yet as heavy as my weight should be. (2.1.194-203)

Editors often gloss Petruccio's assertion that "women are made to bear" as referring to penile-vaginal intercourse and the capacity for reproduction typically associated with it.[72] However, this is not the only way in which Petruccio might "burden" Katherine sexually, and the exact position and genital configuration he has in mind when he commands her to sit on him is open to interpretation—or preference. For the actors playing Petruccio and Katherine, as for the actors playing those actors, anal sex, not vaginal sex, is the more obvious form of intimacy. More to the point, while the acts themselves are functionally, logistically different, and while the cultural significances of these acts differ considerably, the positioning, at least in this instance, is identical. Petruccio's command thus lays bare a propinquity of orifices and acts that undercuts the primacy of procreative sex. The anality of the scene becomes explicit as Katherine declares her "waspish[ness]":

> Katherine: If I be waspish, best beware my sting.
> Petruccio: My remedy is then to pluck it out.
> Katherine: Ay, if the fool could find it where it lies.
> Petruccio: Who knows not where a wasp does wear his sting?
>   In his tail.
> Katherine: In his tongue.
> Petruccio: Whose tongue?
> Katherine: Yours, if you talk of tales, and so farewell.
> Petruccio: What, with my tongue in your tail? Nay, come again,
>   Good Kate, I am a gentleman.
> Katherine: That I'll try.
> *Strikes him* (2.1.208-16)

When Petruccio imagines sticking his "tongue in [Katherine's] tail," which "tail" is it? As Gordon Williams points out, "tail" could refer to male as well as female genitalia.[73] According to Williams, in this instance "tongue in [the] tail" means cunnilingus, but, following Eric Partridge's more capacious exposition of the term in question, I would argue that anilingus is just as likely the referent.[74] For one thing, at the risk of stating the obvious, both acts involve tongues in tails, depending on how one perceives the bottom or back of the body. It is notable, too, that Petruccio genders male Katherine's hypothetical wasp, making anilingus—and also, it turns out, fellatio—a more plausible signification: "Who knows not where a wasp does wear *his* sting? / In *his* tail." In this construction, the wasp's sting is constituted both phallically (in the stinger) and anally ("*in* the tail"). The point here is not that Petruccio's bawdy pun refers to one act or another, but rather that the spectrum of acts is available to all characters and players—and hence to all betrothed and married couples—across the dramatic and dramaturgic configurations *Shrew* parades.

This playfulness characterizes Bianca's courtships as well, even if the character who hopes to seduce her through what we might call assplay winds up with someone else. When Baptista learns that the recently wed Katherine and Petruccio have left in the middle of the nuptial festivities, he recommends that Lucentio and Bianca take their "places at the table" (3.3.119?). In yet another gesture toward the Lord's machinations, Tranio responds, "Shall sweet Bianca practice how to bride it?" (3.3.122). Here again, the diction points to a multiplicity of performances, as Bianca and Lucentio's marriage is "bride[d]" at least twice each time *Shrew* is staged, and each staging requires boy players and female characters to learn the bride's part. "To bride it" obtains on multiple levels. Also like Petruccio and Katherine, Bianca and one of her suitors participate in dialogue that uses anal erotics to queer the process of courtship. In order to gain access to Bianca, Hortensio assumes the identity of a music tutor named Litio. On more than one occasion, Litio uses lewd language to explain his lessons. About Katherine's progress, he says,

> I did but tell her she mistook her frets,
> And bowed her hand to teach her fingering,
> When, with a most impatient devilish spirit,
> 'Frets, call you these?' quoth she, 'I'll fume with them.' (2.1.147-50)

As one might expect, the lesson did not end well, Katherine smashing the lute on her tutor's head, but Litio insists on his trying his hand at teaching Bianca, the woman, after all, he is trying to woo:

> Madam, before you touch the instrument,
> To learn the order of my fingering,
> I must begin with rudiments of art,
> To teach you gamut in a briefer sort,
> More pleasant, pithy, and effectual
> Than hath been taught by any of my trade. (3.1.62-67)

This not-so-subtle attempt at seduction employs music lessons as a euphemism for sexual stimulation.[75] Much like Katherine's tail, however, the site of pleasure here is ambiguous at best. Litio does not specify whether the lute is his or Bianca's, and presumably this affects the kind of "fingering" being taught. Critics tend to view stringed instruments as early modern slang for female genitalia, but as I have been arguing, the play resists this kind of rigid distinction among bodies and pleasures. In fact, the interplay between the dramatic and the dramaturgic privileges what Bianca and boy actors have in common—anality—rather than conventional understandings of the euphemism. And even if one insists that the lute must mean the vagina, Litio takes as his students characters who are also cross-dressed actors in the troupe solicited by the Lord, and so tutorials on how to pleasure oneself, whether vaginally or anally, betray the anatomical difference the bawdy language would have been meant to conceal. Still another possibility is that Litio wants to train Baptista's children how to finger *his* instrument (which one, he does not say), in a lesson that would have resonated in more personal ways for play-boys growing up in the theatrical world.

In the banquet scene—the play-within-the-play's last scene—spectators are confronted not just with queer marriage but with queer domesticity, a domesticity that marks the play's return to its dramatic and dramaturgic beginning. As in the Induction, where Bartholomew is solicited to play the bride and Sly (unwittingly) is compelled to play the husband, spousality in the banquet scene is performed through and against the queer Renaissance dramaturgy I have been examining. In part, this is registered through the play's destabilizing anal erotics, which does not abate after the couples are wed. When Katherine and the Widow commence their battle of wits, Petruccio and Hortensio offer the following remarks:

> Petruccio: To her, Kate!
> Hortensio: To her, widow!
> Petruccio: A hundred marks my Kate does put her down.
> Hortensio: That's my office. (5.2.34-37)

Interpreting "put her down" to mean "have sex with," Hortensio acknowledges the possibility of sex between women, which is also, in keeping with the play's dramaturgy, sex between the Lord's, not to mention Shakespeare's, play-boys. And when Hortensio claims "that's [his] office," he juxtaposes two non-procreative kinds of sex with mixed-sex relations that are, in the context of dramaturgy, also pederastic relations between adult male and boy actor. Like Sly and his wife's erotic banter, this exchange reveals a marital conjugality that is inescapably queer. As it happens, precisely this kind of sexuality is anticipated in Bartholomew and Sly's puns on "stand" in the Induction:

> Bartholomew: [Y]our physicians have expressly charged,
> In peril to incur your former malady,
> That I should yet absent me from your bed.
> I hope this reason stands for my excuse.
> Sly: Ay, it stands so that I may hardly tarry along. (Ind 2.117-21)

As Smith notes, Sly may think he has come up with a clever pun when in fact his boy bride has already delivered it to an audience her/his husband has no idea exists.[76] In light of this performance, the bawdy puns traded at the banquet merely continue what might be best understood as the irreducible performative anality of staged marriage.

A similar moment occurs when the couples bandy about reproductive metaphors. The troping of "conceive" begins seemingly innocently enough, with a request for a clarification:

> Widow: He that is giddy thinks the world turns round.
> Petruccio: Roundly replied.
> Katherine: Mistress, how mean you that?
> Widow: Thus I conceive by him.
> Petruccio: Conceives by me! How likes Hortensio that?
> Hortensio: My widow says thus she conceives her tale. (5.2.20-25)

In the same way that Hortensio imagines Kate "putt[ing] down" the Widow, Petruccio posits the Widow's engaging in reproductive acts with someone who is not her husband. In the fictive realm of the play-within-the-play, the Widow's extramarital affair with Petruccio may be mixed-sex and potentially procreative, but it is also, in the world of the Lord and his players, homoerotic and/or pederastic, an encounter between a man and a boy. In performance, then, the reproductive body is also a sodomitical body, one that is able to "conceive" (or generate) a "tale" (or tail). Perhaps inevitably so, the Widow's capacity for conception and parturition is limited to the excess of her/his queer desires.

And then, of course, there is Katherine's concluding speech, which Shakespeare scholars have pored over for centuries. While this speech continues to engender lively debate about wifely obedience and subjection, it also confuses spousal bodies. Correlating outer and inner, Katherine states,

> I am ashamed that women are so simple
> To offer war where they should kneel for peace,
> Or seek for rule, supremacy, and sway
> When they are bound to serve, love, and obey.
> Why are our bodies soft, and weak, and smooth,
> Unapt to toil and trouble in the world,
> But that our soft conditions and our hearts
> Should well agree with our external parts? (5.2.165-72)

Enjoining everyone in the theater to gaze upon her body, Katherine offers an ambiguous self-examination that confuses her "external parts" and the "soft condition" it signifies with that of the boy actor portraying her. Indeed, "soft[ness]," "weak[ness]," and "smooth[ness]" pertain as much to Bartholomew as they do to Katherine, and here, at play's end, at exactly the moment the former shrew is supposedly lecturing her fellow wives, spectators are looking not at a reformed woman but rather a "master-mistress" not unlike the beloved of Shakespeare's Sonnet 20.

The banquet scene, moreover, is the place where the play's dramatized marriages meet their temporal limits, as the marital futurity imagined for Katherine and Petruccio, Bianca and Lucentio, and the Widow and Hortensio is demolished by Renaissance dramaturgy. In many productions, this return is signaled by the play's ending not with the banquet, which, according to Sly, was merely a dream, but with Sly and his wife. But a full framework is not essential, since Hortensio's and Lucentio's final lines, forming a heroic couplet, mark the end of the action proper (5.2.192-93). At this point, the dramatic and dramaturgic marriages are obliterated, only to be reconstituted in different productions back at the play's beginning. This is not to say that the marriages only signify teleologically, as comedic endpoints toward which the plot moves unswervingly. Rather, it is to acknowledge that the dramatic marriages exist only in the present and only to the extent that they are performed. Like dramaturgic marriage, then, the unions of Katherine and Petruccio, Bianca and Lucentio, the Widow and Hortensio, and even Bartholomew and Sly have no existence apart from or beyond their performative enactment.

The implications for the marriages I have been interrogating extend well beyond the bounds of the stage, as Renaissance dramatists, polemicists, and audiences certainly knew. In exposing all marriages as performances, *Shrew*, like all Renaissance plays, points up the insistence on, as well as the futility of, continually performing marriage and spousality, which exist only to the extent that they are performed. Following Butler, one could say that Renaissance drama problematized relations between "copies," laying open the possibility that offstage marriages might be parodies of onstage marriages, but one might also think of dramaturgic and dramatic marital arrangements as what Jean Baudrillard has called "simulacra"—more specifically, "simulations of the third order" where representation has replaced any semblance of the original.[77] Though Baudrillard associates these simulacra with "postmodernity," this essay has argued that queer Renaissance dramaturgy and the deconstructive project it engendered and sustained punctured the fantasy of reality that both structured and was structured by social arrangements such as marriage. As simulacra, staged marriage served a strikingly postmodern function, annihilating fantasies of the real that govern the lives of spectators who tried so desperately not to acknowledge that the marital performances they observed in the theaters were in fact the queer grounds for their own Renaissance productions. Or to riff on a well-known Shakespeare passage, all the world's marriages are stages, and all the husbands and wives merely players.[78]

Notes

1. Throughout this essay I use a cluster of terms to describe actors who cross-dressed on the Renaissance stage and characters who cross-dress in their respective plays. Like Jennifer Drouin, I use cross-dressing to refer to "the practice of employing boy actors to play the woman's part." Jennifer Drouin, "Cross-Dressing, Drag, and Passing: Slippages in Shakespearean Comedy," in *Shakespeare Re-Dressed: Cross-Gender Casting in Contemporary Performance*, ed. James C. Bulman (Madison, NJ: Fairleigh Dickinson Press, 2008), 23. Drouin further distinguishes cross-dressing from drag and passing. Drag, which Drouin suggests slips between parodic and nonparodic, signifies a self-referential performance that exposes the constructedness of gender; passing is distinctive in its trying to conceal performance, a subversive act that has potentially deadly consequences. While I find these distinctions useful if we follow Drouin in "focusing on the fictional world of the play and setting aside temporarily the question of the audience's reception of the early modern boy actor" (39), part of my argument in this essay is that Shakespeare's plays refuse this kind of bifurcation. Thus, I use cross-dressing and drag interchangeably, not to dismiss Drouin's analysis, but to insist that the instances of cross-dressing I examine are always also forms of drag.

2. On the popularity and diversity of disguise plots in early modern drama, see Victor Oscar Freeburg, *Disguise Plots in Elizabethan Drama: A Study in Stage Tradition* (New York: Columbia University Press, 1915, repr. New York: Benjamin Blom, 1965).

3. Phyllis Rackin, "Androgyny, Mimesis, and the Marriage of the Boy Heroine on the English Renaissance Stage," PMLA 102, no. 1 (1987): 29.

4. Ann Rosalind Jones and Peter Stallybrass, *Renaissance Clothing and the Materials of Memory* (Cambridge: Cambridge University Press, 2000), 207.

5. Will Fisher, *Materializing Gender in Early Modern English Literature and Culture* (Cambridge: Cambridge University Press, 2006), 31.

6. Laura Levine, *Men in Women's Clothing: Antitheatricality and Effeminization 1579-1642* (Cambridge: Cambridge University Press, 1994), 7. See also Mark Breitenberg, *Anxious Masculinity in Early Modern England* (Cambridge: Cambridge University Press, 1996). Breitenberg's argument is that "masculine anxiety is a necessary and inevitable condition that operates on at least two levels: it reveals the fissures and contradictions of patriarchal systems and, at the same time, it paradoxically enables and drives patriarchy's reproduction and continuation of itself" (2).

7. Catherine Belsey, "Disrupting Sexual Difference: Meaning and Gender in the Comedies," in *Alternative Shakespeares*, ed. John Drakakis, 2nd ed. (New York and London: Routledge, 2002), 184.

8. Studies of cross-dressing on the early modern stage are numerous and wide-ranging. Those that pertain most immediately to my argument in this essay are quoted and discussed in text or cited in notes, but there are many others that have shaped my thinking. See, for example, the following: Dympna Callaghan, *Shakespeare Without Women: Representing Gender and Race on the Renaissance*

Stage (New York and London: Routledge, 2000); Marjorie B. Garber, *Vested Interests: Cross-Dressing and Cultural Anxiety* (New York and London: Routledge, 1992); Jonathan Goldberg, *Sodometries: Renaissance Texts, Modern Sexualities* (Stanford, CA: Stanford University Press, 1992); Jean Howard, "Power and Eros: Crossdressing in Dramatic Representation and Theatrical Performance," in *The Stage and Social Struggle in Early Modern England* (New York and London: Routledge, 1994), 93-128; Laurence Senelick, *The Changing Room: Sex, Drag and Theatre* (London and New York: Routledge, 2000), esp. 127-56; Bruce R. Smith, *Homosexual Desire in Shakespeare's England: A Cultural Poetics* (Chicago and London: University of Chicago Press, 1991); and Susan Zimmerman, ed., "Disruptive Desire: Artifice and Indeterminacy in Jacobean Comedy," in *Erotic Politics: Desire on the Renaissance Stage* (New York and London: Routledge, 1992), 39-61.

9. For a few Shakespearean examples, see Loreen L. Giese, *Courtships, Marriage Customs, and Shakespeare's Comedies* (New York: Palgrave Macmillan, 2006); Lisa Hopkins, *The Shakespearean Marriage: Merry Wives and Heavy Husbands* (New York: St. Martin's Press, 1998); and B. J. Sokol and Mary Sokol, *Shakespeare, Law, and Marriage* (Cambridge: Cambridge University Press, 2003).

10. On the appearance of foreign actresses on the English stage, see Stephen Orgel, *Impersonations: The Performance of Gender in Shakespeare's England* (Cambridge: Cambridge University Press, 1996), 5-8, as well as essays in Pamela Allen Brown and Peter Parolin, eds., *Women Players in England, 1500-1660: Beyond the All-Male Stage* (Aldershot: Ashgate, 2005), and Robert Henke and Eric Nicholson, eds., *Transnational Exchange in Early Modern Theater* (Aldershot: Ashgate, 2008). On the inclusion of women in English Renaissance masques, see Suzanne Gossett, "'Man-Maid, Begone!': Women in Masques," ELR 18, no. 1 (1988): 96-113; and Clare McManus, *Women on the Renaissance Stage: Anne of Denmark and Female Masquing in the Stuart Court 1590-1619* (Manchester: Manchester University Press, 2002; and New York: Palgrave Macmillan, 2002).

11. Lady Mary Wroth, *The Countesse of Mountgomeries Urania . . . .* (London: John Marriott and John Grismand, 1621).

12. Michael Shapiro, *Gender in Play on the Shakespearean Stage: Boy Heroines and Female Pages* (Ann Arbor: University of Michigan Press, 1994), 6-7.

13. On the possibility that an adult male actor, rather than a play-boy, assumed the role of Lady Macbeth, see A.R. Braunmuller, ed., *Macbeth, The New Cambridge Shakespeare*, 2nd ed. (Cambridge: Cambridge University Press, 2008), 264. On Cleopatra, see Carol Chillington Rutter, ed., *Documents of the Rose Playhouse*, rev. ed. (Manchester and New York: Manchester University Press, 1999), 224-25n59.

14. Fisher, *Materializing Gender*, 87.

15. A pertinent example of this is Thomas Walter Laqueur's *Making Sex: Body and Gender from the Greeks to Freud* (Cambridge, MA, and London: Harvard University Press, 1990). Although Laqueur's arguments about the predominance of Galen and the one-sex model in Renaissance discourse remain influential, Katharine Park and Robert A. Nye have critiqued the progress narrative charted by such arguments. See Katharine Park and Robert A. Nye, "Destiny is Anatomy," *New Republic*, February 18, 1991, 53-57.

16. See, for example, Carol Thomas Neely, *Broken Nuptials in Shakespeare's Plays* (New Haven, CT, and London: Yale University Press, 1985).

17. Though critics often take Helena at her word, Kathryn M. Moncrief claims in "'Show me a child begotten of thy body that I am father to': Pregnancy, Paternity, and the Problem of Evidence in All's Well That Ends Well," *Performing Maternity in Early Modern England*, eds. Kathryn M. Moncrief and Kathryn R. McPherson (Aldershot, UK: Ashgate, 2007) that the character's "'claim on Bertram' and her 'triumph' may not be as certain as they first appear" (30).

18. Lee Edelman, *No Future: Queer Theory and the Death Drive* (Durham, NC, and London: Duke University Press, 2004). I am also drawing upon Edelman's formulation of "reproductive futurism," which "perpetuates as reality a fantasy frame intended to secure the survival of the social in the Imaginary form of the Child" (14).

19. William Shakespeare, *Romeo and Juliet*, in *The Norton Shakespeare: Based on the Oxford Edition*, eds. Stephen Greenblatt, Walter Cohen, Jean E. Howard, and Katharine Eisaman Maus, 2nd ed. (New York and London: W. W. Norton, 2008), 12. All citations from Shakespeare's works refer to the Norton Shakespeare and appear hereafter in text. References are to act, scene, and line.

20. Judith Butler, *Gender Trouble: Feminism and the Subversion of Identity* (New York and London: Routledge, 1990), 31. Cf. Butler's more recent claims in "Is Kinship Always Already Heterosexual?" *Differences* 13, no 1 (2002): 14-44.

21. On this point, I agree with Rebecca Ann Bach, who argues in *Shakespeare and Renaissance Literature Before Heterosexuality* (New York: Palgrave Macmillan, 2007) that "we must separate out the ideology of 'heterosexuality' (a word not coined until the nineteenth century) from phenomena such as marriage and sexual activity between men and women" (2). For a discussion of, and rejoinder to, the critical tendency to impose heterosexuality on Renaissance texts, see Bach, *Shakespeare and Renaissance Literature Before Heterosexuality*, 1-24. On the recent invention of statistical norms and heteronormativity, see Karma Lochrie, *Heterosyncrasies: Female Sexuality When Normal Wasn't* (Minneapolis and London: University of Minnesota Press, 2005), esp. xi-xxviii and 1-25.

22. Stephen Gosson, *Playes confuted in fiue actions prouing that they are not to be suffred in a Christian common weale . . .* (London: Thomas Gosson, 1582). John Rainoldes, *Th'overthrow of stage-playes, by the way of controuersie betwixt D. Gager and D. Rainoldes . . .* (Middelburg: Richard Schilders, 1599).

23. Arthur L. Little Jr. has published two important essays that locate queer marriages in Shakespeare's comedic plots. See Arthur L. Little Jr., "'A Local Habitation and a Name': Presence, Witnessing, and Queer Marriage in Shakespeare's Romantic Comedies," in *Presentism, Gender, and Sexuality in Shakespeare*, ed. Evelyn Gajowski (New York: Palgrave Macmillan, 2009), 207-36; and idem, "The Rites of Queer Marriage in The Merchant of Venice," in *Shakesqueer: A Queer Companion to the Complete Works of Shakespeare*, ed. Madhavi Menon (Durham, NC, and London: Duke University Press, 2011), 216-24.

24. William Shakespeare, *The Taming of the Shrew*, in *The Norton Shakespeare: Based on the Oxford Edition*, eds. Stephen Greenblatt, Walter Cohen, Jean E. Howard, and Katharine Eisaman Maus, 2nd ed. (New York and London: W. W. Norton, 2008).

25. Michel Foucault, *The History of Sexuality: An Introduction*, trans. Robert Hurley, vol. 1 (New York: Vintage, 1990), 159.

26. See Jonathan Goldberg, "The Anus in Coriolanus," in *Historicism, Psychoanalysis, and Early Modern Culture*, eds. Carla Mazzio and Douglas Trevor (New York and London: Routledge, 2000),

260-71; Jeffrey Masten, "Is the Fundament a Grave?" in *The Body in Parts: Fantasies of Corporeality in Early Modern Europe*, eds. David Hillman and Carla Mazzio (New York and London: Routledge, 1997), 129-45; and Will Stockton, *Playing Dirty: Sexuality and Waste in Early Modern Comedy* (Minneapolis and London: University of Minnesota Press, 2011). Though these studies differ in their application and extension of psychoanalytic theory, they all respond, at least in part, to the governing question of Leo Bersani's "Is the Rectum a Grave?" in Leo Bersani, *Is the Rectum a Grave? And Other Essays* (Chicago: University of Chicago Press, 2010). See also David Hillman, *Shakespeare's Entrails: Belief, Scepticism, and the Interior of the Body* (New York: Palgrave Macmillan, 2007); Gail Kern Paster, *The Body Embarrassed: Drama and the Disciplines of Shame in Early Modern England* (Ithaca, NY: Cornell University Press, 1993), 113-62; and Patricia Parker, "Preposterous Reversals: Love's Labor's Lost," *Modern Language Quarterly* 54, no. 4 (1993): 435-82.

27. My use of the term "sodomitical" is indebted to scholars who have sought to mediate debates about sodomy as a discursive formation registering, on the one hand, sexual acts deemed deviant or nonprocreative, and, on the other, political, cultural, and religious transgressiveness. In addition to the specific studies I cite throughout this essay, see Kenneth Borris and George Rousseau, eds., *The Sciences of Homosexuality in Early Modern Europe* (New York and London: Routledge, 2008); Alan Bray, *Homosexuality in Renaissance England* (London: Gay Men's Press, 1982); Gregory Bredbeck, *Sodomy and Interpretation: Marlowe to Milton* (Ithaca, NY, and London: Cornell University Press, 1991); Mario DiGangi, *The Homoeroticism of Early Modern Drama* (Cambridge: Cambridge University Press, 1997); and Nicholas F. Radel, "Can the Sodomite Speak? Sodomy, Satire, and the Castlehaven Case," in *Love, Sex, Intimacy and Friendship between Men, 1500-1800*, eds. Katherine O'Donnell and Michael O'Rourke (New York: Palgrave Macmillan, 2003), 148-67.

28. For a survey of this trend in Shrew scholarship, see Dana E. Aspinall, ed., "The Play and the Critics," in *The Taming of the Shrew: Critical Essays*, 3-38 (New York and London: Routledge, 2002), 3-38.

29. Karen Newman, *Fashioning Femininity and English Renaissance Drama* (Chicago and London: University of Chicago Press, 1991), 38.

30. Ibid., 50.

31. Michael Shapiro, "Framing the Taming: Metatheatrical Awareness of Female Impersonation in The Taming of the Shrew," *Yearbook of English Studies* 23 (1993): 144; Amy L. Smith, "Performing Marriage with a Difference: Wooing, Wedding, and Bedding in The Taming of the Shrew," *Comparative Drama* 36, no. 3 (2002): 290.

32. See also Frances E. Dolan, *Marriage and Violence: The Early Modern Legacy* (Philadelphia: University of Pennsylvania Press, 2008). While she does not take up the metatheatrics of the Induction, and while she maintains the husband-wife dynamic between Katherine and Petruccio, Dolan encourages us to expand our notion of domesticity and the household and consider the crucial function of, among others, servants. As Dolan writes, "Rather than condemning Katharina's violence or self-assertion entirely, Petruchio redirects her claims to mastery away from him. The two remain equals with regard to their desire to domineer over their own servants and the outside world" (127).

33. John Rainoldes, *Th'overthrow of stage-playes, by the way of controversie betwixt D. Gager and D. Rainoldes . . . .* (Middelburg: Richard Schilders, 1599), 107.

34. Stephen Gosson, *Playes confuted in fiue actions prouing that they are not to be suffred in a Christian common weale . . . .* (London: Thomas Gosson, 1582), G4ᵥ.

35. Philip Stubbes, *The anatomie of abuses . . . .* (London: John Kingston, 1583), M1ᵥ.

36. Foucault, *The History of Sexuality*, vol. 1, 101.

37. The first gloss is from Ann Thompson, eds., *The Taming of the Shrew. By William Shakespeare*, The New Cambridge Shakespeare Series (Cambridge: Cambridge University Press, 1984), 47n11; the second, from William Shakespeare, *The Taming of the Shew*, in Greenblatt, et al., *The Norton Shakespeare*, 170n7. As Shapiro points out, Thompson undermines her own interpretation of the term in admitting it was rarely applied to women ("Framing the Taming," 150-51).

38. Juliet Dusinberre, "The Taming of the Shrew: Women, Acting, and Power," *Studies in the Literary Imagination* 26, no. 1 (Spring 1993): 67.

39. Ibid.

40. According to Dusinberre, "Shakespeare's Sly may in fact have been played by William Sly, a member of both the Pembroke's men in the early 1590s . . . and subsequently of Shakespeare's company, the Chamberlain's Men, later the King's men" (ibid., 69).

41. Shapiro, "Framing the Taming," 151.

42. Ibid., 146 and passim.

43. On the importance and various significations of the marital bed in medieval and Renaissance art and iconography, see Diane Wolfthal, *In and Out of the Marital Bed: Seeing Sex in Renaissance Europe* (New Haven, CT, and London: Yale University Press, 2010), esp. 13-41.

44. *Oxford English Dictionary*, 2nd ed. (Oxford: Clarendon Press, 1989), "husband, *v.*" 1, definition 2.

45. Ibid., "husband, *v.*" 2, definitions 4 and 5. Shakespeare will use the verb "to husband" in a similar sense in *King Lear* and *All's Well That Ends Well*; in fact, the *Oxford English Dictionary* provides the pertinent quotations from these plays to exemplify the term's use in the context I am describing.

46. Barbara Hodgdon, *The Shakespeare Trade: Performances and Appropriations* (Philadelphia: University of Pennsylvania Press, 1998), 4.

47. A. Smith, "Performing Marriage with a Difference," 296.

48. Ibid.

49. On the geographical liminality of the playhouses, see Steven Mullaney, *The Place of the Stage: License, Play, and Power in Renaissance England* (Chicago and London: University of Chicago Press, 1988).

50. Jonas Barish, *The Antitheatrical Prejudice* (Berkeley, Los Angeles, and London: University of California Press, 1981), 118.

51. Gosson, *Playes confuted in fiue actions*, C1ᵣ, C3ᵣ.

52. John Greene, *A Refutation of the Apology for actors Diuided into three briefe treatises . . . .* (London: W. White, 1615), 39.

53. William Prynne, *Histrio-mastix The players scourge, or, actors tragaedie . . . .* (London: Edward Allde, Augustine Mathewes, Thomas Cotes, and William Jones, 1633), 363.

54. Prynne, *Histrio-mastix*, 211-12.

55. Orgel, *Impersonations*, 29. See also Barish, *The Antitheatrical Prejudice*, 82-96.

56. According to Deuteronomy 22:5, "The woman shall not wear that which pertaineth unto a man, neither shall a man put on a woman's garment: for all that do so are abominations unto the Lord thy God," *King James Bible*, London: Robert Barker, 1611). This passage was a favorite among those who objected to the theater's institutionalized cross-dressing. Indeed, it appears prominently in all of the anti-theatrical texts I examine in this essay: Gosson, *Playes confuted in fiue actions*, C3₂; I.G. Greene, *A refutation of the Apology for actors*, 54-55; Prynne, *Histrio-mastix*, 179; Rainoldes, *Th'overthrow of stage-playes*, 32; Stubbes, *Anatomie of Abuses*, F6ᵥ.

   On Elizabethan sumptuary laws, especially in the context of Renaissance theater, see Amanda Bailey, *Flaunting: Style and the Subversive Male Body in Renaissance England* (Toronto, Buffalo, and London: University of Toronto Press, 2007). See also Frances Elizabeth Baldwin, *Sumptuary Legislation and Personal Regulation in England* (Baltimore, MD: Johns Hopkins Press, 1926); N. B. Harte, "State Control of Dress and Social Change in Pre-Industrial England," in *Trade, Government and Economy in Pre-Industrial England: Essays Presented to F.J. Fisher*, eds. D. C. Coleman and A. H. John (London: Weidenfeld and Nicolson, 1976), 132-65; Wilfrid Hooper, "The Tudor Sumptuary Laws," *English Historical Review* 30, no. 119 (1915): 433-49; and Alan Hunt, *Governance of the Consuming Passions: A History of Sumptuary Law* (New York: St. Martin's, 1996).

57. Newman, *Fashioning Femininity*, 38.

58. Anonymous, *A pleasant conceited historie, called The taming of a shrew As it was sundry times acted by the Right honorable the Earle of Pembrook his seruants* (London: Peter Short, 1594), A4ᵣ.

   On the relationship between the 1594 Quarto and 1623 Folio, see Leah S. Marcus, *Unediting the Renaissance: Shakespeare, Marlowe, Milton* (New York and London: Routledge, 1996); Stanley W. Wells and Gary Taylor, "No Shrew, A Shrew, and The Shrew: Internal Revision in The Taming of the Shrew," in *Shakespeare: Text, Language, Criticism: Essays in Honor of Marvin Spevack*, eds. Bernhard Fabian and Kurt Tetzeli von Rosador (Hildesheim, Zurich, and New York: Olms-Weidman, 1987), 351-70.

59. Shakespeare, *Mr. VVilliam Shakespeares comedies, histories, & tragedies* (London: Isaac Iaggard and Ed Blount, 1623), 210.

60. Jones and Stallybrass, *Renaissance Clothing and the Materials of Memory*, 215.

61. Shapiro, "Framing the Taming," 155.

62. To be fair, the stage directions for these kisses, which occur in *Taming of the Shrew* 5.1 and 5.2, do not appear in the 1623 Folio and have been added by modern editors who have taken Petruccio and Katherine's dialogue as their cue. It is certainly possible, especially in *Taming of the Shrew* 5.1, that Katherine rebuffs Petruccio, but this, too, would point spectators back to the play's Induction, where Sly's wife had done the same.

63. Anonymous, *A pleasant conceited historie, called The taming of a shrew*, G2ᵥ.

64. Ibid.

65. On uses of the Induction in more modern productions of Shrew, see Elizabeth Schafer, "Introduction," in *The Taming of the Shrew, Shakespeare in Production* (Cambridge: Cambridge University Press, 2003), 30-76, especially 52-56. Schafer notes Ellen Dowling's study of sixty-five productions of Shrew from 1844 to 1978. Of the productions surveyed, "75 per cent . . . used Sly, many using the full framework from A Shrew, rather than just the three scenes supplied by the Folio" (52).

66. Schafer, *Shrew*, 58.

67. In *Dream in Shakespeare: From Metaphor to Metamorphosis* (New Haven and London: Yale University Press, 1974), Marjorie Garber says of Midsummer's epilogue, "Puck's purposeful ambiguity dwells yet again on a lesson learned by character after character within the play: that reason is impoverished without imagination, and that we must accept the dimension of dream in our lives. Without this acknowledgment, there can be no real self-knowledge" (60).

68. Schafer, *Shrew*, 59.

69. Gordon Williams, *A Glossary of Shakespeare's Sexual Language* (Atlantic Highlands, NJ: Athlone Press, 1997), s.v., "hell." See also Eric Partridge, *Shakespeare's Bawdy*, 3rd ed. (New And London: Routledge, 1968), s.v. "hell."

70. The word "forward" appears eight times in *Taming of the Shrew* (1.1.69, 1.2.90, 2.1.293, 4.5.78, 5.2.119, 5.2.157, 5.2.169, 5.2.183), in each instance modifying "wife" or "woman." Cf. Joseph Swetnam, who in *The araignment of leuud, idle, froward, and vnconstant women* . . . . (London: George Purslowe, 1615), explains that a woman's "forwardness" is not the result of her having a vagina but of her being born of Adam's rib:

    Moses describeth a Woman thus: At the first beginning (saith hee) a woman was made to be a helper vnto man, & so they are indeed: for she helpeth to spend and consume that which man painefully getteth. Hee also saith that they were made of the ribbe of a man, and that their froward nature sheweth; for a ribbe is a crooked thing, good for nothing else, and women are crooked by nature: for small occasion will cause them to be angry (Bi).

71. Stockton, *Playing Dirty*, xix.

72. In addition to the gloss found in the Norton Shakespeare, see the following: Frances E. Dolan, ed., *"The Taming of the Shrew": Texts and Contexts* (Boston and New York: Bedford/St. Martin's, 1996); Brian Morris, ed., *The Taming of the Shrew, by William Shakespeare, The Arden Shakespeare*, 3rd series (Walton-on-Thames: Thomas Nelson and Sons, 1981); and H. J. Oliver, ed., *The Taming of the Shrew, Oxford World's Classics* (Oxford: Oxford University Press, 1998).

73. Williams, *A Glossary of Shakespeare's Sexual Language*, s.v. "tail."

74. Partridge, *Shakespeare's Bawdy*, s.v. "tail."

75. In Partridge, *Shakespeare's Bawdy*, see the entries on "finger," "instrument," and "play." In Williams, *A Glossary of Shakespeare's Sexual Language*, see "finger" and "viol."

76. B. R. Smith, *Homosexual Desire in Shakespeare's England*, 150-51.

77. Jean Baudrillard, *Simulacra and Simulation*, trans. Sheila Faria Glasser (Ann Arbor: University of Michigan Press, 1994), 12-14.

78. *As You Like It*, in Greenblatt, et al., *The Norton Shakespeare*, 2.7.138-39.

'UNUSUAL FIRES'

Ann Batten Cristall's Queer Temporality

Christopher C. Nagle

Recent debates in queer historiography[1] have begun to shift the terrain of literary history and its related cultural forms away from more familiar tropes of space and into the remarkably generative direction of queer temporalities.[2] This movement is exciting for many reasons, not least of which is the promise it bears of continuing an ever-expansive variation on a theme of "reparative" critical reading practices originally spurred by Eve Sedgwick's provocation more than a decade ago. In particular, Carolyn Dinshaw's conceptualization of "touching" history, Carla Freccero's notion of "spectrality," and Elizabeth Freeman's "eroto-historiography" allow for some powerful new ways of exploring a richly embodied engagement with the past, one that can be exuberantly subjective and fully rigorous while refusing the toxic, outmoded scholarly belief that these two qualities are incompatible.[3] By imagining the work of literary and cultural history as an endeavor to establish portals in which history works as (at the very least) a two-way street, with the present informing the past as fully as the past informs the present, such writers continue to make it possible to bring to life formerly occluded or simply unimaginable ways of being in the world.

Working out of what seemed a longstanding impasse between alterity and continuism, this emerging body of supple theoretical work provides something more than new models for other readers to adopt and replicate. Even more stimulating, perhaps, is the anti-systematic character of this work, its explicit refusal to establish the kind of readily sedimentalizing edifice that new paradigms often introduce; to abuse a metaphor slightly, today's more provisional theoretical scaffolding readily becomes tomorrow's critical bedrock, a material substrate akin to adamantine Truth rather than an unfolding network of less predictable truth-effects. This particularly salutary effect of the new queer historiography promises a fresh proliferation of new means to reconceptualize what is queer about history, literature, and culture, by re-working the axes of temporality. Without giving up its multi-valent power and specificity, *queer* is thus expanded through a conceptual diffusion that, paradoxically enough, enriches its "present future" (in Valerie Traub's phrase), making unexpected, unfamiliar uses of a term whose seeming familiarity in the current theoretical lexicon makes it difficult for many people to imagine a queerness comprised of broader matrices of eccentricity and deviance than those which commonly congeal around "sexuality," particularly same-sex erotic activity. In this new work sexuality emerges as embodied not merely in acts or identities, but also *in time itself.* Neither simply universalizing, nor presentist, nor radically anticipatory—but also respecting rather than relinquishing the appeal that each of these perspectives might offer—new directions in queer historiography offer the potential of rethinking the relationship of temporality to sexuality, and in so doing, challenge us to think about the sex *of* time as well.

Towards a Decompositional Aesthetics

Since most of this work to date focuses on Early Modern or twentieth-century texts and contexts, it seems particularly timely to press for similar experiments with both canonical and non-canonical texts of the Long Eighteenth Century. To this end I wish to consider the mostly neglected oeuvre of a late eighteenth-century poet, Ann Batten Cristall, not only because her fascinating work deserves a far wider audience than it currently enjoys, but also because it offers an ideal example of the way that the term *queer*, fitting as it feels in many ways, must be pressed into especially flexible and expansive service to account for its riches,[4] and because it provides a kind of test case for exploring the strange modes of temporality embodied in her work. In fact, both the richness of Cristall's poetry—its bizarre formal innovations and thematic excesses, for example—and its lamentable obscurity are markers of its queerness, though not in some simple, causative sense—as if we could presume her queerness first, and then determine either the quality of her poetry or explain its near disappearance from the literary historical landscape from there. As George Haggerty has so ably shown in his recent work on Horace Walpole's letters,[5] such assumptions ultimately do a disservice to the richly varied (and often quite strange) elements of the quotidian, whether one chooses to minimize or maximize the deviance of these everyday manifestations.

We might be better served, as Haggerty notes elsewhere in a recent study of the gothic, by attending to these historically specific cultural manifestations on their own terms. Rather than simply being dutifully historicist in a familiar, traditional sense, such an approach might shed light on "the peculiar sexual limitations of the present," and thus help to unfold the reciprocity of historicism.[6] In this way we might continue moving beyond the residual traces of essentialist-versus-constructionist debate as well as the equally pervasive—if less commonly explicit—assumptions about "anachronism" and "alterity," and thus about what counts as legitimate literary and cultural history. To put it another way: if one of the animating concerns of literary history is to recover what Walter Benjamin calls an "image of the past that . . . not recognized by the present as one of its own concerns threatens to disappear irretrievably," then what is called for, perhaps, is an *arrest* of critical thought—a suspension of initial assumptions about either the past's intimate proximity to us (critiqued as anachronism) or the past's radical distance from us (critiqued as altericist).[7]

The benefit of doing so might be that literary historians could generate a productive, asynchronous convergence between a "now" with which we too often assume an unwarranted intimacy—and thus too quickly make leaps that seem intuitive, based on more or less unconsciously adopted and even habitual contemporary critical procedures (to "always historicize" or to read "one inch above the text," for example)—and a "then" which seems so distant as to require special protocols of analytical objectivity (however relative, flexible, or even fantasmatic) so as to satisfy the scholarly sense of "critical distance." Call it an act of negative capability, but one that not only abides within a space of Keatsian "uncertainties, Mysteries, [and] doubts, without any irritable reaching after fact & reason," but that also experiences this space as a temporal distortion—not as a timeless obliteration of all considerations apart from Beauty as the poet suggests, but as a dis-placement, a queer sense of asynchrony.[8] Such asynchrony could be key to this heuristic practice, but it also would need to facilitate new habits of attention (thinking *and* feeling) attuned to the ways that temporality presses palpably on form, in addition to the representational life of desiring subjects.[9]

After all, affect and eros manifest through structures of language as well as structures of feeling, as Wordsworth argued famously more than a decade before Keats in his Preface to *Lyrical Ballads*. In this early Romantic manifesto, published shortly after Cristall's poetic volume, Wordsworth insists that the felt sense of meter, its pacing and pleasurable constraint, does two curious things: it helps to mediate the experience of pain readers might feel, depending on the subject, and it draws on the human fascination with "similitude in dissimilitude," and thus is directly connected to "the sexual appetite, and all the passions connected with it."[10] Here, the rhythms of sexuality and poetry are inextricably linked, since what draws people to both experiences is the desire for pleasure and the perception of a sameness shared within difference and, likewise, a difference within sameness.[11] This linkage is explained in part by the pleasure of the reading experience which is enriched by repetition, by re-experiencing the work over time—one would reread a ballad more readily, for example, than *Clarissa*, both because Richardson's novel is distressing and because it is a work of prose. But what is less clear is whether each rereading (the same work read at different times) necessarily produces an asynchronous experience: "similitude in dissimilitude" here understood as similar pleasures being generated over time by different occasions for reading. Unlike Cristall, as we shall see, Wordsworth imagines metrical regularity working to secure a reading that is in synch with the poet's designs—a normative expectation that can be thwarted, of course, by readerly insensitivity, creativity, or even eccentricity. But what happens when a poet actively crafts a nonnormative poetics that frustrates the reader's ability to "synch up" with her irregular designs? This writing would require a more flexible and asynchronous reading practice in tune to the unstable and even chaotic flux of such a poetical landscape—or in Cristall's verse, its *timescapes*.[12]

The most logical place to begin looking in more detail at the queer nature of Cristall's project is in her wild, irregular narrative poetry, an "irregularity" announced both in her preface and in subtitles of various individual poems.[13] Lyric pieces, odes and elegies appear throughout *Poetical Sketches* (1795) as well, but the bulk of the volume is made up of something approximating a dramatic fiction in verse. Among other things, this unconventional poetic project enables her to experiment with the flexibility of generic boundaries and a new voice for articulating female experience. The narrative poems that open the collection function as a centerpiece, forming a sequence that is not characteristic of the rest of the volume, but which nonetheless introduces key themes and figures and thus serves as an apt introduction to Cristall's poetic world. Each piece introduces various quasi-mythic characters which are, on one hand, distanced from readers by their names, their behavior and her idiosyncratic typography; on the other hand, the instincts and urges that motivate their behavior and the contexts in which they find themselves are often very human, common, and familiar: the joys of love, desire, religious faith, and creative inspiration; the trials of suffering, loss, isolation, and disillusionment.

Nevertheless, the poems do not allow readers to forget that these are clearly fictional characters, highly self-aware poetic constructs with names drawn from familiar literary stock (Ianthe, Rosamonde, Lysander), but which more frequently are prone to clever, punning possibilities (Eyezion, Viza), the extra-literary (Holbein [Holbain], Raphael), or the randomly exotic (Thelmon, Carmel, Urban). At least one character in each of the narrative poems is a poet-figure whose self-expression takes the form of song and who serves as a protagonist in similarly configured episodes of dangerous heterosexual courtship. These peculiar rituals are characterized by uncontrollable passion of both female and male characters, pathetic vulnerability of the female, and an alternatively playful and ominous tone that reflects a generally violent psychic-emotional instability as well—an instability reflected in the irregular structure and meter of the poems themselves.

This opening sequence presents a temporal progression from "Before Twilight" to "Morning," "Noon," "Evening," and "Night," an expansion of the conventional daily cycle that begins with a liminal stage that is neither night nor dawn. Indeed, the first line of the volume renders this stage explicitly: "Dawn had not streak'd the spacious veil of night"—though within about ten lines it begins to appear. Likewise, the final stage—or more properly, perhaps, the one that brings the reader back full-circle—is marked distinctly, in the "still and solemn hour" (39) of night, by self-consuming reflections that suggest a dissolution not merely of a diurnal schedule, but of mortal existence altogether. The final line of the sequence touches a conventional theme, mourning "those joys which of themselves decay!" (46). Although tumultuous and often tortuous passions are at the center of each poem—and of the entire volume as well—here readers are left in a state of dissolution, as both affective and material existence dissolve before our eyes.

Despite Cristall's claims for randomness and irregularity (and there is plenty of both to be found), an interesting thematic continuity emerges between these forms of dissolution and those of a later poem, "Elegy on a Young Lady." The "decay" invoked in what might seem like a more moralistic framework in the earlier poem—another version of the paths of glory that lead but to the grave—is here retooled into what best can be described as a grotesque opening to an elegy for a beautiful young woman: "Transcendent beauty moulders 'midst the earth!" Cristall's preoccupation not merely with death, but also with the decay of the flesh, defeats any attempt to renovate or redeem the corruption of the body with an imagined spiritual apotheosis.[14] What we might call the *decompositional* opening of the poem is followed in short order by "blasting death / [that] Dissolves each form" (3-4), "A flower, whose bloom, / By grief untimely nipp'd, / Was hurried to the tomb" (16-18), and the "blighted frame" of the corpse (20).

Beyond its intertextual nods to Shakespeare and Gray among others, Cristall's graveyard aesthetic bears a gothic fruit, proffering a model of unconventional, poetically elevated decay that activates the speaker's desire: "her virgin virtues were exhal'd above, / While o'er her corpse sad streams of bitter woe / Delug'd the relick of our former love" (21-3). In fact this "former love" has been transmuted by not one but *three* related deaths: the elegized young lady who dies of grief, her presumably male lover who is slain by the sword of a jealous rival (Jaspar), and the rival himself who dies of guilt after the murder. This narrative overkill within Cristall's elegy is set in motion not only by a triangulated rivalry, but also specifically by the lady's "constancy [which] no energy can shake" (62), a fortitude which directly precipitates the vengeful actions that follow. The only love remaining, then, is the speaker's lyric embodiment, which strikingly recounts the saturating bath of the corpse in her own tears. Oddly, "the relick of our former love" here seems to refer to the corpse itself, which is treated with a fleeting, almost idolatrous religious fervor—and by locating the ladies' shared love within this sole decaying body, introduces autoerotic as well as necrophilic energies in addition to the more evident homoeroticism.

Rather than moralizing, poems such as this one revel in their morbid extremities, drawing into its orbit a strange erotic attention, and offering no consolation beyond the vague abstraction of a "Mysterious Power" whose "dread will" (89) is perhaps as fearful as "the dire fiend internal" (78). This is one possible explanation for the highly abstracted references to both figures of Good and Evil, a stark contrast to the earthly characters populating her verse, most of whom have highly stylized, suggestive, and specific names. But even when they do, as the seducer-villain Jaspar does in this poem, Cristall's characters are always less significant than the passions which overtake them. One might say they serve as vehicles for the violence of the positive and negative affective states that they embody; or, to borrow one of her favorite figures, they serve as "mansions" for the habitation of emotions. Since the dominant affective register in this verse is heightened—"wild," "unzon'd," even "unnatural"—the body is perhaps best seen as a vehicle, a highly mobile and unstable machine prone to extremes—for both men and women alike. The startling kinds and degrees of oddness performed by this human-machine help to recast nature in its multifarious forms, to rip it 'out of time' rather than rendering it 'timeless,' and thus require a different kind of literary historical accounting attuned to the body's specifically erotic instability.

Of course, for women, the body is a site not only of violent passions—for gifted poets and musicians as well as more average women—but it is also a primary site of potential sexual violence, of corporeal and spiritual violation at the hands of predatory men. This persistent threat manifests itself throughout Cristall's verse tales, beginning with the heroine of "Morning," Rosamonde, whose indeterminate fate is to be left "all wild, sad, weeping, and forlorn!" (45). Indeed, her fate is less clear than that of her nameless corollary (perhaps the same woman?) in "Noon," who is the obvious prey of a nameless seducer who led her to stray "far in vice," and thus, "resolv'd to die— / Rather than (sad alternative!) to lie / Amid the streets, and common insults share" (80, 85-7). Rosamonde's segment ends with the deeply feeling and generous hero, Lysander, promising to revenge her wrongs, but his own powerful emotions also prove contagious and rekindle those of the newly (or nearly) chastened damsel: "Fir'd by his zeal, / extatic feelings tinge her frame; / Whose glow the passions of her breast reveal / Bright blossom of a future ripening flame!" (120-3). The closing image provides an instructive case that helps to clarify why the seemingly positive influence of a well-intentioned hero is itself ambiguous: mixing these metaphors for the growth of love fits her purpose nicely, since it highlights the healthy and unhealthy models of love's development. Ripening like a flower (we might think here of Blake's "The Sick Rose"), her desire also threatens to burn out of control, suggesting a future that repeats her past experience. And as so many moments in Cristall's tempestuous verse insist, good intentions are just as likely to lead to tragic consequences as to happy ends.

The following part of the sequence, "Evening," introduces us to Gertrude, who is connected to Rosamonde by a triangulation of desire with Urban, who serves as the polyamorous fulcrum between the two women. With "his genius fir'd" (19) by Rosamonde, he is also drawn to Gertrude in her state of mourning, "droop[ing], like [a] flowret nipp'd in early spring" (12). The conventional image for lost virginity repeats a motif appearing throughout the sequence and *Poetical Sketches* as a whole, while allowing the poet to pay more attention than ever to the female body on which she lavishes so much attention. Cristall's poetic imagination—it is hard not to call this a specifically Sapphic gaze—produces a kind of alternative blazon, from head to toe:

> The drops which glide down Gertrude's cheeks,
> Mid bitter agonies did flow;
> And though awhile her pallid lips might glow,
> 'Twas as a blossom blighted soon with woe:
> Her disregarded tresses, wet with tears,
> Hung o'er her panting bosom straight and sleek;
> Her faithful heart was all despondency and fears.

> The skies disgorg'd, their last large drops refrain,
> The cloudy hemisphere's no more perturb'd;
> The leafy boughs, that had receiv'd the rain,
> With gusts of wind disturb'd,
> Shake wild their scattering drops o'er glade and plain;
> They fall on Gertrude's breast, and her white garments stain.
> Sighing, she threw her mantle o'er her head,
> And through the brakes towards her mansion sped;
> Unheedingly her vestments drew along,
> Sweeping the tears that to the branches hung:
> And as she pass'd
> O'er the soak'd road, from off the shining grass,
> In clods around her feet the moist earth clung. (20-39)

This intensely earthy erotic attention to Gertrude's body (a precursor, perhaps, of Elizabeth Bennet's famously muddy feet and the flushed glow of exercise that combine to make her an object of erotic interest to Mr. Darcy) is interesting for several reasons. The first is that this scene goes unwitnessed by anyone but the poet and her audience, so the framing perspective shifts away from the more common voyeur/predator dynamic enacted in other poems. The second reason is that this sudden displacement forges a connection between the "irregularity" of the poet's nonnormative desire and the irregular poetic forms such desire takes in her work, producing an early example of what one critic has called "the poetic contours of sapphism" in Romantic-era writing about intimacy between women.[15] Additionally, the spondaic dilation that closes this passage forces a slow-motion shift in the temporality of the scene itself. While the reader's gaze is trained on a woman speeding through the landscape to escape the storm, the poetic line works *against* her forward motion like an undertow, slowing it down almost cinematically as our focus is drawn to the equivalent of a close-up on her feet, where "clods" of "moist earth clung." Lastly, this moment also provides a thematic echo to other solitary, eroticized scenes elsewhere in the volume.

In *Thelmon and Carmel; An Irregular Poem*, for example, both male and female protagonists give reign more explicitly to the kind of solitary and self-generated pleasures that Gertrude does not quite fully indulge, even as Cristall the poet does. Thelmon begins:

> Disowning every tie that link'd the heart,
> He lost in vice the racking sense of smart;

He gave a scope to all his mad desires.
(Perverted genius deepest crimes inspires)
The wanton chords he struck with loose delight,
And wit's strong flashes shed luxuriant light;
Till, satiate with the empty joys of sense,
And oft disgusted with their impotence,
Wearied of follies reap'd without controul,
With self-reproach he smarted to the soul;
With shame and scorn from noisy pleasures flew,
And to the calms of solitude withdrew;
Nature exploring, and with music fir'd,
Lost in research he wander'd as inspir'd. (15-28)

Here we find masturbation as perfect allegory for poetic generation, with erotic pleasure indulged and then regretted. Once satiated by his excessive indulgence, Thelmon's "empty joys"—songs of sound without sense, or rather with *sensation* substituting for rational sense—lead to his shame in the face of such activity's "impotence." Even as he turns to "nature" at the end of this passage, the character is here at odds with his creator in casting these pleasures as impotent, incapable of generation—presumably, of his inspired production of song.

The poem's female protagonist, Carmel, has her own moment of perverse indulgence, fittingly, after listening to Thelmon's "Song":

Remembrance pour'd its influence through her soul;
Her aching bosom heav'd with bitter sighs,
Her agitated thoughts distracted roll;
And to her fev'rish fancy Thelmon rose —
Now lofty verse in strains harmonious flows,
Now passion speaks in his all-potent eyes.

Like an imperfect dream the past appears,
His errors fleet like a dissolving cloud;
His virtues shine like uneclipsed stars:
No more the sense of wrongs secures her heart,
Her bosom burns with unavailing smart,
And all within the hopeless flame avow'd.
Restless she lay, till o'er the mantling skies
The dazzling radiance of the morning rose;
From the broad light she turn'd her weeping eyes,

And, spent with passion and the weight of thought,
The transient comfort of soft sleep she sought,
And listless sunk at length to half repose. (145-62)

Although this passage is perhaps more subtle than Thelmon's corollary expressions—no "perverted genius" or "deepest crimes" are invoked here—the solitary experience of aching, heaving, feverish agitation that leaves Carmel utterly "spent with passion" and "listless" is no less clearly an extended representation of masturbatory fantasy. Remarkably, she seems unaffected by the shame that plagues her male counterpart, which suggests a reversal of normative gender constructions for each character. The other major difference between the two scenes is the way in which they do conform to conventionally gendered expectations: Thelmon responds more actively by flying off into exploration and "research" (of the natural world? of human nature?), while Carmel nearly expires with passivity, sinking into a state of "half repose." Neither character's activity, then, generates poetic self-expression within the work, or perhaps only indirectly if it does at all.

But for Cristall, this representational short-circuiting of pleasure's productivity, its ability to inspire and articulate desire that bears fruit in song, is always being realized at the broader level of this "irregular" collection. The intensity with which she invests her eroticized verse exemplifies a performative aesthetic that not only represents wildly excessive passions but also argues for them as well. This argument is most relevant for poets themselves, whose primal impulses are thematized throughout the poetry. Cristall insists on the inevitability and inherent value of poetic passions for those whose "genius" refuses to brook the conventional restraints of culture. For such creatures, simultaneously blessed and cursed like Byronic heroes of a later era, "'Tis passion, and not virtue, which inspires" ("Songs of Arla" 158). And life devoid of inspiration, even if it is consequently less dangerous, seems like no life at all for her protagonists, many of which are avatars of the poet herself.

For a British woman poet in the 1790s, however, this argument is clearly dangerous, and bears affinities with the radical claims for women's autonomy over their own bodies and desires that contemporary writers explored—often to their peril—during this post-revolutionary era. The literary experiments of the Marys—Wollstonecraft, Hays, and Robinson, to name only the most well-known—share common interests with the poetic tales of Cristall heroines like Arla. In "The Enthusiast," for example, we see the protagonist's tripartite victimization at the hands of patriarchal religion, heterosexual lust, and her father's paternal authority. Even after she is seemingly chastened by her father's admonishments—"resign'd, to simple truth" after her wild transports into the realm of "dire extremes"—Cristall allows her heroine the last wild words and returns her to a state of "frenzied ecstasy" (23).

In a coda-like sequel to Arla's tale and her sequence of Songs, one more piece follows after its neat resolution. The "Song of Arla, Written During Her Enthusiasm" performs disorderly formal excess, flashing back to an earlier point in her history while appending another chapter to a narrative already closed. Its effect is to reconsider the case of Arla's fall and recovery, and to trouble the easy conclusion in which the older, wiser patriarch has the last word. Rather than drawing her sad tale of ruin to a close, this poem adds a new chapter, not merely revisiting but in fact reopening her history of wholly self-authorized effusions of excess. Troubling the logic of containment, restraint, and the proper bounds of both form and feeling, Arla finally insists, "Feelings like mine no virtue can control."[16] The addition and strategic placement of this final Song functions as reflection but also as commentary, insisting that the frenzy of past experience is perhaps not dead after all, and (to follow the Gothic metaphor to completion) it definitely is not buried deeply enough to stay submerged—in Arla's consciousness, or in history—for very long.

Shame's Face: Of Animals and Same-Species Siblings

What helps to keep the ground disturbed is Cristall's elevation of loss, shame, and varied forms of social negativity, key animating principles of her poetry that contribute to the queer decompositional aesthetic I have discussed above.[17] Shame in particular resonates in her verse as a contagious dynamic that simultaneously blocks intimacy while registering the urgent desire to connect, animated by the "double movement" Sedgwick has delineated: "toward painful individuation, toward uncontrollable relationality."[18] It also functions as a performative echo of the authorial shame voiced in the volume's preface, where excesses of feeling are mapped onto excesses of form, thus freezing, looping, or otherwise disfiguring time for her characters while contributing to a suspension of time for the reader in lyric space. This eroto-aesthetic dynamic feeds the formal irregularity for which she apologizes in her preface, as well as the thematic excesses that are colored by consistent homoeroticism and homo-affectivity. These latter registers explore both female *and* male same-sex attraction, and as part of the legacy of the culture of Sensibility, affective bonds even exceed or transcend the realm of human relations. For an important development of this supplemental variant of queer affect, I will turn to a final example, the exemplarity of which is implicit in its advertisement on the title page of the volume.

In one of Cristall's longer narrative poems, *Holbain*, the hero's primary attachments are to his horse (or to be more precise, the memory of his *dead* horse), to a kindly older man who leads him safely through the dark woods during his treacherously stormy midnight travels, and to this patriarch's young son who is wracked by grief over the recent loss of his mother. In part, this poem is a tale of shame, particularly the shame generated by gender deviance.[19] If the "glow" of shame seems conventional enough when stemming from a character's perceived expression of "unmanly woe"—certainly, sentimental tales have beaten this trope nearly to death—Cristall's poem shifts the landscape of this formulaic tableau by recoding its hero, Holbain, as distinctly feminine in his "confusion" when he stumbles upon the nameless youth "gushing tears" alone in the woods. Like countless heroines before him, especially those from gothic and sentimental novels, Holbain's confusion and his subsequent attempt "quickly to depart" from this touching and private scene are explained by an excess of delicacy within: we are told, in a parenthetical explanatory gloss, that "(Sacred he deem'd the feelings of the heart.)" When the youth follows and pursues him, "glowing" with shame, this negative affect seems to be communicable, shared in touching mutuality by both men, who walk off together as kindred souls.

A sad tale of thoughtless youth follows, as Holbain learns that guilt joins shame in feeding the "inward [burn]" of his young friend, who neglected his mother during an outing on a fateful day with wildly unpredictable weather. After wandering off to find food for their picnic, the young man was distracted by encountering a friend, when the idyllic day turned suddenly, violently stormy, and both his mother and the castle ruins in which she awaited her son's return were wholly obliterated.[20] Holbain's response is fitting: he shares "hot tears" with his friend and "with strong sympathy the youth survey'd." This scene of the male homoerotic gaze echoes their first meeting at the dinner table when Holbain is introduced to the family. As he looks around the table "observ[ing] the family by turns; / His fine eyes sparkle, and his bosom burns," and the first sight that attracts him is not the "plain" young daughter with "no roses" in her cheek and "no radiance" in her eyes; rather, he is drawn immediately to "[t]he elder youth, more silent than the rest, / [who] Seem'd with the recent marks of grief impress'd." Clearly, we have the elements of a narrative that counters the more familiar framework of heterosexual courtship that one might expect under similar circumstances.

But there is more at stake in this queer reading than the deep emotional bonds displayed by men of feeling in the late-eighteenth century, though that indeed is part of the tale. Cristall's project is too strange and too varied to be reduced to a landscape of same-sex erotics and affection alone. Consider that this fast friendship actually mirrors—both in its intense expression of individual (and later, of shared) grief, as well as in its high claims for friendship—the bond between Holbain and his dearly departed horse. At the poem's opening, the horse is spooked by the gothic atmospherics of the landscape—a "sighing" gust of wind through the trees sends it bounding away in a mad frenzy, only to be "plung'd, and smother'd in a quagmire." Grief "pierces" Holbain, who is found "Mourning his generous friend, while sad he stood." This position is the one in which the old man originally finds him, and it also serves as the sole illustration to Cristall's volume. Or to be more precise, this line is the quote provided beneath the illustration on the title page, which in fact depicts a moment *before* the horse's demise, approximately ten lines earlier. The effect is thus to produce a framing scene of fantasmatic temporal dissonance that keeps the horse alive at the same time that it pays testimony to its death, or more specifically—and this point is crucial—to Holbain's proleptic commemoration of its death.

The image itself—an engraving by the poet's brother, the well-known watercolor artist Joshua Cristall—depicts a highly stylized pose, with a muscular, half-naked Holbain and his beleaguered horse framed in a perfectly symmetrical triangulation with the "rising moon," which originally bears the Gothic description of "a bloody meteor." Barely visible far in the distance, beyond the quagmire in which the horse is sinking, is an obscure, unidentified edifice much like the one Holbain's human friend had visited with his mother on the fateful day of his own loss—another figure that no longer exists (as we learn, it was destroyed long before Holbain arrived), so this component further disrupts the sense of the poem's linear temporality. The reason for this scene's selection—whether by Cristall the poet, Cristall the artist-brother, or Joseph Johnson, the publisher—will probably never be known. Let me suggest one possible reason, apart from the vagaries of personal taste. In no obvious way is this poem the centerpiece of the volume, whether one considers physical placement, length, thematic significance, or stylistic achievement. The longest individual work, *The Triumph of Superstition*, would stand as the structural centerpiece of the collection, and "The Enthusiast / Songs of Arla" sequence seems especially significant to the poet's designs, as it extends across multiple thematically and stylistically linked segments.

But if the young and inexperienced woman poet did not wish for the sort of attention accorded, for example, to women writers of the same era such as Wollstonecraft and Robinson, it would have been wise to avoid foregrounding the latter poem and its potentially self-promoting poetic persona.[21] The self-evident excesses of Cristall's poetry already bespeak a similarly inspired poetic "genius" like the troubled and transgressive Arla. In fact, nearly any of the longer narrative poems in the collection—those works most likely to draw the interest of readers for their eccentric representation of topical and popular themes (especially the Gothic and sentimental)—also bear the threat of implicit social critique, especially in the highly fraught 1790s, when seemingly every literary production could be conscripted into a political cause. If political subversion and transgressions of both gender and sexuality were on the forefront of those threats, as much recent scholarship has established, then Cristall might well have wished to exempt herself from such attention.[22]

But there is another reason that emerges from reading this odd poem. The illustration to Cristall's "irregular" volume highlights not merely a human figure, his animal companion, and a gothic landscape, but also something less obvious because it is less visually dynamic: the "quagmire" which destroys the horse and thereby animates Holbain's grief and loss. This double loss, both material and affective, also bears an analogue in the early moral provided by the old man who leads Holbain from his errant path: "monstrous crimes in soils luxuriant grow, / Strong powers ill govern'd sink us deep below." Even without the clear link between the literal "sinking" into the quagmire at the poem's opening and the figurative moral slide into depths "below," the trope of "luxuriant" soils—that staple of exoticized (often Orientalized) locales in the British Gothic imaginary—serves as a familiar signpost for deviant desires.

In other words, the quagmire in which Holbain's beloved horse is caught threatens to suck him in as well, suggesting a link between the physical and psychic, with the typical (material and moral) associations of "straying from the path," but also the less typical link—forged in both cases through grief—between man and horse and between man and boy. Both are sympathetic links in the affective chain that connects nature and its inhabitants and binds the latter to this earthly existence. The perversity of this worldview, consistently articulated throughout *Poetical Sketches*, is not merely the poverty and pointlessness of any appeals to a transcendent spirit or a rational check on the passions' dominion. It is also, and perhaps more importantly, a perversity grounded in the most conventional and yet most easily ignored trope of homo-affectivity in the mid- and late eighteenth-century: loss.[23]

Loss of self, loss of the romantic other (one's 'better self'), loss of friendship, loss of place, loss of purpose, loss of time—all of these forms of loss are implicated in the vertiginous chain of associations crystallized in the image on the title page, itself a collaborative endeavor between brother and sister and between the "sister arts."

How, then, to balance the strange combination of the threatening "quagmire" and the exemplary family romance between artistic genres as well as siblings? With such an anti-systematic work that works so hard to sabotage the very didacticism that its vignettes perpetually invite, it is probably best to begin with what is *not* being articulated. Ultimately Cristall's poetry works against the normative logic that insists that rich, luxuriant soils yield "monstrous crimes," and counters such banal moralizing with the warm "glow" of shame transformed by "genius" into benevolent "rapture." Indeed, the cover image of Holbain might be read as the scene of shame's transformation *through time*, and perhaps even throughout time. If this scene is indeed emblematic of Cristall's poetic project as a whole, a paradoxically *systematic irregularity* that is richly diffused throughout the volume—mixing more and less conventional exempla, more and less irregular metric forms, narratives of both homo and hetero coupling, and multifarious emblems of desire—it makes sense to take this one image as a kind of synecdochal "quagmire." Making the quagmire a temporal as well as a spatial figure, it more effectively serves as a sign-post for what dangers—and pleasures—lie ahead for readers imaginative enough to enter into the complex fantasy-scape of Cristall's poetic world.

This central part of the poetic landscape not only crosses the spatial with the temporal, but also disturbs the ground of nature itself. In fact, the representation of nature is crucial to all of this work, since the very notion of "nature" and the "natural" is consistently attacked, dispersed, and reorganized in new terms throughout Cristall's poetry. Nature, it seems, is *never* quite natural. Though she has passages to rival the best of the lush natural world of Keats (who later, like Arla, would "see and sing by my own eyes inspired") and some that anticipate Wordsworth's poetry, the natural realm is also somehow strangely *out of this world*. It is, above all, constructed rather than discovered, and constructed in such a way that it can provide metaphors for artistic creation, ranges of feeling, or moral processes.[24] In other words, it is not merely a serious and strange play with synaesthesia that we see all over her work. What she creates, finally, is a Gothic pastoral verse-world structured through and disfigured by queer temporality. Passions, actions, relationships, and language itself are all shaped by the generative violence of the creative impulse, embodied by many of her protagonists—especially those who are poets or musicians—and equally importantly, performed on the page itself.

Ultimately, I see her poetry providing a case study that might contribute to recent challenges posed to the conventional practices of historicism by literary scholars such as those mentioned at the outset of this essay. As Jonathan Goldberg and Madhavi Menon have recently argued, queer scholarship by Freccero, Traub, Alan Bray, and others working in the Early Modern period provides trenchant and inspiring alternatives to more traditional historiography. In particular, the construction of new narratives about gender and sexuality within histories of affective relations that refuse to reconsolidate familiar binaries (difference/sameness, repression/liberation, past/present, art/science) shifts the critical landscape away from what Goldberg and Menon call "the compulsive heterotemporality of historicism."[25] I hope that the extended examination I have undertaken here suggests that similar kinds of "unhistorical" considerations might be equally useful—though perhaps in different ways—when approaching late eighteenth-century texts as well, especially if a queer historicism can work to undo the persistent "fetishizing of periodization"[26] that too often leads readers to see what they expected to find all along, rather than discovering the newly unexpected pleasures that might await them as well. Ann Batten Cristall's poetry offers such "unusual fires," and their exploration allows us to rethink the historical moment in which her work emerges, as well as the questions and tastes that scholars bring to both conventional and unconventional literary works. Embracing this nearly lost poet and her sole volume of poetry—of which there is but one extant copy—might stimulate a fresh "willingness to be warmed by the afterglow of the forgotten."[27] And warming to her work could offer new decompositional portals to the multifarious times of the past, which are just as surely moments and experiences of feeling knowledge in the continuing *present.*

Notes

for Eve Sedgwick, late and soon

1. I am grateful to the anonymous reader of this manuscript for pressing me to clarify connections and implications of my argument throughout, to the Queer People conference participants who provided valuable feedback to an early version of this work (particularly George Haggerty), to Beth Bradburn and Courtney Wennerstrom for saving me from shameful missteps in the eleventh hour, and to Chris Mounsey above all for his patience and support. All citations for Cristall's poetry are taken from my electronic edition of *Poetical Sketches* (1795), which is part of the University of Virginia's *British Poetry 1780-1910: a Hypertext Archive of Scholarly Editions*, eds. Jerome McGann and David Seaman, (Charlottesville: University of Virginia Library, 1995), http://etext.lib.virginia.edu/toc/modeng/public/CriSket.html.

2. Judith Halberstam, *In a Queer Time and Place: Transgender Bodies, Subcultural Lives* (New York: New York University Press, 2005); Elizabeth Freeman, "Turn the Beat Around: Sadomasochism, Temporality, History." *Differences* 19, no. 1 (2008): 32-70, "Still After," in *After Sex?: On Writing Since Queer Theory.* Special Issue of *South Atlantic Quarterly*, eds. Janet Halley and Andrew Parker (Durham, NC: Duke University Press, 2007): 495-500, and "Time Binds, or, Erotohistoriography," *Social Text* 84-85, nos. 3-4 (October 2005): 57-68, as well as her introductory essay and roundtable discussion with a host of important scholars, both of which are featured in a special issue on "Queer Temporalities," *GLQ* 13, nos.2-3 (2007): 177-95; Valerie Traub, *The Renaissance of Lesbianism in Early Modern England* (Cambridge and New York: Cambridge University Press, 2002) and "The Present Future of Lesbian Historiography," in *A Companion to Lesbian, Gay, Bisexual, Transgender, and Queer Studies*, eds. George E. Haggerty and Molly McGarry (Madlen, MA and Oxford: Blackwell, 2007); Heather Love, *Feeling Backward: Loss and the politics of Queer History* (Cambridge, MA: Harvard University Press, 2007). See also David Halperin's suggestive remarks about "a different relation to time" for histories of female and male homosexuality (*How to Do the History of Homosexuality* [Chicago: University of Chicago Press, 2002], 79). For a related exploration of the political significance of temporality in a non-literary context, see Judith Butler's "Sexual Politics, Torture, and Secular Time," *British Journal of Sociology* 59, no. 1 (2008): 1-23.

   Freeman's recently published *Time Binds: Queer Temporalities, Queer Histories* (Chicago: University of Chicago Press, 2010) draws together the work cited above in addition to some new material.

3. Eve Kosofsky Sedgwick, *Novel Gazing: Queer Readings in Fiction* (Durham, NC: Duke University Press, 1997), and reprinted more recently in *Touching Feeling* (Durham, NC: Duke University Press, 2003). Carolyn Dinshaw, *Getting Medieval: Sexualities and Communities, Pre- and Postmodern* (Durham, NC: Duke University Press, 1999); Carla Freccero, *Queer/Early/Modern* (Durham, NC: Duke University Press, 2005); Elizabeth Freeman, *Time Binds: Queer Temporalities, Queer Histories* (Chicago: University of Chicago Press, 2010).

4. Of course, such expansive work has been initiated already by major figures in queer studies, from the early polemics of Lee Edelman and Michael Warner and the many supple (and highly varied) interventions of Leo Bersani and Judith Butler in the realm of critical theory, to the subtle and searching revisionary literary history imagined in the studies of George Haggerty, Valerie Traub, Heather Love and others. Before all of these important scholars, Eve Sedgwick's body of work provides the exemplary model of the capacious potential of queerness. To be as clear as possible: the problem is not a narrowness of perspective in the field of Queer Studies—whatever its current impasses—but rather a narrow understanding and reductive reception of this work within the broader fields of Anglophone literary and cultural history.

5. George Haggerty, "Queering Horace Walpole," in "Friendship and Same Sex Love," eds. Caroline Gonda and Chris Mounsey, *SEL* 46, no. 3, Special Issue (2006): 543–61.

6. George Haggerty, *Queer Gothic* (Urbana: University of Illinois Press, 2006), 20. Thanks to my anonymous reader for helping me to clarify this formulation.

7. Walter Benjamin, *Illuminations* (New York: Schocken, 1969), 255. The quoted material and the reference to arrested thought are taken from the well-known "Theses on the Philosophy of History," thesis 5 and 17, respectively.

8. John Keats, *Selected Letters*, ed. Robert Gittings, revised, with a new Introduction by Jon Mee (Oxford: Oxford University Press, 2002), Letter to George and Tom Keats, 21, 27(?) December, 1817.

9. See Freeman's related thought: "Ultimately, the most powerful dialectic between sex and temporality may be that as new readerly responses become possible, new modes of writing emerge and
older modes become suddenly, dazzlingly accessible to us. Readerly responses, erotic in the broadest sense of the term, depend on the sensations possible, thinkable, and tangible in a particular
historical period" ("Introduction," *GLQ* 13, nos. 2-3 [2007]: 168).

10. William Wordsworth, "Preface," *Lyrical Ballads with other poems* (London: Longman and Rees,
1800), 47.

11. Elsewhere I have argued for the reactionary heteronormativity of this formulation as part of the
moral imperative underwriting Wordsworth's response to the tradition of Sensibility that precedes
him (see Christopher C. Nagle, *Sexuality and the Culture of Sensibility in the British Romantic Era*
[New York: Palgrave Macmillan, 2007], chap. 3, esp. 84-85).

12. I have found particularly helpful Carolyn Dinshaw's savvy observation that "one way of making
the concept of temporal heterogeneity analytically salient, and insisting on the present's irreducible multiplicity, is to inquire into the felt experience of asynchrony" ("Theorizing Queer Temporalities: A Roundtable Discussion." *GLQ* 13, no. 2 [2007]: 190). For another relevant, challenging
approach to these issues, see Graham Hammill's exploration of a "poesis of the body" in *Sexuality
and Form: Caravaggio, Marlowe, and Bacon* (Chicago: University of Chicago Press, 2000).

13. The few existing critical readings of Cristall's work, with the exception of Jerome McGann's, have
spent more time attending to the way she frames and positions her work in the preface than in
analyzing the poetry itself, so I will not belabor these issues here. See Jerome McGann, *The Poetics
of Sensibility: A Revolution in Literary Style* (New York: Oxford University Press, 1996). Clearly, the
apologia is typical of much writing by women of the period.

14. For example, one might compare this gesture with the famous mock-heroic ending of Pope's *Rape
of the Lock*. Of course, the 1790s Gothic vogue provides a more immediate context.

15. Susan Lanser, "'Put to the Blush': Romantic Irregularities and Sapphic Tropes," *Historicizing
Romantic Sexuality*, ed. Richard C. Sha (January 2006) Pars. 6-8. *Romantic Circles*, April 22,
2006, http://www.rc.umd.edu/praxis/sexuality/lanser/lanser.html. Lanser's focus here is on S. T.
Coleridge and both William and Dorothy Wordsworth, but her analysis is enriched by attention
to a range of other figures, including Anne Lister, the Ladies of Llangollen, and (briefly) Cristall
as well.

16. Cristall, "Songs of Arla," Song I, l.5. The volume's penultimate "Ode" seals this commitment
with a damning couplet: "But reason, truth, and harmony are vain, / No power man's boundless
passions can restrain" (23-4).

17. See Love's *Feeling Backward* for a groundbreaking and original treatment of similar affective forms
of negativity in a later historical context, and Adriana Craciun's *Fatal Women of Romanticism* (New
York: Cambridge University Press, 2003) for a different conceptualization of a poetics of (Romantic) decomposition in the later work of Letitia Landon.

18. Eve Kosofsky Sedgwick, "Shame, Theatricality, and Queer Performativity: Henry James's *The Art
of the Novel*" in *Gay Shame*, eds. David M. Halperin and Valerie Traub, (Chicago: University of
Chicago Press, 2009), 49-62. (originally published as "Queer Performativity: Henry James's *The
Art of the Novel*" *GLQ* 1 [1993]: 1-16), 51. Sedgwick also notes that "shame is itself a form of communication. Blazons of shame, the 'fallen face' with eyes down and head averted—and, to a lesser

extent, the blush—are semaphores of trouble and at the same time of a desire to reconstitute the interpersonal bridge . . . shame is both peculiarly contagious and peculiarly indiv.duating" (50).

19. For an important collection of new work that reframes the theoretical significance of the topic, see *Gay Shame*, eds. David Halperin and Valerie Traub, a volume drawing from the 2003 conference held at the University of Michigan. See especially Halperin and Traub's introduction to the collection, "Beyond Gay Pride," as well as Sedgwick's "Shame, Theatricality, and Queer Performativity" and Michael Warner's "Pleasures and Dangers of Shame." For a more skeptical reading of shame's critical deployment, particularly in the work of these two latter critics, see Leo Bersani's "Aggression, Gay Shame, and Almodovar's Art" in *Is the Rectum a Grave? And Other Essays* (Chicago: University of Chicago Press, 2010).

20. The stunning extremity of the tale recalls the pathos and pyrotechnics of the climactic scene in Bernardin de St. Pierre's sentimental blockbuster, *Paul et Virginie*. This work was translated into English in 1788 by the famous sentimental poet, chronicler of the French Revolution, and "unsex'd female," Helen Maria Williams, and was an international bestseller akin to Rousseau's *Julie* and Goethe's *Werther*.

21. Like their compatriot, Helen Maria Williams, both writers enjoyed notoriety during this period, even if their greatest scandals were yet to come. Robinson's Sapphic persona would supplant her earlier identity as "Perdita," Shakespearean actress and royal consort, with the 1796 publication of *Sappho and Phaon*; Wollstonecraft, already infamous for the radical politics of her earlier *Vindications*, would become irredeemably shamed by Godwin's posthumous biographical *Memoirs*. The latter was also a friend of the Cristalls and a subscriber to *Poetical Sketches*.

22. For extended discussion of these issues see, for example, Claudia L. Johnson, *Equivocal Beings: Gender and Sentimentality in the 1790s, Wollstonecraft, Radcliffe, Burney, Austen* (Chicago: University of Chicago Press, 1995) and Nagle, *Sexuality and the Culture of Sensibility*, as well as Katherine Binhammer, "The Sex Panic of the 1790s," *Journal of the History of Sexuality* 6, no. 3 (1996): 409–34.

23. The classic articulation of this insight is George Haggerty's groundbreaking work, *Men in Love: Masculinity and Sexuality in the Eighteenth Century* (New York: Columbia University Press, 1999).

24. This catalog of late eighteenth-century poetic attributes is indebted to Patricia Meyer Spacks, ed., "Introduction," in *Augustan Poetry* (New York: Irvington, 1979), a list which again brings to mind Blake's work and world, as do the consistently repeated images of human eyes that "roll." The only example of such an other-worldly natural setting I have seen in women's poetry of the period is one that is literally out of this world: Melesina Trench's imagination of an extra-planetary world in *Laura's Dream; or the Moonlanders* (Southampton: J. Hatcher, 1815).

25. Jonathan Goldberg and Madhavi Menon, "Queering History." *PMLA* 120, no. 5 (October 2005): 1608–17.

26. Valerie Traub, "Friendship's Loss: Alan Bray's Making of History." *GLQ* 10, no. 3 (2004): 339–54.

27. Freeman, "Still After," 498.

From Terry Castle's *The Apparitional Lesbian* (1993) to Jennifer Waelti-Walters' *Damned Women* (2000), when reviewing the literary history of lesbianism in France, critics have generally persisted in taking the 18th century as a starting point, claiming Diderot's *Memoirs of a Nun* (1796) to be the first literary work to stage a lesbian as a main character. We know that the lesbian has been erased or "ghosted"—to quote Castle—almost universally. Even Michel Foucault—perhaps one of the most likely historians to tackle the taboo raised by the question of a genealogy of female homoerotic practices in literature—despite the promising title of his book, *The History of Sexuality*, fails to inscribe her presence in seventeenth- and eighteenth-century France. One would therefore have to agree with Catherine A. MacKinnon's response to Foucault's *History* that

> for a man who understands so much about epistemology, power, knowledge, and law, it takes the tenacity of genius to avoid gender as nearly completely as he does. I think his denial of gender is fundamental, and necessary to his perspective.[1]

Despite their lack of presence in literary history and criticism, women who chose to step outside the heterosexual economy were very much known to Old Regime France. The history of Early Modern lesbian representations is, however, a curious one. Attempts to define the lesbian in texts of that period range from the dangerous male imitating tribade, to the abandoned, older, and grief stricken Sappho, inherited from the Ovidian tradition, who plunges into the sea after having been rejected by the man for whom she has forsaken all women.[2] The threatening dimensions of the tribade are particularly obvious in dictionaries and treatises of

Early Modern France. Henry Estienne begins this trend in the Renaissance.³ For Estienne, the "tribade" is guilty of "*meschanceté*" ["wickedness"], that is to say of dressing up as a man, and of penetration, a crime punishable by death by fire.⁴ The real offense for Estienne is not that the tribade loves another woman but that she dares to love her in a masculine disguise, therefore attempting to appropriate the sacred shape of the phallus.

In Old Regime France, Pierre de Bourdeille, known as Brantôme, continues this representational tendency in his posthumous *Vies des dames galantes*, where he paints a peculiar portrait of the tribade:

> *On dit que Sapho de Lesbos a esté fort bonne maitresse en ce mestier, voire, dit-on, qu'elle l'a inventé, et que depuis les dames lesbiennes l'ont imitée en cela et continué jusques aujourd'huy; ainsi que dit Lucian: que telles femmes sont les femmes de Lesbos, qui ne veulent pas souffrir les hommes, mais s'approchent des autres femmes ainsi que les hommes eux-mesmes. Et telles femmes qui ayment cet exercice ne veulent souffrir les hommes, mais s'adonnent à d'autres femmes, ainsi que les hommes mesmes, s'appellent tribades, mot grec dérivé, ainsi que j'ay appris des Grecs, de tribo, tribein qui est autant à dire que fricare, freyer, ou friquer, ou s'entrefrotter. . . .*
>
> [It is said that Sapho of Lesbos was a mighty mistress in this occupation that, and even that she invented it, and that since then, lesbian ladies have imitated her and continued to do so until today; as Lucian says: that such women are the women of Lesbos, who do not want to be near men, but who go near other women just as men themselves do it. And such women who love this practice don't want to go near men, but devote themselves to other women, just as men themselves do it, [they] are called *tribades*, derived from the Greek word, as I have learned from the Greeks, *tribo* and *tribein* which is to say *fricare*, or rub together [. . .]⁵

It is interesting to note that next to the term "tribades" already appears the word "lesbian," a term that will not be used frequently in France for another two centuries.⁶ Brantôme insists that these women act "just as men themselves do it," not simply because they feel erotic love toward the female sex, but mostly because of their very practice of that love. Brantôme creates a clear link between "tribade" and "fricare" insisting that the lesbian imitates the male even in the very act of love itself. In Brantôme's imaginary then, sexual practices between women can only make sense if they are seen to imitate heterosexual love making, the tribade assuming a role clearly associated to the masculine. Under Brantôme's pen, the lesbian has thus become hetero-normalized, the victim of a kind of rationalization of homoerotic practices between women. This hetero-normalization is a recurring practice in French literature portraying the lesbian, for many are those who regard her as an imitator, one that must be recuperated at all costs.[7]

Nowhere is this question of imitation of masculinity and attempt to usurp phallic privileges more obvious than in the play I propose to examine here. The comedy *Iphis et Iante*, first performed at the Hotel de Bourgogne in Paris in 1634,[8] offers France's first Early Modern lesbian character to appear on stage, an unprecedented feat realized by the notorious seventeenth-century French libertine poet and playwright Isaac de Benserade. Though Benserade's characterization of the lesbian has been labeled uniquely sympathetic and avant-garde by some,[9] I hope to show that it is instead extremely damaging, for imbedded in the play is his fearful narrative towards her, a fear that hides behind a prominent satirical discourse around her lack of phallus.[10] Following the analysis of this phallus-identified lesbian, I will then examine Benserade's second and last narrative depiction of lesbianism in his career, in "On Uranie's Love for Philis," a long poem written in the *fin de siècle* which contrasts his first grotesque lesbian with what this narrator sees as a more troubling and incomprehensible behavior. The analysis of both sapphic representations will show that toward the end of his career, Benserade envisioned the lesbian as a more dangerous creature, one that seemed to embody the ideal 18th century libertine, a woman undefined by hetero normative laws.

As the title suggests, Benserade's comedy is based on one of Ovid's metamorphoses in *Book Nine*, the *Fable of Iphis and Ianthe*. Ovid's plot is simple: at the birth of Iphis, her mother Telethusa decides to bring her up as a boy in order to hide the truth from her husband, Lygdus, who, worried by the financial burden of too many daughters, had previously sworn to kill the child at birth were it not a boy. Because the mother is reassured by the goddess Isis that all will end well, she decides to save her daughter and lies to her husband about Iphis' sex. Years go by, and Iphis, who has been disguising as a boy since her birth, falls madly in love with a young woman, Ianthe. Both families decide to wed them. As the day of their wedding draws closer, Iphis is miserable, feeling the shame of this "monstrous passion"[11] and tries in vain to stop her "stupid fires".[12] On her wedding day, Iphis begs the gods for help. In the end, Isis saves the day by transforming Iphis into an adolescent boy. The natural order being restored, the wedding can now safely take place. The Ovidian plot ends here. Ovid recognizes the existence of lesbian love, but the text insists visibly on the feelings of shame and monstrosity from which Iphis suffers because of that love. Valerie Traub is right then to note that with Ovid the sexual impossibility between both young women is always safely maintained.[13] Since lesbian love in the Ovidian fable is a moral crime, one that is deemed to be against nature, the physical contact must remain strictly forbidden.

Seeking to expand on what, in his preface to the reader, Benserade playfully calls *la stérilité* ["the sterility"] of Ovid's subject—referring of course to the assumed sexual impossibility between Iphis and Iante (Ianthe)—the seventeenth-century playwright makes a few important changes to the Ovidian plot. First, he adds three new characters, among which the most significant is Ergaste, a young man who knows about Iphis' sexual disguise and who is madly in love with her.[14] This brings an additional homoerotic twist to the plot, but one that is not really explored by the play. Indeed, aside from the occasional humoristic remark made by Iante's father Téleste (Telethusa) on what he calls Ergaste's *"étrange manie"* ["strange way"][15] (4.5), and by Iphis' father Lidge (Lygdus) for whom Ergaste has *"perdu le sens"* ["lost all reason"] (3.4), it is clearly not male homoeroticism that intrigues Benserade here.[16] For while the changes made by Benserade all add to the overall thematic of homoerotic love in the play, Iphis' age and the chronology of events are the two most crucial changes brought to Ovid's plot, since they accentuate the play's desire to explore the normally forbidden realm of public displays of female homoeroticism. In Benserade's play, Iphis is in fact twenty years old. It is this adult and sexually matured woman who now replaces the young adolescent girl of Ovid's fable. More importantly, Iphis' metamorphosis in Benserade's comedy happens after the wedding, leaving plenty of time for the theatrical exploration and display of female homoerotic love. Iphis' newly created sexual maturity and the fact that she is allowed to wed the woman she loves before the metamorphosis can take place are two factors that will play a determining role in the representation of lesbian love in Benserade's revolutionary drama. Indeed, the love we witness here is intensely physical and erotic. Benserade's play does not shy away from portraying the strong sexual desire that Iphis feels for Iante, as it is the case, for instance, when Iphis recounts the first erotically charged moments of her wedding night to her mother:

> *J'oubliais quelque temps que j'étais une fille,*
> *Je ne reçus jamais tant de contentements,*
> *Je me laissais aller à mes ravissements,*
> *D'un baiser j'apaisais mon amoureuse fièvre,*
> *Et mon âme venait jusqu'au bord de mes lèvres,*
> *Dans le doux sentiment de ces biens superflus*
> *J'oubliais celui même où j'aspirais le plus,*

J'embrassais ce beau corps, dont la blancheur extrême
M'excitait à lui faire une place en moi même,
Je touchais, je baisais, j'avais le cœur content.

[I forgot for a time that I was a young girl,
I have never received so much contentment,
I let myself go to my ravishment,
With a kiss I appeased my feverish love,
And my soul rose up to the brim of my lips,
In the sweet sensation of these excessive goods
I forgot even that, to which I aspired most,
I kissed this beautiful body, whose extreme whiteness
Excited me to open myself to it,
I touched, I kissed, I had a contented heart.] (5.5)

We are witness, here, to an unusual representation of lesbian love for the period, one that seems to pay homage to the physical union of both women. However, far from admitting a possibility that Ovid had so vehemently denied, that is, the female homoerotic possibility, Benserade allows this lesbian erotic representation only to better emphasize what the play portrays incessantly: its ridiculousness and, especially, its lack of phallus. The play obsesses with lexical references that point, time and time again, to the obvious missing agent in this couple. In the end, it is the themes of (phallic) lack, incompleteness and ridiculousness that will mostly define female homoerotic love and the lesbian, herself, comes out as a being marked by the grotesque, the not quite real, the uncanny, that is to say, embodying Baroque traits that depict her very queerness in the eye of society.

Remaining true to the dominant aesthetic in France in 1634, Benserade's representation of the lesbian paints a being defined by the Baroque. Iphis and her passion are rendered supernatural, the play's language marking them with references to notions of instability, disorder, and illusion. Iphis' mother betrays this baroque tendency in her description of her daughter's passion for another woman:

Iphis, que je te plains, et qu'on verra dans peu
De merveilleux effets de ton aveugle feu!
Tu pourrais différer ce triste mariage,
Qui ne sera jamais qu'à ton désavantage,
Aussi bien, cette flamme est une illusion,
Et j'ai peur qu'elle tourne à ta confusion.

[Iphis, I feel for you, and we'll see before too long
The wondrous effects of your blind flame!
You could defer this sad wedding,
Which will only ever be to your disadvantage,
As well, this flame is an illusion,
And I fear it will become your confusion.](1.2)

As the play develops, the lesbian is slowly defined as a baroque being, a woman whose homoerotic passion appears as supernatural, a feeling evoked here by the "wondrous effects." The antithesis contained in "blind flame", and the words "illusion" and "confusion" (suggesting states of instability and disorder) further accentuate the Baroque elements that contribute to the representation of Iphis and her lesbian love. However, Télétuze is not the only character in the play who describes Iphis' erotic passion for Iante in Baroque terms. This type of reference occurs in the text as a whole. A case in point; Iante's words also betray that very aesthetic when, in her soliloquy, she remembers the moment she discovered Iphis' sexual disguise during her wedding night:

Dieux, qui s'en fût douté! que cette tromperie,
Pour s'abuser soi-même est pleine d'industrie,
Qui vit jamais au monde un prodige pareil?
Pour moi je l'attribue aux effets du sommeil,
Et dans l'incertitude où mon esprit se plonge,
Un semblable incident me passe pour un songe.

[Gods, who would have known! that this trickery,
To fool itself is so resourceful,
Who in the world has ever seen such a wonder?
For my part, I attribute it to the effects of slumber,
And the uncertainty in which my mind is thrown,
Such an incident strikes me as a dream.] (5.1)

In Iante's confused and stunned state of mind, this is indeed a strange scenario, one where, following baroque aesthetics, the divisions between reality and fantasy are blurred, and one that reminds us also of the very theatricality of the baroque, of the play within the play, a characteristic noted by Iante herself: "*Et pour faire parler les théâtres de nous /Une telle rencontre est digne qu'on la joue*" ["And to make theaters speak of us / Such an encounter is worthy of being staged"] (5.1). The lesbian, this odd being, must thus be placed on the comic stage, her "*amour bouf-*

fon" ["buffoon love"], as defined by Ergaste, to be witnessed and mocked by all. Indeed, the theatricality of lesbian love reaches its pinnacle when she and her sexual practices are all but exhibited on stage during the fourth act. The play's stage directions indicate that the first scene opens "*dans une chamber*" ["in a bedroom"] (4. 1). Iphis and Iante's wedding ceremony has just been concluded, and the spectators can now witness the two women alone, in the intimacy of their bedroom, ready to consummate their love. In the desperate hope that the goddess Isis will rescue her from this most delicate situation, Iphis (still unable to tell the truth to Iante) abandons herself to her destiny. As noted by Biet, while the nuptial scene ends here, the two women remain on center stage, their sexual encounter hidden only by a curtain that has been lowered in front of their wedding bed to conceal this homoerotic moment.[17] The rest of the act can safely take place in front of that enticing yet morally proper curtain. Although the spectators see the actions of the following scenes unfold before them, what really catches their attention throughout the whole act, what they take pleasure in, is what might be happening behind that tantalizing curtain. This scene produces a kind of collective orgasm, but a pleasure that also becomes a shared laughter between playwright and male spectators on the perceived impossibility of such a situation.

In her study of lesbian representations from the Renaissance to modern day Europe, Lillian Faderman remarked that lesbian love "is a sterile game, the sight serves only as an aphrodisiac to the male spectator, and all the participants tacitly agree that the penis is the *sine qua non* of sexual pleasure".[18] In the case of *Iphis et Iante*, the spectators' curiosity will have to wait an entire act before being satisfied, that is to say, before knowing the outcome of that night. Furthermore, the notion of a "game" suggested by Faderman is particularly appropriate to our analysis of the grotesque being that is the lesbian in Benserade's imaginary, for it is precisely the laughter brought about by such "sterile game" that allows her to be non-threatening to society. From an Early Modern audience perspective, since nothing *meaningful* can take place during Iphis and Iante's wedding night, their female homoerotic performance can safely be simulated (or encouraged to be imagined by means of the stage curtain), without troubling the audience, even during the sacred hetero-normativity of a matrimonial night. This lack of menace stemming from a bizarre lesbian character attempting the impossible is also reinforced by the genre chosen by Benserade for his re-creation of Ovid's fable, since emotional dissociation between spectators and the character labeled ridiculous is essential to achieving laughter in a comedy. Not surprisingly then, it is this very potential for laughter that terrifies Iante the morning after her nuptials: "*Ce mariage est doux, j'y trouve assez d'appâts / Et si l'on n'en riait, je ne me plaindrais pas* ["This marriage is sweet; I find enough enticement in it/ And if one did not laugh at it, I would not complain"] (5.1). Without this risk of a collective laughter, Iante would gladly have accepted the terms of this union. Laughter in the play thus simultaneously allows for the presence of the lesbian on stage and for her banishment.

To his strategic representation of the lesbian as a strange being marked by baroque traits and fearing laughter, Benserade will add the themes of incompleteness and lack, attributes that even precede her appearance in the play. As mentioned earlier, in his preface, Benserade informs the reader that: *"la stérilité du sujet m'a obligé d'y coudre quelques intrigues"* ["the *sterility* of Ovid's subject forced [Benserade] to expand on the plot"]. Indeed, from the first scene in Act one, Benserade uses the concepts of infertility and lack as the dominant traits in his lesbian character. This depiction is particularly apparent when Iphis' mother attempts to convince her husband to call off the wedding of her daughter to Iante:

> *Il me semble*
> *Qu'ils ne pourront jamais s'accommoder ensemble.*
> *Ces amants une fois sous la loi de Vénus*
> *Ne sont pas pour s'aimer après s'être connus:*
> *Je veux qu'ils s'aiment bien et qu'ils soient d'un même âge,*
> *Ils n'ont pas ce qu'il faut pour faire bon ménage.*
>
> [It seems to me
> That they will never manage to fit together.
> These lovers, once under Venus' law
> Will surely not love each other, having known each other:
> I agree that they like each other and are of the same age,
> They don't have what it takes to get along well.] (1.1)

When her husband, not understanding his wife's allusions, replies that Iphis is old enough to become a husband, Télétuze insists:

> *Il est vrai que c'est être à la fleur de son âge,*
> *Mais pour se marier, il en faut davantage:*
> *Il faut être tout fait devant que s'attacher*
> *D'un lien dont jamais on ne peut s'arracher*
>
> [It is true that he is in the prime of his youth
> But to marry, more is needed:

One must be fully formed before getting tied down
With a yoke which can never be severed] (1.1).

The meaning of "fully formed" to which the mother is referring here could not be made clearer. Because her daughter is missing the play's sacred object, the phallus, Télétuze cannot take the physical relationship between Iphis and Iante seriously. Her insistence throughout the play on Iphis' lack reminds the modern reader of the Freudian theory on castration, in which, according to Luce Irigaray in *Speculum of the Other Woman*, woman is but an incomplete being (read man), unfinished, a marker for zeroness:

> Woman's castration is defined as her having nothing you can see, as her *having* nothing. In her having nothing penile, in seeing that she has No Thing. Nothing *like* man. That is to say, no *sex/organ* that can be seen in a *form* capable of founding its reality, reproducing its truth. *Nothing to be seen is equivalent to having no thing. No being and no truth.*[19]

The social refusal to take the lesbian sexual relationship seriously is a characteristic common to masculine writing of the period. According to Faderman, in Early Modern society "men enjoyed a phallocentric confidence which ceased to be possible in the twentieth century. [. . .] The claim of love between women could be seen as very slight in view of the overwhelming importance of the heterosexual bond".[20] Benserade offers the same heterocentric ideology, as his play contrasts incessantly the futility and infertility of lesbian love with the fertility of hetero-sexual married life. But what is perhaps most damaging for the lesbian in his comedy is the fact that, other than Ergaste (Iphis' would-be lover), it is the female characters closest to Iphis who emphasize time and time again what they all perceive to be her physical lack. Her mother, her lover, her friend and even Iphis herself, all take turns denouncing her deficiency, her grotesque nature, and the impossibility of her situation. Mérinte, for instance, cannot resist pointing out to Iphis' mother that the couple about to be wed is deficient: *"Tous deux pour s'accorder ont trop de sympathie, / Il manque à leur hymen la meilleure partie"* ["Both have too much sympathy to fit well together / The best part of their marriage is missing"] (1.3). Not satisfied with her remark on Iphis and Iante's flaw as a couple, Mérinte will also raise the question of chastity. In her eyes, for the lesbian couple is not only infertile, but because it is, it is therefore necessarily chaste:

> *La chasteté fera son trône de leur lit :*
> *Si de semblables nœuds unissaient tout le monde,*

Ce serait bien pour voir la nature féconde;
L'encens aux immortels ne serait plus offert,
Et ce grand Univers serait un grand désert.

[Chastity will make a throne of their bed:
If such ties united everyone,
Wouldn't that be something to see nature's fertility;
Incense would no longer be offered up to immortals,
And this great universe would be a vast desert.] (1.3)

Mérinte, then, clearly equates lesbian sexual practices with chastity. Without what she refers to as the "best part", nothing meaningful, that is to say sexual, can take place. The futility of Iphis and Iante's physical union is thus perfectly emphasized. The consequence of this feminine mob joining up forces and mocking the lesbian cannot be underestimated. The playwright portrays the women characters in his play as the spokespeople of hetero-normativity, and, in addition, he positions them as the principal enemies of female homoeroticism. We are, in a way, reminded of Hélène Cixous' primary accusation toward society's principal means of reinforcing heterosexuality: "Men have committed the greatest crime against women. Insidiously, violently, they have led them to hate women, to be their own enemies, to mobilize their immense strength against themselves, to be the executants of their virile needs".[21] And so, in the end, the being that is most threatening to the very existence of the lesbian character is the female character herself, especially the mother, who speaks most forcefully of Iphis' lack throughout the play.

Crippled by the numerous remarks made toward her physical lack, Iphis comes to feel more and more inadequate. Her own words reveal this feeling of sexual inadequacy:

Je connais ma faiblesse et je me sens coupable
D'accepter un trésor dont je suis incapable,
Et pour n'en point mentir, je ne mérite pas,
Imparfait que je suis, de si parfaits appâts.

[I know my weakness and feel guilty
To accept a treasure of which I am incapable,
And to be honest, I don't deserve,
Imperfect as I am, such lovely enticement.] (2.3)

The closer Iphis gets to her wedding night, the more she fears and curses her lot:

Étrange effet d'amour! je meurs pour cette belle,
Et cependant, hélas! je suis fille comme elle:
J'adore ses beautés, qu'on ne peut trop priser,
Je suis fille, elle est fille et je dois l'épouser.
Ah déplorable Iphis! Iante infortunée!
Qui pourra de nous deux consommer l'hyménée?
Quoi? ce trésor charmant serait entre mes bras,
Je le posséderais, et n'en jouirais pas?
Quoi, je tiendrais l'objet dont mon âme est éprise
Et j'userais si mal d'une faveur acquise?
Quoi, le ciel me rendrait sans éteindre mes feux,
De bienheureux Amant, possesseur malheureux?
Quoi, je m'endormirais auprès de cette belle,
Et je ne ferais pas l'impossible pour elle?
Je serais inutile en un si digne emploi?

[Love's strange effect! I pine for this beauty,
And yet, alas! I am a maiden like her:
I love her beauties, which cannot be overstated,
I am a maiden, she is a maiden and I must marry her.
Oh deplorable Iphis! Oh unfortunate Iante!
Who between us two will consummate this marriage?
What? This charming treasure would be in my arms,
I would possess it, but not fully enjoy it?
What? I would hold the object of my soul's desire
And would use so badly this favor given to me?
What? the heavens, keeping me afire, would change me
From blissful Suitor, to unhappy possessor?
What? I would fall asleep next to this beauty,
And would not do the impossible for her?
I would be useless in such a worthy task?] (2.6)

In Iphis' soliloquy, we find the incompleteness of lesbian love, according to Benserade's premise that the lesbian cannot fully sexually satisfy her partner nor can she be satisfied herself; her sexual completeness can only be granted by the participation of the phallus. The importance of the phallus in Benserade's play coincides with its privileged status in the imaginary of the period. In her study on patriarchal perceptions of the lesbian in Early Modern Europe, Elaine Marks observed that "the tribade has value as a sexual being only insofar as she participates in the worship of the phallus. The phallus is always present as prime mover in the lesbian discourse of male scriptors".[22] In *Iphis et Iante*, the phallus is so present that it becomes the motivating agent (if not the main character itself) in the plot. Since the birth of Iphis, it is the presence of the phallus, or rather its noted absence in her, that dictates the events and brings her despair, and ultimately happiness. Therefore while Benserade grants the spectators the pleasure of observing part of the wedding night in the fourth act, he does so to better underline the extent of the ridiculous situation brought about by the constant missing player. Iphis confides in her mother and tells her about Iante's erotic dissatisfaction on their wedding night, a disappointment caused by Iphis' lack:

> *Hélas, qu'eût-elle dit! elle était occupée*
> *À se plaindre tout bas d'avoir été trompée,*
> *Et son cœur me disait par de secrets soupirs*
> *Qu'il ne rencontrait pas le but de ses désirs.*
> *Je lui baise le sein, je pâme sur sa bouche,*
> *Mais elle s'en émeut aussi peu qu'une souche,*
> *Et reçoit de ma part comme d'un importun*
> *Mille de mes baisers, sans m'en rendre pas un.*
> *Le jour vient, et je la vois qui se lève et s'habille,*
> *Honteuse de se voir la femme d'une fille.*
> *Je fais aussi comme elle, et prends mes vêtements,*
> *Ses larmes sur les siens tombent à tous moments.*

[Alas, what could she have said! she was busy
Complaining softly that she had been misled,
And her heart would tell me in secret sighs
That it was not meeting the end of its desires.
I kiss her breast, I faint on her mouth,
But she is as little moved as a stone,
And receives from me as if a nuisance,
Thousands of my kisses, without giving me even one.
Daylight comes, I see her get up and get dressed,
Ashamed of being the wife of a girl.
I do as she does, and grab my clothes,
Her tears on her own garments fall constantly.] (5. 4)

Iphis' retelling of her story does not stress, as the reader might have expected, Iante's certain shock at finding herself in bed with another woman. Instead it insists on Iphis' incapacity to satisfy her. The play's message is plain to read: sexually speaking, the lesbian couple is not self-sufficient; it needs the phallus for pleasure. It is no surprise then that in Benserade's plot Iphis, feeling ashamed and incomplete, tries to kill herself immediately following her nuptial encounter with Iante. This near fatal endeavor is stopped by her mother, but as Lise Leibacher-Ouvrard has so rightly observed, the knife with which Iphis attempts suicide is a symbolic reminder of the very object for which she longs so desperately.[23]

At this point in the plot, the comedy's imperative is to reinstate the stray being that is the lesbian, an odd woman without her place in society. This reinstatement will happen in a much more convincing way than in Ovid's text. While with Ovid the story ends with the transformation of Iphis into an adolescent boy, Benserade adds a celebration of heterosexual fertility and of masculine virility, as Iphis' last words demonstrate when she is asked by all if she has really become a man:

> *Au reste, si l'excès de ma félicité*
> *Laisse dans vos esprits de l'incrédulité,*
> *Si vous ne jugez pas mes discours véritables,*
> *Je vous en ferai voir des effets bien palpables,*
> *Et ma chère moitié d'une bonne façon*
> *Prouvera dans neuf mois qu'Iphis est un garçon.*

> [Besides, if my excessive happiness
> Leaves a doubt in your mind,
> If you don't judge my words to be true,
> I will have you see for yourselves some palpable results,
> And my dear beloved will in a remarkable way
> Prove in nine months that Iphis is a man.] (5.4)

In the end, the play suggests an established heterocentric representation of the lesbian. While it illustrates lesbian love, it clearly does so as a non-event, an insignificant affair that precedes the coming of the heterosexual experience, a fertile sexuality that promises total completeness to women. Although she did not examine Benserade's play, Faderman is right to note that "far and away the most predominant attitude toward lesbian lovemaking in French libertine literature was that it was merely a prelude to heterosexual lovemaking".[24] The end of Benserade's comedy certainly advocates the same message. Furthermore, whether it be with Ovid or Benserade, the metamorphosis of Iphis also illustrates what Adrienne Rich has called "the control of consciousness," that is to say an act in which "the possibility of a woman who does not exist sexually for men—the lesbian possibility—is buried, erased, occluded, distorted, misnamed, and driven underground".[25] The metamorphosis executes the necessary task; it helps society get rid of a being that has no place within its structures. In this obliteration of the lesbian, Benserade goes even further than Ovid. Not content with simply refusing to acknowledge the lesbian possibility, as Ovid did, his play insists instead on her total sexual incompleteness. The lesbian heroine in Benserade's comedy, though at first glance promising, is in the end brutalized by representations of the grotesque and the ridiculous, a textual assault that finally culminates in the collectively celebrated exile of her much undesired body. In the author's vision, she has no place in society. Disfigured symbolically by her lack of phallus, this eccentric being lives only to await a miracle or death. The play must make space for the much anticipated and desired phallus.

Benserade's obvious fascination with the lesbian would not fade away. Toward the end of his life, he wrote "On Uranie's Love for Philis" (1697),[26] a series of long stanzas in which he offers a different view of female homoerotic love, one where the lesbian no longer attempts to confer upon herself phallic privileges by disguising as a male, and where she is no longer associated with the masculine. Now deprived of male attributes, it is not lack or incompleteness that defines the lesbian in this *fin de siècle* poem, but, rather, nothingness. At the onset of "Uranies' love for Philis," we learn that the narrator's lover has just left him for another woman. His disbelief at his lover's new choice is unmistakable:

> *Je ne murmure pas, infidelle Uranie,*
> *De vôtre trahison;*
> *[. . .]*
> *Si pour un autre Amant vous aviez pris le change,*
> *Je l'aurois enduré:*
> *[. . .]*
> *Mais quoi! vôtre amitié, pour suivre une autre Amante,*
> *Se sépare de nous!*
> *Belle certainement, adorable, charmante,*
> *Mais femme comme vous.*

> [I don't complain, unfaithful Uranie,
> About your betrayal;

[. . .]
If you had traded for another Suitor,
    I would have suffered it:
        [. . .]
But what! Your love, to follow another woman,
    Detaches itself from us!
Beautiful, yes, adorable, charming
    But a woman, like you.][27]

The narrator admits to the beauty and charm of his female rival, but he insists that the very essence of her femininity exist only to satisfy the masculine gaze and its desires:

Elle est, il est bien vrai, digne d'être admirée
    De tous également;
Mais sa divinité ne doit être adorée
    Que de nous seulement.

[She is, it is true, worthy of being admired
    By all, equally;
But her divinity must be adored
    By us only.][28]

Though her beauty can be seen by all, masculine desire is the sole benefactor of her inner beauty, her "divinity," that is to say, the secret temple of her sexuality. Soon the frustrated lover wants to reinstate the supremacy of hetero-sexual relations and thus redirect feminine passion toward its true recipient, himself, the only being able to arouse true desires in her:

Aussi, quoiqu'elle jure et quoiqu'elle vous mente,
    Vous croyez vainement
Qu'elle ait jamais pour vous cette ardeur véhémente
    Qu'on a pour un Amant.

[Thus, whatever she may promise or lie,
    You believe in vain
That she'll ever have for you this fervent passion
    That one has for a male lover.][29]

The narrator quickly warns his lover that she simply does not have what it takes to satisfy her new lover:

> Vôtre flâme est brillante, elle tonne, elle éclaire,
>   Mais elle est sans vigueur;
> Elle peut éveiller et jamais satisfaire
>   L'amoureuse langueur.

[Your flame is bright, it thunders, it shines bright
    But it has no vigor;
It can awaken yet never satisfy
    The amorous languor.][30]

Without the participation of the male partner, these lovers ultimately cannot fulfill each other's desires. Though we may sense the familiar theme of lesbian incompleteness found throughout *Iphis et Iante*, Benserade goes further with his stances as the relationship of the two female lovers becomes entirely null and void, since it opposes the concept of heterosexual complementarity, so dear to the narrator's ideology:

> Vous estes nos moitiez, avec nous assorties
> Vous formez un beau tout ;
>   Séparez-vous de nous, vous n'estes que parties.
> Vous n'estes rien du tout.
>   Séparez-vous de nous, vous n'estes que des ombres
> Sans force et sans pouvoir.
>   Vous estes les zéros, et nous sommes les nombres
> Qui vous faisons valoir

[You are our halves, with us by your side
You become whole
    Separate yourselves from us, you are but lone parts.
You are nothing at all.
    Separate yourselves from us, you are but shadows
Without strength or power.
    You are the zeros, and we are the numbers
That make you worth while][31]

The female lovers portrayed here quickly degenerate into oblivion and the narrator becomes avenged by the very nothingness of the lovers' relationship. The hostility that had been building in the narrator's attack on the lesbian couple culminates at this point. The repetitions of the various expressions of incompleteness, ("zeros," "lone parts," "nothing") as well as the many negative structures used to describe the lesbian lovers show at once the narrator's need for hetero-complimentarity and a depersonalization of the lesbian. The lesbian is more than incomplete; she is a non person, a non being, a 0 against the 1 masculine. Benserade's poem reminds us strangely of a similar process of patriarchal depersonalization of the lesbian, one noted by Pat Califia, who remarks that society sees lesbians as performing "an awkward attempt to achieve pleasure that will forever elude them because [their] bodies don't fit together".[32] Califia quotes the popular *Everything You Always Wanted to Know About Sex* (But Were Afraid to Ask):* "one vagina plus another vagina still equals zero",[33] an ideology that Benserade clearly shared, 300 years before, in his poem.

In her book *Invisible Relations*, Elizabeth Susan Wahl comments on the invisibility of women's intimate and erotic relationships, often known in Old Regime France as *"tendres amities"* [tender friendships],[34] a term notably used when referring to female intimate relationships within the female centered Précieuses movement. I believe that at the end of Louis XIV's reign, one that has become increasingly religiously austere, the lesbian is more than invisible. Rather, she is nothingness, a series of zeros. We witness her presence perfectly well, for she is in plain view. But without her active participation in the worshiping of the phallus—as witnessed in Iphis' behavior throughout the play—that is to say when she is not seen as imitating the male—following the lovers from "Uranie's love for Philis"—she is nothing. Her behavior is simply inexplicable, incomprehensible. In a way then, in Benserade's *fin de siècle* poetic imaginary, the lesbian seems to embody the ideal 18th century libertine. Uranie and Philis' refusal to define their homoerotic desires according to heterosexual relations, or at the very least to imitate the male like the tribade was perceived to do in Early Modern France, make them examples of perfect libertines, since by refusing to reinstate the primacy of hetero relations in their sapphic relationship, they stand outside any laws, but most importantly beyond the law of the phallus.

In the end, whether she is merely grotesque and incomplete, like Iphis, or synonymous with zero, as are the inconceivable Uranie and Philis, in the author's vision, the lesbian has no place in society, even in a comedy. Everywhere he imagines her, her body exists only to be mocked, negated, and banished by his narrative.

Notes

1. Catherine A. MacKinnon, "Does Sexuality have a History?" in *Discourses of Sexuality from Aristotle to AIDS*, ed. Donna C. Stanton (Ann Arbor: University of Michigan Press, 1992), 128.

2. On this archetype of Sappho as the abandoned woman, see Ovid's "XVth Heroide." Ovid, *Heroides,* trans. Harold C. Cannon (New York: Dutton, 1971).

3. Henri Estienne, *L'Introduction au traité de la conformité des merveilles anciennes avec les modernes ou Traité préparatif à l'apologie pour Hèrodote* (Genève : n. p. 1566).

4. Marie-Jo Bonnet, *Les Relations amoureuses entre les femmes* (Paris: Éditions Odile Jacob, 1995), 30.

5. Pierre de Bourdeille, seigneur de Brantôme, *Les Vies des Dames galantes*, ed. Maurice Rat (Paris: Le Livre de Poche, 1962), 121.

6. Brantôme's use of the word lesbian justifies my own usage of the word which I have preferred in my analysis of Benserade's texts over the term "tribade."

7. See for instance Donatien Alphonse François Sade's *Augustine de Villeblanche ou le stratagème de l'amour* (1788) in *Œuvres complètes du Marquis de Sade*, Tome treizième (Paris: Au cercle du livre précieux, 1962).

8. The play would be published for the first time three years later, in 1637, in Paris. See Isaac de Benserade, *Iphis et Iante* (Paris: Lampsaque, 2000).

9. See for instance Christian Biet, "A quoi rèvent les jeunes filles? Homosexualité féminine, travestissement et comédie: le cas d'Iphis et Iante d'Isaac de Benserade (1634)," in *La Femme au XVIIe siècle*, ed. R. Hodgson (Tübingen: Gunter Narr Verlag, 2002), 80; Joseph Harris, "Disruptive Desires: Lesbian Sexuality in Isaac de Benserade's *Iphis et Iante* (1634)," *Seventeenth-Century French Studies* 24, no. 1 (2002): 152; and Elizabeth Susan Wahl, *Invisible Relations: Representations of Female Intimacy in the Age of Enlightenment* (Stanford, CA: Stanford University Press, 1999), 65.

10. I have argued elsewhere that despite being labeled a comedy, Benserade's play, in fact, shares many characteristics of a tragicomedy, its comic aesthetic slowly giving way to the tragic trauma of Iphis, a young heroine struggling with her gender identity, psychologically fragmented and unable to see a way out. Iphis' crisis results in an intense emotional trauma which in turn leads to her suicide attempt in act 5. See Marianne Legault, "Iphis & Iante: traumatisme de l'incomplétude lesbienne au Grand Siècle," *Dalhousie French Studies* (December 2007) 81, 83-93.

11. Ovid, *Metamorphoses Book IX-XII*, (Warminster: Aris & Phillips Ltd, 1999), 145.

12. Ibid., 146.

13. Valerie Traub, *The Renaissance of Lesbianism in Early Modern England* (Cambridge and New York: Cambridge University Press, 2002), 283.

14. The other two new characters are Nise (Ergaste's friend) and Mérinte (Ergaste's would-be lover).

15. Isaac de Benserade, *Iphis et Iante (1634)* (Paris: Lampsaque, 2000). All translations of Benserade's play are mine; I wish, however, to thank my colleague Ramine Adl for his valuable input. Act and scene numbers follow quotes in parentheses.

16. Iphis' lover, Iante, also remarks on Ergaste's "disorderly flame" for Iphis ["feu désordonné"] (3.iv).

17. Biet, "A quoi rèvent les jeunes filles?" 74.

18. Lilian Faderman, *Surpassing the Love of Men: Romantic Friendship and Love between Women from the Renaissance to the Present* (New York: William Morrow,1981), 27.

19. Luce Irigaray, *Speculum of the Other Woman*, trans. Gillian C. Gill (Ithaca, NY: Cornell University Press, 1985), 48.

20. Faderman, *Surpassing the Love of Men*, 29.

21. Hélène Cixous, "The Laugh of The Medusa," in *New French Feminisms: An Anthology*, eds. Elaine Marks and Isabelle de Courtivron (New York: Schocken Books, 1981), 248.

22. Elaine Marks, "Lesbian Intertextuality," in *Homosexuality and French Literature: Cultural Contexts, Critical Texts*, eds. George Stambolian and Elaine Marks (Ithaca, NY: Cornell University Press, 1979), 361.

23. Lise Leibacher-Ouvrard, "Speculum de l'Autre Femme: Les Avatars d'*Iphis et Ianie* (Ovide) au XVIIe Siècle." *Papers on French Seventeenth-Century Literature* MLA Convention 2002, 30, no. 59 (2003): 351.

24. Faderman, *Surpassing the Love of Men*, 26.

25. Adrienne Rich, "Compulsory Heterosexuality and Lesbian Existence," in *The Lesbian and Gay Studies Reader*, eds. Henry Abelove, Michèle Aina Barale, and David M. Halperin (New York: Routledge, 1993), 448.

26. Isaac de Benserade, "Sur l'Amour d'Uranie pour Philis (1697)," in *Poésie* (Genève: Slatkine Reprints, 1967), 165-73.

27. Ibid., ll. 1-2, 5-6, 13-16.

28. Ibid., ll. 37-40.

29. Ibid., ll. 45-48.

30. Ibid., ll. 57-60.

31. Ibid., ll.129-36.

32. Pat Califia, "Identity Sedition and Pornography," in *PoMoSexuals: Challenging Assumptions about Gender and Sexuality*, eds. Carole Queen and Lawrence Schimel (San Francisco: Cleis Press, 1997), 98.

33. Ibid., 98. Califia quotes from David R. Reuben, *Everything You Always Wanted to Know About Sex, But Were too Afraid to Ask* (New York: McKay, 1969).

34. Wahl, *Invisible Relations*, see in particular 107-110.

UNQUEERING SAPPHO AND EFFEMINIZING THE
AUTHOR IN EARLY MODERN ITALY

Alessandro Verri's *Le Avventure di Saffo, Poetessa di
Mitelene* and the Defense of Women Poets in Arcadia

Clorinda Donato

HIS ARTICLE ANALYZES Alessandro Verri's novel *Le Avventure di Saffo, Poetessa di Mitelene* (1782) as an apology for the women poets of the Arcadia, which was the most important literary and cultural academy in eighteenth-century Italy. Verri's characterization of Sappho as a respected woman of letters rather than a depraved lover of other women operates as an implicit defense of the status of women in the Republic of Italian and European letters. Such an analysis is particularly timely, as the status of what is known as Sapphic literature, or the literature of same-sex relationships among women in the overarching field of eighteenth-century studies, has targeted Alessandro Verri's *Le Avventure di Saffo* with unsubstantiated readings that neglect to consider the literary and cultural context of eighteenth-century Rome and the practices of sociability in which the transplanted Milanese nobleman, Alessandro Verri, engaged during the writing of this novel. By the same token, Italian criticism of *Le Avventure di Saffo* has overlooked the multiple implications associated with the name and persona of the Greek poet from the island of Lesbos who wrote passionately about and to the women she loved. Instead, they have continued to read the Sappho persona as symbolic of the essence of poetry, devoid of corporeal desire, in the way that romantic poet, Giacomo Leopardi, would write of her in his poem, *L'Ultimo Canto di Saffo* [*Sappho's Last Song*] (1822).

Limiting the interpretation of Verri's work to an esthetic reading of Sappho denies the density of the European literary and cultural knowledge, particularly British, that he had meticulously acquired, first in his years as an astute and outspoken leader of the Milanese Accademia dei Pugni [The Academy of Fists] in the periodical *Il Caffè*, and later as the author of three novels written during the second half of his life. As a novelist he resided in Rome, a city whose pulse and intricate web of cultural and political interests inspired his literary genius in ways that Austrian-ruled Milan never had.[1] While Alessandro Verri actively participated in the cultural and political struggles championed in the periodical *Il Caffè*, which he spearheaded with his brother, Pietro, and with Cesare Beccaria, renowned author of the 1764 *Dei Delitti e delle pene* [*On Crimes and their Punishment*], the posture and rhetorical sparring of a Milanese philosophe against the austere authority of the Hapsburgs, proved, ultimately, to be ill-suited to his temperament. A cultural force who penned some of *Il Caffè's* more memorable articles, Alessandro's militant genius would evolve in the direction of engaged romanticism, splitting from the enlightenment polemics of his brother, Pietro. In sharp contrast with Milan, Rome was imbued with a lingering baroque culture that had moved seamlessly into first romanticism, with little concern for the latest rhetorical fireworks of French *philosophie*, with the exception of a modest flutter of interest when yet another French work was placed on the Index. Vatican intrigues, the burgeoning art market created by hoards of grand tourists, and an active underworld of illicit love, sexual daring, and fantasy made Rome a far more enticing environment for Alessandro, who would never return to Milan to live. Within this environment, the desire to invoke, revisit, and recreate a heathen past as a source of inspiration for artistic innovation and experimentation led artists and writers alike to seek fresh energy in the myths, statues, and writings of antiquity. Alessandro Verri's *Le Avventure di Saffo* must be read within this Roman context, not only as his contribution to this particular cultural movement, but also as a significant, but little studied moment in the evolution of the Italian novelistic genre.[2]

There is no more protean figure in the history of western literature than Sappho. Not only does her legacy nearly date from the origins of the western literary tradition in Greece, but it continues to evolve and inspire, resonating more profoundly than ever at a time in scholarship when gender fluidity, transition, and transgression within a literary context have produced new readings of virtually every text in the canon, while at the same time breathing new life into heretofore little known authors, texts, and national contexts. Alessandro Verri's *Le Avventure di Saffo* can be counted among those texts that have been deemed worthy of a fresh look. A resounding success when first published in Rome, translations and multiple editions of Verri's novel reflected its wide recognition both at home and abroad.[3] This far-reaching success can initially be traced to the growing interest in revisiting Greek culture and literature through the lens of a new genre's modernity, which recontextualized Sappho for an eighteenth-century audience. This sentiment was particularly strong in Rome, where the artistic and cultural ties to antiquity permeated the work of artists and art historians such as Johann Joachim Winkelmann; innovations on the theme abounded in the art of Giovanni Battista Piranesi, where antiquity was consistently reinvented as a means of responding on the side of Italy in the *anciens-moderns* debate with concrete examples of antiquity as fodder for modernity, with adaptations and new applications.[4] Like Piranesi in sculpture, printmaking, and theoretical reflection on the interface between antiquity and modernity, Alessandro Verri set out to reinvent literature, first, through the recasting of Homer into prose, and second, through the marriage of topoi from antiquity, such as Sappho, with the modern genre of the novel.

Tatiana Crivelli has studied the difficult departure from the epic for Italian writers in the eighteenth century who found themselves torn between loyalty to traditionally Italian genres and the need to reach a broader sector of the reading public through new genres, even if it meant cloaking familiar themes in new styles. Crivelli attributes Verri's success with Italian audiences to his adherence to classical themes that he imbued with romantic appeal through a modern resignifying of Sappho; French audiences were likewise drawn to this figure, for she embodied many traits of the French women of letters.[5]

Until recently, however, Verri's novel had received scant attention, cited only as an influence on nineteenth-century authors Giacomo Leopardi and Germaine de Staël, whose own Sapphic creations have received far greater critical attention than Alessandro Verri's.[6] Thanks, however, to Joan DeJean's inclusion of Alessandro Verri's novel in *Fictions of Sappho*, her study of the trajectory of the personae of the Sappho figure throughout literary history, Verri's Italian novelistic treatment of the Sappho legend has been analyzed alongside the predominantly French renderings that make up the fictions DeJean discusses in her book.[7] While DeJean has brought Verri's text into the international critical arena alongside texts that are more accessible and better known, her claims that Verri's choice to prefer a heterosexual Sappho to Sappho, the poet of same-sex desire, are based on homophobic sentiment and the desire to advance a male aesthetic agenda cannot be sustained when tried against the information we now have about Alessandro Verri, his literary ambition, his critique of the French novelistic tradition and *philosophie*, and his participation in the academic milieu of Rome with his companion, the Marchioness Margherita Gentili Boccapaduli.

In this article we will interpret Alessandro Verri's unqueering of Sappho through the Italian lens that Joan DeJean and others have missed. The cultural, historical, and national complexities of this lens have been disregarded under the assumption that the Italian model cohered neatly with the French context (De-Jean) or the German one (Reynolds), not to mention the subliminal tendency to view Italy from the gaze of French or German readings of the Italian eighteenth and nineteenth centuries, as both Joseph Luzzi and Nelson Moe have made abundantly clear in recent monographs.[8] Instead, the Italian eighteenth-century reality requires knowledge of multiple contexts due to Italy's polycentrism, with vibrant centres of cultural production spanning the entire peninsula as the series of studies that make up the collection *Italy's Eighteenth Century* has shown.[9]

Specifically then, this study offers a counter reading to the one proffered by Joan DeJean and Margaret Reynolds, who have interpreted Verri's novel through the prism of negativity and innuendo associated with Sappho in eighteenth-century Britain and France in which Sappho's poetic genius is thoroughly denigrated as a function of the object of the female love that inspired it. Instead, Verri's "unqueering" of Sappho must be read within the specific context of Rome as a site of prolific literary and performative activity for women. Sensitive to the attacks on the creative genius of women and their performance of such genius publicly in salons or *conversazioni* and the halls of the Arcadia and similar academies, Alessandro Verri unqueers Sappho as a way of bolstering female poetic and performative agency.[10] His choice, indeed, has little to do with heteronormativity and should not be read as an assault on same-sex female love. Verri "unqueered" his Sappho as a gesture towards the female cultural authorities with which he had become familiar, surrounded as he was by powerful women whose artistic genius he greatly admired and upon whose friendship and love he greatly depended.

Through a reconstruction of Verri's Roman social and literary relationships in which female authorial and cultural agency was both commonplace and expected, and a comparison with the disparaging British view of women who wrote, Verri's Sappho is restored to the genealogy of female literary and heteronormative sexual agency that informed Madame de Staël's travels to Italy as well as her own experiences in Italian academies and salotti.[11] However, this unqueering constitutes a powerful political gesture in its support for female agency, not merely reducible to what might appear to be a superficial return to heteronormativity. Verri "unqueered" his Sappho to endorse the literary work of the female cultural authorities with whom he engaged both privately and publicly. It is significant in the Italian context that he experiments with the novel, a genre that he recognizes as the most capable of spreading his message to a broad audience. Indeed, such unqueering adds an important dimension to our understanding of Sapphism as a literary trope, yet we can only access that dimension reliably by attending to the historical nuances of Verri's work that will be laid out here.[12]

Scholarly work on the "grand tour" in Italy has highlighted the extent to which this cultural pilgrimage had become a veritable industry that fed tourists' image of Italy and its antiquities, enhancing foreigners' preconceived notions of culture while nourishing their illusions of bourgeois grandeur. The travel guides and voyages of numerous visitors can be thought of in the same category of cultural artifact as the commissioning of artist Pompeo Batoni for a portrait while seated in front of one of Rome's most notable monuments.[13] Most importantly, however, the focal point on the "grand tour" for study of the long eighteenth century by necessity brings numerous cultures and sub-cultures into contact in a continual dialogue of music, books, récits de voyage, and images borrowed, exchanged, adapted and transmitted from one generation of travelers to the next for well over a hundred years. While Mme de Staël was a consummate consumer and producer of products for the "grand tour" machine, her contacts in Italy were limited to Italians of her same class and to the small segment of the population that catered to grand tourists.[14] Neither Reynolds nor DeJean considered the Italian literary context of Verri's Sappho, which praised the intellect of the woman poet. Verri's novel restores a positive connotation to the term Sapphic as the descriptor of the woman who writes poetry. This reappropriation of the term served Madame de Staël, for whom Verri's work became the model for the novel *Corinne, ou l'Italie*. This highly autobiographical account of Staël herself, embodied in the poet, Corinne, was fashioned on the biography of Maria Maddalena Morelli, or Corilla Olimpica, her name in Arcadia.[15]

Histories of Sappho

Known as "the Poetess" to Homer's epithet "the Poet," Sappho's personae have never enjoyed the monolithic status of Homer, an epic poet whose life is unknown to his audience. A singer of heroic rather than personal tales, there is little in Homer's poetry to invite speculation about his daily existence, let alone his sentimental life. Despite the fact that we know very little about Homer, "The Poet" and his name conjure up without ambiguity, "the sex that is one" in much the same way that Adam's oneness before Eve is never tainted by history; instead, we come to know Eve through her history with the serpent, her relationship with Adam, and the ensuing story of the Fall. In like manner Sappho, as a writer of love poetry, and ultimately, human vulnerability, has always been directly implicated in her own artistic creation; indeed, her life story and her art reside together, open for casting and recasting in any number of fictions, as DeJean has so aptly called them, in ways from which men have been thoroughly excluded. Thus Sappho's

[95]

life history and the ensuing personae that have been built upon the Sappho pa-limpsest have imbued both her name, Sappho, and her name by anatomasia, "The Poetess" with meanings that have always resulted from a conflation of her lifestyle and her poetic genius. Mapping the performance of gender and genius associated with Sappho in any period or national context, then, has become one of the most important efforts of queer studies, for the representation and reception of Sappho serve as barometers by which an entire culture's attitudes toward female same-sex relationships may be viewed. For early modern scholars such mappings are particularly complex, since the culture, science and performance of gender often share simultaneous sites of activity.

Queering Sappho and The Early Modern Woman Who Writes

Queer Theory's contribution to eighteenth-century studies, particularly in the British and French fields, has spurred the systematic reading and rereading of what is now known as Sapphic literature, resulting in monographs, collected volumes and countless articles over the past twenty years.[16] This current of research has led a number of feminist scholars to pick up Alessandro Verri's novel, *Le Avventure di Saffo, Poetessa di Mitelene* for an understanding of what eighteenth-century Italian fiction might add to the debate on eighteenth-century Sapphism. Glenn Most reminds us that nowadays, Verri's novel "is largely forgotten, but at the time it was an enormous success—it went through at least fifteen editions in Italian and was translated, adapted, and plagiarized into a number of languages."[17] Most used Verri's novel to dispel the notion that there was anything prejudicial about Verri's choice to make of Sappho the heroine of unhappy, heterosexual love rather than the victim of unrequited, same-sex love, a position with which we agree and expand upon in this article. His view is based upon the oft-cited complication of the existence of two Sapphos residing on the island of Lesbos at the same time, both of whom were poets. Most bases his explanation of Verri's choice of a heterosexual Sappho on this dichotomy. However, Most overlooks the fact that Verri references Sappho, the tribade, in his novel, and that this reference indicates that he was fully aware of the European implications of the debate about Sappho, writing, and sexuality.

As the numerous studies quoted here provide ample documentation about how the eighteenth-century read representations of Sappho or used the figure of Sappho, Most's study and, we might add, the Italian case regarding Sappho, would appear to be an anomaly in this debate, but one, that we argue, makes sense when analyzed in the proper cultural context. It is thus important to revisit Alessandro Verri's Sappho in order to better situate his choice to represent a heterosexual Sappho within an Italian context, not only in light of Most's findings, but primarily in opposition to Margaret Reynolds' and Joan DeJean's readings of Verri's Sappho. Reynolds and DeJean both see in Verri's choice to prefer the heterosexual Sappho to her lesbian persona, (which is explicitly stated in the novel as will become apparent further ahead on our analysis), as a valorization of the male over the female body. They view this as a means of establishing a new genealogy of male physicality, one that ultimately displaces Sappho from the center of her own narrative, bumping her from a role of strength and agency to one of accessory to the undoing of her own subjectivity as both literary symbol and icon. Reynolds and DeJean trace Verri's representation of Phaon's body to the Nazi and Fascist male body (think of the visual representations of Mussolini's torso, currently the subject of provocative work on art and fascism), which they relate to the discourse on twentieth-century nationalisms.[18] While an intriguing interpretation, Reynolds and DeJean have not only neglected the Italian and specifically Roman context within which Verri's novel was written, but they have ignored the intertextual clues in Verri's text, which, if anything, valorize the female subject by endowing her with a strength of poetic genius and sexual desire, albeit heteronormative, which builds on the Renaissance legacy of female poetic genius found in the work of Veronica Franco, Vittoria Colonna and Tulia Aragona to name only a few of the women poets who fought for, and won, their place in the pantheon of illustrious poets in the Italian republic of letters. Verri reconnects Sappho to this illustrious group of female poets, establishing her as a "capo scuola" in a serious tradition of women poets.

Arcadia and Women Poets

In eighteenth-century Rome the parallel between Verri's Sappho and the women poets of the Arcadia Academy was obvious to all. The *Accademia dell'Arcadia* had first opened its doors in 1690 to honor Queen Christina of Sweden, establishing from its inception, the importance of women as cultural protagonists. Susan Dixon summarizes the situation: "The first Italian academy to admit women was the *Accademia degli Arcadi*. Founded in 1690, the Arcadian Society was primarily an institution dedicated to the reform of Italian literature. For almost forty years after its founding, the heyday of the Society's growth and activity, it fostered and promoted the poetic output of its female members."[19] Women poets, however, had been critiqued and lampooned in increasingly vitriolic attacks from the inception of the *Accademia dell'Arcadia*. Neither De Jean nor Reynolds has made an attempt to consider the illustrious history of female poets in the Italian literary tradition, where women were renowned authors of poetry penned in both Latin and Italian, and where Sappho, in Renaissance Italy, symbolized classical, female poetic genius rather than homosexual depravity. Here it is important to distinguish between the hypersensitivity to same-sex female love in eighteenth-century British and French literature as deviant, and the tendency to blame Italy and lax Italian sexual mores for it.[20] The danger of tainting women's writing by evoking the specter of Sappho was reserved for the eighteenth century through the influence of British and French attributions of the practice of same-sex, female love as centered in the Italian peninsula.

The Italian Tradition and Alessandro Verri's Sappho

Locating the Sappho figure in early modern Italy reveals itself as one of the most complex endeavors of such mapping quests, one that requires the isolating and understanding of any number of ancient and contemporary representations of Sappho before an attempt at deciphering the figure of Sappho in the Italian eighteenth-century can be made. Indeed, in Italy, the figure of Sappho was appropriated as a classical model of excellence for women writers of the Renaissance. Representations of Sappho on medals and coins were sought as symbolic reminders of the noble calling of poetry, a calling that was ungendered. In a Renaissance context, this particular representation of Sappho was easily transposed into the image and likeness of the Renaissance poet-courtesans, such as Veronica Franco. While her power of literary seduction might be compared to her power of sexual seduction, for Renaissance Italy, this power remained heterosexual in nature. Indeed, in Italy, collections such as *Memorie di Safione*, celebre *cortigiana*, reinforced this model.[21] However, the model was transposed and corrupted by English- and French-language adaptations of Sappho's life and legend. Among the most representative of them were the two anonymous novels, *Sapho ou l'Heureuse inconstance*, published in La Haye in 1695 and *L'Histoire et les amours de Sapho de Mitilene*, Paris 1724. Though these have been cited as unofficial sources for Verri's novel, there are other sources that should also be considered, especially Johann Christoph Wolf's *Saffo, Saphus*, 1733.[22] The importance of these two models lies in their thoroughly divergent appropriations and applications of the Sappho figure. At one pole we find the French-language models which mapped Sappho onto the scurrilous anecdotal type of literature that is reminiscent of the numerous anecdotes that circulated about Mme Du Barry in France and about any number of actresses in Britain, narrative treatments that can be considered precursors to novels such as Prevost's *Manon Lescaut* or Cleland's *Fanny Hill.*

Wolf, instead, in the German neoclassical tradition, edited and translated Sappho's Greek poetry into Latin in a facing-page translation, replete with an engraved frontispiece copiously decorated with various coins and medallions carrying her countenance, surrounding a bust of "SAPFW ERESIA" [Sappho the Eresian] (1733). Wolf's publication of this volume was followed in 1739 by a three-volume collection of translated poetry by eight Greek women and prose pieces by Greek women orators.[23] Wolf's desire to memorialize the writings of female poets and orators through the translation of such a comprehensive assemblage of the most important women poets and speakers of ancient Greece offers an ennobling portrait of the woman as writer and public speaker, the two roles for erudite women in Arcadia that were under attack.[24] Italy's ongoing homage to antiquity and respect for the primary exponents of the Greek and Latin literary traditions make novels like Verri's *Saffo* an interpretive challenge for the reader who is accustomed to the British and French emphasis on bourgeois heroes and heroines in novels that reflect experiences from the daily lives of their readership. While the Italian literary public read the novels and *contes* of Defoe, Richardson, Diderot, Rousseau and Voltaire, there was little in terms of character selection and development in them with which they could completely identify, a problem of particular acuity with regard to female characters. Alessandro Verri's correspondence with his brother, Pietro, contains numerous references to this problem, which he addresses by first going back to Shakespeare, and then to antiquity for inspiration, having definitively excluded modern prose sources as potential fodder for his novelistic projects.[25] Concerning the figure of Sappho, both British and French authors focused their attention on her as an example of vice, relegating to the most minute of details her career and renown as a poet of majestic proportions. Instead, for Alessandro Verri, her career and renown are precisely what were at stake and what presented themselves to him as the ideal source for novelistic treatment as part of a new proposal for both female characters and the novelistic genre. Indeed, Sappho's *career* as a writer inspired Verri as a way of bridging the old and the new. The classical tradition of Sappho and her poetry became relevant once again through Verri's emphasis on her work as a writer and a performer of poetic recitations, not unlike the heavily scrutinized women writers and improvisers who populated Italian academies and who were emulated by travelling British women in Italy. However, these women met with a mixed reception as *improvisatrici* once they returned home. Hannah More sought to provide women with guidelines for maintaining a sense of proportion in their emulation. The need to do so "demonstrates the ambiguous social status of female sensibility and enthusiasm in the second half of the eighteenth century . . . carefully regulated sensibility was a desirable and necessary attribute in an exemplary woman, but undisciplined and excessive sensibility could easily degenerate into a vulgar and dangerous enthusiasm."[26]

Through Sappho, Verri had found a way to evoke the quotidian through an exemplary life from antiquity. He was highly critical of the female characters who populated the contemporary novels as lacking in those attributes that could render them models of behavior. He was explicitly critical of Rousseau's *Julie, ou La Nouvelle Heloise*, and of the bourgeois novel in general.[27] He sought to establish a novelistic genre that would definitively break with the models coming out of Britain and France to embrace topoi and prose styles that would resonate more profoundly with new audiences at the end of the eighteenth century in the period 1780-1820, now defined as "*premier romantisme*" [first generation romanticism], and studied as a fully-fledged literary moment in which the coalescing of elements from the periods of *lumières* and romanticism are finally being given their due from critics, as opposed to the notion of "pre-romanticism," which, coined by the French, conferred an amorphous and transitory notion to the period in which Alessandro Verri's novelistic career flourished. Recapturing and reclaiming this period and its works constitutes an important step in restoring to their proper place the writings of so many British, German, and now, Italian authors whose legacy has suffered from the heretofore universally accepted French periodization applied to European literature of the seventeenth and eighteenth centuries, and which glossed over a period in which its own national production was less than brilliant.[28] Addressing the persona of Sappho in early modern Italy through the 1780 novel *Le Avventure di Saffo, Poetessa di Mitelene* we are also dealing with any number of interpretive gaps that can only be bridged when the delicate interplay of images of Sappho is unpacked against the backdrop of Italian literary history and culture as it intersected with the Grand Tour practices with which Alessandro Verri was intimately familiar.

Christina of Sweden and the Queering of the Female Intellectual in Rome

A nexus of influences and experiences in eighteenth-century Italy came to bear on the image of Sappho as Alessandro Verri contemplated writing his novel.[29]

Dominant among these influences are the early modern Franco-British legends of Sappho, with numerous attributions to the Italian origin and continuation of female same-sex relationships. Much like the shifting origins of venereal disease, breaches of female heteronormativity were inevitably traced back to the Italian peninsula in the early-modern European mind. Among the numerous examples, noteworthy is the one taken from Brantôme's *Le Dame galanti*: ". . . in our France, such women are very common, although it is said that this practice only began here a short time ago, and that it was imported from Italy by a certain lady of quality who shall go unnamed."[30] The "lady of quality" Brantôme referred to is in all likelihood Maria de' Medici.[31] She is important when referenced in this context of love "donna con donna," as she begins a line of early modern women monarchs who are transplanted from their native lands to other national contexts in which they alternately thrive and suffer.[32] The case of Marie Antoinnette, feted for her beauty and fashion acumen, but later accused of bringing down the French nation with her voracious sexual appetite, tinged also with a taste for same-sex lovemaking, constitutes a point of culmination in the exasperated scapegoating frenzy that provided a sexual parallel to the political demise of the French monarchy. Yet the third woman to complete this triptych, Christina of Sweden, is the most important for our purposes, for she resided in Rome 1654-1689 after abdicating the throne in her native Sweden for reasons that immediately called into question her sexuality.

In 1654, at the age of twenty, Christina of Sweden peremptorily declared that she would never marry. She left the Swedish throne for reasons upon which she refused to elaborate. Contemplating the expected semblance of heteronormativity conferred by the marriage contract, she famously stated: "that which belongs to oneself should not belong to another". She soon departed for voluntary exile in Rome. Speculation that she was a hermaphrodite abounded, her purported hermaphroditism becoming one of the rationalizations for her numerous liaisons with other women, amply documented by a variety of eyewitnesses both prior and subsequent to her departure from Sweden. Disinterest in cultivating a feminine look, she preferred instead a tomboyish, unkempt appearance and is often depicted in masculine guise. Her proficiency at riding and military exercises coupled with intellectual acumen and the drive to develop the life of the mind through engagement in the nascent Republic of Letters cast her at the centre of the most important academy in Rome, the Arcadia. Her fearless and brilliant intellect rather than her same-sex love affairs sealed her reputation in Rome. Indeed, the most remarkable aspect of contemporary descriptions of Christina is the absence of incrimination for her sexual preference. Rather, her status as erudite queen elevated to the level of "honor" those who enjoyed lesbian affairs with the Swedish monarch.[33] In a unique case of cultural and intellectual acumen in a woman flaunting an unorthodox sexual appetite, Christina earned a well-deserved reputation as a patroness of the arts, whose artistic acumen was considered by the sculptor Bernini to be as profound as his own.[34] She spoke several languages, which she employed in her cultivation of the arts and sciences, both in word and deed. In 1656 she left her greatest legacy to literature by establishing an academy devoted to good taste in literary pursuit. In 1690, one year after her death in 1689, the most prominent members of this academy officially founded it in her memory, naming it "Arcadia," harking back to the simplicity of nature and a return to a fresh poetic style, devoid of the trappings of "seicentismo" or as it was known in English, "Euphuism". However, over time, Christina of Sweden's role as patroness of the arts was to emerge as conflated with her preference for same-sex liaisons, and was thus explicitly linked to Sappho's homoerotic, poetic persona. As Joan DeJean states in her preface to *Fictions of Sappho*, Christina of Sweden's reading of Sappho's poetry is distinctly homoerotic. While she is rightly wary of using such readings as indicators of the Swedish monarch's own sexuality, in the case of Christina of Sweden, her reading of Sappho, combined with her lifestyle and strong leadership as patroness of the arts in Rome, made identifications of her with "mascula Sappho" a foregone conclusion.[35]

In Alessandro Verri's world some one hundred years later, the legacy of Christina of Sweden's "mascula Sappho" had cast in a subaltern light the scores of erudite women who participated in Arcadia. Though they composed and performed alongside their male Arcadians to the acclaim of many, their compositions and performances prompted the scorn and disdain of others. Defense of the status and persona of the erudite and cosmopolitan Roman woman lies at the crux of Alessandro Verri's desire to explicitly unqueer Sappho in his novel. The politics of this unqueering become apparent through a gendered reading of Arcadia's history, a reading which may begin to unravel the curious lack of attention that the Arcadia has received in eighteenth-century studies, both in Italy and beyond.

Arcadia

The fate of Arcadia was mixed even at the height of its splendour. Recognized as a firmly established cultural institution by Europeans on the grand tour, represented in paintings and literature alike, the history of eighteenth-century Italian literature has paid cursory attention to the role of this academy and the reception of its culture and practices among the traveling, foreign elite. An academy that proposed a return to simplicity and good taste through the seeking of refuge in the idyllic past of poet-shepherds in the mythical pastoral Greek expanses of Arcadia offered a playful, erudite diversion to traveling nobility in Italy. By the same token, however, its rituals and practices must have seemed odd to French and British travelers who sought modernity in scientific prose. The Arcadia only served to exacerbate what had been erroneously seen as an embarrassing legacy of static poetic expression and elitist nostalgia for a noble past. Much of Arcadia's inability to establish a strong presence among the ranks of eighteenth-century scholars today can be traced to the fact that the moment of its formation coincided with simultaneous attacks on Italian poetry coming from France, immortalized in Pere Bouhours' *Manière de bien penser dans les ouvrages de l'esprit* (1687). The Arcadia was known for practices that many, including Ugo Foscolo, ridiculed as childish and archaic, such as the assigning of Arcadian names to its "shepherds" and "shepherdesses" as its members were called.[36] Easily construed as thoroughly ridiculous and frivolous, these practices fanned the flames of French contempt for Italian poetry at this culminating moment in the war for literary hegemony waged by the French against the Italians at the end of the seventeenth century.[37] As seen through the eyes of the French enlightenment, adamant in its bashing of Italian culture, the institution could easily be construed as striking a strident, anachronistic chord when compared with the scintillating sociability of the salon culture of Enlightenment Paris and its attendant philosophes, or the public visibility of the London coffeehouse where poetry certainly did not constitute a topic of burning importance. Instead, it suffered from facile approximations with seventeenth-century poets such as Marino, who was considered the height of Italian poetic decadence by French critics.[38] However, recent attention to the surprisingly significant presence of women in Arcadia and the discovery of the debate that surrounded their inclusion, performance, and power has become more perceptible as scholars study the copious records and treatises, both in published and manuscript form, as well as debates and correspondences through which the Arcadia meticulously documented every aspect of its existence.[39] Every history of Arcadia needs to be rewritten to reflect this significant feature of its membership and of the politics of its literary production and performance.

While the Arcadia's activities, practices, and principles were performed primarily within the Academy's private chambers, the expanded arenas of Roman sociability brought the Arcadia to more public attention.[40] Well-connected travelers on the Grand Tour were invited to participate in Arcadia's gatherings, where they were often feted with honorary membership, as well as the very public performances of some of Arcadia's most renowned *improvisatrici*, known today primarily through Mme de Staël's modeling of her protagonist Corinne on Corilla Olimpica in her novel *Corinne: ou l'Italie* (1807).

Sappho, l'Improvisatrice, and the Castrato

While the preponderance of references to Sappho in the Italian literary tradition make no mention of her status as a tribade, emphasizing, as we have said, her inner beauty, which matched the perfection of her poetic voice, the delicate beauty and physicality of the stereotypical muse of the Italian poetic tradition, Petrarch's fair Laura, remains a male poetic objective, one that lies in sharp contrast to the Sappho, the creator and singer of verse who is homely and unattractive in a traditional feminine sense. A female victim of the choice between art and life, she is physically "e-feminated," in the same way that the sweet-voiced castrato has been emasculated. Yet like the castrato, she enthralls, and transgresses through her performance. The comparison of Sappho with the castrato lends much to our understanding of the reception accorded to the improvising female poet in Arcadia, which oscillated between euphoria and scorn; it also may help our understanding of the extremity and violence of these reactions. Is improvisation a performance art—fluctuating and improvisatory—or is it an art of authorship, concerned with property and permanence? St. Augustine confessed that listening was effeminizing when the auditor cared more for the voice being heard than the song. The castrato improvised and ornamented, substituting one aria for another, ignoring dramatic plausibility while disrupting the fourth wall separating performers from their audience. In Algarotti's famous *Essay on the Opera* (1755), he condemns virtuoso singers for their "monstrous inversion of things"; these creatures "over do, confound, and disfigure every thing"; they "pervert to a quite different meaning and complexion from what was intended by the air." Thus it was considered effeminate to take the ear's delight seriously. Algarotti calls the musical element in opera "effeminate and disgusting," and a "despotic sovereign". Algarotti's attack on the castrati can be easily appropriated to explain the alternating reactions of acclamation and revulsion sparked by the public performances of the *improvisatrici*. Indeed, Algarotti was one of the most vocal detractors of female membership in Arcadia as shall be seen in the concluding portion of this essay.

Alessandro Verri's *Le Avventure di Saffo*

We meet Sappho, the teenager, an innocent girl, at the cusp of her sexual awakening. Verri presents to us a girl, whose desire has been formed by the reading of love stories and poems. She knows about the effects of love second hand. However, when she spies the burnished, well-muscled body of Phaon, who has been miraculously transformed into a perfect physical specimen, thanks to a special oil provided to him by Venus, she is overcome by desire, the desire which inspires her to write her first poem. After many trials, she attempts to follow Phaon to Sicily. But he is delayed by a shipwreck, and she is taken in by Eutychius, a wise and enlightened scholar who tries to divert Sappho from her passion. The novel ends with a delirious Sappho jumping to her death from the white rock of Leucas.

This plot summary has been extracted from Reynolds' and DeJean's discussions of Verri's novel. Both emphasize the same elements, while leaving out those passages of Verri's novel that instead support a reading that has nothing in common with Dejean's and Reynolds's presentation of what they see as Verri's masculinist, anti-same-sex Sappho. Let us recall their reading. Reynolds and De-Jean both underscore the fact that in Verri's rendering, Sappho does not become a poet until she is consumed by desire at the sight of Phaon's body. Indeed, they gloss over Verri's very careful descriptions of the quality of Sappho's intellect, underscored from the outset of the novel in chapter two, when she first sees Phaon at the games of Mitilene:

> . . . .Errava così il suo cuore disciolto e leggiero come un'ape sui fiori; e quantunque non bella, pure perchè giovine, e di pregevole intelletto, poteva in altri ispirare delle passioni tanto più profonde, quanto più cagionate non dalla fragile esterna forma, ma dalla perpetua bellezza interiore.

> [Thus wandered up and down her heart, light, and fickle as the bee upon the flowers; and though not handsome, yet being young, and of superior intellect, she was calcualted to inspire others with a passion, so much the deeper as not being caused by fragile external form, but by perpetual, internal beauty.][41]

Verri's Sappho is smitten by Phaon at first sight. From that moment on she is driven by pure physical desire. Indeed, Verri's Sappho is one among few female characters so thoroughly consumed by sexual desire, reminiscent of Boccaccio's *Elegia di Madonna Fiammetta*, the first psychological novel in which Boccaccio, posing as a woman, writes of the desperation felt by Fiammetta once she realizes that she has been abandoned by her lover, Panfilo. Verri has assigned to Sappho the desire-motivated role that had heretofore been the domain of Ariosto's Orlando, who becomes crazy when he realizes that Angelica loves another. Indeed, she has traded roles with Orlando, and begins to chase the elusive Phaon, much as Orlando chased Angelica in the *Orlando Furioso*. Sappho's desire forges her destiny and drives her intellect, in sharp contrast with a scenario that in the French novel only plays itself out for male protagonists such as Des Grieux in *Manon Lescaut*, a novel in which Manon's only agency is her possession of beauty and feminine wiles. Thought and speech are never attributed to Manon at all, who is remarkable for her antics, but is never heard defending them or justifying herself. She is silent. Instead, Verri's Sappho is bold, a woman who heeds the advice of no one, not even her mother. Unlike Mme de Lafayette's *La Princesse de Clèves*, who, equally tormented by desire, heeds her mother's wishes and the strict code of Louis XIV's court by silently committing herself to a convent. She is condemned by inaction, her only agency being that of removing herself from any possible action that would confirm her right to love. Verri's Sappho, instead, constitutes the bold embodiment of expressive and physical action, a woman who cannot be stopped in her pursuit. While one might be tempted to read her fearlessness to seek her destiny in the classical sense of the tradition of Greek tragedy and its French seventeenth-century metamorphoses in Corneille and Racine, Verri's choice of the novelistic genre as opposed to theatrical tragedy, and his ability to graft the narrative strategies and appeal of the bourgeois novel onto the classical model, make such conjectures unfounded upon close, comparative readings. Verri's previous experiments with classical tragedy prior to his decision to test his prose narrative mettle are also sufficient proof that he had considered the dramatic genre for his Sappho, but rejected it in favor of prose, given his objectives.

Joan DeJean is making an ahistorical reading of Verri's Sappho when she focuses on what she calls Verri's transfer of the "fiction" of Sappho to Phaon's masculine beauty: "In the tradition initiated by Alessandro Verri's 1782 novel *Le Avventure di Saffo*, Phaon, the mythical lover presented by Ovid as the poet's downfall replaces her at the heroic center of the Sapphic plot. In this new fiction, there is no mention of Sappho's political activities; narrative energy is concentrated instead on a hypermasculinized Phaon. Authors from Verri to the fanatical Napoleon loyalist J.-B. Chaussard, whose *Fêtes et courtisanes de la Grece* appeared in 1801, linger over the powerful beauty of Phaon's young flesh in a protofascist hymn to the male body as well-oiled machine for the domination of anyone, for example female revolutionaries, who threaten the patriarchal order."[42]

DeJean's analysis suffers from the dearth of knowledge about the eighteenth-century literary tradition outside of Italy, following, instead the unfortunate tendency to read from the anachronistic position of Fascist culture and iconography in the typical privileging of twentieth-century sensibilities in the absence of greater knowledge about Italy's unique position in European enlightenment culture. While one might be sympathetic to such an analysis, especially in consideration of the state of queer studies in the 1980s and the preponderance of studies on male homosexuality, the ever-growing body of knowledge about the Italian eighteenth-century makes it difficult to promote DeJean's reading in light of what has been unearthed. The negative literary models of Sappho that Verri was combating cannot be emphasized enough, nor can the ancillary historical, medical, and scientific debates that influenced Verri's decision. When Pierre Bayle critically approached the question of Sappho's sexual identity and orientation in the article he devoted to her in his late seventeenth-century *Dictionnaire Historique et Critique*, published in fifteen editions, Sapphism, or same-sex love among women, was reintroduced as a topos that would dominate the dual arenas of fictional and scientific writing during the eighteenth century. Bayle specifically responded to the erotic quality of Sappho's poetry, pointing out that it was hard to read about her feelings for girls without finding expressed in it what he called "l'Amour de concupiscence."[43] In the age of seventeenth-century science, the attempt to match physiological symmetry to lustful female desire fuelled scientific speculation. Autopsies and dissections of the female genitalia sought to understand if the make-up of lesbian anatomy differed in any way from that of the heterosexual woman. Pamphlets, poetry, and fictional prose of every genre filled the pages of same-sex female erotic literature, particularly in England, but also in France and Italy. The judgment was negative and degrading. The term "Sapphic" became an insult within the English context where it was used exclusively as a term employed to designate women who engaged in same-sex relationships, rather than women who wrote poetry.

Verri, a discerning consumer of eighteenth-century British literature, was certainly aware of the negative connotations that the term Sapphic had come to assume in England. Gianmarco Gaspari has even suggested that the title of Verri's novel, *Le Avventure di Saffo*, adds an Italian title to the highly popular Greek romances that were circulating in Italian, such as *Le Avventure di Cherea e Calliroe* and *Le Avventure di Leucippe e Cleofonte*, and of particular note, the trio of Tobias

Smollett's *The Adventures of Roderick Random* (1748), *The Adventures of Peregrine Pickle* (1751), and *The Adventures of Count Fathom* (1753). Pope's condemnation of Lady Mary Wortley Montagu, who travelled extensively throughout Europe, was well known in erudite circles, particularly in Italy as Algarotti's friend and lover. Lady Mary was a writer, to be sure, but Pope's use of the term Sapphic to refer to her was fully intended to disparage and discredit her as undesirable. Reynolds herself reports in her book *The Sappho Companion* the following accusations that Pope published against Lady Mary, all under the name of Sappho. He began with personal hygiene:

> As Sappho's diamonds with her dirty smock;
> O Sappho at her toilet's greasy task,
> With Sappho fragrant at an evening mask[44]

continued with the state of her health:

> Slander or Poyson, dread from Delia's Rage,
> Hard Words or Hanging, if you Judge by Page
> From furious Sappho scarce a milder Fate,
> Poxed by her Love, or libell'd by her Hate . . . [45]

and finished with her morals and appearance:

> When I but call a flagrant Whore unsound,
> Or have a Pimp or Flaterer in the Wind,
> Sapho enrag'd crys out your back is round,
> Adonis screams—Ah! Foe to all Mankind!
>
> Thanks, dirty Pair! You teach me what to say,
> When you attack my Morals, Sense or Truth,
> I answer thus—poor Sapho you grow grey,
> And sweet Adonis—you have lost a Tooth.[46]

Lady Mary as a writer never stopped identifying herself with Sappho, and Pope never stopped using Sappho as a term of abuse for women writers. The negative connotation of the term was certainly known to Verri. Instead of seeing his choice to make Sappho a heterosexual poet as an expression of homophobia, however, Verri, used the figure of Sappho as a positive model of female freedom who chose her fate when she consciously refused to fulfill the expectation of Venus by sacrificing a pair of doves to the goddess and was thus condemned to die. Much like Arcadian poet Maria Fortuna's tragedy *Saffo* (1776), Verri's Sappho has been thoroughly recast in this work that invokes the muse of history rather than poetry to tell Sappho's life story utilizing new information about the poet that Verri claims had been gleaned by a scholar who had travelled to Lesbos. By proposing a new and modern source for Sappho's life story, Verri is free to challenge Sappho's negative legacy as a tribade who wrote for other women. In Book 3, Chapter 4, entitled "La Poesia," Verri's most explicit rehabilitation of women poets appears following the representation of a performance by Sappho of two odes, which Verri reproduces in his novel. In these performances, Verri shows us the female poet and *improvisatrice*, who is as moved to create by her passion as she is by the accolades of her public:

> Ma il sincero applauso che questi (versi) ottennero, le fece ragionevolmente credere che quanto Venere le era contraria, altrettanto le fossero favorevoli le Muse; e però stimolata non meno dalle ripetute lodi, che dalla interna vampa, che pure sembrava esalando in lamenti poetici, alquanto calmarsi, compose quell'altra sua chiarissima ode a Faone:
>
> Felice al par de' Numi chi dappresso
> Ascolta il dolce suon di tua favella:
> Più felice di lor, se gli è concesso
> Destar su quella
>
> Bocca il soave riso . . . e che ragiono,
> Se ragion più non ho! la prima volta
> Che ti vidi rimasi, come or sono,
> Misera e stolta.
>
> Chiuse il silenzio le mie labbra, aperte
> Solo ai sospiri, e sol per lor faconde
> D'ogni altro favellar furo inesperte.
> L'amor m'infonde
>
> Sottil fuoco vorace entro le vene,
> Mi benda gli occhi, più non odo, sento
> Che vivo ancor, ma vivo delle pene
> Coll'alimento.
>
> Scorre per le convulse membra il gelo
> Delle stille di morte, io mi scoloro
> Siccome il fior diviso dallo stelo:
> Ecco già moro.

Oh, benché estremo, avventuroso fiato,
Se giunge ad ammollir quel cuor spietato![47]

[But the sincere applause which there obtained, made her reasonably believe, that though Venus was adverse, yet the Muses were favourable to her; and therefore, stimulated not less by repeated praises, than by the internal flame, which seemed, in exhaling into poetical lamentations, somewhat to calm itself, she composed that other, her most celebrated ode to Phaon.

Bless'd as the immortal Gods is she,
The maid who fondly fits by thee,
And hears and sees thee all the while,
Softly speak, and sweetly smile.

'Twas this depriv'd my soul of rest,
and rais'ed such tumults in my breast;
That while I gaz'd, In transport toss'd
My breath was gone, my voice was lost.

My bosom glow'd; the subtle flame
Ran quick through all my vital frame;
O'er my dim eyes a darkness hung,
My ears with hollow murmurs rung.

In dewy damps my limbs were chill'd,
My blood with gentle horrors thrill'd;
My feeble pulse forgot to play,
I fainted, sunk, and dy'd away.][48]

Following the recitation of this ode, Verri makes his case for Sappho's heterosexuality by rejecting previously held notions about the nature of the passion that inspired its creation and improvisational recitation:

Questa ch'io dico ode a Faone, ben so che altri asseriscono dedicata ad una fanciulla da lei amata con disdicevole delirio. E tanto crebbe questa fama contraria al nome di così leggiadro ingegno (forse promossa dalla invidiosa malignità de' garruli poeti), che fu asserito da taluni, come prima dell'infelice amore, che io descrivo, ella fosse stata immersa in dissoluti costumi a segno, che le rimanesse l'ignominioso titolo di Tribas.[49]

[This, which I call an Ode to Phaon, well I know that others assert to have been dedicated to a girl by her beloved with inexpressible delirium. And this report, so unfavourable to the name of so bright a genius, increased to that degree (promoted perhaps by the invidious malignity of the babbling poets) that it was asserted by some, that before the unhappy love which I Describe, she had been so deeply plunged in dissolute habits, that she had obtained the ignominious appellation of τριβάς][50]

Verri's reference to the connecting of Sappho's poetic genius to the "title of Tribas," reminds us of the transfer of the term from the Greek, Tribas, to tribade in French, and then tribade in Italian. As Valerie Traub explains, "The female same-sexual practice that imperial Greek and Roman writers alike singled out for comment was "tribadism". According to Traub, knowledge of this practice entered western Europe during the Renaissance through the discovery of Greek and Roman classical literature, and the rediscovery of female anatomy in medical texts. Same-gender female desire loomed large, re-entering literary discourse as we have seen in Brantôme's collection in the sixteenth century, and in the seventeenth century, through Pierre Bayle's article on Sappho in the *Dictionnaire historique et philosophique* and his reference to her wrongly directed lustful love.

Verri's description of the genesis of female poetry through a novelistic biography of Sappho is as significant for its contents as it is for its genre. Verri chose the modern genre of the novel to offer performative and lived examples of a woman poet in Arcadia, flesh and blood women who both think and love, as expressed by their poetry. This vibrant, powerful voice of the female poet who was deemed to have conquered the same heights as any male imitator of Petrarch, is feted in Verri's Sappho. Verri is exhorting women to follow their own tradition of excellence in poetry, a tradition whose roots are found in Sappho. The pedagogical intent of Verri's novel as a recasting of the novelistic genre has already been noted in this article. We would like to add Verri's purpose which extended to female readership. Here, he offers a pedagogical novel to women, one that does not condescend to them, as did Francesco Algarotti's treatise *Newtonism for Women*, but rather, one that offers them an image of themselves as the revered intellects that the women in his circles were striving to become.[51] The ability to tell a life story through the novelistic genre makes of Verri's Sappho a model for women to follow. The heroines of tragedy are too far away for identity to be sparked. His choice of Sappho and not Phedre, for example, stems also from his own experience in Rome in the aristocratic circles of his companion, the Marchioness Margherita Gentili Boccapaduli, whose intellectual prowess is finally emerging in the critical work cited above. Verri's novel offered women a literary model and an invitation to go forth boldly, taking up the mantle of renowned, Renaissance female poets Veronica Franco, Vittoria Colonna and Tullia D'Argona that Alessandro Verri invoked through his Sappho. Through his novel, Verri also took a position on the pro-feminine side of the "feminization" debate that was raging in Arcadia over the ongoing admission of women to its ranks.

The Debate over Women in Arcadia [garruli poeti]

As Elisabetta Graziosi has reminded us, the Arcadia was the first academy to admit women per its statute, with Rome the site of an expanding array of salons and "conversazioni" in which the shared private space for cultural and intellectual exchange had moved into the public arena. Indeed, numerous, recent studies have begun to uncover the unique terms of Roman eighteenth-century culture and politics as they played themselves out in various institutions of erudition and sociability. Maria Pia Donato's social history of the Roman academies offers a comprehensive look at sociability in Rome in the period of first romanticism; her work also documents Alessandro Verri's life in the academies and in Arcadia, including his assiduous attendance at the social gatherings that took place at the home of the Marchioness Margherita Gentili Boccapaduli, the woman for whom he remained in Rome until his death.[52] Paola Giuli's studies on Arcadian women, and in particular, the scandal surrounding the crowning of the improvisatrice Corilla in the Sala Capitolina in 1776, offer a culminating event in the public display of female erudition, one that certainly influenced Verri's writing of *Le Avventure di Saffo*.[53] We are reminded by Paola Giuli that Corilla was the first and last poet to be honoured in that way, accused, as she was, of sexual promiscuity and child abandonment, and thus implicitly of having sacrificed motherhood for public glory. The most pertinent of recent discussions about women in Arcadia, however, is Susan M. Dixon's 2006 study of this literary academy, which has made available for the first time a valuable summary of women's roles in Arcadia in the seventeenth- and eighteenth-centuries, as well as the history of the gendering of criticism which targeted women and their literary production in vitriolic attacks penned by some of the most famous men of letters in the peninsula.[54] As we have seen, women's involvement was part of the Arcadia's platform from the moment of its founding, in honor of its first patron, Christina of Sweden. The memory of sixteenth-century Roman poet Vittoria Colonna was also evoked at its inception.

However, upon the demise of founder Giovanni Maria Crescimbeni in 1728, women's presence, which had reached eight percent of the academy's membership under Crescimbeni, was attacked, and Arcadia: ". . . became gendered to such an extent that the presence of women as members of the Accademia degli Arcadi was often identified as the major impediment to the Society's success."[55] Criticism of women members came from outside the academy post 1730 in the form of treatises by three of the most well-known figures in the Italian enlightenment, albeit, the northern enlightenment: Francesco Algarotti, Sergio Bettinelli and Giuseppe Baretti.[56] Though their critiques of Arcadia are well known, the extent to which they drove the backlash against scholarly women had not been explored before Susan Dixon's analysis: ". . . they poke fun at the emasculation or feminization of the arcadian men and put the blame on the arcadian women."[57] Dixon explains that the Arcadia, in keeping with its democratic rhetoric, embraced female membership upon its founding and in its early years; it promoted women's writing, recitation, and improvisational performance of poetry, first within the exclusive circles of its membership, and later through performances that were open to attendance by non-members, as acts that would promote the public good. However, through public performances, a number of male poets made remarkable careers for themselves, among them Metastasio, whose public acclaim garnered for him none other than Maria Teresa of Austria as patroness. We celebrate his professional trajectory, forgetting, instead, the potential careers of two of Arcadia's greatest female poets, Faustina Maratti and Corilla Olimpica, both of whose careers and reputations were destroyed from the furore their public acclaim provoked. While Metastasio continued at his craft into maturity, women never had an artistic career beyond their youth, nor were they engaged at foreign courts as were composers and castrati. By exhibiting career ambitions, ". . . they lacked the appropriate modesty required of their gender. To their critics, Arcadia had allowed them to ignore or supersede established gender roles."[58]

Yet in Alessandro Verri's world, the perception of women was changing through the exemplary practices of a number of erudite, Arcadian women. His companion, Margherita Gentili Boccapaduli, successfully negotiated a public presence and erudite persona well into her sixties. She has been immortalized in one of the most striking portraits of an erudite woman to have been painted in the eighteenth century, a 1777 full length likeness by Laurent Pécheux that leaves no detail to the imagination in the establishment of her intellectual and mondaine credentials. She has been captured in a stately pose within her cabinet of scientific curiosities, performing the role of expert and hostess as she shows her collection of butterflies to an observer. She is dressed fashionably, yet comfortably, having been one of the first women to adopt a less constricting bodice, as well as a skirt devoid of the cumbersome fixed hoops that impeded rapid movement or made· cumbersome the close observational work required of a collector and scholar of curiosities. Laurent's portrait of the Marchioness was painted only one year after Corilla Olimpica's infamous performance.

As Verri wrote his novel in the late 1770s, this is the image of the erudite woman that he had before him, one that surely inspired his writing, as well as his lifestyle at her side. Indeed, in Rome where he lived with the Marchioness, Alessandro Verri had become the image of the feminized, emasculated writer who served a new type of muse, his Arcadian companion of the heart and mind, Margherita Gentili Boccapaduli. Alessandro's first encounter with the Marchioness, which he described to his brother Pietro in a 1768 letter as a profound *coup de foudre*, was so powerful that it changed his vision of the world, together with his role and future in it. The Marchioness and Roman forms of sociability and erudition in which women like her figured prominently in the *conversazioni* they oversaw, which they directed, and of course, in the Accademia dell'Arcadia, had become his world; despite the exaggerated laments about the bond to the Marchioness that held him prisoner, he never made any serious attempt to return to his former life.[59] The portrait painted of the Marchioness in 1777 by Laurent Pécheux, has been shown in two exhibitions over the past 25 years, "Fasto Romano: Dipinti, sculture, arredi dai palazzi di Roma" in 1991 and "Il Neoclassicismo in Italia: Da Tiepolo a Canova" in 2002.[60] The contents of this arresting portrait are best emphasized by reporting the description of it that appeared in a review of the show: "In 1777 Laurent Pecheux painted one of the most curious paintings in the exhibition, the portrait of the Marchioness Margherita Gentili Boccapaduli, companion of the Milanese Alessando Verri and a woman of high intelligence. We see her at the center of her cabinet of curiosities as she is showing an observer her collection of butterflies. She is dressed in an elegant outfit in the latest fashion. Behind her can be seen well known ancient statues, shells and acquatic fossils; at her feet a silver pool full of gold fish."[61] The painting has often been cited because of the presence of the Egyptian-motifed inlaid table designed by Piranesi; instead, the Marchioness herself commands our attention as a new kind of woman, one who is performing an act of erudition, the demonstration of the cabinet of curiosities, that had previously been the exclusive domain of men. The cabinet and its curiosities are clearly hers and she shows them off with a modest, yet authoritative gesture whose agency is not mediated through a male superior. As documented in Alessandro's correspondences with Pietro, the development of the cabinet of curiosities and the pursuit of erudition in natural philosophy were activities that the Marchioness and Alessandro shared together. Yet the cabinet was identified as hers, as was her possession of the knowledge about its contents. Alessandro played a supporting role in these endeavors while she commanded center stage, as shown in the portrait.

Alessandro's thorough conversion from a male-based, private and exclusive Milanese-style erudition to the more eclectic and inclusive social scene in Rome greatly chagrined his brother Pietro, who, over time, had begun to realize the extent to which he and his brother had parted ways, physically, intellectually and emotionally, a gap he blamed directly on the Marchioness Gentili Boccapaduli. In an epistolary dispute over the nature of the contemporary Romans and the practices of their government, an exasperated Pietro chided his brother in an early letter: " . . . if it weren't for the Marchioness, you would agree with Voltaire as much as I do, and you would have left [Rome] after a few weeks' time."[62] Alessandro Verri's decision to abandon Milan in favor of Rome signaled a significant life-style change, one that manifest itself most clearly in his decision to write novels in contrast with his brother Pietro's pursuit of more philosophical topics and genres, as well as his choice in women.

Conclusion

Alessandro Verri's death on Novembre 23, 1816 in Rome was solemnly commemorated by both the Accademia dell'Arcadia and the Accademia Tiberina. These honors constitute a tribute that carries both literary and gender significance. From his earliest days at his brother's side in the redacting of the periodical *Il Caffè*, his effeminate manners and literary taste provoked the scorn of Venetian journalist Giuseppe Baretti who described him as "an itsy, bitsy weakling" who echoed his brother Pietro's every word, "picking up each one with two fingers and showing it as if he were showing off one of Cleopatra's pearls."[63] In his life he had succeeded in embodying a model of the writer that was attacked by his peers: "Both Baretti and Bettinelli suggested that there was much too much concern with praising the female members [of Arcadia], who did not deserve it, and thus the praisers must be insincere and obsequious flatterers. Bettinelli insinuated that by 'faking being in love,' men were being kept from useful manly activities: military service, politics and civic service, farming and engineering."[64] If we reflect on Alessandro Verri's life, the effusive love he often expressed for the Marchioness, his defense of women poets in the *Avventure di Saffo*, and his pursuit of activities that fell far from the definition of manly, we might conclude that his defense of Sappho is also a defense of a gender dynamic and new forms of agency, both male and female, in a cross-cultural context in which the unqueering of Sappho and the effeminizing of the male author are equal partners in the evolution of a new, early romantic paradigm.

Notes

1. Both the Accademia dei Pugni [the Academy of Fists] and *Il Caffè* were spearheaded by Alessandro's brother, Pietro, as a reaction against the rigid rule of the Austrian monarchy in Lombardy. The spirit of the movement and the ensuing satire of its organ, the periodical *Il Caffè*, are the closest examples of Italian enlightenment literature to French *philosophie*. Alessandro's interest in French literature and thought reached its culmination during this period of his activity in the journalistic endeavor. He accompanied Cesare Beccaria (author of *On Crimes and their Punishments*, 1764) to Paris in 1767, experiencing first hand, with Beccaria (dubbed the Italian Rousseau by the French) the distance separating French *philosophie* and Italian letters.

2. See Gilberto Pizzamiglio, "Le fortune del romanzo e della letteratura e della letteratura d'intrattenimento," in *Storia della cultura veneta. Dalla Controforma alla fine della repubblica. Il Settecento*. 5, no. 1 (Venice: N.Pozza, 1986): 171-96.

3. I have used the most recent edition of Verri's novel, Alessandro Verri, *Le Avventure di Saffo Poetesse di Mitilene a cura di A. Cottignoli*, (Roma: Salerno Editrice, 1991). For details about the publishing history of the work see Bruno Toppan's *Du "Caffe" aux "Nuits romaines:" Alessandro Verri romancier*, (Nancy: Presses universitaires de Nancy, 1984), especially chap. 2, *"Les Aventures de Sapho*: Un Roman "Experimental,"* 53-94, cites brother Pietro Verri's running commentary on the extraordinary success of the novel in his correspondence with Alessandro, as well as the first review of the novel which appeared in the "Nuovo giornale letterario d'Italia" in 1789 proclaiming it "il primo" among the Italians, 92n63. The year of this review (1789) coincides with the publication of the novel's English translation.

4. See Clorinda Donato, "Fresh Legacies: Giovanni Battista Piranesi's Enduring Style and Grand Tour Appeal," *Eighteenth-Century Studies* 43, no. 4 (2010): 508-11.

5. See Tatiana Crivelli, "Sappho, ou le mythe de l'ancienne Grèce: L'Ecriture Romanesque entre orient et occident, antiquité et lumières," *in Les Lumières européénnes dans leurs relations avec les autres grandes cultures et religions*, eds. Florence Lotterie and Darrin M. McMahon (Paris: Honoré Champion Editeur, 2002), 145-64.

6. Within the Italian tradition, Giacomo Leopardi's poem *L'Ultimo canto di Saffo*, 1822, is the most well-known representation of the Saffo legend. Treasured element of the Italian poetical canon, recited by school children and victims of unrequited love alike, *L'Ultimo canto di Saffo* betrays no trace whatsoever of the Greek poet's same-sex longings. While Verri explicitly states his choice to paint a heterosexual Sappho, thus clearly referencing her queer legacy, Leopardi has thoroughly adapted the Sappho persona to his own image and likeness both in physical and spiritual terms (i.e., high poetic genius and intellectual powers trapped in a repulsively ugly body and face). Staël's *Corinne ou l'Italie*,

1807, comfortably adapts Verri's morally rehabilitated, heterosexual poetess with her explicit references to the culture of women in Arcadia to her own self-promoting embodiment of this female, poetic inheritance. Staël, like Verri, clearly fought to cast off all lesbian connotations associated with the term Sapphic, fully aware, like him, of the threat it continued to pose to women writers.

7. Two articles that offer new information about the genesis of Verri's *Sappho* and the novel's place within the Italian and European literary traditions respectively are Bianca Danna, "Saffo, l'"alter ego" al femminile," in *Metamorfosi dei Lumi. Esperienze dell'"io" e creazione letteraria tra Sette e Ottocento, ed. Simone Carpentari*, (Messina and Alessandria: Edizioni dell'Orso, 2000), which analyzes the 1776 tragedy based on Sappho which Verri, in all likelihood, was aware of; and Gianmarco Gaspari's "La Prosa del Settecento, Dalla Negazione alla Rivolta," in *Il mito nella letteratura italiana, Vol. II: Dal Barocco all'illuminismo*, ed. F. Cossutta (Brescia: Morcelliana, 2006), 265-84, which argues that Verri's Sappho, despite the numerous treatments of the Sappho figure that may have influenced him, remains an original treatment, one which reflects a series of national and personal concerns regarding the novelistic genre, its past and future. We share this view and in the present article underscore yet another aspect of the novel's singularity in its treatment of gender.

8. See Joseph Luzzi, *Romantic Italy and the Ghost of Italy*, (New Haven, CT: Yale University Press, 2008); and Nelson Moe, *The View from Vesuvius*, (Los Angeles: University of California Press, 2002).

9. See Paula Findlen, Wendy Wassyng Roworth, and Catherine M. Sama, eds. *Italy's Eighteenth Century: Gender and Culture in the Age of the Grand Tour*, (Stanford, CA: Stanford University Press, 2009).

10. Italian *conversazioni* differed greatly from French salons where women hosted, but never performed, leaving men of letters to carry on their debates and discussions in front of them. Though many of the *salonnières* became famous, their role tended to be ornamental rather than active, whereas women both hosted and actively participated in the *conversazioni*.

11. Mme de Staël embraced Verri's unqueered Sappho twice, first for one of the few theatrical works she wrote entitled *Saffo*, as well as for the novel, *Corinne, ou l'Italie*, which can also be considered an artifact of similar intention, not to mention her portrait playing the lyre crowned with laurel in the tradition of the Italian academy l'Arcadia. Her grand tour view of Italy resonates in these works. See Pierre Chessex, "The Grand Tour," in *Encyclopedia of the Enlightenment*, ed. Michel Delon, (Chicago: Fitzroy Dearborn Publishers, 2001), 622-25.

12. See Serena Baesi, "Italian Improvisatrici and their Influence on English Romantic Writers: Letizia Elizabeth Landon's Response," in *British Romanticism in Italian Literature: Translating, Reviewing, Rewriting*, eds. Laura Bandiera and Dieco Saglia (Amsterdam and Atlanta: Rodopi, 2005), 82, for a discussion of how the perception of Italian women as "improvisitrici" in the eighteenth century limited their agency as authors.

13. See Edgar Peters Bowron, *Pompeo Batoni-Prince of Painters in Eighteenth-Century Rome*, (New Haven, CT: Yale University Press 2007).

14. Germaine de Staël's experiences of sociability in early nineteenth-century Italy were limited to the "salotti" in which noble friends, such as Vincenzo Monti, introduced her. Staël can be considered a victim of underexposure to the reality of Italian culture and overexposure to the superficiality of grand tour culture, an "Italy" made in the image and likeness of tourists.

15. See Paola Giuli, "Tracing a Sisterhood: Corilla Olimpica as Corinne's Unacknowledged Alter Ego," in *The Novel's Seductions. Staël's 'Corinne' in Critical Inquiry,* ed. Karyna Szmurlo (Lewisburg, PA: Bucknell University Press, 2001).

16. Among the most noteworthy we can count Joan DeJean's *Fictions of Sappho, 1546-1937* (Chicago: University of Chicago Press, 1989); Lisa Moore's *Dangerous Intimacies: Toward a Sapphic History of the British Novel* (Durham NC: Duke University Press, 1997); Margaret Reynolds' *The Sappho Companion* (Basingstoke and New York: Palgrave Macmillan, 2000); Harriette Andreadis' *Sappho in Early Modern England: Female Same-Sex Literary Erotica, 1550-1714* (Chicago: Chicago University Press, 2001); Valerie Traub's *The Renaissance of Lesbianism in Early Modern England* (Cambridge and New York: Cambridge University Press, 2002); as well as the two collected volumes edited by Ellen Greene, *Reading Sappho, Contemporary Approaches* and *Re-Reading Sappho, Reception and Transmission,* both published in 1996 (Los Angeles: University of California Press).

17. Glenn W. Most, "Reflecting Sappho," in *Rereading Sappho: Reception and Transmission,* ed. Ellen Greene (Los Angeles: University of California Press, 1996), 11-35.

18. Jeffrey Thompson Schnapp *Anno X. La Mostra della Rivoluzione fascista del 1932: genesi - sviluppo - contesto culturale-storico – ricezione,* afterword by Claudio Fogu (Rome-Pisa: Istituti editoriali e poligrafici internazionali, 2003).

19. Susan M. Dixon, *Between the Real and the Ideal. The Accademia degli Arcadi and Its Garden in Eighteenth-Century Rome* (Newark, DE: University of Delaware Press, 2006), esp. "Women in Arcadia," chap. 5, 105-12.

20. See Celia R. Daileader, "Back Door Sex: Renaissance Gynosodomy, Aretino, and the Exotic," *ELH* 69, no. 2 (2002): 303-34.

21. Adolfo Albertazzi, "Il Romanzo," in *Storie dei generi letterari italiani,* (Milano: Marzorati, 1902), 126.

22. Sappho, *Sapphus, poetriae Lesbiae : fragmenta et elogia, quotquot in auctoribus antiquis graecis et latinis reperiuntur, cum virorum doctorum notis integris / cura et studio Jo. Christiani Wolfii . . . qui vitam Sapphonis & indices adjecit* (Hamburgi : apud Abrahamum Vandenhoeck, 1733).

23. Johann Christoph Wolf, *Muliervum Græcarum quae Oratione Prosa Usae Sunt Fragmenta et Elogia Graece et Latine cvm Viorvm Doctorvm Notis et Indicibvs* (Göttingen: Abrahamum Vandenhoeck, 1739).

24. Johann Christoph Wolf (1689-1770) directed the municipal library in Hamburg and substantially increased its holdings in the 1750s; before his directorship, Wolf taught poetry at Hamburg's Akademischen Gymnasium, focusing in particular on works by Greek and Latin poets of classical antiquity.

25. See Toppan, *Du "Caffè" aux "Nuits romaines,"* 43-48.

26. Corvey Women Writers on the Web, "British Women Writers and Eighteenth-Century Representations of the Improvatrici," explains how the Italian improvisatrice, whose performances won over even the most recalcitrant British travelers on the Grand Tour, became a suspect figure once British women began to imitate their emotional performances. The article cites the difficulty of maintaining the proper balance between decorum and virtuosity as described by Hannah More ". . . I will even go so far as to assert, that a young woman cannot have any real greatness of soul,

or the true elevation of principle, if she has not a tincture of what the vulgar would call Romance, but which persons of a certain way of thinking will discern to proceed from those fine feelings, and that charming sensibility, without which, though a woman may be worthy, yet she can never be amiable (http://www2.shu.ac.uk/corvey/CW3/. Accessed 10 October 2012)." The only fault with this otherwise extremely useful British-Italian cross-cultural discussion of the *improvisatrici* is that assumption that these female performers were universally revered in Italy. Instead, they were as reviled in Italy in the second half of the eighteenth century as they were in Britain, as we are attempting to demonstrate here.

27. Toppan, *Du "Caffè" aux "Nuits romaines,"* 61.

28. The opening paragraph of Jacques Voisine's review of *Metamorfosi dei Lumi. Esperienze dell'"io" e creazione letteraria tra Sette e Ottocento*, ed. Simone Carpentari, (Messina and Alessandria: Edizioni dell'Orso, 2000) provides a succinct overview of this recent shift away from the previously felt need to tie literary movements to the history of events, which for the French, and for that matter, European eighteenth centuries, the historical watershed of the French Revolution was also imposed on literature.

29. Leopardi's *Ultima Canto di Sappho* is a highly personalized site of self-reflection and intellectual narcissism. Leopardi writes Sappho as his spiritual sister, ugly and unappealing, but endowed with "alto e raro genio". As direct influences on Leopardi's poem, *Verri's Le Avventure di Saffo* and Mme de Staël's *Corinne* are always referenced. Such references are, however, not based upon close readings of either Verri or Staël as in neither is Sappho tormented over her appearance, and the discrepancy between physical and intellectual beauty. Once again, Sappho, in the hands of Leopardi, has been filled with his own desire.

30. De Bordeille Pierre di Brantôme, *Le Dame galanti*, trans. Alberto Savinio (Milan: Adelphi, 1994). The first French edition of this monumental collection of licentious anecdotes was first published in Leiden between 1666 and 1667.

31. Daughter of the self-fashioned Florentine line of nobiliy 'De' Medici, Maria de' Medici is often cited as the source of French culinary excellence; nonetheless, her foreignness does not go unnoticed, a theme with regard to women monarchs that is exacerbated in the case of Marie Antoinnette.

32. See Dora Polachek, "A la recherche du spirituel: L'Italie et les *Dames Gallantes* de Brantôme," *Romanic Review* 94, nos. 1-2 (2003): 227-43.

33. See Daniela Danna, *Amiche, Compagne, Amanti, Storia dell'amore tra donne* (Trento: UNI Service 2003), 64, provides the testimony of the niece of a wealthy Portuguese merchant who lived in Hamburg where he conducted business with the Court. When questioned by her family about her liaison with Christina who was passing through Hamburg she purportedly told them "any acts committed with one of the most glorious sovereigns of Europe offer greater honor than shame."

34. Lilian H. Zirpolo, "Christina of Sweden's Patronage of Bernini: The Mirror of Truth Revealed by Time," *Women's Art Journal* 26, no. 1 (2005): 42.

35. DeJean, *Fictions of Sappho*, 11.

36. See Ugo Foscolo, 'Life of Pius VI', *Scritti vari di critica storica e letteraria* (1817-1827), in *Edizione nazionale delle Opere di Ugo Foscolo*, ed. Uberto Limentani (Florence: Felice Le Monnier, 1978),

1–131. Published in English during Foscolo's exile in England, in the *Edinburgh Review* 62 (1819): 271-95 without the author's name, the treatise offers Foscolo's views of the Arcadia, which certainly echo the impressions he had heard from his British hosts: 'Pius was a patron of genius; but preferred the fine arts to literature or science: and he was neither a very learned nor a very impartial patron. His greatest weakness was in patronising or tolerating the *Arcadians*. The name is not very celebrated, we believe, in this country. Yet all the curious are aware, that here has existed at Rome, for a hundred and fifty years, an academy or corporation of poets, under that fantastic appellation – and richly deserving all the ridicule with which it is pregnant. It was established at a time when such affectations were more easily tolerated, and for a good enough purpose; but for many years it had become a liability and a nuisance, filling Italy with its shepherds and affiliated societies. Any blockhead who could produce a sonnet and a sequin gained easy admittance into the Arcadia, the credentials and patent of the poet, a pastoral name, and a grant of lands in some romantic district of the ancient Arcadia. Even now, a visitor no sooner arrives in Rome, than he receives a visit from the Secretaries of this Academy, who offer him the Laurel and a copy of verses already prepared, which are to be recited in the name of the generous visitor. Now and then too, at their public meetings, they place the crown on the head of some traveller, who is vain and silly enough to play the hero in these farces. But those who submit to this coronation, are generally *improvisatori* by profession, who, to increase their cache at home, go to Rome to purchase this honour, much in the way that quacks in medicine purchase their degrees from some third-rate university.'

37. At the end of the seventeenth century, the prestige and hegemony of the Italian language and of Italian literature in Europe began to wane dramatically. As poetry yielded its place of prominence to an age of prose at the cusp of the eighteenth century, the Italian peninsula's literary heroes and innovators were relegated to the ranks of amusement rather than exemplary model. Poets whose names once stirred awe and admiration, i.e., Dante, Petrarca, Ariosto, Tasso, and the Renaissance women poets Veronica Franco and Vittoria Colonna, lost both readership and status as French essayists, novelists, and philosophes ushered in a new era of form and content. Within eighteenth-century Italy, this crisis of perception of the literary canon sparked debate throughout the enlightenment centers of the Italian peninsula. Among those who most vociferously and strategically took on the debate were the Jesuits Lodovico Antonio Muratori and Girolamo Tiraboschi. To this end, Muratori's *Primi disegni della repubblica letteraria d'Italia* [First Designs of the Literary Republic in Italy] (1703) and Tiraboschi's sixteen-volume *Storia della letteratura italiana* [History of Italian Literature] (1772-82), the first history of Italian literature, deserve consideration within the context of the literary debates raging both inside and outside of the Italian peninsula. The controversy over modernity was sparked at the end of the seventeenth century, by Père Domenique Bouhours, a French Cartesian Jesuit, who attacked baroque literature, and the Italian language in particular, in his *Entretiens d'Ariste et d'Eugène* (1671), a position that was reinforced a few years later in 1674 by Nicolas Boileau's *Art poétique*. But the most devastating blow was delivered by Bouhour's *Manière de bien penser dans les ouvrages de l'esprit* (1687), which categorized Italian language, literature and culture as solidly belonging to a defunct past, inaugurating French as the language and literature of the future. Moreover, Bouhours, in this work, attributed to Italian literature a very precise responsibility for having spread throughout Europe the bad taste of the seventeenth century, which might not have provoked such a strong reaction if Bouhours had not added to his litany of complaints the negative influence of Petrarca. In 1693 Camillo Ettori, a Jesuit from Bologna, published *Buon gusto nei componimenti rettorici* [Good Taste in Rhetorical Compositions]; in 1703 Gian Giuseppe

Felice Orsi, a marquis from Bologna, responded with a volume of *Considerazioni* [Considerations] which conceded to the critique of seventeenth-century bad taste, but defended poets of previous generations such as Tasso, and most especially Petrarch. Orsi would publish three other volumes on this same topic, one in 1707 and two in 1735. In 1703 Muratori's *Primi disegni* were published, as we have mentioned, and in 1708, his *Riflessioni sul buon gusto* [Reflexions on good taste]. The examples cited here constitute but a very few samples of the proliferation of writing on this topic that emanated from the academies and learned societies of Italy. These literary clubs, of which the most famous was the Arcadia, had been accused by Muratori as bearing the brunt of the responsibility for the sorry state of affairs in Italian literature by promoting within their ranks the practice of bad taste and bad poetry through prizes and public ceremonies. Ultimately, Italy was in competition with its own past. Among the ranks of intellectuals, the desire to move beyond its poetic legacy prompted lively discussion in the learned correspondences throughout the century culminating in Ugo Foscolo's.

38. See Francoise Waquet, *Le Modèle français et l'Italie savante. Conscience de soi et perception de l'autre dans la république des lettres (1660-1750)* (Rome: Ecole francaise de Rome, 1989).

39. Rome's oldest public library, the Biblioteca Angelica, houses the records of both the first and second phases of Arcadia activity in Rome, which are contained in over 4,000 volumes of material. Scholars have begun working with this material to uncover the history and evolution of this literary institution.

40. See *Carteggio di Pietro e di Alessandro Verri*, ed. Emanuele Greppi and Alessandro Giulini, vol 1 (Milan, 1923), pt. 1.

41. Alessandro Verri, *Le Avventure di Saffo, poetessa di Mitilene, Traduzione dal Greco originale, nuovamente scoperto*, Padova, 1782; *The adventures of Sappho, poetess of Mitylene. Translation from the Greek original, newly discovered,* London (Cadell) 1789, 2 vols, vol I, pp. 60-63. The volume quoted from here in Italian with English translation is a facing page translation that reprints the Italian edition of 1782, still carrying the fictitious imprint of Padua, with the English translation of 1789 published in London, as was the entire work. Speculation abounds as to the reason for maintaining the fictitious Padua imprint for the Italian original. The translator is unknown, though it was once thought that it might be Verri himself, while Gilman Parsons has speculated that the translator may be John Nott, though there is no explicit reference to him as translator. Even-numbered pages are reflective of the Italian original, and the odd numbered pages are reflective of the English translation, bound together and numbered consecutively.

42. Greene, *Re-Reading Sappho*, 12.

43. Ibid., 19.

44. Margaret Reynolds, *The Sappho Companion* (Basingstoke and New York: Palgrave Macmillan, 2000), 124.

45. Ibid., 124.

46. Ibid., 124.

47. Verri, *Le avventure di Saffo*, 60-63.

48. Alessandro Verri, *The adventures of Sappho, poetess of Mitylene*, trans. from the Greek original, newly discovered . . . (London, 1789), 2.209-11.

49. Verri, *Le avventure di Saffo*, 212.

50. Verri, *The adventures of Sappho*, 213.

51. Francesco Algarotti, *Newtonianismo per le dame* (Bologna, 1737).

52. Several scattered notices about the Roman *salotto* of Margherita Gentili-Boccapaduli appear in publications on eighteenth-century Rome. Arturo Pompeati-Lucchini mentions the attachment of Alessandro Verri to the Marchesa until his death, in *Vincenzo Monti*, (Bologna: N. Zanicchelli, 1928), 141. However, direct knowledge about the lives and literary production of the women such as Gentili-Boccapaduli has been difficult to procure. Fortunately, numerous projects are underway that should substantially improve our understanding of women's roles in eighteenth-century Rome. Among the most recent and propitious for future research is *Scritture di donne: La memoria restituta*, eds. Marina Caffiero and Manola Ida Venzo (Roma: Viella, 2007), which contains an article about Marchesa Margarita Gentili-Boccapaduli and her travel writings by Marina Pieretti, "*Il Viaggio d'Italia* di Margherita Sparapani Gentili Boccapaduli," 61-78. See also Marina Pieretti, "Margherita Sparapani Gentili Boccapaduli. Ritratto di una gentildonna romana (1735-1820)," *Rivista Storica del Lazio* 8-9 (2000-2001): 13-14.

53. See Elizabeth Graziosi, "Arcadia femminile: presenze e modelli," *Atti e memorie dell'Accademia degli Arcadi* 9, nos. 2-4 (1991-94).

54. Dixon, "Women in Arcadia."

55. Ibid., 105.

56. See Francesco Algarotti, *Newtonianismo per le dame; Sergio Bettinelli, Lettere Virgiliane*, 1757; and Giuseppe Baretti, *La Frusta letteraria*, 1763-1764.

57. Dixon, "Women in Arcadia," 109.

58. Ibid., 111.

59. See Andrea Cortellessa, "L'Antiquario fanatico e l'ombra di Vitruvio. Sincretismo estetico nelle *Notti romane*," 349n64, http://www.disp.let.uniroma1.it/fileservices/filesDISP/327-364_COR-TELLESSA.pdf (accessed September 16, 2012), in which Alessandro described the Marchioness as "the poison of my life" (il veleno della mia vita) in a letter to Count Antonio Greppi dated May 23, 1778. The description only underscores Alessandro's dependency on the Marchioness.

60. See the exhibition catalogue, A. González-Palacios, ed. *Fasto Romano: Dipinti, sculture, arredi dai palazzi di Roma* (Milano-Roma, Leonardo De Luca Editori, 1991), table xxiv, caption 60, 141-42.

61. The description of the portrait is my translation of an excerpt of a review of the exhibit Ilaria Sgarbozza, "Il Neoclassicismo in Italian: Da Tiepolo a Canova," (Milano, Palazzo Reale, March 2–July 28, 2002). The translation of the following text, which appears in the body of this article, is mine. "Laurent Pecheux dipinse nel 1777 quello che è uno dei più curiosi quadri in mostra, il ritratto della marchesa Margherita Gentili Boccapaduli, compagna del milanese Alessandro Verri e donna di grande intelligenza. Vestita di un elegantissimo abito all'ultima moda è rappresentata nel suo gabinetto di curiosità, mentre mostra allo spettatore la sua collezione di farfalle. Alle sue spalle note statue antiche, conchiglie e fossili acquatici; ai suoi piedi una vasca d'argento piena di pesci rossi."

62. See Emanuele Greppi, and Alessandro Giulini, eds. "Prefazione," in *Carteggio di Pietro e Alessandro Verri*. (Ottobre 1766-luglio 1767), vol. 1, pt. 1, (Milano: Cogliati, 1923), xlv.

63. This is my translation of Greppi, "Prefazione," "tanto riderà vossignoria e tornerà a ridere quando sentirà come il conte Pietro Verri non ne dica una, mai, a cui il conte Alessandro Verri suo fraellino mosciolino, piccin, ppiccino non faccia subito eco e nn la pigli su condue dita e non la mostri come si mostrerebbe una delle perle di Cleopatra." xxix, n 1.

64. Dixon, "Women in Arcadia," 109.

SINCE ITS INITIAL HEARING, the 1811 trial of *Miss Marianne Woods and Miss Jane Pirie against Lady Helen Cumming Gordon* has generated a proliferation of responses: the essay, the play, the film, and of course, scholarly papers. For a trial that took place behind closed doors and that was, as William Roughead—who published an essay summarizing the trial in 1930—claims, "swept out of existence"[1] by Edinburgh society due to its scandalous nature, it has remained persistently in circulation, under various forms, for nearly two centuries.

The facts of the trial are as follows: in 1809, Marianne Woods and Jane Pirie opened a girls' day and boarding school, containing fourteen pupils, in Drumsheugh, a wealthy, unspoilt neighbourhood of Edinburgh. In 1810, Lady Helen Cumming Gordon, an influential aristocrat who had helped recruit students to the school, suddenly withdrew her own 'natural' granddaughter, Jane Cumming, and soon all the other parents followed suit. Based on evidence from her granddaughter, Dame Cumming Gordon had accused Woods and Pirie of "improper and criminal conduct",[2] and Woods and Pirie, facing ruin, sued Dame Cumming Gordon for libel in 1811. A key factor in the trial was that the main witness, Jane Cumming, was the biracial and illegitimate child of the late George Cumming, Dame Cumming Gordon's son, and a young East Indian woman. There was an initial trial in the Court of Session, the highest civil court in Scotland, in which Woods and Pirie lost their libel suit by one vote. The closeness of the vote allowed Woods and Pirie to appeal the decision in 1812, where the verdict was reversed again by one vote—the shift being based on the idea that Jane Cumming was an unreliable witness—and Dame Cumming Gordon was asked to pay damages, although the amount was not determined. Dame Cumming Gordon then launched her own appeal to the House of Lords, and the financial and legal wranglings dragged on until 1819, at which point Dame Cumming Gordon is thought to have settled out of court for a considerably smaller sum than that initially recommended by the Court of Session.[3] In the meantime, the school was never reopened, and Woods and Pirie not only lost their livelihood but separated; while Marianne Woods returned to London and eked out a living as a governess, Jane Pirie remained in Edinburgh, but was not well enough to work again. As Frances B. Singh has recently uncovered, Jane Cumming appears to have been the least affected by the trial's outcome, remaining under the protection of Dame Cumming Gordon, marrying a Presbyterian clergyman in 1818, and bearing three children. Jane Cumming died in 1844.[4]

Recent readings of the trial and of its subsequent incarnations have focussed on the ways in which the colonial context of the period as well as early nineteenth-century discourses around race shaped and fashioned its outcome. As Geraldine Friedman has argued: "The case [. . .] provides an exceptional opportunity to explore not only women's same-sex sexuality, but also the ways in which it intersects with issues of race, class, and the constitution of the British nation within the frame of colonial geopolitics."[5] Mikko Tuhkanen has also suggested that the trial anticipated the eugenicist and sexological discourses appearing at the end of the nineteenth century, when the categories of "racial difference" and "sexual perversity"[6] became linked in inextricable ways. According to Tuhkanen, the trial's later incarnations—as popular essay by Roughead in 1930, as Lillian Hellman's 1934 play, *The Children's Hour*, and as William Wyler's 1961 filmed version of *The Children's Hour*—each revisit the connections between race and deviant female sexuality to varying degrees.

This essay builds on these post-colonial readings of the Woods/Pirie trial by examining its various generic mutations as it has travelled through history, and by analyzing the role and function of hybridity in relation to questions of race, sexuality and textuality. On the one hand, the concept of hybridity is what made the trial intelligible in 1811—by positioning the biracial Jane Cumming as the 'instigator' of perverse female sexual knowledge—and on the other, it is also what made the trial's verdict unstable, as evinced by the symmetrical votes of four to three in both the initial ruling and the subsequent appeal. At no point, therefore, did the judges rule unanimously in favor of, or against, the two schoolteachers. As Martha Dobie argues in Hellman's reinterpretation of the trial: "It's all mixed up."[7]

As a term that came into use with Charles Darwin's theory of evolution in the nineteenth century, the concept of hybridity is particularly apposite for an understanding of the Woods/Pirie trial. 'Hybrid' could mean, among other things, the child of parents of two different races. However, when applied to animals, the term seemed to encompass both reproduction and sterility. In his *Life and Letters* (1887), Darwin wrote to his correspondent: "I think there is rather better evidence on the sterility of hybrid animals than you seem to admit."[8] In biological and evolutionary terms, hybridity is the result of reproduction, but the hybrid product itself may not have the capacity to reproduce. In the animal kingdom, hybridity tended to be seen as an endpoint, a potential death of the species. In human terms, hybridity was thought to produce a weakening of the species rather than outright sterility. By contrast, in nineteenth-century horticulture, a hybridist was someone who cross-fertilized different kinds of flowers to improve their bloom or their color, thereby creating a 'better' or more distinct product. Even there, however, the question of successful reproduction remained an issue; it could be very difficult to create the perfect hybrid strand. A hybrid product is therefore something that goes against nature, in that it is the result either of an accident of nature, or of a controlled manipulation of nature. One question, then, is whether the hybrid object can form a family and have a lineage, or whether it is one of a kind. As a hybrid subject, Jane Cumming both eventually produces offspring—as recent scholarship has uncovered—and produces a 'one of a kind' narrative—in her accusations against Woods and Pirie. For the defense, the accusations against Woods and Pirie are the direct result of Jane Cumming's hybridity; only her mixed-race background could lead her to construct this most perverse and un-English of narratives. The defense wants Jane's story to be unproductive, and not capable of leading to any kind of truth. The truth in question would entail a recognition of the existence of a non-reproductive lesbian sexuality, which returns the argument to the underlying fear of the effects of hybridity.

Human hybridity—as in the mixing of the races or miscegenation—was rarely seen as an improvement of the species, even though there were key differences among respective geo-political configurations in relation to this issue. For example, while the legacy of slavery in the United States made miscegenation not only taboo but illegal in certain states until the mid-twentieth century, in Britain the East India Company initially encouraged—up to about the time of the Woods/Pirie trial—marriages between British men and East Indian women, a group who became known as Anglo-Indians. However, as the British colonial empire expanded over the course of the nineteenth century, anxiety around miscegenation increased, and as Robert Young has argued, miscegenation was increasingly thought to produce sexual as well as racial aberrations.[9]

Human hybridity over the course of the nineteenth century was therefore associated more closely with the idea of falling away and of degeneration than with improvement, as in the horticultural model. The dangers attributed to hybridity also had their parallel in the way homosexuality was being conceived. According to Guy Hocquenghem, homosexual desire would become particularly threatening to notions of proper lineage, "because it produces itself without reproducing."[10] Queerness, in other words, spreads horizontally rather than vertically, invoking disease and contamination rather than healthy offspring. Homosexuality therefore coincides with hybridity—with the same fear of contaminating the species—while being distinct from it, in that it is not engaging in biological reproduction. It is also predicated on a model of sameness rather than difference. Nevertheless, as sexological discourse developed later in the century, the figure of the invert became a variation on the hybrid subject, both female and male, neither fully the one nor the other. Furthermore, in a trial where the key figures are a biracial adolescent and a couple accused of lesbian acts, a new kind of hybrid mixing occurs in the encounter between these two socially unacceptable identity categories. Throughout the trial, the judges superimpose the logic of hybridity onto this potentially lesbian pairing through the language of contamination, the unnatural and the exotic, so that both the biracial subject and the lesbian subject are cast in terms of an improper mixing, which it is the judges' task to disentangle.

Yet for all the focus on the body—on Jane's racialized body and on Woods' and Pirie's sexualized bodies—this is a trial as much about textuality as sexuality, about the concrete and real effects produced by the telling of a story. It is important to remember that this is a libel trial, a trial about words and their potency. The trial transcripts, largely based on a schoolgirl's report, are over a thousand pages long, which begs the question of why such a disproportionate response. In this sense, the trial's textual proliferation—in the transcripts themselves and in their later cultural incarnations—hybridizes the terms of the original accusation, mixing fact and fiction and ensuring that the initial incident—a possible sexual encounter between two women—has not been contained as one of a kind, but rather endlessly reproduced. Yet it is arguably the 'non-event' at the centre of the trial that has led to its compulsive reiterability over the last two centuries. What has become real is not the 'facts' of the case, but the various narratives it has generated, with their resulting cultural influence. In this sense, the judges failed where they most wanted to succeed; rather than closing this queer narrative down, they wedged it open.

Even in its initial incarnation as a libel trial, the case was defined by a paradox, in that the libel suit was asking for an accusation to be withdrawn, the terms of which were not representable by law. In the Scottish and British legal systems, in contrast to their European counterparts, the prohibition against sodomy, which—although rarely implemented—was punishable by death, did not apply to sexual acts between women.[11] It is nevertheless worth noting that the early nineteenth century was a particularly homophobic period, during which, according to A. D. Harvery, "more than fifty men were hanged for sodomy in England," making it a time when "trials and executions for sodomy were much commoner than they had been in any earlier period."[12] In 1806, "there were more executions for sodomy than for murder."[13] The Woods/Pirie trial was therefore taking place in a climate of extreme anxiety about homosexual behavior, reflected in the immediate closing down of Woods' and Pirie's school. However, the intelligibility of their act within the legal system could only take place under cover of another judicial category, in this case that of libel. When judges such as Lord Gillies state that "no such crime was ever known in Scotland, or in Britain,"[14] they are correct in that the vice in question could never come directly under the aegis of Scottish or British law.

Therefore, can an accusation be libelous if the accusation in question is not recognized by the law as a crime? While the judges on both sides were unanimously repelled by this "disgusting subject",[15] it nevertheless eluded the epistemological frame of the law itself. The task of the judges, therefore, was to rule on the truth or falsehood of the accusation of deviant female sexuality while simultaneously confirming that its non-representation within the law was the logical reflection of its non-existence. To this extent, the subject of the trial compromised the discursive legal apparatus by which the law acquired its authority; the court was being asked to confront a subject that should never have come to light. By holding the trial behind closed doors—which Roughead highlights in the title of his essay, "Closed Doors; Or, the Great Drumsheugh Case"—the judges physically restage the drama of deviant female sexuality under the aegis of invisibility. In keeping the subject-matter from prying eyes and a public audience, they create a literal and metaphorical closet, a space *of* and *for* the secret that is deviant female sexuality. In his reconstruction of the trial, Roughead emphasizes that "[n]o word of it is to be found in contemporary journals, letters, or biographies;"[16] that it was crucial for Edinburgh society to behave as though the trial had never taken place suggests that the anxiety around female same-sex desire lay at the centre not only of the trial's narrative logic but also defined the social climate within which it took place. What was at stake, as Lord Meadowbank argues, was public morals, and the need to keep "the purity of female manners [. . .] free from suspicion,"[17] particularly when 'behavior' between men appeared to be out of control.

Yet the judges' insistence on invisibility underscores the fact that lesbian sexuality was itself becoming all too visible, reinforcing the idea that, as Lynda Hart argues: "That which a culture negates is necessarily included within it."[18] The judges, in fact, were being confronted less with impossibility than with degrees of probability, of whether it is "more improbable that Miss Cumming should have invented the story, or that the pursuers should have been guilty of the crime?"[19] In either case, the judges are faced with what Lisa Moore calls "two equally problematic forms of [women's sexual] agency."[20] It is in the process of navigating the terms of this agency, in the space between the actual—the performance of sexuality—and the possible—the imagining of sexual acts—that the trial itself becomes a hybrid discourse of fact and fiction, reality and fantasy, knowledge and innocence, the seen and the unseen.

Furthermore, as Roughead argues, this case represents "uncharted territory"[21] in that it has no locatable referent. Emerging from an exclusively female community, there is no man through whom this desire has passed, there is no phallus. The underlying epistemological question is: how can something visible come out of what is invisible? In sifting through the evidence, the judges on both sides repeatedly stumble on the trope of visibility, which is also the defining trope of legal discourse. In order to reach a verdict on a case, something has to be made representable; empirical truth has to have an object. When Lord Meadowbank makes his initial summation of the trial in 1811, he argues that the act would be possible either by "women of a peculiar conformation, from an elongation of the *clitoris*" or conversely that, "by means of tools, women may artificially accomplish the venereal gratification".[22] Cast entirely within the Lacanian framework of the symbolic order, Lord Meadowbank's logic constructs the phallus—and its simulations—as the only possible mode of representation, so that the limits of sexual representation are also the limits of language and of legal argument.[23] By making 'lesbian' sexuality articulable only through the figure of the phallus, Lord Meadowbank can also ensure its invisibility by taking the phallus away: no phallus, no sex, no transgression. The crime, which is not a crime, could not have taken place. The judges therefore literalize the impotence of the law before the fact of deviant female sexuality by configuring it as invisible and by logical extension, as impossible. Furthermore, by interpreting lesbian sexuality exclusively in terms of the heterosexual model of penetration, as the only possible proof that sex can have taken place, Lord Meadowbank is also ignoring evidence based on 'discursive weight', whereby, as was the case in this trial, an event or action could be acknowledged as having occurred if two or more witnesses came forward to testify.

Yet the juridical staging of denial by the pursuers is also at odds with the discursive repercussions of the accusation prior to the trial itself, in that everyone Dame Cumming Gordon tells is uncannily receptive to hearing about a sex act that was not supposed to be intelligible. As Eve Sedgwick argues, the 'coming out' narrative, which is what Dame Cumming Gordon 'does' to Woods and Pirie, "can bring about a powerful unknowing *as* unknowing, not as a vacuum or as the blank it can pretend to be but as a weighty and occupied and consequential epistemological space."[24] The extreme reaction of the other parents, who all immediately withdraw their girls from the school, and the consequent reaction of other schools, who are unwilling to take on pupils who have attended Drumsheugh,[25] points to a knowingness that simultaneously needs to be cast off, expelled and recast as an "unknowing". As Sedgwick goes on to argue: "The pathogenic secret itself, even, can circulate contagiously *as* a secret,"[26] so that deviant female sexuality comes to occupy the space between knowledge and ignorance. As Roughead explains in terms of one of the parents', Lady Cunynghame's, reaction to the news: "Scarlet fever her ladyship was prepared to face; moral contagion was another story."[27] In this metaphor of disease, to admit to the knowledge in question is to risk becoming contaminated, yet it is also a knowledge that is always already there, ready to be heard.

The libel trial, in turn, takes place because through the closing down of the school, society has already performed its judgment and sentencing. The judges are being asked to function outside the rhetoric of contagion and to control the spread of the disease. However, while they can recast the events into juridical language, they cannot circumvent the paradoxical binary of knowledge and innocence, of knowing and unknowing. The judges for the pursuers therefore argue that there is nothing to know because there is nothing to see, whereas those for the defendant suggest that no schoolgirl could have invented such tales. For the latter, invention is more troubling than reality. On each side, therefore, a version of female innocence is being protected.

Yet the relations among doing, seeing and imagining are precisely what get collapsed as the trial unfolds. To begin with, what the schoolteachers 'do' and what the girls 'see' becomes the least reliable form of evidence; as Lord Hope reveals concerning a key piece of ocular evidence, that of the maid, Charlotte Whiffin's, claim to have witnessed Woods and Pirie on the drawing-room couch through a keyhole: "We saw this with our eyes. We who visited and inspected the house, saw that the story of the key-hole was physically impossible."[28] The judges discovered that while one of the doors to the drawing-room had no keyhole, the other door had a keyhole which did not provide a view of the couch. Here, while the act of 'seeing' by the judges refutes that of 'seeing' by the female domestic and the girls, as Friedman points out, the very act of looking through the keyhole compromises the disinterested authority of the judges, so that "[t]he sifting of evidence consequently becomes the imagining of the other's imagination."[29] Furthermore, the servant's and schoolgirls' keyhole testimony paradoxically participates in a long tradition of keyhole testimonies used in sodomy trials, which, according to George Haggerty, were a key framing device for "the versions of these trials produced for public consumption."[30] On the one hand, by creating their own keyhole testimony, the female servant and pupils of the Woods/Pirie trial are ironically participating in a trope belonging to male homosexuality, and dangerously aligning themselves with a sodomitical imagination. On the other hand, the judges, who can find no evidence of a keyhole, are symbolically reiterating their disbelief that female 'sodomy' can take place. The sexual symbolism of the keyhole therefore becomes a way of constructing and delimiting the possibilities of sexual deviance according to prescribed gender norms.

Furthermore, as Tuhkanen has argued, most of the concrete evidence for the trial is oral and/or aural rather than visual. The girls hear words—as in Jane Cumming's witnessing of the phrase: "O do it, darling" —and sounds—Jane's description of hearing a sound like "putting one's finger into the neck of a wet bottle"[31]—a simile which invokes the visual through the aural, and which hovers between heterosexual intercourse and lesbian penetration with fingers. This simile also reveals that oral and/or aural evidence, in contrast to visual proof, is more closely aligned with the realm of the possible than the actual, with imagination rather than fact, and with feminine rather than masculine modes of knowing. Words and sounds are not transparent; they are subject to mishearing and misinterpretation. The judges themselves want Jane to have misheard the phrase: "You are putting it *in* the wrong place" as "*on* the wrong place".[32] Here, the oral slippage between *on* and *in* highlights rather than erases the easy transition between female innocence and female lust. Oral and/or aural cues therefore generate a proliferation of possibilities and interpretations, activating the imagination of the judges and the witnesses alike. In the case of the schoolgirls, seeing is often the result of hearing rather than the other way around. As Lord Boyle notes of Jane's friend, Janet Munro's, testimony: "I cannot conceive but that [Miss Munro] was from the beginning a witness whose mind had been misled and tainted with regard to the actions of the pursuers."[33]

As Hellman will also exploit in her play, orality is connected to gossip; words circulate and in the process, shift their meaning; language is fundamentally unstable, so that the girls' testimonies repeatedly subvert the court's will to knowledge. Furthermore, in spite of their institutional authority, the judges, like the schoolgirls, also occupy the position of believing what they hear, for all they have as testimony are the girls' stories. While Lord Meadowbank talks of the "extreme facility with which credit is given in schools of all descriptions, and particularly female boarding-schools, to whatever is there circulated or surmised,"[34] the judges are engaged in a parallel process of conjecture, which in the judges' terminology is cast as 'theory' whereas in the schoolgirls' is called 'gossip'. The very subject of the trial—deviant female sexuality—therefore produces endless deviations away from the certainty of juridical discourse.

It is at this intersection of the juridical and the fictional that the figure of Jane Cumming is inserted as a 'solution' to the case. Jane's excessive visibility as a hybridized and biracial subject serves as a material embodiment of the uncontrolled hybridization that defines much of the trial. On the one hand, Jane's racial and cultural differences are over-determined to such an extent that she appears intelligible only within those categories. She is "wanting in [. . .] a European complexion",[35] defined by her "Eastern constitution",[36] and seen as sexually precocious on account of her "Eastern education".[37] On the other hand, her paternity, although illegitimate, gives her access to the Scottish aristocracy, so that it is less her absolute otherness than her hybrid status that produces discomfort. As Friedman has argued, British colonialism in India was reaching a point where the Indian idiom of colonial rule—in the form of having British administrators and civil servants assimilate into the native way of life—was being questioned.[38] In particular, there was an increasing anxiety of assimilation around "sexual relations between British men and Indian women".[39] As a direct product of such a union, Jane Cumming embodies a more public, political anxiety around the formation of empire and nation-building.

Jane becomes not only the grounding figure of errancy and of un-belonging, but she also challenges the intelligibility of Scottish womanhood by her filiative connection to it. Jane's body is cathected in terms of what Anne McClintock describes as "the simultaneous dread of catastrophic boundary *loss* (implosion) [. . .] and attended by an *excess* of boundary order and fantasies of unlimited power."[40] This duality structuring the male imperial imaginary is evidenced in Lord Meadowbank's reading of Jane: he "detect[s] something inscrutable and disturbing about this child of India."[41] While Lord Meadowbank warns against "the charge [being] the evidence of its own truth"[42] as in witchcraft trials, he performs the same gesture with Jane Cumming, reading her body as "evidence of its own [lies]". However, while Jane's testimony literally and symbolically disrupts the coherence of Scottish womanhood, her hybridity—both in terms of her assumed precocious sexual knowledge, and her mixed-race background—paradoxically also secures the trope of visibility; for the pursuers, Jane becomes the only object the judges can see, thereby ensuring that the schoolteachers' sexuality and race can remain invisible. This is literalized by the fact that only Jane and the other pupils could physically appear in court, whereas the schoolteachers could not testify on their own behalf. This was part of a broader policy of keeping parties to a case out of court, as they were assumed to be too biased to give evidence. To this extent, Jane's hybrid instability makes her a stable referent of otherness and impurity, enabling Scottish femininity to remain pure.

In contrast, the counsel for the defense attempt to recuperate Jane as a properly socialized British subject: "I am certain," argues Lord Robertson, "that her upbringing, here rather than in India, must render her different from her female parent."[43] However, while Britishness is seen as able to erase Indianness, in his notes Lord Robertson also describes Jane as "entirely dark [with] little trace of British features," and questions the veracity of her paternity: "One wonders if her mother did not invent a tale for young Mr. Cumming."[44] This locating of duplicity in the mother rather than the daughter suggests a certain interchangeability between female subjects, depending on the requirements of the court. The fact that, as Tuhkanen argues, "the true nature of close female friendships was potentially hidden from the disciplinary gaze,"[45] also enabled an element of substitution. Mother, daughter and female lover all become sites of potential disorder and transgression, so that 'difference' becomes locatable as much in feminine as in racial otherness. Within this logic, the counsel for the defense can seamlessly position Jane Pirie in the place of Jane Cumming. In a clear echo of Jane Cumming's "Eastern imagination", Miss Pirie is taxed by George Cranstoun with having "a morbid irritability of feeling" and "an overheated imagination."[46] Yet it is the judges themselves who privilege imagination over observation by imagining the potentially perverse behavior of their witnesses. They become fully implicated in the discourse they seek to regulate and discipline, hence the compulsion to locate the workings of the imagination in figures of otherness.

While Jane Cumming is taxed with having an excess of sexual knowledge, Jane Pirie is seen as having an excess of sexual feelings. According to Cranstoun, in such persons, "the romance of friendship, or rapture of devotion, alternates with the gratification of the lowest sensuality."[47] In each case, the domain of virtuous femininity is under threat. By placing the blame of deviant female sexuality on particular bodies, and by constructing the racialized and the hysterical body as mutually collapsible categories, both sides seek to contain the fear articulated by Lord Gillies: "Are we to say that every woman who has formed an early intimacy, and has slept in the same bed with another, is guilty! Where is the innocent woman in Scotland."[48] Here there is both rhetorical flourish and genuine anxiety, as Gillies navigates his way through intangible evidence. As colonized and gendered subjects, Jane Cumming and Jane Pirie respectively come to embody, on the one hand, the trial's only intelligible source of resolution and on the other, they are what prevent its satisfactory closure. The very fact of the differences between the two women confirms the hybrid quality of female same-sex desire and paradoxically ensures that it cannot be contained in one location.

The trial, along with its victims, did sink into oblivion for just over a century, before being resurrected by William Roughead, whose forty-year career as a chronicler of the more unusual crimes and misdemeanors of Edinburgh society attracted him to the Woods/Pirie case. Housed in a collection entitled *Bad Companions*, the story of Woods and Pirie appears to maintain its anomalous status, in that Roughead reads these particular 'bad companions' as innocent. Yet this innocence, coupled with Edinburgh society's desire to forget the trial, becomes Roughead's justification for bringing it back into circulation. Roughead may want Woods and Pirie to be innocent, but he cannot stay away from the tantalizing theme of lesbian desire. His occasionally salacious descriptions reenact much of the judges' extravagant language with regard to the nature of the 'crime'. While for the judges it is an "extraordinary and distressing case,"[49] for Roughead it is "at once so monstrous and extravagant as to baffle belief."[50] Already, we see the trial entering the realm of the unbelievable and the fantastic, its discursive register shifting away from the legal and the factual. Roughead also positions himself as final judge and arbiter of the case; his text enacts a restaging of the trial—he literalizes this metaphor by talking about "the grotesquely limited stage upon which this tragi-comedy was played"[51]—in order to reach the final verdict. "My interest in the case," claims Roughead, "resides in the fact that *the charge was false*."[52]

Therefore, this compulsion to reaffirm a verdict that the judges of 1812 had already reached and to close the case down once and for all, is precisely what keeps it open. The very fact that lesbian activity was found, once again, not to have taken place, generates further discursive activity. Roughead also positions himself as a colonial explorer attempting to map out this obscure terrain: "As a conscientious explorer of the dark continent of crime, having discovered this uncharted territory, I feel it my duty to divulge my find."[53] In this conflation of colonial and Freudian metaphors, Roughead ensures that the "uncharted territory" of female sexuality remains open while simultaneously exculpating Woods and Pirie. Yet Roughead's desire to exonerate the schoolteachers also involves a turning away from contemporaneity, and a recognition of himself as an historically hybrid subject, caught between two world-views: "I fully realize that I am between two fires: belated Victorians will account me overbold; resolute psychologists will deem me not bold enough."[54] In his recognition of the paradigm shift to modernity and of the making visible of lesbian desire, Roughead implies that he is in the wrong historical moment. Although he invokes and simultaneously questions the findings of the sexologists—"I make no claim to the license granted to Professor Krafft-Ebing, Mr. Havelock Ellis, and other scientific exponents of such problems"[55]—his awareness of their work on sexual inversion suggests Woods and Pirie might not have been read in the same way within a modern idiom. By reaffirming the verdict of the appeal judges, Roughead draws a line not only between perversity and normality, but also between modernity and a more 'innocent' era.

At the same time, Woods and Pirie are perceived by Roughead as having been as much the victims of aristocratic arrogance as of "the imaginings of the Indian",[56] so that Jane Cumming's racial hybridity becomes part and parcel of a decadent aristocracy's refusal of proper form. In contrast to his euphemisms around sexuality, his description of Jane's parentage is blunt: "Her [Dame Cumming Gordon's] son had died in India, bequeathing to his aristocratic parent a bastard, borne to a black woman."[57] Here, Roughead's unusual spelling of "borne" suggests both reproduction and the burden of miscegenation. While Roughead duplicates the judges' orientalist discourse, he also taxes Lady Cumming Gordon with reinforcing Jane's sexual knowledge with unnecessary research of her own, research which "would provide pleasant reading for winter evenings round the fire in Charlotte Square."[58] Here, Lady Cumming Gordon's search for proof of lesbianism is recast as a prurient interest that merely reinforces Jane Cumming's already compromised identity. Whereas the judges showed a marked respect for Lady Cumming Gordon, Roughead's modernity can be seen in his attack on aristocratic privilege. In fact, research into the school's inception shows that Woods and Pirie were always at Lady Cumming Gordon's mercy, in that, as mentioned, she was instrumental in bringing in most of the pupils, just as she was in having them removed.[59] To this extent, Roughead correctly reads Lady Cumming Gordon and Jane Cumming as partners in crime, so that Jane's position as a bastard child of the aristocracy becomes an expression of the aristocracy's illegitimate relationship to power and privilege.

While Roughead's popularization of the trial is essentially faithful to the court transcripts, Hellman's dramatization, *The Children's Hour*, situates it firmly in the modern era, and in the literary rather than the historical. However, in spite of these shifts, the structures of disavowal embedded in the original libel case remain relatively intact. By Hellman's own admission, the theme of lesbian desire in the play is intended as an allegory for the broader issue of bullying—the play was responding to the increasingly fascist political atmosphere of the 1930s—and of the malicious power of gossip. Cast in this light, lesbianism becomes the marginal factor used to structure more central themes.

Yet, as Mary Titus has shown, female homoerotic desire also permeates the play, and reflects the concerns of the period over the dangers of same-sex communities such as boarding schools 'breeding' lesbian desire. Titus reads the three figures of Mrs. Tilford, Mary Tilford and Martha Dobie as representations of an 'abnormal' femininity, in contrast to Karen Wright's 'normal' heterosexuality. *The Children's Hour* represents Hellman's own complex navigation of being a Jewish female playwright in a male-dominated artistic world, her own half-recognized desires for her friend Julia, narrated in her autobiography *Pentimento* (1973), and her generation's turning away from the figure of the New Woman towards a 'liberated' embracing of unfettered heterosexuality. Roughead's Drumsheugh Case, Titus suggests, offered "an impersonal Scottish lawsuit" as "a safe medium for exploring very personal issues."[60] Yet, in contrast to Roughead, who rejects the possibility of same-sex desire in the Woods/Pirie case, Hellman foregrounds the fears articulated in the original trial, that lesbian desire is potentially everywhere, and that, as Tuhkanen argues: "the routes of proliferation are unpredictable, concealed, ghostly, telepathic."[61] Although their respective texts are only four years apart, while Roughead remains deliberately within the Victorian idiom of denial, Hellman locates herself firmly in modernity, where lesbianism becomes rather the visible expression of the "outcast, whose difference threatens all social order, not just that constructed by gender."[62]

In *The Children's Hour*, the question of hybridity, in terms of discourse, race and sexuality, takes on both a more muted and a more pervasive form. In contrast to the judges of the original case and to Roughead's summary, who use the terms of juridical discourse to effectively deny deviant female sexuality, Hellman uses fiction in order to acknowledge it. Yet this acknowledgment is also fraught with other forms of denial, such as the denial of any pleasure in the acknowledgment.

Acknowledgment, in fact, brings about death in the form of Martha Dobie's suicide. Hybridity, in turn, rather than being located in a singular biracial body, permeates the entire play. Paradoxically, the fact that Hellman erases the racialized subject from her narrative—the pupil Mary Tilford is white—radically complicates questions of visibility and answerability. In *The Children's Hour*, there is no one subject who can take on the burden of lesbian desire. Instead, it is articulated more pervasively in terms of a contagion with no fixed origin.

In Hellman's play, the Western world is already corrupted, in the same way that the judges perceive Indian domestic society to be. As Lord Meadowbank confidently states: "I hold myself entitled to assume it as an historical fact, and matter of notoriety, that the language of the Hindoo female domestics, turns chiefly on the commerce of the sexes."[63] While the original judges could comfort themselves that corruption comes from without, where, as Tuhkanen has argued, "racial otherness infects white femininity with illicit sexual knowledge,"[64] the incursion of decadence for Hellman now comes from within; hybridity is the means by which Western society is constituted, it is no longer safely located in the outer geographies.

This is dramatized in the play through the connections between the theme of childhood—associated as it is with innocence—and that of culture—associated with knowledge and civilization. In *The Children's Hour*, these associations are deliberately questioned and undermined; childhood is not a time of innocence but of confusion, of misunderstandings, and of boredom. Hellman used her own childhood memories in the creation of Mary Tilford, described as "the world of the half-remembered, the half-observed, the half-understood."[65] It is also the world of half-knowledge, in which information is tantalizingly there and yet beyond one's full grasp. The play's title, *The Children's Hour*, also invokes the hybrid space of childhood, existing as it does between the real and the imagined, between waking and sleeping, what Karen describes as "that dark hour of the night, when, half awake, you struggle through the black mess you've been dreaming."[66] Childhood is less the place of innocence than the place where fact and fiction are entirely interchangeable and where the meaning of things is constantly shifting.

Within this context, lesbian desire becomes an embodied expression of hybridity, as both real and fictional, spoken and unspoken, seen and unseen. Furthermore, the theme of lesbian desire exposes the failure of the school to educate the girls in the realm of culture. While the play opens with the girls reciting Portia's speech on mercy, it is their complete failure to understand or respond to the speech's content that is foregrounded. Education, and in particular feminine education, encapsulated by the flighty ex-actress Mrs. Mortar, is presented as form without content. As Mrs. Mortar says: "Women must learn these tricks."[67] The only moment of authentic education that occurs in the play is an illicit one, in the form of Mary's secret reading of Théophile Gautier's *Mademoiselle de Maupin* (1836). This text is circulating among the schoolgirls as a counter-cultural narrative—as the other of Shakespeare—with Mary as its source. As she says to her friend Evelyn: "You can have it. That's what I was doing this morning—finishing it. There's one part in it—"[68] Mary becomes the educator, telling her friends exactly which section to read. In parallel with Jane Cumming's 'exotic' Indian world, this French—and therefore almost equally exotic—novel will offer a fantasized world of knowledge that will inform the boarding-school world. Written at the height of the decadent period, Gautier's novel revels in the theme of hybridity, featuring a woman who passes as a man, deliberately confusing heterosexual categories, and ending with a scene of lesbian activity: "Instead of going back to her room, she went to Rosette's. What she said there, what she did there, I have never been able to discover, although I have done the most diligent research."[69]

In Hellman's choice of this scene, knowledge of lesbian desire in *Mademoiselle de Maupin* is figured in terms of the trope of the unknowable. In an echo of the Woods/Pirie trial's juridical discourse, the narrator can find no proof of lesbian activity. All he has are traces or imprints: "But a chambermaid of Rosette's informed me of this singular circumstance: although her mistress hadn't slept with her [male] lover that night, the bed was rumpled and disturbed, and it bore the imprint of two bodies."[70] Yet again, lesbian activity is manifested as simultaneously present and absent, hinted at but not fully apprehendable. It is not simply the allusion to this scene which informs the play but the very way in which the scene is structured, as a site of simultaneous knowing and unknowing. In their circulation of information resulting from Gautier's novel, the schoolgirls continue to re-enact its ambiguity. As with the illicit act of reading, Mary has to whisper the 'truth' to her grandmother: "I'd tell you, but I've got to whisper it."[71] This whispering—a particularly resonant gesture in a dramatic form where the spoken word conveys meaning—duplicates not only the original schoolgirls' oral form of communication, but also the judges' inability to understand them clearly, as in the unresolved distinction between "on" and "in". From the audience's perspective, the act of whispering is both full and empty, like lesbian sexuality itself.

In *The Children's Hour*, the acknowledgment of lesbian desire—on the part of the grandmother, Mrs. Tilford, as well as Martha Dobie—brings not just shame but an epistemological crisis. Not only do the characters suffer, but so does meaning itself. As Joe, Karen's doctor fiancé, says to her after Martha's revelation of her desire for Karen: "Everything I say to you is made to mean something else."[72] Karen further claims that "every word will have a new meaning. You think we'll be able to run away from that? Woman, child, love, lawyer—no words that we can use in safety any more."[73] Having just lost the libel case off-stage, Karen's invocation of the word "lawyer" exposes the ways in which neither private nor public categories can retain the same sense, much in the same way as the judges of the original trial feared that "the purity of female manners" could never mean the same thing again. In each case, what lesbian desire seems to destabilize is less the integrity of the heterosexual body than the category of knowledge itself. Because lesbian desire is presented in these texts as unknowable, its incursion into the public sphere challenges the grounds upon which knowledge is formed.

The shifting meaning of words, in turn, underlines the indeterminacy of lesbian desire, as not being fully one thing or another, as not quite dangerous and not quite safe. As Karen says to Joe: "You didn't know for sure; you thought there might be just a little truth in it all."[74] Unlike the categorical act of sodomy, lesbian desire is perceived as that which can be "a little truth" and a little true; it can insinuate itself in places where it is assumed to be exempt, such as girls' boarding-schools. Equally, this process of insinuation has played itself out in the cultural trajectory of the trial itself. In the journey from court-case to play to film—from 'fact' to 'fiction'—the story has become increasingly lesbianized. Since Lord Woodhouselee's statement that such "unnatural commerce [. . .] in this part of the world is a thing unheard of,—a thing perhaps impossible,"[75] the trial has been culturally recuperated under a lesbian lens. William Wyler, who was finally able to make a film of the play in 1961—after making a heterosexual version in 1936 called *These Three*—is recognized as having reinterpreted the figure of Karen in terms of what Jennifer A. Rich has called a "not-not heterosexual".[76] In Wyler's film, Rich argues that Karen Wright—her surname alluding to her 'correct' sexuality—rather than representing a stable heterosexuality, becomes uncategorizable, inhabiting a "fissured sexual definition."[77] In particular, critics are agreed that the film's final scene—a lingering shot of Karen walking slowly yet firmly through the mourners, away from Martha's grave and from her ex-fiancé towards the gate and the world beyond—situates Karen in a position of defiance with regard to social norms and heterosexual expectations. In this sense, Karen has been queered as a way of bringing Hellman's play, and Wyler's film, into post-modernity.

The play of *The Children's Hour*, in turn, continues to be produced regularly in Britain and North America. Rather than being relegated to the historical archives, the Woods/Pirie trial, as a cultural event, has circulated in ways that would have baffled and horrified its judges. However, the excessive length of their own court transcripts points to the early modern compulsion to turn "sex into discourse"[78] in a drive to manage and to contain that which was exceeding discursive and legal parameters. Had the judges themselves not expressed such an acute ambivalence over the subject, it is possible the closure they sought might have been achieved. As it is, the original trial continues to speak volumes.

Notes

1. William Roughead, "Closed Doors; Or, the Great Drumsheugh Case," *Bad Companions* (Edinburgh: W. Green, 1930), 112.

2. Marianne Woods, Jane Pirie, and Helen Cumming Gordon, *Miss Marianne Woods and Miss Jane Pirie against Dame Helen Cumming Gordon* (New York: Arno Press, 1975), 1:1. The sections of the trial have been numbered as follows: (1) The Petition of Lady Cumming Gordon of Altyre, (2) Speeches of the Judges, (3) The Speeches of Lords Robertson, Glenlee, Newton and Polkemmet, (4) Answers for Dame Helen Cumming Gordon to the Additional Petition of Miss Marianne Woods, and Miss Jane Pirie.

3. According to Lillian Faderman, the Court of Session recommended damages of 9,233 pounds sterling, in *Scotch Verdict: Miss Pirie and Miss Woods v. Dame Cumming Gordon* (New York: Columbia University Press, 1993), 302-3.

4. For information about Woods and Pirie after the trial, see Faderman, *Scotch Verdict*, 312. For an excellent account of Jane Cumming, see Frances B. Singh, "Recovering Jane," *Notes and Queries*, January 22, 2011, 1-2; and "Digging for Jane and Finding Yorrick," *Nineteenth-Century Contexts* 33, no. 1 (2011): 53-78.

5. Geraldine Friedman, "School for Scandal: Sexuality, Race, and National Vice and Virtue in *Miss Marianne Woods and Miss Jane Pirie Against Lady Helen Cumming Gordon*," *Nineteenth-Century Contexts* 27, no. 1 (March 2005): 54.

6. Mikko Tuhkanen, "Breeding (and) Reading: Lesbian Knowledge, Eugenic Discipline, and *The Children's Hour*," *Modern Fiction Studies*, Special Issue 48, no. 4 (Winter 2002): 1001-40. *Literature Online,* http://lion.chadwyck.com.

7. Lillian Hellman, *Four Plays by Lillian Hellman. The Children's Hour. Days to Come. The Little Foxes. Watch on the Rhine* (New York: Modern Library, 1942), 79.

8. Charles Darwin, *The Life and Letters of Charles Darwin, Including an Autobiographical Chapter*, ed. Francis Darwin, vol. 2 (London: J. Murray, 1887), 96.

9. Robert J. C. Young, *Colonial Desire: Hybridity in Theory, Culture and Race* (London: Routledge, 1996), 5, 26, 136.

10. Guy Hocquenghem, *Homosexual Desire*, trans. Daniella Dangoor (Durham, NC: Duke University Press, 1993), 107.

11. In England, Henry VIII passed the Buggery Act of 1533, which made the act of sodomy punishable by death. However, this act did not include same-sex acts between women. In Europe, however, sodomy laws included women, although they were rarely implemented against them.

12. A. D. Harvey, "Prosecutions for Sodomy in England at the Beginning of the Nineteenth Century," *Historical Journal*, 21, no. 4 (1978): 939.

13. Ibid.

14. Woods, Pirie, and Cumming Gordon, *Miss Marianne Woods and Miss Jane Pirie*, 2:93.

15. Ibid., 3:11.

16. Roughead, "Closed Doors," 112.

17. Woods, Pirie, and Cumming Gordon, *Miss Marianne Woods and Miss Jane Pirie*, 2:2.

18. Lynda Hart, *Fatal Women: Lesbian Sexuality and the Mark of Aggression* (Princeton: Princeton University Press, 1994), 11.

19. Woods, Pirie, and Cumming Gordon, *Miss Marianne Woods and Miss Jane Pirie*, 2:95.

20. Lisa L. Moore, *Dangerous Intimacies: Toward a Sapphic History of the British Novel* (Durham: Duke University Press, 1997), 81.

21. Roughead, "Closed Doors," 113.

22. Woods, Pirie, and Cumming Gordon, *Miss Marianne Woods and Miss Jane Pirie*, 2:7.

23. In relation to lesbian desire and the law, it is worth noting that in *The Psychogenesis of a Case of Homosexuality in a Woman* (1920), Sigmund Freud wrote: "Homosexuality in women, which is certainly not less common than in men, although much less glaring, has not only been ignored by the law, but has also been neglected by psychoanalytic research." Sigmund Freud, et al., *The Standard edition of the complete psychological works of Sigmund Freud (1920-1922), Beyond the pleasure principle, Group psychology and other works*, trans. James Strachey, vol. 18 (London: Hogarth Press, 1955), 147.

24. Eve Kosofsky Sedgwick, "Epistemology of the Closet," in *The Gay and Lesbian Studies Reader*, eds.. Henry Abelove, Claudia Barale, and David Halperin (New York: Routledge, 1993), 51-52.

25. In the deposition of Mrs Cunynghame, one of the parents who removed their daughter from the Drumsheugh school, we learn that Miss Weston, the principal of another school, "had very great difficulty in taking the witness's daughter into her school, some of the parents of her scholars having objected; and the witness understood from what Miss Watson said, that if her daughter had been examined as a witness in this case, she must have left the school." (Deposition of Dame Mary Cunynghame, in Woods, Pirie, and Cumming Gordon, *Miss Marianne Woods and Miss Jane Pirie*, 129).

26. Sedgwick, "Epistemology," 53.

27. Roughead, "Closed Doors," 126.

28. Woods, Pirie, and Cumming Gordon, *Miss Marianne Woods and Miss Jane Pirie*, 2:56.

29. Friedman, "School for Scandal," 36.

30. George E. Haggerty, "Queering Horace Walpole," in *Friendship and Same-Sex Love*, SEL 46, no. 3, Special Issue (2006): 543.

31. Woods, Pirie, and Cumming Gordon, *Miss Marianne Woods and Miss Jane Pirie*, 4 91.

32. Lord Hope notes that: "I myself put the question to Miss Cumming, whether she was sure of the words '*in* the wrong place,—whether they might not be '*on* the wrong place'." (Woods, Pirie, and Cumming Gordon, *Miss Marianne Woods and Miss Jane Pirie*, 2: 57).

33. Ibid., 2:112.

34. Ibid., 2:13.

35. Ibid., 2:1.

36. Ibid., 2:73.

37. Ibid.

38. Friedman, "School for Scandal," 59.

39. Ibid., 60.

40. Anne McClintock, *Imperial Leather: Race, Gender and Sexuality in the Colonial Context* (New York and London: Routledge, 1995), 26.

41. Faderman, *Scotch Verdict*, 189. Although Faderman's text is both modernized and edited, there is no other published source for the judges' notes on the testimony of different witnesses.

42. Woods, Pirie, and Cumming Gordon, *Miss Marianne Woods and Miss Jane Pirie*, 2:4.

43. Faderman, *Scotch Verdict*, 187.

44. Ibid.

45. Tuhkanen, "Breeding (and) Reading," 4.

46. Woods, Pirie, and Cumming Gordon, *Miss Marianne Woods and Miss Jane Pirie*, 4:27.

47. Ibid., 4:30.

48. Ibid., 2:92.

49. Ibid., 3:1.

50. Roughead, "Closed Doors," 122.

51. Ibid., 118.

52. Ibid., 127.

53. Ibid., 113.

54. Ibid., 127.

55. Ibid.

56. Ibid., 132.

57. Ibid., 116.

58. Ibid., 136.

59. Faderman writes: "By the spring, largely through Lady Cumming Gordon's recommendations, the school enrolled the two Miss Dunbars, Miss Dewar, Miss Anstruther, Miss Hunter, the two Miss Edgars, Miss Cunynghame, and the two Miss Frasers," *Scotch Verdict*, 29.

60. Mary Titus, "Murdering the Lesbian: Lillian Hellman's The Children's Hour," *Tulsa Studies in Women's Literature* 10, no. 2 (Autumn 1991), 217.

61. Tuhkanen, "Breeding (and) Reading," 2.

62. Titus, "Murdering the Lesbian," 222.

63. Woods, Pirie, and Cumming Gordon, *Miss Marianne Woods and Miss Jane Pirie*, 2:16.

64. Tuhkanen, "Breeding (and) Reading," 2.

65. Hellman, "Introduction," in *Four Plays by Lillian Hellman*, viii.

66. Hellman, *Children's Hour*, 67.

67. Ibid., 6.

68. Ibid., 30.

69. Théophile Gautier, *Mademoiselle de Maupin*, trans. Joanna Richardson (Harmondsworth: Penguin, 1981), 344.

70. Gautier, *Mademoiselle de Maupin*, 344.

71. Hellman, *Children's Hour*, 42.

72. Ibid., 73.

73. Ibid.

74. Ibid., 74.

75. Woods, Pirie, and Cumming Gordon, *Miss Marianne Woods and Miss Jane Pirie*, 2:73.

76. Jennifer A. Rich, "'(W)right in the Faultlines': The Problematic Identity in William Wyler's *The Children's Hour*," in *The Queer Sixties*, ed. Patricia Juliana Smith (New York: Routledge, 1999), 194.

77. Rich, "'(W)right in the Faultlines'," 196.

78. See Michel Foucault, *The History of Sexuality: An Introduction*, trans. Robert Hurley, vol. 1 (New York: Vintage Books, 1978), 36.

THE MOLLY AND THE FOP

Untangling Effeminacy in the Eighteenth Century

Sally O'Driscoll

Introduction: The Rise of Effeminacy Rhetoric

EFFEMINACY BECAME A PARTICULARLY pressing cultural problem in England in the late seventeenth and early eighteenth centuries.[1] What constituted appropriate masculinity was not a new question, since references to and concerns about "womanly" men had periodically entered into public debate for at least the preceding two hundred years.[2] Yet with the Restoration, and on into the eighteenth century, the discourse of effeminacy—defined tautologically as a lack of appropriate masculinity—became more widespread: it appeared in all kinds of popular print, acting as a focus for concerns about what kind of man was appropriate to govern the nation state under emerging modern forms of political and economic institutions. Middling-class masculinity struggled to differentiate itself from aristocratic masculinity, and for the length of the eighteenth century, *effeminacy* repeatedly arose as a term in that struggle.

During this period, male gender presentation came to be associated with the new category of sexual identity. Since the publication of Alan Bray's groundbreaking *Homosexuality in Renaissance England*,[3] modern debate about sexual identity (the shift from sodomy as general category of acts to, eventually, homosexual as a specific type of individual) has centered on self-consciousness: that is, on the extent to which men who had sex with men considered themselves to be different from other men, and whether such a recognition of difference would constitute at least the beginnings of what we would call, in modern terms, a sexual identity. The question of whether gender presentation might function as the sign of this sexual self-consciousness has been crucial; in the work of Alan Bray and Randolph Trumbach especially, the connection between gender presentation and sexual identity has been fundamental. Both use the molly as a central figure in their arguments,

[145]

for the molly is supposedly the proto-homosexual figure par excellence, whose outlines emerge tantalizingly from the court records and pamphlets of the early decades of the eighteenth century. The molly (unlike the Restoration rake) both presents himself as "effeminate," in that he wears women's clothes, and also (as an avowed sodomite) seems to embody the self-consciousness of a sexual identity in the modern sense, the claim that one is defined by one's choice of erotic object.

The molly, then, is my focus in this discussion, for the molly can be used as a prism for differentiating various aspects of effeminacy. He is the linchpin of a modern retrospective narrative that begins with two important figures of the Restoration—the libertine, pansexual, aristocratic rake (with his wives, mistresses, and male lovers) and the sexually ambiguous effeminate fop; following on the heels of rake and fop, the molly supposedly combines sodomy with effeminacy, providing modern readers with a recognizable figure—one who is familiar because the language of sexuality and the language of gender presentation come to seem inseparable by the twentieth century.

Yet the molly is actually a problematic representative of effeminacy. If *effeminacy* is defined by the fop—a very visible figure of theater and polite society—it is hard to see how the same term can be applied to mollies, who are laboring-class or lower middling-class men participating in a specific London-based culture of taverns and cruising grounds. In eighteenth-century texts, mollies appear as a subgroup within the broader discussion of sodomites, men who are unambiguously represented as having sex with other men in that culture of cruising. Yet in the narrative of sexual identity, mollies are also assumed to be effeminate, an assumption I question. It may seem peculiar to question molly effeminacy, since the available representations of mollies describe them as dressing in women's clothes, calling each other by women's names, and staging elaborate rituals for birthing babies (using dolls). But when one compares a molly to a fop, it is clear that their styles of effeminacy are hardly commensurate, and that a contemporary observer would not equate the two. It is also clear that fops are not necessarily assumed to be sodomites, whereas mollies are, which suggests that the molly form of effeminacy was essentially linked to sodomy while the fop form of effeminacy was not; to put it another way, *fop* is a term related to manners and presentation, whereas *molly* is a term related to sexual practice. These differences are the puzzle I address here, in an attempt to tease out the various elements of effeminacy and evaluate the ways class shapes the definition of the term: for fops are not laboring class, while mollies are. *Effeminacy* is too narrow a term to cover the gender presentations and popular representations of both the laboring-class molly and the aristocratic fop.

Popular print sources show that the effeminacy of fops is an effeminacy of style and gesture, an exaggeration of manners that makes the gender boundaries between masculine and feminine seem dangerously porous. This is an effeminacy of similitude, of absorption, of merging, an effeminacy that suggests the lack of meaningful difference between men and women. This form of effeminacy refuses to acknowledge any distinction that reinforces the gender binary. The effeminacy of mollies, however, needs a new name, for it designates something utterly different: it is a substitution of femininity for masculinity, a celebration of the gender binary rather than a rejection of it. This distinction between foppish effeminacy and molly transvestism is analogous to a modern tension between transgender and transsexual identities, a tension that can be summed up as an opposition between a postmodern, transgender, queer celebration of the dissolution of sex and gender binaries, and a transsexual reclamation of precisely those binary identities.[4] Nonetheless, as Laurence Senelick reminds us, there is no transhistorical meaning of cross-dressing, and it is dangerous to posit one: each example of the phenomenon of transvestism must be read in its own historical and cultural context.[5] Thus I choose not to use the anomalous word *drag* for mollies, or to assume that the meaning of their transvestism matches modern cultural meanings of similar activities. Comparing fops and mollies in the context of contemporary commentaries allows us to disentangle two very different things that modern narrative confuses by naming both *effeminacy*.

What Stephen Shapiro calls "the moment of the molly" lasts only a few years, from the 1690s through the 1730s: then the word *molly* disappears, along with any evidence of the molly himself.[6] The figure of the molly comes down to us in an exceptionally shadowy form, filtered through court trial records, hostile pamphlets, and newspaper accounts. There is a far broader and longer discourse about fops, from the Restoration through the nineteenth century, in novels, plays, pamphlets, and popular print—but never in court records. Contemporary commentaries also appear in broadsides, ballads, cheap pamphlets, and newssheets that would have been available to the broadest range of semi-literate and literate cultural consumers; exploring these sources gives modern readers the broadest available understanding of the cultural meaning of these figures.

The problem of disentangling the molly from the fop disappears later in the century, as the molly figure disappears from public representation along with the term itself: by the late 1760s, a new figure emerges—the macaroni. The macaroni figure is originally an aristocrat, but by the 1770s, men from all social classes borrow macaroni style; the terms *macaroni* and *fop* become almost indistinguishable for a while, and class is no longer a crucial element for distinguishing between different types of effeminate male presentation. But the focus of the current discussion is the "moment of the molly," a period that lasts for less than fifty years, in which fops and mollies are separate creatures, and the term *effeminacy* does not mean the same thing when applied to each.

The Effeminacy of Fops

Even when applied to fops, the term *effeminacy* was not static: during the Restoration, it still drew on some connotations that later became obsolete, and could mean a man who loved women too much, and spent too much time either chasing them sexually or adopting their pursuits[7]; or a man who cared too much about dress, and thus was not manly enough; or a man who was physically weak and undeveloped, rather than a brave warrior, and thus insufficiently masculine.[8] *Effeminacy* did not necessarily suggest transgressive or sodomitical sexuality. The term did always, however, signify in relation to masculinity, as a perceived deviation from a norm of masculinity that was itself constantly in flux. Effeminacy is stable in its designation of deviance, yet mutable in the content of its deviation.[9] The arena of deviation is also fairly consistent: clothes and manners are where spectators locate the problem, and these also distinguish the fop from other transgressive male figures such as the rake.

A fop may be defined by his clothes, but those clothes changed their meaning. The specific significance of clothes and manners shifted through time, as the relationship between outer form (self presentation) and inner qualities (masculinity) was renegotiated. Susan Staves, in an early and astute commentary on theatrical fops, notes the devolution of the fop figure from comedy of manners during the Restoration to farce by mid eighteenth century, and concludes that the function the fop played changed as the aristocracy lost control of clothes and manners as signifiers of class and wealth.[10] From the mid seventeenth century on, clothing gradually lost its ability to identify the social status of the wearer with any accuracy; the fop could be interpreted by spectators as a symbol of cultural anxiety about the shifting meaning of clothes as representative of class, and of aristocracy as power. David Kuchta argues that this change began with Charles II's invention of the three-piece suit, a "sartorial revolution [that] shifted elite masculinity from a regime that valued sumptuous display as the privilege of nobility to one that rejected fashion as the concern of debauched upstarts; from a world that reserved fine fabrics for honorable aristocrats to one that abandoned them to those considered effeminate fops."[11] As men's fashion changed its significance, men who dressed fashionably were also seen differently, as more threatening.

Clothes became a commodity, a luxury: the problem was to find a way for manliness to steer a path between the dangers of the increased luxury made available through the development and importation of commodities, while adhering to the new politeness and refinement of manners that were becoming the norm—and yet still be "manly." This question occupied thinkers throughout the century, from Shaftesbury to Mandeville to Hume and Adam Smith.[12] Luxury—as demonstrated through one's clothes, goods, and amusements—was no longer a proclamation of birth rank but marked one as a tasteful consumer. As industry became increasingly important to Britain's economy, consumers of luxury goods and services might be either denigrated as vicious or praised for playing a part in the economy and raising the standard of living, and thus "luxury" and "effeminacy" became epithets in political debate, laden with baggage and ready to fling at one's opponents. The fop's clothes were part of this interpretational instability.

Manners were a crucial part of the fop's presentation, and also a point of tension, for manners were associated with the Continent (the polished manners of France, for example), and with women—the question was how closely the public might associate appropriate masculinity with these dangerous areas. As Michèle Cohen puts it, "The fop is a parody of the man who has, precisely, followed the prescriptions for achieving politeness: he seeks the company of ladies, whom he resembles, and he is Frenchified."[13] Manners became a mark of nationality: the theme of nostalgia for the bygone (supposed) martial glory of Englishmen, the stalwart John Bull figure who bravely fought for his country, was to become a standard of effeminacy discourse for the next hundred years.

Popular print discussion of foppish effeminacy and gender transgression began to be widely disseminated in the seventeenth century with the publication of pamphlets such as "Hic Mulier: or, the man-woman" and "Haec Vir: or, the womanish-man" (both 1620). These pamphlets critiqued each sex's deviations from appropriate gender presentation, and provided a vocabulary and set of concerns framing the discussion. A spate of similar pairs followed: for example, "The Character of a Town-Gallant: Exposing the extravagant fopperies of some vain self-conceited pretenders to gentility and good breeding" along with "The Character of a Town Miss" (1675); and "Mundus Muliebris" along with "Mundus Foppensis" (1691).

These sources illustrate the concerns about the fop's dress, manners, habits, and untrustworthy slide away from Englishness. In "The Town Gallant," as it was already the case in "Hic Mulier" and "Haec Vir," the source of the contamination that has ruined English men is placed firmly as the fault of France. In "Haec Vir," the problem was identified as venereal disease, with its debilitating effects, supposedly imported from France. In "The Town Gallant," the problem is more subtle, a question of French taste rather than a literal disease:

> [I]nstead of true *Gallantry* (which once dwelt in the Breasts of Englishmen) he is made up of compliments, *Cringes, Knots, Fancies, Perfumes, and a thousand French* Apish Tricks. . .[14]

The town gallant—the fop—embodied both the dilemma and the danger of politeness: in becoming polite (evidenced here by his obsession with fashion), he risked forfeiting his identity as *English* and as a *man* and becoming "all outside, no inside."[15] This notion of politeness is class-based—the type of foppish effeminacy that is feared here is associated with the middling classes and their relationship with the manners of court and aristocracy, not with mollies or the laboring class.

But "The Town Gallant," like other popular pamphlets, is most concerned about the porous boundary between masculinity and femininity: the fop crosses that boundary when his concern with dress leads him into the feminine position of turning himself into a spectacle, becoming an object rather than a subject. The town gallant epitomizes this:

> Till noon he lies a *Bed* to digest his overnight's *Debauch* and then having *Dressed* himself, and paid half an hour's adoration to his own sweet *Image* in the *Looking-glass*, he *Trails* along the streets, *observing* who *observes* him, to the *French Ordinary*, where he swills his paunch with good cheer and Burgundy.

The concern with the admiration of others is fully developed here: it is not only that the town gallant takes too much time dressing and thinking about clothes, as women do, but he goes further and "Trails along the streets," making sure that he is watched. In the economy of masculinity—an economy of power—only the weak and powerless (women) need to use clothes and appearance as a way of drawing attention to themselves and attracting a husband. For a man to perform these behaviors and court attention suggests that he needs to toady to someone else more powerful than he—for what sense does such behavior make otherwise? The fop's dress is a signal of need for admiration, and of his desire to turn himself into a powerless object for spectators; this self-objectification is the underlying concern of effeminacy discourse, and is referred to obsessively in many texts over the ensuing years.

Foppish Effeminacy Linked to Sodomy

Effeminacy was sometimes associated overtly with sodomy: the changes in the representation of the fop suggest that while the fop may not have been *necessarily* seen as sodomitical at mid-century, the association of over-nice dress with effeminacy and also with a possibly transgressive sexuality could by then be publicly made.[16] George Haggerty phrases the changes thus: "Restoration fops are comically monstrous and later fops are morally monstrous."[17] Although there are many examples in popular print of fops who love only women, there are also—even in the earlier period—texts that make an explicit link between foppish effeminacy and sodomy.[18]

The texts that make a link between foppishness and sodomy are not essentially different from those that simply discuss effeminate foppishness: they differ only in that they pursue the implications of where clothes and manners (self-objectification), if improperly managed, can lead. The pamphlets have different ways of articulating this—the fop's overdeveloped interest in clothes makes him so much like a woman that other men are attracted to him; or he fails to restrict the gesture of kissing to women, and thus starts kissing men; or he takes up womanly pastimes instead of athletics. Whatever the variation is, the message is that clothes and manners are a slippery slope. This suggests that in the popular imagination, sodomy is not related to an internal quality, but is an acquired habit; not a desire or a drive, but a tendency that has been allowed to spin out of control. "Mundus Foppensis" (1691) is blunt in connecting foppishness with sodomy:

> Since Men are much more blam'd in History,
> For tying up their Slipper peaks
> With Silver Chains, that reach'd their Necks.
> Was't not, d'ye think, a pleasant sight,
> To see the smiling Surgeon slit
> The swelling Figs, in Bum behind,
> Caught by misusing of his Kind? (3-4)

The end result of self-objectification is specifically stated here: a man's inappropriate desire to be admired (by, for example, wearing silver chains) indicates that he is the passive partner in a sodomitical relationship. Not only that, but the relationship leads to unpleasant physical side effects, and to the mockery of the "smiling surgeon."

In this pamphlet, inappropriate gestures are the sign to onlookers that a man has entered the gray area of confusion between masculinity and femininity, and that since he no longer knows his own proper place in the world, it is likely that his sexual practice will be as confused as his understanding of how men and women should behave. Kissing—an appropriate gesture when a man uses it with a woman—is a sign of sexual transgression when it occurs between two men. The kiss as social greeting quickly blurs in the poem into the kiss as erotic caress, a forerunner to oral sex:

> The World is chang'd I know not how,
> For Men kiss Men, not Women now;
> And your neglected Lips in vain,
> Of smugling Jack, and Tom complain:
> A most unmanly nasty Trick;
> One Man to lick the other's Cheek;
> And only what renews the shame
> Of J. the first and Buckingham:
> He, true it is, his Wives Embraces fled
> To slabber his lov'd Ganimede;
> But to employ, those Lips were made
> For Women in Gomorrah's Trade;
> Bespeaks the Reason ill design'd,
> Of railing thus 'gainst Woman-kind:
> For who that loves as Nature teaches,
> That had not rather kiss the Breeches
> Of Twenty Women, than to lick
> The Bristles of one Male dear Dick? (12-13)

The definition of "unmanly" behavior lies in the inappropriate transfer of a gesture (kissing) that has been marked as acceptable when applied to women, and as unacceptable when applied to men. The "unmanly" man does not change his own gestures, merely the choice of who will receive those gestures. This inappropriate transfer of object choice for an affectionate gesture is the bridge to sodomy: the custom of men kissing men is explicitly associated with James I's reputedly homosexual relationship with his favorite (his "mignon"), the Duke of Buckingham. This pamphlet thus repeatedly associates effeminacy (defined in this particular way) with sodomy, not stating that one leads to the other but intimating that where one sees "unmanly" (or inappropriately directed) behaviors or gestures, then sodomy must also be present.

"Almonds for Parrots" (1708) takes a slightly different tack while connecting effeminacy with sodomy. Aimed at a group of unnamed writers, this pamphlet describes the poets it attacks as too pretty and flirtatious, effeminate in the sense of being too much with women, too interested in women and womanly accouterments. They know all about cosmetics and hairdressing, clothes and style: at first, the function of all this womanly knowledge is always aimed at conquering women. But in the process, the modish young men become dangerously like women: one young fop is so successful at his pretty ways that he can now be mistaken for a woman—and the final couplet of this section suggests that he might do well in a military camp, where men are forced to turn to each other for sexual satisfaction:

> Thus pretty S—d—y reigns among the fair,
> And passes for the bright Idalian Star,
> The Men are apt to take him for a She,
> And pay false Homage to the Deity.
> 'Tis pity *Nature* so mistook her Way,
> To make at once both Sexes go astray,
> That when she did the Masculine create,
> He should turn Tail, and prove effeminate.
> But this in Camps may of more Service prove,
> Where Male with Male are forc'd to kindle Love. (4)

"Almonds for Parrots" makes a different link between effeminacy and sodomy: effeminacy—in the sense of men spending too much time with women and eventually becoming exactly like them—will lead to sodomy, because once a man becomes like a woman, other men will be attracted to him.

This is not an uncommon argument: another pamphlet that presents effeminacy as not only related to sodomy but specifically its cause is "Plain Reasons for the Growth of Sodomy in England" (1728).[19] "Plain Reasons" shows effeminacy as a set of manners that are inculcated into well born boys, thus arguing that education is key to strengthening the manliness of the ruling classes. The pamphlet describes nostalgically how boys used to be brought up to be both tough and athletic and do their lessons, whereas now they are kept with their mothers too long and made soft, playing with dolls and drinking tea. Thus the race becomes effeminate:

> Thus, unfit to serve his King, his Country, or his Family, this man of
> *Clouts* dwindles into nothing, and leaves a Race as effeminate as himself;
> who, unable to please the Women, chuse rather to run into unnatural

Vices with another, than to attempt what they are but too sensible they cannot perform. (9-10)

In this case, effeminacy—physical weakness, bad upbringing, lack of training in manly pursuits—is what leads men to sodomy; they have sex with men because they are unable to satisfy women. This makes male same-sex relations a fallback position for impotent men; heterosexuality requires strength, sex with men does not. Both early training and education, and later social pressure from peers contribute to effeminacy, which apparently is learned rather than innate. Effeminate, foppish fashion is also a cause of sodomy in "Plain Reasons":

> But what renders all more intolerable is the Hair strok'd over before and cock'd up behind, as if it were just ready to receive a Head-Dress: Nay, I am told, some of our Tip Top Beaus dress their Heads on quilted *Hair Caps*, to make 'em look more Womanish; so that Master *Molly* has nothing to do but slip on his *Head-Cloaths* and he is an errant Woman, his rueful face excepted; but even that can be amended with Paint, which is as much in Vogue among our Gentlemen, as with the Ladies in *France*. (11)

This is one of the rare occasions where the term *molly* is used to refer to a man other than the specific group of laboring class cross-dressers found in the court records. For this effeminate "Master *Molly*," the choice of clothes leads inevitably to sodomy: external gestures or behaviors—behaviors that could easily be changed by proper education or social enforcement—lead to a sexual act. There is no notion of an innate sexual identity here. Nonetheless, habit can lead to effeminacy, and thence toward sodomy, in a downward slide. The pamphlet also claims that the gesture of kissing between men is "the first Inlet" to sodomy (12); one behavior leads to the worse. This is a slightly different interpretation than we saw in "Mundus Foppensis," which associated the two but did not mark out a cause/effect sequence.

The effeminate fop plays an important function in the long eighteenth century: he is a colorful figure whose deviation from the norm of an uncertain masculinity makes visible the boundaries for onlookers. Popular print sources present fops with a certain complexity: they depict men who have the proper manners and clothes to move in the upper classes (or who at least claim to have them), and yet the display of those manners seems to inspire a profound unease in those who watch the fop. The fop causes one to question the relationship between internal qualities and external accouterments. If manners can be acquired by any man, then men may pass for something they were not born to be; if manners are acquired from conversation with women, then men may become like women; if men become like women, they may be sodomites; French-style manners may overcome the traditional warrior-like virtues of the Englishman, and leave the nation vulnerable—the concerns are various, yet they are all consistent with a social sea-change related to the rise of the middling classes and the transformation of their role in the economy and governing structures.[20] In this context, the rhetoric of foppish effeminacy provides a channel for the discussion of what kind of man was needed; the foppish man may be seen as problematic, threatening, or inadequate, but he is still seen as human. Foppish effeminacy may lead to sodomy, and sodomy is "beastly," but the fop is not thereby assumed to be intrinsically an animal. In contrast, mollies in popular print sources are presented as an utter anomaly: they come from the laboring classes, and are presented as vile, beastly, almost inhuman, and completely beyond the pale.[21] The molly embodies—in his specifically designated criminal body, often put on public display in the pillory—the rhetorical excesses of anti-sodomitical discourse from the previous two centuries, made even more virulent by the molly's transvestism. There is little relationship between a fop whose clothes veer dangerously close to womanliness, and a molly who wears women's clothes: the term *effeminate* cannot usefully be applied to both.

Mollies

The discourse about mollies takes place in a very narrow range of print sources: pamphlets, broadsides, and newspapers that relay court proceedings and the court records themselves.[22] Everything that is said in print about mollies takes for granted their criminality and their need for punishment. The other striking aspect of the evidence is that much of it was produced not in the normal course of the judicial system's activities, but as a result of targeted entrapments by members of the Societies for the Reformation of Manners, who sent spies to bawdy houses, pick-up places for prostitutes of both sexes, and taverns in an attempt to find evidence for the prosecution of sexual sins, swearing, and Sabbath breaking.[23] It is hard to tell how much the zealotry of these informers colored their testimony about mollies.[24] The paucity of available sources makes it difficult for modern historians to judge exactly how mollies were understood by their contemporaries. Nor are the available sources neutral: they follow the well established conventional rhetorical style of criminal pamphlets, whose stories of criminal apprehension, confession, and execution were produced in abundance. One would hardly choose to look to such sources for the historical truth of mollies, yet there is no other type of evidence; thus there is no alternative but to try to read the records of mollies with an ear for the nuance of the rhetoric.

Mollies, however sketchy the evidence delineating their existence, play a larger role than any other figure in scholarly work on the development of the modern concept of sexual identity. Alan Bray's *Homosexuality in Renaissance England* is one of the most important presentations of the argument that a homosexual subculture emerges during this period, that mollies are the first people who have a gay identity, and that they are felt (and feel themselves) to be different from other people because of this—no longer is sodomy a vice that any person could fall into, it is now a sign of one's membership in this club (as Ned Ward put it in his famous pamphlet on mollies).

Describing the evidence, Bray argues that mollies have distinctive places to go, clothes or other signs to point each other out, and a special argot. The molly houses, along with the piazzas of Covent Garden, part of St. James's Park, the latrines at Lincoln's Inn, and a section of Moorfields, created what Bray calls "a coherent social milieu. [. . .] The molly houses and the casual meeting-places such as St. James's Park were not separate entities but were part of a specifically homosexual world, a society within a society".[25] Bray's argument has shaped modern scholarship about same-sex sexuality, and the narrative he sketches out is not what I want to argue with. Rather, I wish to push a little harder on the question of the molly's effeminacy, and contrast it to the very different effeminacy of the fop. Even if the contemporary sources sometimes use the word *effeminate* to describe mollies, and even if Bray's description depicts mollies "in drag"[26] and aping women's manners, molly self-representation and transvestism do not constitute the same type of effeminacy as that of the carefully dressed fop.

The difference between the molly and the fop turns on the distinction between transvestism and effeminacy: the mollies' practice of wearing women's clothes and calling each other by women's names does not make them *like* women, and does not even mean that they wanted to be like women. Bray himself makes this important distinction very briefly, but does not pursue it: discussing the effeminacy of mollies, he points out that molly transvestism takes place in molly houses, not on the streets, and that it was not intended to enable mollies to pass as women. The transvestism of the eighteenth-century molly houses was "about homosexuality; it was not intended to deceive and, as the molly houses themselves, was widely kept as unobtrusive as possible. Effeminacy and transvestism with specifically homosexual connotations were a crucial part of what gave the molly houses their identity".[27] The mollies' effeminacy consists mainly of their wearing of women's clothes, and their exaggerated (we would now say campy) borrowing of women's gestures and names. These elements, however, are crucially different from the effeminacy of fops.

Molly and *sodomite* were not synonymous terms at the time. Randolph Trumbach argued in his early work that although many may possibly have been effeminate, "the majority of sodomites could not have been effeminate, let alone transvestite."[28] Yet these other, non-effeminate sodomites tend to be ignored in scholarly discussions of the genesis of modern sexual identity. Mollies are more compelling to modern readers than other sodomites because of their colorful representation: the transgressive act of a man donning an item of women's clothing acts as a lightning rod, drawing attention to the molly's sexuality and to the molly's apparent refusal to abide by boundaries. The combination of transvestism and same-sex sexuality has made mollies obscure other varieties of male sexual behavior. And the mollies' visibility has brought them to the center of theories of early modern sexual identity.

Fops do not put on women's clothes (even though popular print sources make exaggerated claims about the similarity between a fop's clothes and a woman's). Foppish effeminacy is a way of expanding the boundaries of what is considered appropriate gender behavior, and makes those boundaries porous; it works by synecdoche and produces similitude: the fop allows himself to develop characteristics that have been assigned as feminine, as appropriate to women; that is, he chooses to give free rein to qualities such as concern for appearance, concern for the admiration of others, concern for manners and witty conversation, etc. These concerns exist in all people of a certain social rank: the problem is the degree to which they are cultivated—the fop is out of balance (out of humour, one could say, in seventeenth-century terminology), because he has allowed the wrong concerns to come to the fore; he has allowed himself to overdevelop aspects of himself that he should have restrained and held in check. By developing qualities that should have been moderated, he moves, step by step, toward similitude with women (who are, according to humoral theory, less moderate and rational than men). This question of balance is what all commentators on fops are worried about: the fop is not innately wrong, rather he needs to be put back into harmony, just as he would need to be bled if he were too sanguine. Certainly there are serious consequences to his lack of balance, and these could even include sodomy, so foppishness should not be condoned. Nonetheless, foppish effeminacy functions within the realm of everyday problems, and rarely rises to the level of freakishness.

Mollies are different from fops. Similitude is not in question here: transvestism does not make mollies like women, nor do they try to pass as women.[29] Putting on a woman's dress, adopting a name such as "Old Fish Hannah"—these are surely not attempts to be taken for a woman. It is impossible to reconstruct the personal and psychological meaning these gestures might have had for an individual man, but in an external sense the gestures function as a public (to the group, not in the broader sense) declaration of a willingness to identify oneself to one's peers, to take a step so shocking to contemporary mores that it burns one's bridges. One could say that molly transvestism is analogous to minstrelsy, in which the application of blackface by a white performer suggests an appropriation of another's identity for one's own purposes: the purpose can be mockery, among other things, but is not an attempt to pass. The molly and the minstrel do not blur boundaries when they adopt the trappings of the "Other": rather they remind spectators, and make visible for them, the gap between male and female, black and white. The complex appropriation involved in these cases reinforces boundaries rather than blurring them.

Many scholarly discussions of early modern cross-dressing focus on the boy players of the theatre. Yet this work is not of much use for explaining mollies, because it necessarily deals with the situation of boys playing women on stage, in public, for an audience, within the conventional boundaries of a theatrical performance: how they inhabited the roles, and what they might have thought about doing so; and particularly the way audiences responded to them.[30] The boy players were ephebes: beautiful young men, delicate and graceful. Their assumption of female dress or feminine gestures did not make them pass as women, but made them public objects of erotic attraction because it threw into relief their compelling and specifically male beauty. Fascinating as this is, it does not adequately address the way male cross-dressing functions in non-theatrical situations, or in the particular situation of the molly tavern, which one might characterize as somewhere in between cross-dressing done in solitude and drag done on stage—a performance for a small audience of peers. No existing record of mollies suggests that they were young or beautiful, or that youth or beauty were important elements of molly socializing. Thus the function of transvestism for mollies does not have the same meaning as it does for the boy players.

To modern readers, the mollies' apparent claiming of a proto-modern sexual identity is seductive and compelling precisely because it suggests that mollies, like modern people, use gender transgression deliberately to signal sexual transgression. This anachronistic interpretation obfuscates what the evidence suggests. It is not clear what molly transvestism meant to their contemporaries: certainly, the available representations of mollies claim that they are both transvestites and sodomites—the question is how their contemporaries understood the link between those two facts. It does not appear (as the evidence below indicates) that wearing women's clothes signaled that the molly intended to play the sexually passive partner, nor does it indicate any attempt to take on feminine gender characteristics—the lisping and gossiping that the sources describe have little to do with the real behavior of women. Mollies are not seen as weak men—as the fops were seen to be, through their gradual similitude with women—but rather as monstrous and beast-like. As we shall see in the popular print sources, it is the particular combination of sodomy, transvestism, and what one might call *revelry* that makes mollies so shocking in their time (and thus such good fodder for hack writers). I suggest that the mollies' use of women's clothes functions not so much as a signal of their sodomitical tastes—that is the modern link, an anachronism here—but as a sign that they are not ashamed of those tastes: the brash, rowdy parties where the mollies masquerade and play make it clear that they do not wish to hide, at least from each other. This flaunting of sexuality—not the sexuality itself—sets them apart from other sodomites who used the cruising grounds, and from male prostitutes (cross-dressed or not). To use the word *effeminacy* to describe this use of clothes obscures the differences between mollies and fops.

Mollies in Popular Print

The popular print descriptions of mollies are striking in their repetition of certain words: *vile, beastly, unnatural, monstrous,* and *filthy.* The insistence, in multiple sources, on these adjectives—along with a refusal to describe in detail some of the scenes of molly life—falls within the conventional rhetoric for criminal pamphlets but also serves to remind the reader that mollies are indeed beyond the pale.

There are many popular print sources that describe sodomites: these too draw heavily on reports of court cases, portraying sodomites (like mollies) as criminals in need of punishment, examples to deter the wicked. These often use the same terms that are used for mollies, describing the sodomites as *beastly* and *vile*: these are the terms commonly used for non-procreative sex practices. What distinguishes mollies from sodomites (in their popular print representations) are two things: their use of women's clothing, and their gatherings at molly parties in taverns where their social rituals seem to have been shared by all participants. These distinguishing factors indicate that molly identity is *performative*: sodomites might have strolled the London cruising grounds looking for sex with other men, but mollies planned and created a social scene that marked them as outcasts, before sexual practice was even involved. Their appropriation of women's clothes and manners parallels the foppish use of clothes and manners, but inverts it: molly transvestism is not *effeminate* in the sense of making mollies like women, nor do mollies like women too much; it does not even make mollies less masculine, if masculinity is defined as physical strength.

The most famous description of mollies is found in a pamphlet by the Grub Street hack Ned Ward, called "The Second Part of the London Clubs" (1709?), which includes the description of the Mollies Club among a series of descriptions of other fictitious clubs.[31] The original version of Ward's pamphlet at first seems to see mollies as clearly effeminate, but the reader soon sees that molly effeminacy is more complex than it first appears: the "Mollies Club" section begins,

> There are a particular Gang of sodomitical Wretches in Town, who call themselves *Mollies*, and are so far degenerated from all masculine Deportment, or Manly Exercises, that they rather fancy themselves Women, imitating all the little Vanities that Custom has reconciled to the Female Sex, affecting to speak, walk, tattle, curtsy, cry, scold, and mimick all manner of Effeminacy. (5)

Ward describes this affectation of women's clothes and manners in more detail, adding his famous scene of the fake lying-in (resulting in the birth of a wooden "Jointed-Baby" [6]), and the gossiping of the mollies about "husbands" and "children."[32] However, the reason given for this appropriation of feminine behavior is not that the mollies are becoming like women (as effeminate fops were accused of doing), or that they enjoy acting like women; rather, it is a way to make fun of women so that they can justify their preference for men. As Ward says,

> Thus every one in his turn makes Scoff of the little Effeminacies, and Weaknesses, which Women are subject to: when gossiping o'er their Cups, on purpose to extinguish that Natural Affection which is due to the fair Sex, and to turn their Juvenile Desires, towards preternatural Polotions [sic]. (6)

Only after this mockery of women has been performed do the mollies turn to the "Beastly Obscenities, that no Man who is not sunk into a State of Devilism can think on without Blushing" (6). In other words, far from being effeminate in the ways fops are (either in the sense of being like women, or the sense of liking women too much), these sodomites are pictured as hating and mocking women, and needing to reenact that hatred before they can enjoy sexual acts with men. The link between effeminacy and sodomy is here portrayed as a reverse link or anti-connection.[33]

Ward also mentions mollies in "The London Terrae-filius, Number V" (1708), a forty-page pamphlet from a series published between 1707-1708.[34] Each number in the series is a compilation of character sketches of people to be seen on London's streets; in this case, the mention of mollies is a brief aside included in a study of a woman who keeps her adult son tied to her apron strings:

> Notwithstanding the great Boy is upwards of Twenty Years of Age, she keeps him thrice a Day to his *Geneva Bible* and *Assemblies Catechism*, as if he had not been crept above two or three Years out of his *Hanging-Sleeves* into more Manly *Britches*; and has Hatch'd him up under her own Wing after so Effeminate a manner that he behaves himself more like a *Catamite*, an *Eunuch*, or one of those Ridiculous Imitators of the Female Sex, call'd *Mollies*, than like a Son of *Adam*; and at all times stuffs his womanish Dialect with so much *O dear, O fie*, and *forsooth Mother*, that a Stranger would take him, by his Feminine Deportment, to be some Tall two Handed *Chamber-Maid* Dress'd up in Man's Cloths to make Sport for the Company. (11-12)

The line between behavior and sexual practice is blurred here; a catamite is a boy who is a passive sexual partner in a relationship with a man (the connotations are of a lack of agency on the boy's part); a eunuch is a castrated male; and a molly is a sodomite who appropriates women's clothes and gestures. The three terms are not equivalent—the only thing that they have in common is that all three terms refer to men who do not occupy a position of privilege and power. The focus of Ward's contempt seems to be misogyny rather than sexuality: he scorns men who have come, through whatever practice, not to be *like* women but to occupy a woman's powerless position, and he uses these epithets in a confused diatribe to shower contempt on a man who has allowed this to happen to him.

Long descriptions of mollies and their activities are found in two well known conventional criminal narratives: Jonathan Wild's "An Answer to a Late Insolent Libel, Entituled, A Discovery of the Conduct of Receivers and Thief-Takers" (1718), and "A Genuine Narrative of All the Street Robberies Committed Since October Last, by James Dalton, and His Accomplices . . . Taken from the Mouth of James Dalton" (1728). These focus on the fascination that mollies held for men who were themselves criminals, but who are presented as finding the mollies' flouting of social mores much more extreme than their own.

"An Answer to a Late Insolent Libel" is mostly a discussion of Wild's career as thief-taker and receiver of stolen goods. However, the last part involves the protagonist's visit with the city marshal to a molly house, which describes for the reader's titillation the protagonist's shock at the wanton behavior of the mollies. It also gives us a detailed description of their clothes—one of the few texts to do so. After the protagonist and the marshal have engineered the arrest of some of the mollies, the prisoners are forced to appear in front of the judge in the clothes they had worn to the party:

> About the usual hour of their separation, several of the sporting Sodomites were siez'd, by the *M---l* and his Man, and their Assistants; in Women's Apparel, and Convey'd in these same Dresses to the Compter. The next Morning they were carried before the Lord Mayor in the Dresses they were taken in by his Lordship's Order; some having Gowns, Petticoats, Head Cloths, fine lac'd Shoes, Furbelow Scarves, Masks, and compleat Dresses for Women; others had Riding Hoods; some were Dress'd like Shepherdesses; others like Milk-Maids, with fine Green Hatts, Wastcoats and Petticoats, and others had their Faces painted, and patch'd, and very extensive Hoop petticoats, which were then very lately introduc'd. Appearing in these dresses of Redicule [sic] before my Lord Mayor, (after Examination) his Lordship Committed them to the Workhouse there to continue at hard Labour during pleasure, and as a part of their Punishment, Order'd them to be publickly convey'd thro' the Street in their various Female Habits.[35]

The description suggests the elaborate nature of the cross-dressing supposedly undertaken by mollies. Some of them apparently have complete outfits of everyday city women's clothes, along with makeup and accessories; others have outfits that seem more like masquerade costumes, such as shepherdesses and milkmaids. The women's clothes are worn only in the privacy of the Holborn house where the molly ball took place; part of the deliberate humiliation and punishment is the broad publicity—the hauling of the mollies into court and through the streets in these outfits, where they would presumably be subject to the scorn and vilification of the public as if they were in the pillory.[36]

Not only do these mollies wear women's clothes, but they do so to titillate other men. As the pamphlet puts it, "there was a noted house in *Holborn*, to which those sorts of persons us'd to Repair, and Dress themselves in Women's Apparel for the Entertainment of others of the same Inclinations, in Dancing, &c. in imitation of the Fair Sex" (31). In this, the representation of mollies comes close to that of fops, as the molly entertainer, like the town gallant who *trailed* along the streets looking out for admirers, performs for the pleasure of other men. To turn oneself into the object who aims to please the subject (the one who has power) is a profound refusal of the power dyad that defines the binary opposition of masculine and feminine. In this case, though, the molly is far more public and explicit than the fop in his demand for admiration from his peers; the social aspect of molly revelry indicates a group acceptance that legitimates sexual transgression, and it is this legitimation that is of such concern to contemporary commentators. Molly socializing and legitimation—what I have been calling molly revelry—convince modern commentators that mollies are proto-homosexuals; yet this revelry is not effeminacy.

The second pamphlet, "A Genuine Narrative," is supposedly James Dalton's confession to his own crimes, when he turned witness against his accomplices to save himself. The first half describes his methods of mugging people on the street and holding up coaches, in tedious detail. Then, surprisingly, the narrative turns to his association with "Susannah Haws," often called "Sukey,"[37] whose real name is never given, and who is described as a "bug to the mollies" (32)—that is, a man who pretends to be a molly or a molly-lover, picks up mollies in the street (rather than in a molly club), but who then blackmails his marks. The account that follows names an extraordinary number of names, and supplies many details of the mollies' lives, supposedly to make it easier for them to be recognized and punished. What or who exactly Sukey is remains unclear: "Dalton knowing him to be unsound in his Principles (that is, he was neither a down-right Pick-pocket, a downright sodomite, or a downright bug, tho' a Part of every one of them), told him, There was no faith to be held with Hereticks. . ." (34).

The narrator claims that the continued interest Dalton shows in Haws is due to his desire "to discover something of the Intrigues between these Beasts in the Shape of Men" (35). He interrogates Sukey, but finds the information too disgusting to pass on to his readers:

> This made Dalton urgent with Sukey to discover what they did together, and in what manner they behav'd themselves, when in their most private Meetings: But, good God! the relation was so astonishing, and so shocking to human Nature, that it is impossible any man should hear it (that is not abandon'd to all manner of Vice,) without shuddering,

and his Blood running chill at the very Thoughts of it: Therefore as the Relation exceeds all Bounds of Modesty, and is too shocking to appear in publick, it is hop'd the Reader will excuse the Author's not exposing the damnable, unnatural, and beastly Appetites of these Wretches, whose Filthiness exceeds more than Imagination can conceive. (36-37)

It is frustrating to be denied the details that so shocked his narrator; the narrator uses the conventional epithets of *unnatural* and *beastly*, but does not even indicate whether these social occasions included transvestism, and if so what it might have meant to the participants. The narrator does, however, depict Dalton's "urgent" curiosity to see as much as he could, which suggests how compelling the mollies' revelry was to their contemporaries, as well as to modern readers.

Sukey Haws gives Dalton much information, including this description of a molly wedding,

> between *Moll Irons* and another *Molly*, a butcher; and that one *Oviat* (who sometime since stood in the Pillory) and another *Molly*, a Butcher of Butcher-Row, near *Temple-Bar*, stood as Bridemaids [sic], and that *Oviat* went by the Name of *Miss Kitten*, the Butcher by the Name of the *Princess Saraphina*; and that one Powell, who was call'd *St. Dunstan's Kate*, pretended to be deeply in Love with Madam Blackwell, the Person who was evidence against John Potter, convicted last Sessions for stealing the D—ke of M-----u's rich Hangings. (37-38)

These mollies are butchers or thieves, clearly laboring-class men, and the text focuses on the performative aspects of their socializing: it gives long lists of their female pseudonyms, along with the areas they supposedly frequented.[38] It also presents the story of a molly "lying-in," when a doll is supposedly birthed as part of a ceremony—as we have already seen in Ward's *History of the London Clubs*. The social rituals by which mollies communally transgress conventional mores are what fascinate the narrator and readers: the *revelry* aspect of molly sociability signals not so much their sexuality but their willingness to celebrate transgression. In this sense the molly is more like a laboring-class rake than a fop.

Finally, the narrator offers a song sung in the molly clubs—said to be carefully selected from among others that were supposedly too disgusting to be published:

> Let the Fops of the Town upbraid
> Us, for an unnatural trade,

We value not Man nor Maid;
    But among our own selves we'll be free,
    But among, &c.
We'll kiss and we'll Sw---e,
Behind we will drive,
And we will contrive
    New ways for Lechery,
    New ways, &c.

How sweet is the pleasant Sin?
With a Boy about Sixteen,
That has got no Hair on his Chin
    And a Countenance like a Rose,
    And a Countenance, &c.
Here we will enjoy
The simpering Boy,
And with him we'll toy;
    The Devil may take the Froes,
    The Devil &c.

Confusion on the Stews,
And those that Whores do chuse,
We'll praise the Turks and Jews,
    Since they with us do agree,
    Since they, &c.
They're not confin'd
To Water or Wind,
Before or Behind,
    But take all Liberty,
    But take &c.

Achillis that Hero great,
Had Patrocles for a Mate;
Nay, Jove he would have a Lad,
    The beautiful Ganymede,
    The Beautiful &c.
Why should we then
Be daunted, when
Both Gods and Men

Approve the pleasant Deed,
Approve the &c. (42-43)

Note that in this song the molly persona who is singing is the active sexual partner; in fact, the song describes the kind of sexual relationship between an adult male and an adolescent boy that was assumed to make the older partner *not* effeminate. The song is a celebration of the major elements of molly identity, as it appears in the popular texts: it extols the freedom of mollies ("among our own selves we'll be free"), their socializing and revelry, their self-legitimation, and their sexual tastes.

In "Hell Upon Earth: Or the Town in an Uproar" (1729), the narrator also notices that mollies are interested in finding young men:

> It would be a pretty Scene to behold them in their Clubs and Cabals, how they assume the Air and affect the Name of *Madam* or *Miss, Betty* or *Molly*, with a chuck under the Chin, and *O you bold Pullet I'll break your Eggs*, and then frisk and walk away to make room for another, who thus accosts the affected Lady with *Where have you been saucy Queen? If I catch you Strouling and Caterwauling, I'll beat the Milk out of your Breasts I will so*; with a great many other Expressions of buffoonry and ridiculous Affectation. If they can procure a young smug-fac'd Fellow they never grudge any Expence, and it is remarkable these effeminate Villains are much fonder of a new Convert than a Bully would be of a new *Mistress*. (42-43)

In this case, the narrator presents mollies whose manners and gestures are exaggerated versions of conventional femininity. Again, the juxtaposition of the "effeminate" gestures is contradicted by the notion that these mollies are more interested in converting young men to their cabals than in playing a "feminine" sexual role. Molly self-presentation is not actually effeminate, if that term is defined by physical weakness or sexual passivity: molly transvestism and exaggerated appropriation of womanly gestures function not as signs of effeminacy but as reminders of masculinity.

Eighteenth-century commentators who were concerned with male sexuality and self-presentation categorized gender and sexual transgressions according to the axes of similitude and contiguity (metonymy) or substitution (metaphor), and evaluated the transgressors accordingly. Fops who blurred the boundaries and became like women were ridiculed, but mollies who substituted elements of femininity for elements of masculinity were demonized. The ways fops and mollies used markers of conventional femininity are fundamentally and functionally different, and surely cannot fit under the umbrella of *effeminacy*.

Notes

1. A brief review of the eighteenth century's rich, complex language to designate male effeminacy suggests the importance of the topic in the culture. Apart from the word effeminate itself, the available terms included *fops, beaux, dandies, pretty gentlemen, fribs, macaronis, neuters,* and *amphibians.* The word fop, however, is the most important and frequently used of these.

2. The *Oxford English Dictionary*, 20 vols. 2nd ed. (Oxford: Clarendon Press, 1989), lists the first use of *effeminate* as an adjective c. 1430, but the majority of the examples given come from the sixteenth and seventeenth centuries.

3. Alan Bray, *Homosexuality in Renaissance England* (New York: Columbia University Press, 1995).

4. The tension and what lies at stake behind it are powerfully described by Jay Prosser:

   > Queer theory's embrace of the transsexual for dehomogenizing sexual and gender identities and deconstructing the narrative of gendering strikes me as a misreading, indeed, a failure to read transsexual stories as narratives with plots centered on embodied becoming. Transsexual subjects themselves have traditionally figured their transition as a final going home, a trajectory that is only worth its risks, complications, and intense pain (somatic and psychic) because it will allow one to finally arrive at where one should have always been: the destination, the telos of this narrative (being able to live in one's 'true gender identity') is all.

   in "Queer theory's embrace of the transsexual 'No Place Like Home: The Transgendered Narrative of Leslie Feinberg's *Stone Butch Blues.*'" *Modern Fiction Studies* 41, no. 3-4 (1995): 488.

5. Laurence Senelick, *The Changing Room: Sex, Drag, and Theatre* (London and New York: Routledge, 2000).

6. Stephen Shapiro, "Of Mollies: Class and Same-Sex Sexualities in the Eighteenth Century," in *In a Queer Place: Sexuality and Belonging in British and European Contexts*, ed. Kate Chedgzoy, Emma Francis, and Murray Pratt (Aldershot and Burlington, VT: Ashgate, 2002), 158.

7. The Restoration fop—frequently an aristocrat in class status—was often portrayed as effeminate in the seventeenth-century sense of liking women too much; of shading into the libertine or rake. As Peter McNeil puts it, "extravagant 'male' dress in the early years of the century, no matter how 'feminine' in its focus on adornment and affectation, was read as potentially alluring to women. Fringed gloves, red heels, the open waistcoat and affected behavior were seductive until at least the 1740s; they were the props of the ladykiller." See "That Doubtful Gender: Macaroni Dress and Male Sexualities," *Fashion Theory: Journal of Dress, Body & Culture* 3, no.4 (1999): 418. The reference to some of these decorative elements comes from *Spectator* 16:

   > I have received a letter, desiring me to be very satyrical upon the little muff that is now in fashion; another informs me of a pair of silver garters buckled below the knee, that have lately been seen at the Rainbow coffee-house in Fleet Street; a third sends me an heavy complaint against fringed gloves. To be brief, there is scarce an ornament of either sex which one or other of my correspondents has not inveighed against with some bitterness, and recommended to my observation. I must therefore, once for all, inform my readers, that it is not my intention to sink the dignity of this my paper with reflec-

tions upon red-heels or top-knots, but rather to enter into the passions of mankind, and to correct those depraved sentiments that give birth to all those little extravagances which appear in their outward dress and behaviour. Foppish and fantastick ornaments are only indications of vice, not criminal in themselves." (London: 2nd ed., 1713).

8. Susan C. Shapiro explores the various meanings of effeminacy in literary texts from the sixteenth century through the nineteenth in an article entitled "'Yon Plumed Dandebrat': Male 'Effeminacy' in English Satire and Criticism," *Review of English Studies*, New Series 39, no. 155 (1988): 400-412. Thomas A. King offers a broader and more nuanced set of connotations: "gelded," "weake, vnperfite," "of womanly and childish conditions," "wanton," "delicate," "nice," "sweete-smelling, comely araid, wantonly drest vp, smug," "soft, pliant or loose," "effeminate and nice as a woman," "fearful, vnconstant, wauering, slippery," in *The Gendering of Men 1600-1750: Volume 1, The English Phallus* (Madison: University of Wisconsin Press, 2004), 75-76.

9. As King asks, "How might we account for the apparent continuity of the term across the difference of history?" (*Gendering of Men*, 64). King rethinks the public/private divide in his discussion of effeminacy (see esp. chap. 2); he suggests that modern thinkers have not paid enough attention to the ways in which male subordination to other males was a part of public life, and constituted a different type and degree of effeminacy than is usually acknowledged.

10. Susan Staves, "A Few Kind Words for the Fop," *Studies in English Literature, 1500-1900* 22, no. 3 (1982): 427. Fops were originally discussed mainly as stage characters: see for example George E. Haggerty, "Gay Fops/Straight Fops," in *Men in Love: Masculinity and Sexuality in the Eighteenth Century* (New York: Columbia University Press, 1999); Laurence Senelick, "Mollies or Men of Mode? Sodomy and the Eighteenth-Century London Stage," *Journal of the History of Sexuality* 1, no.1 (1990): 33-67; Kristina Straub, *Sexual Suspects: Eighteenth-Century Players and Sexual Ideology* (Princeton, NJ: Princeton University Press, 1992). For discussions of fops and the social meaning of their clothing, see Elizabeth Wilson, *Adorned in Dreams: Fashion and Modernity* (Berkeley: University of California Press, 1985), esp. 22-26, for a discussion of the history of sumptuary laws and their disappearance. See chp. 1 of David Kuchta, *The Three-Piece Suit and Modern Masculinity: England, 1550-1850* (Berkeley: University of California Press, 2002) for a further discussion of sumptuary laws and the Renaissance understanding of clothes as a means of proclaiming (rather than creating) a person's status.

11. Kuchta, *The Three-Piece Suit*, 4.

12. G. J. Barker-Benfield demonstrates this in *The Culture of Sensibility: Sex and Society in Eighteenth-Century Britain* (Chicago: University of Chicago Press, 1992), chap. 3.

13. Michele Cohen, "Manliness, Effeminacy and the French: Gender and the Construction of National Character in Eighteenth-Century England," in *English Masculinities 1660-1800*, eds. Tim Hitchcock and Michele Cohen (London and New York: Longman, 1999), 51.

14. Charles Hindley, ed. *The Old Book Collector's Miscellany: Or, a Collection of Readable Reprints of Literary Rarities*. vol. 4 (London: Reeves and Turner, 1873), 4.

15. Cohen, "Manliness and Effeminacy", 51.

16. As Straub notes in *Sexual Suspects*, "Satires on effeminate men are more likely, after mid-century, to associate foppishness with sexual perversion. *The Pretty Gentleman* (1747), *Sodom and Onan* (1776), *Love in the Suds* (1772), *The Fribbleriad* (1761), *The Spleen* (1776), and other satires on

'macaronis' and 'effeminate' actors tend to resolve the earlier fop's sexual ambiguity all too conclusively as homosexual," 56.

17. Haggerty takes this further than I would when he says, in Restoration comedy, "Fops are always portrayed as sexually confused gender misfits" (*Men in Love*, 45).

18. Some scholars argue that effeminate sodomites in the early modern period made that link culturally available far earlier than the late seventeenth century; see for example Michael B. Young, *King James and the History of Homosexuality* (New York: New York University Press, 2000). However, the assumption that effeminacy and sodomy went together was not universally made until much later.

19. Anonymous, *Plain Reasons for the Growth of Sodomy in England, to which is added, The Petit Maitre, an odd sort of unpoetical Poem, in the trolly-lolly stile* (London, 1728). Further references to this work are given in parentheses in the text. This entire pamphlet is reprinted as the second part of the 1749 edition of a different and well-known pamphlet, "Satan's Harvest Home": the first 45 pages of "Satan's" are new; then comes "Plain Reasons," verbatim, then a 2-page addition—"The Game at Flats"—then the "Petit Maitre" poem verbatim. The juxtaposition of old and new material explains the fragmented quality and repetitiveness of "Satan's Harvest Home."

20. David Kuchta defines non-effeminacy as "fitness to rule." Kuchta, *The Three-Piece Suit*, 112; King puts it this way: "...effeminacy has indicated those bodies that could not bear civil virtue and utility" (*Gendering of Men*, 66).

21. Bray claims that molly house society was "composed of individuals drawn from the whole spectrum of the lower and lower-middle classes" (*Homosexuality in Renaissance England*, 86).

22. Many of the records are now available online in the Old Bailey trials: http://www.oldbaileyonline. org/. Bray notes that the sources he uses for his description of molly houses come from trial records and a handful of pamphlets (many of which are cited here); as he says, these sources "should not be taken uncritically. They were intended as a form of entertainment; and their editors naturally gave prominence to the sensational aspects of the molly houses, as indeed did the prosecution at the trials themselves. [. . .] However, while one may doubt the reliability of particular details, the picture that emerges of the molly houses as a whole is almost certainly reliable. It is impossible to believe that a compilation of this size could have been a fabrication; it is far too consistent, both within itself and with the literary accounts, as well as with the contemporary newspapers used by Trumbach in his article, for it to be other than substantially accurate" (*Homosexuality in Renaissance England*, 136-37n1). The Randolph Trumbach article Bray refers to is "London's Sodomites: Homosexual behavior and Western Culture in the 18th Century," *Journal of Social History* 11, no. 1 (1977): 1-33.

23. For a description of the development of the societies for reforming manners in the late seventeenth century, see Edward J. Bristow, *Vice and Vigilance: Purity Movements in Britain since 1700* (Totowa, NJ: Rowman and Littlefield, 1977), esp. chap. 1.

24. Many sermons preached to the *Societies for the Reformation of Manners* praise these informers in no uncertain terms; a representative sermon by Joseph Wilcocks says of informers: "What Praises therefore and Encomiums may we not justly offer to those faithful Servants and valiant Soldiers of the Lord, who have lifted themselves under the Banners of Christ for this particular Service, and have determined, at all Hazards, by *Honour and Dishonour, through evil Report and good Report,*

to engage the Powers of Darkness, and harrass the Tents of Ungodliness, and with an undaunted Valour and indefatigable Industry, to carry on the Attack against Vice and Irreligion, though covered with the *fiery Darts of the Wicked*, and the Hatred and Opposition of a corrupt World." Joseph Wilcocks, *The Righteous Magistrate, and the Virtuous Informer; A Sermon Preached Before the Societies for the Reformation of Manners, in the Parish-Church of St. Mary-le-Bow; On Monday, December 31, 1722* (London, 1723), 17.

25. Bray, *Homosexuality in Renaissance England*, 85.

26. Ibid., 95.

27. Ibid., 88.

28. Randolph Trumbach, "London's Sapphists: from three sexes to four genders in the making of modern culture," in *Body Guards: the Cultural Politics of Gender Ambiguity*, eds. Julia Epstein and Kristina Straub (London: Routledge, 1991), 119. Trumbach later revised his thinking on the topic of molly effeminacy arguing that effeminate mollies in fact constitute a third gender:

> The new effeminate adult sodomites can be documented among the London poor because of the attacks against them made by the Societies for the Reformation of Manners. These sodomites constructed around themselves a protective subculture of meeting places and ritual behavior. A few who seem to have been involved in prostitution played out a largely feminine identity. They took women's names, spent nearly all their time in women's clothes, and were referred to as 'she' and 'her' by their male and female acquaintances. Their male customers in some cases must have known that these prostitutes were genital males, but in other cases perhaps they did not, since some sodomites worked the streets as members of a group of female prostitutes. The gender identity of these transvestite males was not entirely feminine because they sometimes wore men's clothes and were prepared to take the active or inserter's parole in sexual intercourse. They were neither male nor female but a third gender that combined some characteristics from each of what society regarded as the two legitimate genders. A few such men may have existed before 1700. . . (Randolph Trumbach, *Sex and the Gender Revolution*, vol. 1, Chicago Series on Sexuality, History and Society [Chicago: University of Chicago Press, 1998], 6-7).

The concept of the "third gender" moves the discussion away from the usual definition of effeminacy and thus away from the argument I am pursuing here.

29. There are modern analogies here: Leslie Feinberg has written about the large and almost invisible population of heterosexual male crossdressers who wear women's clothes as part of an erotic preference, yet who are almost never included in discussions of transvestism because they remain mostly private and because they do not fit preconceived concepts of gender and sexuality transgression. Yet there are surely interesting parallels to draw between a middle-aged male ironworker who lives in the suburbs and wears women's clothes (with no intention of passing as a woman), and a seventeenth-century butcher who wears women's clothes in a molly house. Leslie Feinberg, "Allow Me to Introduce Myself," in *Trans Liberation: Beyond Pink or Blue* (Boston: Beacon Press, 1988), 14-35.

30. See Senelick, *The Changing Room*, 133, for a summary of recent scholarship on boy players. See also Beth H. Friedman-Romell, "Breaking the Code: Toward a Reception Theory of Theatrical Cross-Dressing in Eighteenth-Century London," *Theatre Journal* 47, no. 4 (1995): 459-79.

31. The original edition took only eight pages to describe six different clubs; Ward expanded and reprinted the two parts in a 395-page volume published the same year. The added material is in the same vein, but I refer here to the original because it was a short, cheap pamphlet that could have

been read by a broad popular audience. James Sambrook in the *Oxford Dictionary of National Bi-ography* claims that the only real one of the 32 clubs and societies Ward discusses in that pamphlet and the later book is the Kit-Kat Club; the others were therefore satirical inventions, (Edward [Ned] Ward, *The Secret History of Clubs: particularly the Kit-Cat, Beef-Stake, Vertuosos, Quacks, Knights of the Golden-Fleece, Florists, Beaus, &c. with their original*, 2 parts [London: 1709]). For a further discussion of Ward's rhetorical evasions and possible intentions, see Craig Patterson, "The Rage of Caliban: Eighteenth-Century Molly Houses and the Twentieth-Century Search for Sexual Identity," in *Illicit Sex: Identity Politics in Early Modern Culture*, eds. Thomas DiPiero and Pat Gill (Athens: University of Georgia Press, 1997), 256-69.

32. This scene is cited or repeated in later eighteenth-century texts, as if it were a known historical fact—for example, in the pamphlet *Ten Plagues of England: Plague III, Effeminacy* (London, 1757).

33. Trumbach glosses this passage thus: "Sodomitical effeminacy therefore threatened the boundaries of culture as much as did sodomy itself. Ward could only conclude that the behavior of the trans-vestite was satirical and intended to 'extinguish that natural affection which is due to the fair sex'" (*London's Sodomites*, 13). I would suggest rather that Ward (while always satirical and certainly hostile to sodomites) was aware that mollies were not trying to become like women, or to like women too much; in a sense, Ward is the first to point out the difference between the transvestism of mollies and the effeminacy of fops, a distinction that later became blurred. King offers a dif-ferent explanation of this passage, focusing on Ward's mention of the mollies' "Juvenile Desires," and reading mollies as men who failed to emerge from juvenile subordination to other men in the hierarchy of patriarchy (*Gendering of Men*, 108).

34. The *Oxford English Dictionary* lists this excerpt from "Terrae-filius" as the first use of *molly*; how-ever, there are earlier examples. Thomas D'Urfey used the term in *The Old Mode and the New, or, Country Miss with her Furbeloe* (London, 1703); it appears in the epilogue, as an actress looks around the theatre and talks to and about all the men there:

> Don't swear, nor say, a Pox, for he'll inform;
> He hates all Oaths, and such rude blustring Folly;
> But cants and lies like any side-box Molly.

In this instance, "molly" appears to refer more to a fop or a beau than a sodomite; it is a typical description of fops at the playhouse, who care only about their outfits and the impression they make, rather than about the play. Thomas Brown uses molly in "A Satyr Upon the French King," (London, 1697). The poem begins:

> And hast thou left Old Jemmy in the Lurch?
> A plague confound the Doctors of thy Church.
> Then to abandon poor *Italian Molly*,
> That I had the firking of thy Bum with Holly.

The sexual connotation is here suggested by the addition of "Italian," since Italy was so often mentioned as the origin of sodomy; Brown also adds the image of flagellation ("firking") with holly for the man (a nonconformist parson) he is excoriating in the poem. These earlier brief references suggest that *molly* was originally a broad (though rarely used) term that could refer to a foppish man but that could also have sexual overtones. Ward seems to have been the first to use the term consistently in print, and to ascribe to it the limited meaning of sodomites who wore women's clothes.

35. The page number is marked as 32, but the pamphlet is mispaginated: the actual page number should be 40.

36. The pillory was a dangerous place for sodomites. As Bray notes in *Homosexuality in Renaissance England*, even though the police were supposed to restrain the crowd, some people were killed in the pillory.

37. Note that John Dunton in "The He-Strumpets" says all male prostitutes address potential tricks in the street as "Sukey."

38. The names are fascinating: "Elinor Roden, Orange Mary, an Orange Merchant near London-Bridge, China Mary, Flying Horse Moll, Small Coal Mary, Old Fish Hannah, and Young Fish Hannah, Johannah the Ox-Cheek Woman, Kate Hutton an Old Man that never wears a Shirt, Tub Nan, Primrose Mary, Thumbs and Waste Jenny, Sukey Pisquill, Queen Irons, alias Pippin Mary, Garter Mary, Hardware Nan, Hanover Kate, Spouse to Pippin Mary, Pretty Criss, a Soldier of the 2d Regiment, Miss Kitten (Oviat), Aunt England, a noted Soap Boyler, Rose Gudger, Pomegranate Molly, Black Moll, &c." (Ward, *History of London Clubs*, 39-40).

PROTO-BUTCH OR TEMPORALLY-CHALLENGED TRANS? CONSIDERING FEMALE MASCULINITIES IN EIGHTEENTH CENTURY BRITAIN

Katharine Kittredge

I F I WERE TO WEAR MY brother's clothing, what would you see? Will it make me winsome or unsettling? If you pass me on the streets do you think I am a man, a butch lesbian, a transgender individual, or merely a fashionista exhibiting the latest menswear fad? As you walk away from our encounter, will you find yourself questioning what you thought you knew of gender, or will you continue on, secure in your certainty that all is set and safe?

The answers to these questions will vary not only with who the "I" may be physically and behaviorally (am I large or small?, do I mince or swagger?) and with the nature of the clothing which I borrow (his dress coat or his biking shorts), but also with who *you* are and what your personal perceptions of gender codes might be. The interpretation will also vary according to the setting in which the cross-dressing occurs—a drag show or a corporate meeting—and the activities in which we engage. Deciding what a person's gender deviation means either to that individual, or to the state of gender in the society as a whole, is never an easy task. The situation becomes even more complicated when the cross-dressing individual and her audience are separated by a span of centuries. When we, as modern viewers, view an image of a female person from the eighteenth century who is wearing pants as she gathers oysters, or another woman donning stockings, breeches, and a waistcoat to strut across a stage, the difficulty of determining the contemporary interpretation of her gender performance should be daunting. One of the shortcomings of modern academic writing about incidents of female cross dressing in past centuries has been a tendency to disregard the wildly variable meanings that may be conveyed by donning gender-transgressive clothing in favor of constructing an interpretation which is consistent with the critic's own theoretical orientation. As Fraser Easton points out,

> Studies of early modern cross-dressing, borrowing heavily from literary and theatrical contexts, as well as from anthropological theory, have commonly interpreted the phenomenon of passing women in terms of a carnivalesque disguise of sex—that is, as a socially significant (and occasionally disruptive) mode of symbolic sexual inversion.[1]

More specifically, scholars studying female people who dress, act, or pass as men in the eighteenth century have taken two routes, interpreting them either as (1) women whose overt masculinity represents their same-sex desire, or (2) women whose cross-dressing is a challenge to the binary gender roles which are becoming more rigid during this period.

The reading of masculine female-bodied individuals from the past as lesbians has been an important element in the critical and historical work that has been done toward recovering a lesbian heritage. Martha Vicinus stated definitively in her 2004 book, *Intimate Friends: Women Who Loved Women 1778-1928*: "Well before the late eighteenth century, it was widely accepted that some women were born more masculine in appearance and aptitude. Same-sex sexual desire was associated with gender inversion."[2] Other historians and literary critics followed her lead. In her *A Lesbian History of Britain*, Rebecca Jennings asserts "Masculinity and the appropriation of a masculine image and persona offered women from the sixteenth to the twentieth century a means of expressing and acting upon same-sex desires."[3] Most recently, however, there has been movement away from such sweeping statements towards a more nuanced reading of the relationship between sex and gender. In a 2010 essay, Sally O'Driscoll describes how, in the early eighteenth century, "transgressive female eroticism turns out *not* to be found where we expect it, tied to female masculinity: the early modern system of identity does not link gender presentation with same-sex sexuality."[4] However, O'Driscoll believes that by the mid-eighteenth century, "transgressive sexuality is signaled by transgressive gender presentation . . . this connection between gender and sexuality is one of the hallmarks of the new configuration of sex, gender and sexuality that was set in place in the eighteenth century."[5] This description of the eighteenth century as a time of transition for the interpretation of gender as an indicator of sexuality makes the close examination of those who deviated from the emerging gender norms during this time both more important and more difficult. Our awareness of the wide variations in the readings of transgender identities and performances within this time period should prevent us from making the kind of sweeping statements about female masculinity that have been prevalent in previous critical and historical works.

The perception of the eighteenth century as the time of emerging modern gender norms has led a number of scholars to examine female masculinity through the lens of gender theory. Many twenty-first century critics have started (as Christine Cloud does in her consideration of Charlotte Charke) with the contention that transvestite characters are important because they represent "a space of possibility, a type of 'third space' that resists binary thinking. The tendency to minimize the breach of transvestite power has been detrimental to the understanding of the destabilizing agency of [the] cross-dressed."[6] Such readings, while valuable, choose to focus on transgender acts which aim at a flawless reproduction of the "opposite" gender—creating an alternative gender persona which allows one to "pass" as a person of the opposite biological sex. Such an approach disregards other forms of gender transgression which are more theatrical and less thus less disruptive: drag and impersonation. In her landmark work, *Gender Trouble*, Judith Butler suggests that "drag fully subverts the distinction between inner and outer psychic space and effectively mocks both the expressive model of gender and the notion of a true gender identity."[7] Yet, as Marjorie Garber points out in reference to "power elite" theatrical performances of Harvard's Hasty Pudding Club: "To cross-dress on the stage in an all-male context . . . is a way of asserting the common privilege of maleness."[8] Transgender activist Leslie Feinberg elaborates on this:

> There is a difference between the drag population and masculine men doing cruel female impersonations . . . the burlesque comedy of cross-dressed men is as *anti-drag* as it is *anti-woman*. In fact, it's really only drag performance when it's transgender people who are facing the footlights.[9]

With regard to the act of putting on the clothing (and grooming and mannerisms) of the opposite gender, one person's cultural assimilation is identical to another person's act of rebellion. Because all acts do not have the same impact (on their subject), the refusal to recognize the differences between various acts of gender transgression is a refusal to acknowledge what Kate Bornstein has called "the full rainbow that is gender outlawism."[10]

In reopening the consideration of some of the most visible masculine female-bodied figures of the past, I hope to avoid some of the totalizing tendencies of past scholars. Ultimately, rather than try to make any definitive statement about the "trans____" nature of these cross-dressing women from the past, I hope to create a wide-ranging theoretical context for them which will allow compassionate representation, if not academic coherence. I will begin by considering the way that class identity and gender identity interact in a variety of eighteenth century masculine female performances: butch, drag, and passing. I will then look at the way that scholars from various time periods have "read" the female masculinity of Sarah Ponsonby and Eleanor Butler, the "Ladies of Llangollen," with a particular eye to identifying the ways in which the cultural contexts and academic/political agendas of these authors may have influenced their readings of their subjects. Finally, I will offer a trans-inflected queer reading of the various gendered identities presented by the notorious Charlotte Charke as a way of demonstrating the insight that can be gained from trans-historical reading. I use as my starting point Judith Halberstam's 1998 book *Female Masculinity.* In this text, Halberstam seeks to develop "the perversely presentist model of historical analysis" in which one "can apply insight from the present to the conundrums of the past."[11] This flies in the face of the more traditional critical stance of Dekker and Van der Pol, who wrote in their important work, *The Tradition of Female Transvestism in Early Modern Europe,* that

> Much energy has been expended on problems of terminology—and not without reason if we are to avoid the danger of using modern sexological terminology in an anachronistic way. This especially holds for words like "homosexuality," "lesbianism," and "transsexuality," which not only have no early synonyms, but include meanings and connotations which simply did not exist at the time.[12]

But, as Jason Cromwell remarked in his essay "Passing Women and Female-bodied Men: (Re)claiming FTM History": "to refuse to name something may effectively render it invisible, but it does not make it impossible."[13] Furthermore, as Halberstam herself says, the refusal to acknowledge distinctions between different forms of female gender deviance (even though this means using terms and concepts which were certainly not contemporaneously available)

> denies them [gender deviant individuals] their historical specificity and covers over the multiple differences between earlier forms of same-sex desire . . . [this] also funnels female masculinity neatly into models of sexual deviance rather than accounting for the meanings of early female masculinity within the history of gender definitions and gender relations.[14]

The acknowledgement of a wide range of female masculinities creates another cluster of problems. Much was written in the late nineties about the "Border Wars" between the FTM (female to male transgender/transsexual) community and the gay and lesbian communities over how one was to define all terms of gender performance and identity—who could be considered "female" and how their gender performance was to be represented. This was especially true when it came to deciding how deceased individuals from other eras should be written into queer history. For example, the passing woman/butch lesbian jazz musician Billy Tipton and author Radclyffe "John" Hall have been cited as forerunners and icons in *both* lesbian and transgender histories.

Furthermore, any attempt fully to comprehend these terms is itself fraught. In 1998, Judith Halberstam and C. Jacob Hale published the manifesto "Butch/FTM Border Wars" in *GLQ: A Journal of Lesbian and Gay Studies* in which they derided "the highly questionable cultural projects . . . of stabilizing the terms *transsexual, transgender,* and *butch.* We believe that there is more play between and among these labels than some transsexual and gay/lesbian activists would have us believe."[15] As Bornstein has also remarked,

> All the categories of transgender find a common ground in that they break one or more of the rules of gender: what we have in common is that we are gender outlaws, every one of us. To attempt to divide us into rigid categories is like trying to apply laws of solids to the state of fluids: it's our fluidity that keeps us in touch with each other.[16]

One positive result of the FTM/Butch Border Wars has been a wider understanding of gender difference, which has led to a spirit of inclusion which David Valentine believes has enabled "transgender-identified and gay and lesbian activists simultaneously to come to an agreement and recognition of shared histories while insisting on their differences."[17] Or, as Halberstam states: "There are a variety of gender-deviant bodies under the sign of non-normative masculinities and femininities, and the task at hand is not to decide which represents the place of most resistance but to begin the work of documenting their distinctive features."[18]

The need to reconsider female-bodied masculine women from the past—and the pitfalls of the project—are clear. For too long gender-deviant individuals have been considered only for the ways in which they impact normative gender roles or for their significance as likely homosexual forebears; this has been detrimental to developing a narrative of transgender history, which leaves contemporary transgender communities without a sense of heritage or continuity. We may agree with David Valentine that the current lack of a coherent "transhistory" is a sign of the marginalization of transgender people within modern society:

> The more general absence of female-bodied people in the anthropological record is the legacy of the historical dominance of men in the field as well as broader gendered patterns of inequality which make it harder for female-bodied people to engage in gender/sexual non-normative practices.[19]

Or, we may sympathize with Judith Halberstam's 2005 reflection on the difficulties inherent in the

> somewhat paradoxical, but necessary project of transgender history: paradoxical because it represents the desire to narrate lives that may willfully defy narrative, but necessary because without such histories, we are left with only a bare trace of a life lived in defiance of gender norms.[20]

Ultimately, the creation of a multi-faceted gender history which is informed by, but separate from, both lesbian history and gender theory should enable us to reach a clearer understanding of the behaviors of the past, and also to contribute to the ongoing project of creating a history for modern individuals who are outside of contemporary gender norms.

Towards this goal, I will be identifying three distinct aspects of the performance of female masculinity in the eighteenth century: (1) the cross-dressing female actors who resemble our modern "drag kings", (2) female-bodied individuals who exhibited "butch" behaviors and attributes, and (3) the transgender women who passed as men. To understand all of these examples of gender transgression, we must place the primary emphasis on the people who are performing gender so that we are looking at both their intentions and the effects of the performance. David Harrison makes the following distinction: "The lesbian/gay communities are based on who one relates to, whereas the transgendered experience is different; it's about identity—relating to oneself."[21] Unlike gender theory, trans-informed queer theory asks us to consider the effect which the performance has on the performer him/herself; the gender presenter must be ceded the ultimate authority in determining his/her own status. In the end, all individuals must be allowed to say for themselves how their external appearance reflects their internal identity. This belief complicates our consideration of apparently transgender individuals from the past, since very few individuals from the eighteenth century obliged us with clear statements about how they "identified." Thus, when considering these individuals, one must combine close reading with a careful consideration of context, and take into account the role that one's own beliefs may play in interpreting the unspoken messages of the past. Towards this end, I will be considering the messages conveyed by each of these forms of gender transgression during the eighteenth century (drag, butch, passing) before moving on to a more tightly focused consideration of contemporary examples of female masculinity.

Theatrical Drag

Theatrical cross-dressing has perhaps received more than its fair share of scholarly attention. Pat Rogers, Kristina Straub, Lynne Friedli, and Marjorie Garber have all written at some length about the eighteenth century vogue for putting women in male dress on the stage. Thomas A. King, in an essay "Performing 'Akimbo': Queer Pride and Epistemological Prejudice" (Meyer 23-50) makes a sophisticated connection between the encoding and reading of homosexual masculinity through the theatrical and aristocratic sartorial/behavioral customs of the eighteenth century. [22] Trans theory allows us to see the similarities between early modern female theatrical transvestism and the modern "drag king shows" which emerged in the 1980s and achieved their height of popularity in the mid-to-late 1990s.[23] Specifically, we can see a resemblance in the way in which an underlying awareness of biological identity informs the audience's response to performed gender.

Both the eighteenth century cross-dressing actresses and modern drag kings operate outside the more traditional areas of dramatic performance; that is, they depend less on the development of actual distinct character personalities than on the audience's familiarity with certain stylized character types. As we know, the essence of drag performances is the esthetic of camp which, according to Kim Michasiw, "depends on a relatively stable ironic context."[24] Both female actresses' performance of "breeches parts" and modern drag performances focus attention on the dual nature of the image presented—the heightened tensions created by the gender/sex disparity. As Oscar Montero remarked about a Drag Queen show:

> The imperfection of her [the drag queen's] imitation is what makes her appealing, what makes her eminently readable. Foolproof imitations of women by men, or men by women, are curious, but not interesting. There has to be some telltale, not the gross . . . something readable . . . a subtle gesture or a peculiar grain of the voice.[25]

Eighteenth-century scholar Pat Rogers presents a very similar view of the act of female cross-dressing in Restoration theater:

> There was no attempt to portray anything other than a notional or stylized masculinity . . . It was central to the effect that the actress's femininity showed through. Its raison d'etre lay in the imperfect masculinity of the performer.[26] (256).

Similarly, Randolph Trumbach has stated that the aim of cross-dressing female actors was purely to be "sexually appealing to men,"[27] or as Dekker and van der Pol have stated, "male disguise by women was used to create piquant situations."[28] In addition to the titillation which may have arisen from seeing two women in a romantic encounter on stage, there was the sartorial fact that male dress allowed the display of the female form in ways that were not appropriate or possible in female dress. As Rogers remarks, ". . . the display of leg enhances the sexual display of womanhood, even as it pretends to mimic manhood."[29]

Although they may play to different audiences—eighteenth century straight men versus twentieth century queer women—both forms of performance ultimately create a transgender effect which blurs gendered response. An eighteenth-century theater goer is quoted by Kristina Straub as saying: "it was a nice point to decide between the gentlemen and the ladies, whether she [Peg Woffington] was the finest woman or the prettiest fellow."[30] Unlike the many satirical images from the time that mocked effeminate men or masculine women by making them appear grotesque or pathetic, theatrical cross-dressing provided an image of gender transgression that was aesthetically and sexually appealing. It is likely that these very public, socially sanctioned forms of female masculinity may have encouraged actual cross-gendered performances by those women who felt themselves to be masculine by nature. Dekker and Van der Pol speculate that early modern theatrical cross dressing was a kind of "gateway" behavior introducing a number of actresses to the pleasures of life in breeches, which they extended into various degrees of lived masculinity offstage.

Butch Behaviors

Today, "Butch" is a loaded word freighted with very specific historical mid-twentieth century connotations: the 2007 *Routledge International Encyclopedia of Queer Culture* defines "butch" only in the context of "butch/femme": "Lesbian identities based on highly masculinized and feminized gender. The term is widely associated with British and American bar culture in the 1950's."[31] However, "butch" remains the only available term for describing (in Gayle Rubin's words) "women who are more comfortable with masculine gender codes, styles, or identities than with feminine ones. The term encompasses individuals with a broad range of investments in 'masculinity.'"[32] More specifically, I use the term "butch" to describe women who feel that both their biological femaleness and their masculine gender are intrinsically part of their identity.

Gayle Rubin notes that "[n]ational, racial and ethnic groups differ widely in their definition of what constitutes masculinity, and each has its own system for communicating and conferring 'manhood.'"[33] Each century also defines masculinity and femininity in its own way. In eighteenth century Britain, femininity was an expensive commodity. In order to be recognizably female one had to have the money to purchase women's dress and its accompanying accoutrements and the leisure to perform the feminine roles of ornament or nurturing care-giver. At this time, class was the most important determining factor in dictating appropriate feminine gender performance.

As a result of the association of femininity with the attributes of the leisure classes, the eighteenth century was "an environment in which the enforcement of domestic femininity for plebian women was still weak."[34] An eighteenth-century working class woman did not have the luxury of being feminine; her energy and her money had to go into more important endeavors like reproduction, sustenance, and survival. Furthermore, working-class women played different roles within society than their aristocratic sisters, and frequently they could only succeed in these roles if they cultivated characteristics which were coming to be explicitly identified as masculine: courage, physical strength, stoicism, and stamina.

Eighteenth-century Britain was home to a host of highly visible working-class women who participated in "unwomanly" activities like hunting, fishing, rowing, boxing, and dueling with both swords and cudgels.[35] Professions open to women varied from region to region, but even into the late eighteenth-century there were women plowing fields, building walls, and shoeing horses. As historian Dorothy George has observed, "When we reach the level of the 'labouring poor' it can almost be said that there is no work too heavy or disagreeable to be done by women, provided it is also ill-paid."[36] The prevalence of the narratives of female soldiers who excelled in combat while disguised as men (discussed in the next section as "transgendered") may also have given rise to expectations that women's competence in these "heavy" tasks indicated that they also had the capacity to take up arms in self-defense. It is recorded that Henry Addington, First Viscount of Sidmouth, received the following petition from the women of Neath in 1803, who requested permission:

> To defend ourselves as well as the weaker women and children amongst us. There are in this town 200 women who have been used to hard labour all the days of their lifes such as working in coal-pits, on the high roads, tilling the ground, etc. If you would grant us arms, that is light pikes . . . we do assure you that we could in a short time learn our exercise.[37]

Rather than being criticized for their masculine behaviors, rural and working class women who took on physically demanding tasks were praised for not "putting on airs" by emulating the feminine dress or behaviors of their "betters." Eighteenth-century working class women were respected for their butch characteristics, even by their more appropriately gendered aristocratic female counterparts. Lady Caroline Hamilton, writing about her kinswoman Sarah Ponsonby, notes the usefulness of the masculine female servant whom they hired

> As soon as they [Eleanor Butler and Sarah Ponsonby] were settled in Llangollen they wrote to Ross for Mary Caryll, who was dismissed from Woodstock for throwing a candlestick at a fellow-servant, wounding him severely. At Ross she was known as Molly the Bruiser. Her masculine qualities afforded them protection till they were well known and established in a village not remarkable for sobriety. [38]

In contrast, among the upper classes, visibly masculine behavior was seen as deviant and less than admirable. Aristocratic women who incorporated any "masculine" articles of clothing—riding jackets, hats, cravats, or hairstyles—were criticized for their "hermaphrodite dress." In Maria Edgeworth's novel, *Belinda*, an unfortunate young woman has her reputation irreparably damaged when she is

> persuaded by Mrs. Freke [a notorious cross-dressing woman] to lay aside her half boots, and to equip herself in men's whole boots; and thus she rode about the country, to the amazement of all the world. These are trifles; but women who love to set the world at defiance in trifles seldom respect its opinion in matters of consequence.[39]

The same is true of women who exhibited intellectual tendencies which were viewed as masculine—the upper class women who used their positions as society hostesses to break the rules governing appropriately feminine conversation and comportment. It is not a coincidence that the "Bluestockings" took their name from an article of masculine dress. Although the Bluestockings were careful to maintain most of the characteristics of aristocratic femininity—being courteous, proper, attentive to social form—these women also exhibited characteristics which were decidedly masculine. Writing in 1776, Nathaniel Wraxall said of Elizabeth Robinson Montagu, the "Queen of the Bluestockings,"

> All the lines of her countenance bespoke intelligence, and her eyes were accommodated to the cast of features, which had in them something satirical and severe . . . [her] manner was more dictatorial and sententious, than conciliating or diffident. There was nothing feminine about her.[40]

Upper class women who crossed the gender line were the subjects of much scrutiny, but were nonetheless tolerated and acknowledged if they exhibited superior abilities. Conversely, women who exhibited masculine characteristics without exceptional abilities were depicted as grotesque. Sister Western, a minor character in Fielding's *The History of Tom Jones*, is as butch as they come:

> [H]er masculine person, which was near six feet high, added to her manner and learning, possibly prevented the other sex from regarding her, notwithstanding her petticoats, in the light of a woman. However, as she had considered the matter scientifically, she perfectly well knew, though she had never practiced them, all the arts which fine ladies use when they desire to signal encouragement . . .[41]

Sister Western is ultimately a failure in terms of both genders: her masculine academic and political "learning" are exposed as fraudulent, and her feminine "scientific" knowledge of the ways of the world is insufficient to allow her to control or protect her niece. Contemporary personal writing, journalism, and fiction indicate that while butch behavior was visible, if not prevalent, among aristocratic women, it was rarely considered as positive a trait as it was among working class women.

Transgendered Women

The eighteenth century's many popular tales of women who passed as men—presented in pamphlets, ballads, plays and lectures—were often highly laudatory. This may have been largely due to the fact that virtually all of these women were middle or lower class, but the positive tone of these accounts seems to indicate a tolerance for what we have now come to recognize as "transgendered" behavior. The lives of eighteenth-century women who passed as men in order to serve in a military capacity have been extensively documented and discussed by Dekker and Van de Pol, Julie Wheelwright, Carolyn Williams, Fraser Easton, and Diane Dugaw. Although their success in passing as men is the primary way in which these military women violated conventional gender norms, their subsequent public visibility through memoirs, speaking tours, and exhibitions in which their successful performance of masculinity was displayed to audiences who knew of their biological female identity makes their ultimate gender performance even more complicated. In *Warrior Women and Popular Balladry*, Dugaw speaks of how the "Female Warrior is a model of virtues both 'manly' and womanly. She is an hermaphroditic ideal. . . Looking like a man, acting like a man, being celebrated as a man, she is the perfect woman."[42] Unfortunately, the extent to which these passing women thought of themselves as male, or wished to become biologically male can never be known. We know that many of them excelled while in their male roles, did not voluntarily resume female dress, and that many of them seemed eager to display their masculine image in public, but we do not have any record of their resuming male dress or personas after their "ruse" was revealed.

The persistence of the desire to pass as male beyond military service would have allowed us to clearly identify these women as "transgender." Unlike the butch individual who identifies as female in spite of her masculine gender performance, the masculine female-bodied transgender person feels his/her masculine gender performance is her/his "true" identity. For such women, having male status in public (employers, colleagues, neighbors) and female status in private (lovers, family) may feel like the most honest way to present themselves. As Jason Cromwell writes in *Transmen and FTMs*:

> Within transsexual discourses, passing means blending in and becoming unnoticeable and unremarkable as either man or a woman . . . that one has succeeded and become a "real" man or woman. In transsexual discourse, a person lies to become real; in mainstream discourse, realness is a lie.[43]

Trans theorist Jay Prosser presents this as specifically opposing traditional queer theory's focus on "performance": "there are transsexuals who seek very pointedly to be non-performative, to be constantive, quite simply to be."[44] This desire to "simply be" the opposite sex is reflected in the testimony of Maria van Antwerpen, an eighteenth-century "passing" woman who wrote that she was "by nature and character a man, but in appearance, a woman . . . It often made me wrathful that

Mother Nature treated me with so little compassion against my inclinations and the passions of my heart."[45] This conviction that one might be biologically female, but more suited by "nature and character" to male pursuits was recorded across many countries and every class.

In his 2003 essay, "Gender's Two Bodies: Women Warriors, Female Husbands and Plebeian Life," Fraser Easton notes that the presence of working-class cross dressing women has been largely neglected by modern historians even though during this period: "Women routinely worked in a range of plebeian and lower middle-rank occupations in male disguise. . . [their professions included] labourers, butchers, cooks, porters, shipwrights, plasterers, ploughmen, stone-cutters, bricklayers, coachmen, pedlars, servants, and East India Company recruits."[46] Easton states that during this time popular opinion maintains that "cross-dressing is a viable and even appropriate way for a poor woman to overcome the obstacles to female employment," and he further notes that "family, friends and even fellow workers sometimes supported a woman's decision to work as a man."[47] This positive response to working class "passing" women is not surprising in light of the extent to which working-class female masculinity—both in terms of professions and in personal attributes—was valued during this time. It seems a small step to go from being a butch woman exhibiting masculine traits and performing masculine tasks to being a female-bodied person assuming a masculine identity. However, although the gender-permeability of working class roles is not to be denied, there is more at stake with gender-identity than dress or occupation. As Easton is at pains to assert, for laboring-class women assuming a male persona is "a personal and ideological choice, *not* just an economical one": "cross-dressing represented both a socially tolerated way to get by (as a reputable and industrious subordinate) *and* a way to escape some aspect of paternalistic control of female power."[48] As Easton summarizes:

> . . . passing-women workers used male garb to alter directly their socio-sexual status, giving themselves, in male disguise, immediate access to better work and pay, to alternative living arrangements . . .and to transgressive sexual relationships.[49]

Unfortunately, once again, we have very few personal accounts of the thinking or intentions of these cross-dressing women, so we have no way of knowing how big a role freedom, economic security, gender identity or same-sex desire played in their decision to pass as men.

Both Lynne Friedli and Kristina Straub have noted that it was the usurpation of male "social and sexual privileges" which lay at the heart of the prosecution of the "Female Husband" Mary Hamilton.[50] It may be that the lack of criminal cases brought against working-class women reflects the fact that working as a bricklayer or a ploughman is not considered an expression of "social privilege" by the dominant (aristocratic) eighteenth century culture. In contrast, upper-class women who chose to live masculine lives did so under the threat of community disapproval, legal action, and personal hardship. There can be little doubt that there have always been transgendered individuals, but the transgender historical record has been skewed by the working class's acceptance of such individuals (since they were unremarkable there were few accounts of their lives recorded) and the aristocratic class's intolerance for such individuals—which would have discouraged aristocratic transgendered individuals from expressing their "true" identity in any visible way. The paucity of publically prominent examples of female masculinity in the eighteenth century has caused the two most famous cases—Ladies of Llangollen and Charlotte Charke—to be both highly visible in their own time, and extensively studied in ours. Their cases are interesting both for the contributions that they make to the history of transgendered individuals and for the ways that they have been appropriated and re-interpreted by subsequent generations with varying degrees of toleration for a "multiplicity of female masculinities."

Ladies of Llangollen

Eleanor Butler and Sarah Ponsonby, the Irish "Ladies of Llangollen," differ from other proto-lesbian couples of the eighteenth century primarily in their unusually high profile; if, like other early modern lesbians, they can be said to have been "hidden from history," it must be recognized that they "hid" in plain sight. World-Cat lists over eighty books, including multiple editions and translations, devoted to Ponsonby and Butler with publication dates ranging from 1847 to 2007. As a result of this intense scrutiny, the writing about the "Ladies" offers an interesting case study in the varying interpretations of female masculinity across the centuries. The diversity of images that are presented—and the extent to which they contradict each other—also reveals the benefit that can be derived from a trans-informed reading which takes into consideration the intention as well as the reception of any given gender performance.

The way that the Ladies of Llangollen were depicted by scholars across three centuries is of particular interest in light of O'Driscoll's assertion that the interpretation of female cross-dressing as a sign of lesbianism became more prevalent as the eighteenth century progressed. Butler and Ponsonby spent their youths in Ireland in the middle of the century, dressing and acting in conventionally feminine ways. In 1778, the two took up residence in Wales and began their lives together. At that time, they adopted the dress that would make them so distinctive in later years—they wore plain men's hats and sturdy "riding habits" as their daily dress. Such habits were an accepted part of aristocratic ladies' wardrobes—although not usually adopted for everyday wear—but they still carried some taint of "hermaphroditic dress." These costumes, initially seen as merely "eccentric," were increasingly identified as both a sign of gender deviance and as an indicator of lesbian desire as the eighteenth century progressed. In private, the perception of the ladies (particularly Butler) as performing masculinity was often expressed in a loving way, as when their friend Harriet Bowdler "teasingly referred to Butler, the older and more outspoken, as 'my *Veillard*' (my old man) and 'him.' Bowdler so admired their relationship that she sighed, 'I wish I knew where to get another husband.'"[51] Similarly, an article published in July of 1790 in *The General Evening Post*, a local Welsh paper, described Butler as: "tall and masculine, she wears always a riding habit, hangs her hat with the air of a sportsman in the hall, and appears in all respects a young man, if we except the petticoats which she still retains."[52] Historian Rebecca Jennings reports that Butler and Ponsonby were "concerned by the implications of the article and wrote to the Tory politician Edmund Burke to request advice on how to prosecute the paper."[53] Jennings does not specify whether "the implications" made were of cross-dressing or lesbianism; perhaps by 1790 the two had already become implicitly intertwined. Chronologically, the next account we have of them is by Madame de Genlis, whose description of her visit to Llangollen was published in her 1804 volume, *Souvenirs de Felicie L——*:

> I perceived in them none of that vanity which takes delight in the surprize of others . . . I was likewise much struck with the little resemblance there is between them. Lady Eleanor has a charming face, embellished with the glow of health; her whole appearance and manner announce vivacity and the most unaffected gaiety. Miss Ponsonby has a fine countenance, but pale and melancholy. (44-45)[54]

Genlis speaks of their fluency in French, their interior decoration, musical accomplishments and extensive library, but never indicates that they appeared unfeminine or inappropriately garbed. Her depiction of Butler as healthy, vivacious, and "unaffected" communicates Genlis's approval of her appearance; and seems to stress that the way that Butler dressed indicated a lack of artifice rather than serving to construct an "unnatural" masculine identity.

Genlis's comments are in marked contrast to the clearly derogatory account written in 1822 by their guest Charles Mathews who describes their "manified dress."[55] Mathews' account reflects how completely early nineteenth-century society had come to equate same-sex female couples with masculinity:

> As they are seated, there is not one point to distinguish them from men: the dressing and powdering of the hair; their well-starched neckcloths; the upper part of their habits, which they always wear, even at a dinner-party, made precisely like men's coats; and regular black beaver men's hats. They looked exactly like two respectable superannuated old clergymen; one the picture of Boruwlaski. (23)

It is true that he calls them "respectable" and elsewhere refers to them as "dear old gentlemen,"[56] but overall the tone is mocking, and the comparison to the dwarf Joseph Boruwlaski is particularly unkind. From this distance it is hard to tell if this presentation of the Ladies is due to Mathews' desire to be humorous (and his personal tendency towards cruelty), or to the larger culture's growing discomfort with gender-blurring performances. Mostly likely, it is a bit of both.

The next description that we have of them was written by the novelist Walter Scott, who visited Llangollen in 1825 and wrote the following description in a letter reproduced by his biographer, J. G. Lockhart, in 1837:

> Imagine two women, one apparently seventy, the other sixty-five, dressed in heavy blue riding habits, enormous shoes, and men's hats, with their petticoats so tucked up, that at the first glance of them, fussing and tottering about their porch in the agony of expectation, we took them for a couple of hazy or crazy old sailors. On nearer inspection they both wear a world of brooches, rings, &c., and Lady Eleanor positively *orders*—several stars and crosses, and a red ribbon, exactly like a K.C.B. To crown all, they have crop heads, shaggy, rough, bushy, and as white as snow, the one with age alone, the other assisted by a sprinkling of powder. (27)

Walter Scott's electing to present the Ladies as humorous figures much in the vein of Mathews' account, rather than as objects of pathos or sentimentality, seems to hint at a larger cultural shift away from seeing their appearance (and perhaps their relationship) as socially acceptable.

In 1828, Prince Puckler-Muskau of Prussia visited the ladies and left this description:

Both wore their still abundant hair combed straight back and powdered, a round man's hat, a man's cravat and waistcoat, but in the place of 'inexpressibles,' a short petticoat and boots: the whole covered by a coat of blue cloth, of a cut quite peculiar,—a sort of middle term between a man's coat and a lady's riding-habit. Over this, Lady Eleanor wore, first, the grand cordon of the order of St. Louis across her shoulder; secondly, the same order around her neck; thirdly, the small cross of the same in her button-hole, and 'pour combe de gloire,' a golden lily of nearly the natural size, as a star,—all, as she said, presents of the Bourbon family. So far the whole effect was somewhat ludicrous. (31-32)

Although Puckler-Muskau concludes by saying "the whole effect was somewhat ludicrous," he also seems to attribute their strange appearance to their having "that air of the world of the 'ancien regime,'" (32) which he goes on to praise as being "courteous and entertaining, without the slightest affectation" and "which, in our serious hardworking age of business, appears to be going to utter decay" (32). Puckler-Muskau appears far more aware of fashion than Mathews or Scott, which allows him to give a description of the ladies which is both much more precise and also more aware of the way individual garments convey both gender and class. He not only details exactly which of the Ladies' accessories belong in the "menswear" category, but he also is able to distinguish between the cut of a men's riding habit and a woman's. While Mathews records an impression of their "manified" appearance, Puckler-Muskau can interpret not only the waistcoat but also the "orders" which Butler displays. As a man who is aware of fashion, Puckler-Muskau sees them primarily as "without the slightest affection" (which echoes Genlis' view of them as "without vanity" and "unaffected") in that they persist in wearing antiquated dress after the rest of the world has moved on to other styles. Unlike Mathews or Scott, he does not imply that the Ladies could actually be mistaken for men; to him, they may be fashion-transgressive, but that does not necessarily mean that they are gender-deviant. The fact that the Ladies' two non-British visitors, Puckler-Muskau and Genlis, seem to be less likely to interpret cross-dressing as an indication of masculinity may hint that perhaps Europeans of this period had a more flexible view of the relationship between clothing and gender—or sexual—identity.

As the nineteenth century progressed, and the Victorian era loomed, accounts of the Ladies' appearance shifted again to emphasize their strange appearance, rather than their transgender performance. In 1847, John Hicklin published a slim volume (67 pages) titled THE "LADIES OF LLANGOLLEN," *as sketched by many hands; with notices of OTHER OBJECTS OF INTEREST in "THAT SWEETEST OF VALES."* The volume contains a wide variety of accounts of the Ladies (including most of the accounts quoted above); and is also used as a marketing tool to promote the sale of other "Ladies" merchandise:

> We commend these pen and ink portraits to the notice of our readers without controversy; and the more especially, as they may gratify their curiosity still more in this matter, by purchasing from our Publisher a well-executed engraving representing, with all due fidelity, excellent likenesses of the "Ladies of Llangollen;" each, as *Hamlet* would say, "in her habit as she lived." (54)

Although Hicklin is abundantly aware of the "curiosity" readers may have about the Ladies, and reproduces accounts such as Mathews' and Scott's which clearly identify their female masculinity, Hicklin, himself, eschews gender-related commentary when describing his impression of a portrait of the ladies: "Disguised as they are by the strangeness of their costume, we should not like to hazard any opinion of our own as to their personal charms" (53). This gender-coyness seems to be a chronologically emergent property which will also be evident in the subsequent mid-Victorian accounts of the Ladies. For example, Lady Caroline Hamilton (1771-1861), whose biographical essay describing their lives was affixed to the 1930 volume *The Hamwood Papers of the Ladies of Llangollen and Caroline Hamilton*, ignored the masculine attributes of her kinswoman, Sarah Ponsonby and her "friend" Eleanor Butler in her accounts of the couple. When she describes their response to the newspaper article's references to Butler as "masculine," Hamilton does not reproduce either the gender-slur or the actual article, but tells her readers that the Ladies were wounded in their "pride—feminine sophisticated and intolerant."[57] Hamilton also removes all gender references when she reproduces the descriptions quoted in Hicklin so that Mathews is recorded as calling them "ridiculous" and we are told that Prince Puckler-Muskau "saw their clothes only as 'somewhat ludicrous.'"[58] While Hamilton felt comfortable in her celebration of the "sweet retirement" of these "celebrated virgins"[59] who broke with contemporary norms of affinity and family, she did not want to acknowledge their evident gender deviance.

Similarly, early twentieth century author Mary Gordon says that she wrote *The Llangollen Ladies* (1936) explicitly to "do justice to the main feature of the Ladies' lives, their great and abiding love for one another"[60] and to debunk the "exaggerated or untrue stories" (11) which had circulated about the pair. Gordon interprets the Ladies' dress as an indicator of their aristocratic class and aesthetic innovation rather than as a sign of their deviant gender or sexuality:

> Neither a Butler nor a Ponsonby proposed to make an impression of lowliness or humility in their new sphere. *Noblesse oblige* was to extend to personal appearance, and what they wore was worthy of their status . . . .as Butler and Ponsonby had set the fashions at the Dublin ball [in their youth], so they proposed to set them now on the London to Ireland highroad. (142)

We can place this alongside M.C. Bradbrook's 1949 assertion that the Ladies' sartorial choices reflected the style of dress which was in fashion when they retreated from society:

> Their manners and outlook, formed in the 1770's, when sentiment and the cult of the Gothic ruled, grew outmoded as the years passed, even as their unvarying costume of riding-habits and beaver hats, piquant in youth seemed by 1829 "somewhat ludicrous" even to the sympathetic observer.[61]

Thus, Bradbrook maintains (much as Puckler-Muskau did), that we should see the attention their appearance attracted in their later years as due to their failure to change with the times, rather than as a failure or refusal to dress in an appropriately feminine fashion.

In the late 1970's and 1980's many feminist academics began "the process of restoring the full range of lesbian options" to an historical record from which "entire communities of women were simply erased."[62] In making Butler and Ponsonby visible as practitioners of same-sex desire, many of these authors strove to depict their cross-dressing as part of their larger rebellion against social norms. For example, Doris Grumbach's *The Ladies* (1984), a fictional account of Butler and Ponsonby's lives, shows their being deliberately transgressive in their clothing choices; she imagines the following exchange between Eleanor and the proprietor of the upscale tailoring firm, D.D. Sutton & Son, Ltd.:

> Eleanor said, "We shall require habits and all the accoutrements. Do you provide shirts and stocks, such things?"
>
> "For ladies? No, my lady, but there is a fine ladies' place a square distant from here that—"
>
> "No matter, we prefer those made for men, in suitable sizes, of course," said Eleanor firmly.

"For ladies, yes. Of course," said Mr. Sutton the son, sounding dubious. (68)

Grumbach undercuts her picture of transgression by later having Eleanor reflect that "they had found a comfortable and satisfying costume that they could wear on all occasions, suitable and acceptable, she was sure, to the world at large"(70). The effect is to present Eleanor as naïve rather than revolutionary, making her sartorial choices for financial and pragmatic reasons rather than as expressions of her gender identity.

The project of re-claiming of the ladies as proto-lesbians continued throughout the rest of the twentieth century in works such as Lillian Faderman's *Surpassing the Love of Men* (1981), Emma Donoghue's *Passions Between Women* (1993), and Martha Vicinus's *Intimate Friends* (2004). More recently, Rebecca Jennings' *A Lesbian History of Britain* (2007) posits that accounts of the Ladies' masculine appearance "indicate suspicions regarding the nature of the couple's relationship, rather than providing an accurate account of their appearance." Rather than seeing the couple as deliberately transgressive, Jennings depicts Butler and Ponsonby as an early lesbian couple who "engaged in an ongoing public relations campaign intended to diffuse any potential scandal surrounding them" and thus became known as "the epitome of virtuous romantic friendship."[63] This reading is in line with Jennings' assertion that "Gender inversion and cross-dressing provided one significant medium for the expression and representation of female same-sex desire in the early modern period."[64] Because her work is focused on sexuality, she is looking at non-typical gender expression as a signifier of lesbianism and is not interested in what it may be saying about the subject's sense of a gendered self.

In the 1990's, the drive to re-examine the Ladies grew out of the intersection between queer and trans theory, and their strange garb was once more re-interpreted. The Ladies are featured prominently in Marjorie Garber's *Vested Interests: Cross-Dressing & Cultural Anxiety* (1992). Garber identifies them unequivocally as cross-dressing women and cites them as an example of the way in which "cross-dressing seems often to have been itself an enabling element in contextualizing and realizing gay marriage" (143). Garber further notes:

Clearly, they were protected by their class and their distinguished acquaintance from the obloquy that might have greeted a less socially acceptable *ménage*, and their dress and appearance, while in some sense "male," were also sufficiently "singular" to make them legible as "keeping to the middle," as identifiable cross-dressers rather than women passing for men. (145)

It is interesting that Garber sees the Ladies as "protected" by their class, given what we know about the relatively positive manner in which eighteenth century society viewed working class female masculinity. In fact, the Ladies were only "singular" for their failure to reproduce upper-class femininity; had they been two spinster washerwomen sharing a home and a bed and dressing in comfortable, utilitarian garb, they would doubtless have passed their lives without being noticed by anyone outside of their own neighborhood. However, Garber's assertion that they were creating a "middle" gender for themselves rather than emulating masculinity or attempting to pass as male is an important distinction that comes out of an awareness of transgender issues.

The progression of the portraits of the Ladies of Llangollen reveals much about the interpretation of gender when each tome was penned, but ultimately we are left knowing little more about their intentions when they adopted male dress. While they were still alive, references to their gender-deviant dress tended to be straight-forward and affectionate. As time passed and female masculinity began to be more closely associated with lesbianism, however, observers in the early and mid-nineteenth century commented more explicitly on their resembling men and tended to speak of them derisively. In contrast, authors in the late nineteenth and early twentieth century erased any mention of gender in their descriptions, choosing to depict them as "quaint" or "eccentric" instead. In more recent times, the desire to recover lesbian history has led to a renewed focus on their appearance since their gender deviance has been seen as evidence of their transgressive sexuality. Most recently, trans-influenced queer theorists have discussed the Ladies as less deviant (and interesting) than the women from their generation who "passed" as men. So, depending on each scholar's perspective, the images we receive of the ladies have ranged from admirably masculine to ludicrously frumpy and they have been presented as everything from fashion innovators or fashion anachronisms to daring cultural re-inventors.

Although some of the myriad interpretations swirling around the Ladies may seem more plausible than others, we must be wary of adopting any one as the "true" view of their gender identity. Trans-criticism has taught us that we must not assume that we have a clear understanding of Eleanor Butler and Sarah Ponsonby until we can understand how they viewed themselves. Fortunately, additional insight into the matter is provided by a piece of evidence unavailable to previous researchers. In a 1798 letter which Sarah Ponsonby (usually identified as the more "feminine" of the two) wrote to her fellow Irish-woman Melesina St. George (later Trench), she requested that Melesina visit the London tailors Messrs Allen and Collier:

> They are punctual, reasonable, and give us very fine and good material, but sometimes equip us in habits of somewhat puritanical form. To avoid this evil for the present, our hopes rest in you, for though we doubt whether this masculine garb ever had a place in your wardrobe, having never yet had the happiness of beholding you so attired, we doubt not your having the goodness to obtain for these gentlemen a sight of one which, my better half [Eleanor Butler] voluntarily claims for you, shall be neither of the Bath or Dublin cut—cuts she holds in equal detestation—but such a one as should not disgrace your line.[65]

This letter indicates that although the ladies were aware that riding habits were "masculine," they considered them within the range of acceptable female garb (hence their willingness to suggest a young widow appear in one), and furthermore, they wanted garments which would emphasize rather than conceal their female curves. In terms of our current understanding of female masculinities, we see a number of recognizable patterns: (1) The Ladies had no interest in replicating existing male personae or styles of dress, although they understood that their dress style would be interpreted as masculine; furthermore they made no effort to appear wholly masculine, since they retained skirts. Thus, although they were wearing men's clothes, they cannot be seen as being in drag. (2) The Ladies' desire for masculine garb which enhanced their feminine "line" indicates that in spite of their taste for male clothing they continued to be proud of their female forms. They may have been butch in their appearance, but there is no indication that they saw themselves as temporally challenged FTM transsexuals. (3) The Ladies were actively engaged in creating a gendered performance that would be unique— "neither of the Bath or Dublin cut"—one which they hoped would accurately reflect their identities.

These observations seem to indicate that (however much the Ladies would certainly have blanched at the term) "transgender" may indeed be the only applicable term that can be applied to Butler and Ponsonby, not because it is the single, perfect label for their "hermaphrodite dress" and proto-lesbian behavior, but because it is a term that reminds us how complicated and situation-specific the presentation of gender can be. The clothing which the Ladies of Llongollen chose could only be worn by upper class individuals, and the shapes that they revealed were clearly female, but the clothing choices that they made were those of both male (cloth, gloves, hats) and female ("habits," skirts) individuals engaged in the act of presenting their gender to the world. They took great care in using their dress to communicate with the rest of society: their social status was clear, their biological/sexual identity was evident, but their gender status—how they wanted the world to respond to them—remained ambiguous. We cannot know whether these choices are evidence of a deeper internal strain of gender-deviance indicating that one or both of the ladies thought of themselves as "actually" male or mentally masculine, but we can say that it shows that they were adamant in their desire to signal their rejection of ideological gender norms to the world. The fact that their lives included both a rejection of the heteronormative imperative that they marry men and the choice to present themselves as gender-ambiguous should not be interpreted as cause-and-effect or seen as an indication that lesbianism and cross-dressing were necessarily connected for Anglo-Irish women in the late eighteenth century. All we can say for sure was that Sarah Ponsonby and Eleanor Butler were two individuals who were not bound by contemporary ideologies and who made little or no effort to hide their desires for men's tailoring and female companion-ship from the world at large.

Charlotte Charke

The title page of the 1755 edition of the autobiography of Charlotte Charke reads:

> A Narrative of the Life of Mrs. Charlotte Charke
> (*Youngest* Daughter of Colley Cibber, *Esq;*)
> containing:

I.   An Account of her Birth, Education, and mad Pranks committed in her Youth.

II.   Her coming on the Stage; Success there; and sundry Theatrical Anecdotes.

III.   Her marriage to Mr. *Charke* and its Consequences.

IV.   Her Adventures in Mens Cloaths, going by the name of Mr. *Brown*, and being belov'd by a Lady of great Fortune, who intended to marry her.

V.   Her being Gentleman to a certain Peer.

VI.   Her commencing Strolling-Player with various surprizing Vicissitudes of Fortune, during nine Years in Peregrination,

VII.   Her turning pastry cook *&c* in *Wales*. With several extremely humourous
         and interesting Occurrences.[66]

What does a trans-oriented/queer gender reading have to tell us about Charlotte
Charke as she shifted locations, professions, and genders during her lifetime? The
crux of trans-informed gender inquiry is: (1) How does she identify or, "What Did
S/he Think s/he was doing?" (2) Can we recognize within her *Narrative* any aspects
of the butch/drag/transgender "multiplicities" of female masculinity? and (3) How
does the application of these terms change the way that we see her both within her
own historical context and as part of a larger project to create transhistory?

Charke as a Butch Woman

Charlotte Charke's dissatisfaction with the roles available to a traditionally feminine girl, and her subsequent embracing of masculine or "butch" roles represent
some of her earliest rebellions against social norms. Although she does not adopt
male dress during her teen years, she does take on the (male-identified) roles of
marksman (29), physician (35), gardener (37), and groom (38). Over and over
during her early years she participates in masculine activities with some measure
of success—like the time she "divert[ed] myself with Shooting; and grew so great
a proficient in that notable exercise, that I was like the Person described in *the
Recruiting Officer*, capable of destroying all the Venison and Wild Fowl about
the Country" (29). This activity is forbidden to her after one of the neighboring
women informs her mother that it is "inconsistent with the Character of a young
Gentlewoman to follow such Diversions." Charke records with chagrin that "[u]
pon this sober Lady's Hint, I was deprived of my Gun" (29). Charke consoles
herself over the loss of her gun by devoting herself to the family's horses, despising
"the Young Ladies of the Family" for their inability to curry a horse or "ride in a
race" (32).

   The estrangement Charke felt from her female relatives extended to a rejection of all of their gender-appropriate "housewifely Perfections" which included
cooking, interior decoration, embroidery. Charke does not frame her rejection
of these activities as a commentary on the shallow pursuits of contemporary
gentlewomen, but rather as a result of her own unsuitability for such a role. She
compares her dexterity with a needle to that of a monkey handling a kitten (19)—
indicating that her attempts to perform female activities are acts "against nature."
Although Charke does not depict herself as alienated from her biologically female

body—she never expresses dissatisfaction with the physical changes of puberty or describes any dissatisfaction over her female traits—she believes that she "naturally" possesses a number of masculine gender traits. She is proud of these traits and identifies them as her "true" or "best" self.

In a recent article on Charke, Christine Cloud has noted that Charke uses a "stereotypically feminine voice"—"very humble, very timid . . . whenever she wishes to project the role of the forlorn daughter"[67] or abandoned wife. However, "whenever Charke desires to highlight her adventurous side she speaks as if she were a typical male; it is at these times that she principally calls herself by her male moniker, Mr. Brown."[68] Feminine dress, voice, and behavior required Charke to identify herself via her relationship to men—daughter, wife, mother of a man's child—and consequently to emphasize her role as the victim of male abuse or neglect. When she is wooed by the man who will become her faithless husband, she bewails the fact that she believed him "as foolish young Girls are apt to be too credulous"(50). This is in sharp contrast to the gender-neutral "couragious [sic] Person" she aspired to be within her family. In contrast, when she allowed her masculine characteristics to rise to the fore in her "Mr. Brown" persona she could be autonomous and even powerful. "Charlotte Charke" was a singularly unsuccessful woman who was unable to convincingly perform the socially prescribed roles of daughter, wife, or mother. Thus, it is not surprising that she chose to pass a considerable part of her life in this alternative persona which allowed her to better express the masculine traits that she saw as an intrinsic part of her personality.

Charke as Drag King

We know that Charlotte Charke was a cross-dressing female actor on stage, but are there also elements of drag in her daily wearing of "mens cloaths"? Many modern scholars have made a distinction between her theatrical cross-dressing and her creation of a masculine persona, claiming that when she donned male clothing outside of the theater, she was dedicated to passing as a man, whereas her theatrical cross-dressing was taken on in response to the public's demand for women playing male roles. In contrast, Joseph Chaney believes that Charke's theatrical cross-dressing should be seen as part of her personal gender expression, noting that Charke's "attitude toward impersonation was devout rather than ironic."[69] Chaney's view is supported by Polly Fields' assertion that even in her theatrical cross-dressing, Charke "did not specialize in the types of drama featuring cross-dressing as titillation."[70] More recently, Caroline Gonda noted that Charke's roles included not only "breeches parts" (i.e. female characters who adopt male disguise) such as Silvia in Farquhar's *The Recruiting Officer* (1706) but also numerous male roles ranging from Roderigo in Shakespeare's *Othello* to the murderous apprentice Barnwell in George Lillo's *The London Merchant* (1731) and dashing figures such as Lothario in Nicholas Rowe's *The Fair Penitent* (1703) and MacHeath in Gay's *The Beggar's Opera* (1728).[71]

Clearly, Charke was appearing on stage in roles where her masculine identity was an integral part of the plot of the performance. These characteristics align her with drag performance in that it appears that she is not expressing a "male self," but performing a series of stylized masculine types. Also, unlike Hasty Pudding-style impersonators or actresses setting out to titillate their audiences with the exhibition of a shapely leg, she was not trying to evoke either laughter or illicit desire; reports of the roles that she played indicate that she was trying to create as perfect an illusion of masculinity as her skills (and her purse) would allow. And yet, the goal was not to "pass" as a male actor: when she performed male roles during her time on the London stage, it was always under her own name with her female status highlighted. Thus, although the elements of camp esthetic or ironic spectacle may not have been present in these performances, she still can be understood as performing "drag" because her audience was always aware of her biological status as a female, even while they judged her on her ability to create the illusion of a stylized male character.

Outside of the performance space of the theater, there are other elements of Charke's gender presentation which can be seen as exhibiting drag characteristics. First of all, there is the fact that Charke tended to choose distinctly masculine (as opposed to androgynous) roles when she was passing as a man—Gentleman secretary, farmer, baker, or suitor. As Erin Mackie has noted, "Charke's transgressive male postures, most prevalent in the *Narrative,* reproduce conventional figures of the male rogue."[72] She does not seem to be interested in merely living a quiet male life; for Charke there is always an element of public performance—whether it be in fooling the owner of a tavern, the customers buying pastry or sausage, or the young ladies who wish to marry him/her. In contrast to the numerous descriptions of the many people who mistake Charke for a man, are the collaborators who know her biological sex (Mrs. Brown, Lord A—-A, the "Person who knew me from childhood") and who benefit from, enable, or applaud her adopting a male persona. She may have been engaged in a straight-forward/"devout" effort to pass in her various new communities, but she always had a core, "safe" audience—similar to the audience attending a drag performance—witnessing her performance with an insider's eye for the gender/sex disjunction. Even more importantly, as Theresa Braunschneider points out in her essay "Acting the Lover: Gender and Desire in Narratives of Passing Women,"

> Each of these narratives [of eighteenth century passing women] establishes an epistemological drama in which the narrator and readers "know" that the body in question is female while the characters within the narrative "know" it is really male. . . Such a discrepancy of knowledge between the characters and readers creates a dual status for the passing woman's disguise: for the narrator and readers her clothing, manners, and in some cases prosthetic penis are signs of impersonation; for those characters internal to the narrative, they are signs of manhood.[73]

Thus, even if the performance which the narrative is recording is one in which Charke is able to flawlessly pass as a man to all who encounter her, the illusion cannot be extended to the readers of the narrative, who open the book with the knowledge that they are reading the autobiography of a biologically female person who is merely creating the illusion of being a man. Reading an autobiography of a person who tells us they are cross dressing always positions us as the audience in a drag show rather than as the casual observer on the street. Charke's decision to frame her narrative so that her female biology and masculine gender are always juxtaposed makes her as canny as any drag king who ever swiveled across a 1990's stage to a driving Elvis beat.

Charke as Transgender

Charke's account of her earliest act of cross-dressing describes how she wore her father's clothing at age four and paraded outside of their country home until "borne off on the Footman's Shoulders, to my Shame and Disgrace, and forc'd into my proper Habiliments" (20). It is significant that even in this youthful prank, Charlotte states that her primary goal was to create a "perfect Representative of my sire"(18) and that she is distressed because "'twould be impossible for me to *pass* [emphasis mine] for Mr. Cibber in Girl's Shoes" (19). The adult Charke plays up the comedy of her early attempt by describing "The Drollery of my Figure" and her "Grotesque Pigmy-state," but she also recounts how happy she was at the "Thought of being taken for the 'Squire'" (19). Over and over in this account, presented as an anecdote that will "raise a Laugh" in her reader, there is an undertone of seriousness—we see Charke as having a desire to leave behind her biological identity as a young girl and to re-make herself into a credible masculine figure. It is also important to note that Charke herself links this childish behavior to her later cross-dressing, stating that this "small Specimen of my former madness" shows that she had "even then, a passionate Fondness for a Perriwig" (17).

There is no doubt that Charlotte Charke qualifies as a "passing woman" in that she sustained a male identity as "Charles Brown" which was, according to her account, "real" enough to pass with even those with whom she was in close contact. She proudly recounts how the young woman who falls in love with her male persona is entirely taken in by her masculine performance:

> . . .when I positively assured her that I was actually the youngest Daughter of Mr. Cibber, and not the [male]Person she conceived me! She was absolutely struck speechless for some little Time; but when she regained the Power of Utterance, entreated me not to urge a Falsehood of that Nature. (111)

Charke smugly asserts, "She was, poor Thing! an Instance, in regard to me, *that the Wisest may sometimes err*" (112). It is hard to know whether Charke's pride in her ability to fool others is evidence of a woman asserting the "truth" of her cross-dressed identity, or the pride of a gifted actress who takes her craft beyond the stage.

Like many of the laboring-class women of her time, Charke frequently had strong economic reasons for donning male clothing, but, unlike them, her extreme poverty also made it necessary for her to pass herself off as a person of another class. Sometimes this was done for reasons of safety, as when, having earned a guinea and being afraid that she might be robbed on her way home, she "changed Cloaths with a person of low Degree, whose happy Rags, and the kind covert of Night, secured me from the Dangers I might have otherwise encountered" (105). In this case, cross-class-dressing is a way to overcome the vulnerability that a privileged person—of either sex—would experience if they were out at night without the protections (carriage, servants) that their rank provided.

More often, cross-dressing, combined with her willingness to take jobs below her rank as the daughter of "Colley Cibber, Esq." represents one of the few ways that Charke manages to support herself outside of the role of wife or daughter. One example of this is when "Lord A———a" takes her on as a "Gentleman" or personal secretary, which means that Charke is a servant,[74] or as she optimistically puts it, "the Superior Domestick" in the family, bearing a rank on par with the Lord's concubine or "Fille de Joye" (135). This is followed by a stint as a street vendor of sausages, much to the disgust of "the Arch-Dutchess of our Family" who considers Charke's entering laboring-class professions as a "disgrace" to the "Honour of Their Family" (139). This same person scolds Charke for wearing masculine garb: "My being in Breeches was alledged to me as a very great Error" (139), but it is significant that of the two faults, the class transgression is discussed first, and at greater length than Charke's cross-dressing. Charke continues her masquerade through stints as a Waiter in a Public House—a job she almost doesn't get, since her employer thinks she is too "well born and bred" for such "Service" (157)—a strolling player, and a Pastry Cook. Her lack of practical knowledge in various working class endeavors is often the cause of her failure—as when she embarks on pig farming with the purchase of an animal which she believes is a pregnant sow, but which turns out to be an old barrow (a neutered male pig).

Like the cross-dressing working-class women discussed by Easton, Charke believes that she deserves applause because she is able to make "an honest Livelihood, as I did not prostitute my Person, or use any other indirect Means for Support that might have brought me to contempt and Disgrace" (140). But we are aware that her refusal to play the role of a privileged person is as large a social transgression as her passing herself off as "Mr. Brown." It is significant that the frontispiece of the *Narrative* contains a mixture of accounts of Charke's crossing gender (Mens Cloaths; Mr. Brown; Gentleman) and references to her taking jobs (Gentleman, Strolling-Player, Pastry Cook) which are unsuitable for a woman of her class. Charke frequently claims that she puts on male clothes out of economic necessity, coupled with a mysterious "Secret, which is an Appendix to one I am bound . . . by all the Vows of Truth and Honour everlastingly to conceal" (139). Yet, given the variety of gender transgressions which she commits—the combination of butch, drag, *and* transgender performances that we see throughout the narrative—it seems likely that her repeated embracing of alternative forms of gender expression must be rooted in some degree in a desire to redefine herself outside of traditional feminine roles.

And yet, Charke never explicitly indicates that wearing masculine clothing is a way for her to express her inner masculine or "true" self; instead, she consistently identifies an external motivation for her transgender appearance, as when she claims that "the original Motive [for cross-dressing] proceeded from a particular Cause" (139). At the same time, her interest in male clothing (particularly the procuring and retaining of attractive, well-fitting hats) seems to indicate that a measure of self-representation is actually present. She clearly uses her masculine identity to express herself—as when she says she is "proud to cock my hat in the Face of the Bailiffs" (112). There seems to be a level of investment in the production of a credible male image that goes somewhat beyond a desire to fool her audience and which incorporates elements of self-representation.

At the same time, there is also evidence that in spite of her alienation from much of the female community, she still thinks of her female identity as "my proper Character" (195), and "who I was" (128); elsewhere she describes cross-dressing as the act through which she would "forsake my sex" (206). These statements indicate that although she exhibits a wide range of female masculinities, she does not fully embrace an identity which we could term "transgender" as we understand its twenty-first century implications. She cannot be said to pass the test proposed by Jason Cromwell for identifying "the historical forerunners of contemporary FTMs": "Did the individual make statements that (contrary to their physiology) they are men or have always felt themselves to be men?"[75]

We know that Charlotte Charke's gender presentation ranged through "Young Gentlewoman" dress, drag performances on stage and real life, a masculine, "butch" adolescence, and the adoption of an alternative male persona. The wide range of female masculinities she exhibits makes it virtually impossible to apply a single label to her gender representation and identity. We know beyond a shadow of a doubt that the genders that Charke presented to society were at variance with both her biological sex and her role as a member of the social elite, but her inconsistent shifting from self to self both in her social interactions and in her personal narrative makes it impossible to define her in any more specific category. Although she exhibits characteristics and behaviors which we currently identify as belonging to butch lesbians, drag kings, and pre-operative transsexuals, her early modern sense of her own identity makes it impossible to choose among these labels. Ultimately, Charlotte Charke belongs in transhistory as an example of a woman who experimented with a number of alternative forms of gender expression. As such, Charke must be considered "transgender" because our current understanding of the term explicitly welcomes individuals whose varied gender performances represent a range of "physical and emotional changes that the individual might experience over a lifetime."[76]

Conclusion

As Jamison Green, an FTM transgender educator, has recently said,

> Rather than trying to control gender expression, or to enforce conformity between gender identities and bodies, opening up to acknowledge and accept a variety of gender/body combinations that exist allows

more people to fully experience their gendered and sexual selves. Every person's experience of their own gender is a vital component of their humanity, whether people are gender-variant or gender-congruent, and whether or not they need to change their bodies to become visible—or invisible.[77]

Those of us who work with images from the past have much to learn from the newest generation of trans-queer theorists. Part of our mandate as scholars is that we must try to look beyond the labels and assumptions of previous generations so that we can more fully appreciate the "variety of gender/body combinations" which existed in the past. The wildly variant interpretations bestowed on gender-deviant performers like the Ladies of Llangollen by three centuries of admirers, academics, and gossip-mongers makes it clear that gender is very much in the eye of the beholder, but that it is still possible to reach a deeper understanding of the significance of a transgressive performance by focusing on the identity of the individuals involved rather than their sexuality or transgressive impact.

The application of trans-queer language and its attendant conceptions to the complex gender-transgressions of Charlotte Charke allows us to identify the many ways in which gender could be flexed during the course of the eighteenth century. It also makes us aware of the many motivations that may lie behind these performances and the benefits and risks that may accompany a shifting of gender, class, or rank. Charke's performance of multiple female masculinities may not help us to reach any final conclusions about her status as a "gender outlaw" of the past, but it does remind us that, as much as possible, we must continue to strive to see the gender performances of the past through the eyes of the performers themselves, even if the world-view they reflect may seem wholly alien compared to that of our own century. Just because their dress is different from ours and our language is different from theirs does not mean that we have nothing to learn from them regarding the past, present, and future possibilities of gender. The closer we move to a post-gender society, the more we need to remember that the starting point for the future is always found in the past.

Notes

1. Fraser Easton, "Gender's Two Bodies: Women Warriors, Female Husbands, and Plebeian Life," *Past and Present* 180 (August 2003): 134.

2. Martha Vicinus, *Intimate Friends: Women Who Loved Women 1778-1928* (Chicago: University of Chicago Press, 2004), 3.

3. Rebecca Jennings, *A Lesbian History of Britain: Love and Sex Between Women Since 1500* (Oxford and Westport, CT: Greenwood World Publishing, 2007), xvii.

4. Sally O'Driscoll, "A Crisis of Femininity: Re-Making Gender in Popular Discourse," in *Lesbian Dames: Sapphism in the Long Eighteenth Century*, eds. John C. Beynon and Caroline Gonda (London and Burlington, VT: Ashgate, 2010), 52.

5. Ibid., 46.

6. Christine Cloud, "The Chameleon, Cross-dressed Autobiography of Charlotte Charke," *Women's Studies* 38, no. 8 (2009): 857.

7. Judith Butler, *Gender Trouble: Feminism and the Subversion of Identity* (New York and London: Routledge, 1990), 174.

8. Marjorie B. Garber, *Vested Interests: Cross-Dressing and Cultural Anxiety* (New York and London: Routledge, 1992), 60.

9. Leslie Feinberg, *Transgender Warriors: Making History from Joan of Arc to Dennis Rodman* (Boston: Beacon Press, 1996), 115.

10. Kate Bornstein, *Gender Outlaw* (New York: Routledge, 1994), 68.

11. Judith Halberstam, *Female Masculinity* (Durham, NC: Duke University Press, 1998), 52.

12. Rudolf M. Dekker and Lotte C. Van de Pol, *The Tradition of Female Transvestism in Early Modern Europe* (New York: St. Martin's Press, 1989), 47.

13. Jason Cromwell, "Passing Women and Female-bodied Men: (Re)claiming FTM History" in *Reclaiming Genders: Transsexual Grammars at the Fin de Siecle*, eds. Kate More and Stephen Whittle (New York: Cassell, 1999), 55.

14. Halberstam, *Female Masculinity*, 46.

15. Judith Halberstam and C. Jacob Hale, "Butch/FTM Border Wars: A Note on Collaboration." *GLQ: A Journal of Lesbian and Gay Studies* 4, no. 2 (1998): 283.

16. Bornstein, *Gender Outlaw*, 69.

17. David Valentine, *Imagining Transgender: An Ethnography of a Category* (Durham, NC: Duke University Press, 2007), 174-75.

18. Halberstam, *Female Masculinity*, 148.

19. Valentine, *Imagining Transgender*, 171.

20. Judith Halberstam, *In a Queer Time and Place: Transgender Bodies, Subcultural Lives* (New York: New York University Press, 2005), 49.

21. Quoted in Bornstein, *Gender Outlaw*, 67.

22. Thomas A. King, "Performing 'Akimbo': Queer Pride and Epistemological Prejudice" in *The Politics and Poetics of Camp*, ed. Moe Meyer (New York: Routledge, 1994), 174-75.

23. Richard Ekins and Dave King, eds. *Blending Genders: Social Aspects of Cross-Dressing and Sex-Changing* (New York: Routledge, 1996), 211.

24. Kim Michasiw, "Camp, Masculinity, Masquerade," in *Feminism Meets Queer Theory*, eds. Elizabeth Weed and Naomi Schor (Bloomington, IN: Indiana University Press, 1997), 165.

25. Quoted in Garber, *Vested Interests*, 149.

26. Pat Rogers, "The Breeches Part," in *Sexuality in Eighteenth-Century Britain*, ed. Paul-Gabriel Boucé (Totawa, NJ: Manchester University Press, 1982), 249, 256.

27. Randolph Trumbach, *Sex and the Gender Revolution*, vol. 1, Chicago Series on Sexuality, History and Society (Chicago: University of Chicago Press, 1998), 115.

28. Dekker and Van de Pol, *Tradition of Female Transvestism*, 54.

29. Rogers, "Breeches," 248.

30. Julia Epstein and Kristina Straub, eds. *Body Guards: The Cultural Politics of Gender Ambiguity* (New York: Routledge, 1991), 144-45.

31. *Routledge International Encyclopedia of Queer Culture*, ed. David A. Gerstner (New York: Routledge, 2007), 112.

32. Quoted in Joan Nestlé, *Persistent Desire: A Femme-Butch Reader* (Boston: Alyson Publications, 1992), 466.

33. Ibid., 468.

34. Easton, "Gender's Two Bodies," 140.

35. Dianne Dugaw, *Warrior Women and Popular Balladry, 1650-1850* (New York: Cambridge University Press, 1989), 125.

36. Easton, "Gender's Two Bodies," 139.

37. Julie Wheelwright, *Amazons and Military Maids: Women Who Dressed as Men in the Pursuit of Life, Liberty and Happiness* (Boston and London: Pandora, 1989), 8-9.

38. G.H. Bell, ed. *The Hamwood Papers of the Ladies of Llangollen and Caroline Hamilton* (London: Macmillan and Co., 1930), 42.

39. Maria Edgeworth, *Belinda*, The Literature Network, http://www.online-literature.com/maria-edgeworth/belinda/19/ (accessed April 26, 2008), chap. 19.

40. René Louis Huchon, *Mrs. Montagu and Her Friend, 1720-1800: A Sketch* (London, John Murray, 1907), 266.

41. Henry Fielding, *The History of Tom Jones*, ed. R. P. C. Mutter (New York: Penguin Books, 1989), 255.

42. Dugaw, *Warrior Women*, 157.

43. Jason Cromwell, *Transmen and FTMs: Identities, Bodies, Genders, and Sexualities* (Urbana: University of Illinois Press, 1998), 38-39.

44. Quoted in Judith Halberstam, "Telling Tales: Brandon Teena, Billy Tipton, and Transgender Biography," in *Passing: Identity and Interpretation of Sexuality, Race and Religion*, eds. Maria Carla Sanchez and Linda Schlossberg (New York: New York University Press, 2001), 16.

45. Dekker and Van der Pol, *Tradition of Female Transvestism*, 68.

46. Easton, "Gender's Two Bodies," 136-37.

47. Ibid., 138-39.

48. Ibid., 142.

49. Ibid., 134.

50. Lynne Friedli, "Passing Women: A Study of Gender Boundaries in the Eighteenth Century," in *Sexual Underworlds of the Enlightenment*, eds. G. S. Rousseau and Roy Porter (Chapel Hill: University of North Carolina Press, 1988): 234-60. Kristina Straub, "The Guilty Pleasures of Female Theatrical Cross-Dressing and the Autobiography of Charlotte Charke," in *Introducing Charlotte Charke: Actress, Author, Enigma*, ed. Philip E. Baruth (Urbana: University of Illinois Press, 1999).

51. Vicinus, *Intimate Friends*, 9.

52. Jennings, *Lesbian History*, 46.

53. Ibid.

54. All of the late eighteenth and early nineteenth century accounts which I will be quoting in this paper are taken from Rev. John Pritchard, *An Account of the Ladies of Llangollen* (Llangollen: Printed and Published by H. Jones at the Atmospheric Gas Printing Works, 1884), all page numbers refer to this volume.

55. Garber, *Vested Interests*, 144.

56. Ibid.

57. Bell, *Hamwood Papers*, 256.

58. Ibid., 370.

59. Ibid., 1.

60. Mary Gordon, *Chase of the wild goose; the story of Lady Eleanor Butler and Miss Sarah Ponsonby, known as The Ladies of Llangollen* (Ruthin, North Wales: John Jones, 1936), 13.

61. M. C. Bradbrook, "The Elegant Eccentrics," *Modern Language Review* 44, no. 2 (1949): 185.

62. Blanche Wiesen Cook, "'Women Alone Stir My Imagination': Lesbianism and the Cultural Tradition," *Signs* 4, no. 4 (1979): 720.

63. Jennings, *Lesbian History*, 45-46.

64. Ibid., 21.

65. Melesina Trench, "The Recollections of Melesina Trench with extracts from her Diary and Correspondence," unpublished manuscript, ref. MS 23M93 (Hampshire Record Office: n.d. 19th century), 90.

66. Charlotte Charke, *A Narrative of the Life of Mrs. Charlotte Charke* (Gainsville, FL: Scholars' Facsimiles & Reprints, 1969). All subsequent references refer to this edition.

67. Cloud, "Chameleon," 864.

68. Ibid., 866.

69. Joseph Chaney, "Turning to Men: Genres of Cross-Dressing in Charke's narrative and Shakespeare's The Merchant of Venice" in *Introducing Charlotte Charke: Actress, Author, Enigma*, ed. Philip E. Baruth (Urbana: University of Illinois Press, 1999), 220.

70. Polly S. Fields, "Charlotte Charke and the Liminality of her Bi-Genderings: A Study of Her Canonical Works," in *Pilgrimage for Love: Essays in Early Modern Literature in Honor of Josephine A.*

Roberts, ed. Sigrid King. Medieval & Renaissance Texts and Studies Series, vol. 213 (Tempe, AZ: Arizona Center for Medieval and Renaissance Studies, 1999), 233.

71. Caroline Gonda, "The Odd Woman: Charlotte Charke, Sarah Scott and the Metamorphoses of Sex," in *Lesbian Dames: Sapphism in the Long Eighteenth Century*, eds. John C. Beynon and Caroline Gonda (London and Burlington, VT: Ashgate, 2010), 113.

72. Erin Mackie, "Desperate Measures: The Narratives of the Life of Mrs. Charlotte Charke," *ELH* 58, no. 4 (1991): 842.

73. Theresa Braunschneider, "Acting the Lover: Gender and Desire in Narratives of Passing Women," *The Eighteenth Century* 45, no. 3 (2004): 211-29.

74. Easton's comments when discussing working-class women reveals how radical this choice really was. He says: "Going into service was commonly viewed as a last resort for poor women seeking work in London; another was prostitution." (138)

75. Cromwell, "Passing Women," 58.

76. Marilyn Morris, "Transgendered Perspectives on Premodern Sexualities," in "Friendship and Same Sex Love," eds. Caroline Gonda and Chris Mounsey, *SEL* 46, no. 3 Special Issue (2006): 586.

77. Jamison Green, *Becoming a Visible Man* (Nashville, TN: Vanderbilt University Press, 2004), 196.

THE SOUND OF MEN IN LOVE

Thomas A. King

I HAVE LONG BEEN MOVED by Prospero's oral transactions with Ariel in Shakespeare's tragicomedy *The Tempest* (1610?), among them, these:

> *Ar[iel]*. Doe you loue me Mafter? no?
> *Pro[spero]*. Dearely, my delicate *Ariell*: doe not approach
> Till thou do'ft heare me call.

and—

> *Pro.* Why that's my dainty *Ariel* : I fhall miffe
> Thee, but yet thou fhalt haue freedome : fo, fo, fo.[1]

Moved, corporeally relocated: The assonance of Ariel's loving and the affirmations that Prospero returns, with their chiasmic and echoing assurances of wholeness across difference, reverberate, surrogating the bare structural function of opposing the good and the bad servants, Ariel and Caliban, air and earth, the "mimic man" and the resistant savage:

> de – y, y – de
> ear-l, el, ar-ll
> dainty – miffe Thee
> I fhall miffe [not have] thee – thou fhalt have [yourself, that is] freedome

Moved, I might say, by a sound irrational and other to the modern place of my listening: these oral transactions, beginning from another place in which love and subjection between two male-bodied individuals may be consonant—"love" here binds together the asymmetrical vocatives "you" and "thou," where "you" instates distance and "thou" performs intimacy or condescension—end by recognizing that love between two male-bodied individuals is incompatible with either's freedom. The love that binds *thee* to a subordinate position should give way to your autonomy, which Prospero cannot quite yet pronounce, even at the end of the play, for doing so will end the play:

> *Pro.* That is thy charge: Then to the Elements
> Be free, and fare thou well: pleaſe you draw neere. (*F* 19)

Turning from the boy player Ariel to the audience and beginning his Epilogue, Prospero addresses us as "you," the colon after "well" indicating the forward thrust of his speaking into the present time and space of the audience opened up by this transition from "thou" to "you:" "pleaſe *you* draw neere." As if to say: Attend you to this crossing over and realignment of pronominalizations, to this space opened up for the emergence of your subjectivity.[2] As if to ask: Does the universalizing of male freedom require the renunciation of the sound of men in love, necessitate an ethics abjuring its own felicitous pronunciation?

As Alan Bray showed, male-male friendship in early modern England, however intimate the bond, was a publicly performed event.[3] Friendship, constituted in a complex and fraught field of speech-acts (where speaking was understood, in early modern theories of eloquence, to include gesturing and other modes of bodily signification), established and affirmed the bonds, obligations, and expectations of favor holding among men who, in other spaces and times, would hold distinctly unequal positions through birth, social status, or occupation. Publicity, in fact, established the site- and occasion-specific conditions of mutuality and intimacy among men; friendship was articulated through signifying practices locating the body of one friend in proximity to the body of the other, ranging, as Bray documented, from the oral swearing of oaths and kinship and the bestowal of favor; to the recording and narrating of those speech-acts in familiar letters, wills, and memorial inscriptions; to the gestural language of public kisses and embraces or the sharing of one's table or bed; and to what Bray called "the gift of the friend's body" in iconizing practices promising the continued proximity and presence of the other's body beyond separation or death, including the exchange of handwriting, portraits, and effigies, bodily tokens such as cuttings of hair, or, the ultimate gift, the provision of one's corpse for burial by one's friend.[4] After he sends all other suitors and spies away, segregating the public spaces of the court to create a (fragile) situation of intimacy, Hamlet solicits a hearing from a hesitant Horatio: "Dost thou hear? / Since my dear soul was mistress of her choice / And could of men distinguish her election, / Sh' hath seal'd thee for herself. . . ."[5] This is not to suggest that the humanist ideal of male-male friendship was easily or ever achieved by men or that the rhetoric of friendship was leveling.[6] Prospero's affirmation of love for Ariel is immediately followed by the reinstatement of distance: "doe not approach." Represented as a mimetic progression toward an ideal form, the sound of men in love played out as an ongoing activity of corporeal discipline. Friendship was a way of practicing a structure of super- and subordination among men, between men and women, and between men and boys that invariably reinforced that structure. In this sense the terms "friendship" and "love" figured different discursive worlds than those in which we tend to locate the equivalent words today. Here, I want to stress the mimetic quality of the acts and events constituting friendship, that is, the imitative and emulative activities by means of which male-bodied persons claimed for themselves and for their friends forms of embodiment carrying public significance.[7]

According to the Ciceronian and Neoplatonic thought underlying Baldessare Castiglione's *Book of the Courtier* (translated into English by Sir Thomas Hoby, 1561), a courtier's delight in the "comeliness" of another's speech and person incited her or him to an agreeing comeliness; as Hoby emphasized in his dedicatory epistle to his patron Lord Henry Hastings, Castiglione's discourse would provide "a mirrour" for gentlemen and gentlewomen of all ages "to decke and trimme themselves with vertuous condicions, comely behaviours and honest enterteinment toward al men. . . ."[8] Eloquence, as staged in *The Courtier*, placed speaker and addressee within the same enunciative field, enabling the lover's and beloved's joint recorporealization, within and by the field of comely speaking, as desiring bodies suited to mobilize subjectivities construed as mutual despite, or across, their apparent status differences. This recorporealization of self and other—as "I" and "thou" or "I" and "you"—was, and is, specific to the speech situation, a consequence of those deictic aspects of utterances "that relate utterances to the spatiotemporal coordinates of the act of utterance"; examples include the pronouns "I" and "you," the temporal markers "now" and "then," and the spatial markers "here" and "there." Through deixis, to draw on Emile Benveniste, the "empty signs" of "I" and "you" become "full," embodied by a specific addresser and a specific addressee; deixis offers the (conventional) promise that one can become "I" by addressing a particular "you" in a specific time and space (here and now).[9] To note the conventionality of deixis is to remark its performativity; through deixis, derived from the Greek for "pointing" or "indicating," attributes of "here-ness" and "now-ness" accrue to the corporeal desires, gestures, and voices occupying the "I" and "you" of the speech act. A kind of pronominalization in which I become addressable by my qualities of being in and activating time and space, deictic conventionality is not (as post-rhetorical models of language as spontaneous and expressive might have it) the antithesis or inhibition of the (emergence of a) thinking, feeling, imagining self. Deixis is an aural event, performed by more than one speaker, a dialogic marking of movements in time and space whereby corporeal desires, gestures, and voices make demands on each other in the here and now.

The subject is specific to the space and time of its speaking. In the particular places and occasions of classical quotation, above all the Renaissance grammar schools and universities, the exchange of rhetoric constituted—that is, gave a material practice and location to—the sound of gentle men in love. Castiglione specified the conversational place and occasion of the dialogues he had reconstructed, by contrast, as producing heterosocial courtliness, displacing the places and topoi of male homosocial conversation. In *The Courtier,* "love" was the idealized scene and sign of the male-bodied speaker's (fraught) participation in those modes of deixis by which he constituted himself as "I" in relation to, and in presence with, the "you" of the female-bodied prince or patron, on the one hand, and in relation to the "thou/you" of a particular female-bodied beloved, on the other. Thus the corporeality of love would differ across the available sites for speaking. Because the modes of deixis whereby the positions "I" and "you" may be occupied and addressed were, and are, specified by the place and occasion of speech, love also entailed emulating a particular topos of love, becoming an image or copy of that common place, or, to change from the visual to the aural register, becoming a recitation of the places and occasions for speaking love.

According to Neoplatonic models of embodiment, the body of the one friend would be discovered within the body of the other, in an exchange of likeness occurring through the eyes, ears, and breath: an event familiarly described as ravishment. To prepare his readers to withstand the temptations of lust, Robert Burton ironically cited an anecdote borrowed from Marsilio Ficino's *Commentarium in Convivium Platonis* (*Commentary on the Symposium of Plato,* written 1474-75, pub. 1484) about the friendship of an older man, Lycias, for a youth, Phædrus. Here is Burton's version, from his *Anatomy of Melancholy* (1621):

> Lycias *hee stares on* Phædrus *face, and* Phædrus *fastens the balls of his eyes upon* Lycias, *and with those sparkling rayes, sends out his spirits. The beames of* Phædrus *eyes are easily mingled with the beames of* Lycias, *and spirits are joyned to spirits. This vapour begot in* Phædrus *heart, enters into* Lycias *bowels; and that which is a greater wounder,* Phædrus *bloud is in* Lycias

> *heart, and thence come those ordinary love speeches, my sweet heart* Phæ-
> drus, *and mine own self, my deare bowels: And* Phædrus *againe to* Lycias,
> *O my light, my joy, my soule, my life.* Phædrus *followes* Lycias, *because his*
> *heart would have his spirits, and* Lycias *followes* Phædrus, *because he loves*
> *the seat of his spirits*[.][10]

Within the topos, or citational space, of male-male friendship, gentle male embodiment was a (re)incorporation of the other man, imaged in those ordinary,
ready-to-hand acts of deixis, "*my* sweet heart . . . and *mine own* self, my deare
bowels," and in the apostrophe that makes what is *there* (or, in the case of abstract
concepts, nowhere) present *here*, "*O my light, my joy, my soule, my life.*" Locating
my heart, my bowels, my soul in your flesh, the apostrophe pointed to the ideal
(if impossible) reciprocity and interpenetrability of "I" and "you" within the
compassionating event of deixis. One might think that such utterances represent
a more primary, less mediated, responsiveness of the flesh and thus a distinction
between embodiment and representation, such that the words imitate the materiality of a phenomenon rather than produce it ("*and thence come those ordinary*
love speeches"). But, here, utterances, reduplicating the paths of the spirits, are
vehicles for reshaping bodies in the likeness of the trope ("*O*"). Thence come such
speeches because the speakers' bodies have already adhered to the commonplace;
the performativity of the commonplace, resonating among and locating bodies in
relation to each other, recovers the circuit of breath, vapour, spirit, and bowels.
Nor are the passionate utterances constitutive of friendship necessarily or merely
verbal. An utterance may be silent or gestural; it may already have occurred prior
to speaking; it may be a yearning of the bowels (the seat of the passions) bringing
Lycias and Phædrus together here and now, face to face, which speaking then affirmed and sealed.

Other critics have explored emulation and eloquence as a chief criterion of
early modern civility and sketched the debates about the role of rhetorical speech
in constructing the liberality, politeness, and modernity of British civil society in
the eighteenth century.[11] I want to consider here the ways early modern rhetorical discourses produced both desiring bodies and the kinds of bodies considered
desirable. This was a speaking that mapped the distinction between civility and
the uncivil or unlearned pleasures of the body onto the difference of comely and
uncomely voices. In an important analysis of John Florio's 1603 translation of
Montaigne's essay "On Friendship," Jeffrey Masten has shown how Florio divided
Montaigne's singular term for the pleasures of male friendship, "*jouissance*," into

two incompatible pleasures: on the one hand, a corporeal enjoyment of the friend's body and, on the other, a spiritual *jouissance* remarking the reciprocity that was the proper end of male homosocial friendship. Here is Florio:

> As soone as it [lustfull love] creepeth into the termes of friendship, that is to say, in[to] the agreement of wills, it languisheth and vanisheth away: enjoying doth lose it, as having a corporall end, and subject to satietie. On the other side, friendship is enioyed according as it is desired, it is neither bred, nor nourished, nor increaseth but in jovissance, as being spirituall, and the minde being refined by vse and custome.[12]

Florio distinguished *jouissance*, which Masten has understood as "an erotics of similitude" through which "[g]entlemen friends are identically constituted," from (what I have called elsewhere) residual pederastic pleasure, or, here, enjoyment, which, in Florio's words, reinstated "a disparitie of ages and difference of offices betweene lovers" by taking a youth or another, more lowly positioned male-bodied person as he might a woman, that is, as an erotic object or possession (to "enjoy" was to use another's body for one's own pleasure).[13] If loving similitude was one end of a rhetorical transaction—Hamlet to Horatio: "Give me that man / That is not passion's slave, and I will wear him / In my heart's core, ay, in my heart of heart, / As I do thee"—the potential for enjoying acknowledges and reinstates an asymmetrical corporeality that ends the rhetorical exchange: "Something too much of this" (3.2.71-74, 1162). Note Florio's phrase "agreement of wills": If the "will" names not only volition but also "carnal desire and appetite" and by metonymy the genitalia,[14] an "agreement of wills" would entail a likeness of intention and action between two male-bodied persons reduplicated by a bodily resemblance (an agreement of genitals and genital desire never signaled in pederastic discourses of male super- and subordination) and thus a similitude of male embodiment that cannot exist in a situation of the inequality or dependence of one male-bodied person vis-à-vis another.

In the absence of love construed as *jouissance*, there is only enjoying and the potential for servitude (using another male-bodied individual as a boy)—and it is this, I think, that suggests the material urgency of Ariel's question, "Do you love me, master? No?" Does Prospero love or enjoy Ariel? When a drunken Stephano stumbles on "a most delicate monster" with "[f]our legs and two voices" on the shore of Prospero's island—his mate Trinculo spread-eagled across the prostrate Caliban, their bodies inverted under the slave's gabardine—the butler's figure for what he sees points specifically to the possibility, or failure, of the speech-acts constituting male homosocial friendship. This is Trinculo: "His forward voice now is to speak well of his friend, his backward voice is to utter foul speeches and to detract."[15] The comely voice is always, no matter what its "content," one man speaking well of another. The anality of the backward voice, explored by Maurice Hunt, recalls the proximity of the sound of men in love to sodomy, that limit or boundary, already located within the rhetorical voice as its fundamental trope, marking the end of comely speaking.[16]

The sound of men in love was the rhetorical place of the arousal, through and as citation, of one male-bodied person's subjection to another man's voice (eloquence being mastery of an other's judgments and passions) *and* it was the rhetorical place for the disciplining and redirecting of that yearning toward comely speech: a disciplining that might establish the autonomy and integrity of the (male) body, on the one hand, and (his) maturation toward the possession and display of civic virtue, on the other. In bodying forth the sound of the play, Ariel raises the critical question of his freedom (as does Caliban): does Ariel envoice Prospero or does he have his own voice? Having explored recent postcolonial responses to *The Tempest* elsewhere,[17] I am concerned here with another question: why does Prospero need a boy (why does the theatre need a boy) to stage these questions about the freedom of male-bodied beings? The critical elision of Ariel's seemliness of mind and body recalls that discomfort with the comely boy and with the material pleasures of the linguistic signifier (a linguistic "body" typically opposed to the thought or substance it ostensibly holds within itself and externalizes as communicable sense) that has plagued literary criticism since (at least) Samuel Johnson's criticism of the metaphysical poets' "perverseness of industry" and Shakespeare's "quibbles."[18] It repeats, too, the reformulation of Ariel's charms, by the eighteenth century, as properly feminine, to be bodied forth on the stage by female-bodied and -identified actors, and thus the rediscovery of aural pleasures as properly heteroerotic. Ariel's contributions to our pleasure as hearers of the play is coextensive with his (pederastic) role vis-à-vis Prospero: the ideal boy student whose tender mouth has been shaped by his Latinate education and who demonstrates his progress by performing (as all boys in University did) roles in the Latinate plays that his (school)master had written for him.

What does Prospero renounce when he "abjure[s]" his "potent art" and "rough magic" and vows to "[b]ury" his staff and "drown [his] book," vows we do not *see* fulfilled in the play (5.1.50, 51, 54, 55, 57; 190)?[19] Although Shakespeare probably took the idea of the play from travel and exploration narratives, the only books directly cited and employed by Prospero himself in the action of the play are the classical Latin texts read by every schoolboy as part of the standard program of rhetoric, particularly Virgil's *Aeneid* and Ovid's *Metamorphoses*, the latter providing the basis for the very speech in which Prospero decides to abjure his art and drown his books.[20] These rhetorical texts provided the performative conditions of oral authority, through recitations that both rehearsed prior recitations and enabled future ones. The Latin texts (and their English translations) held *loci commune* (common places) for rhetorical invention, defined by Walter J. Ong as "finding in the store of arguments that others had always exploited those arguments which were applicable to your case."[21] The visual format of the printed book in the Renaissance—already "the commitment of sound to space" that Ong thought complete by the eighteenth century—nevertheless served oral performance, providing quotations for every schoolboy to memorize, copy into a commonplace book, recite aloud, and cite both in oral and written arguments.[22] Rehearsing the figure, Hoby designed his translation of *The Courtier* to be "a storehouse of most necessary implements for the conversacion, use, and training up of mans life with Courtly demeaners" (4-5); likewise he noted that Castiglione himself "hath folowed Cicero, and applied to his purpose sundry examples and pithie sentences out of him" (5). Such recitations—from speech to print and back again—constituted a mobilization and spatialization of the given and available places for speaking.[23]

To "cite" in classical rhetoric involved a recitation with persuasive and thus constitutive force. To adduce as an authority, to bring forth an instance, to allege by way of example or proof: all these early modern senses of the word "cite" are closely related to its even earlier sense, "To summon, call; arouse, excite," as when Prospero first brings forth Ariel and Caliban by calling them by their names and attributes and charging them to speak: "What ho, slave Caliban! / Thou earth, thou, speak!" (the deictic marker "thou" performing a hierarchic function, and the vocatives "slave" and "earth" locating the body of the addressed within a received rhetoric of the differential social, economic, and moral worth of persons) (Shakespeare, *Tempest* 1.2.313-4, 118).[24] Prospero's speech exercises the art of vocalizing one's authority in the shared, or common, place of a precedent vocalization. To cite is to appeal to the conventional authority behind the "I" (the crown, canon, legal precedent, classical passage, proverb, or rational or customary knowledge that, into the seventeenth century, constituted and circumscribed the field of the persuasive), bringing what is prior into the here-and-now, and at the same time to the passion excited in the auditor, who is (ideally) to have found himself or herself in that place cited by the speaker. What Prospero's speech—his "art"—imitates, and what it says it will abjure, is the citational power of rhetoric: the art simultaneously of situating the subject position "I" within a citational chain and of inducing passionate effects in "thee," one's auditor—the art of bringing "I" and "thou" together in an exercise of power based in inequality but potentially exciting similitude.

The sound of men in love could be the sharing of the figure or citation toward the production and publicizing of amity across asymmetrical positions (where the production of amity, it bears repeating, does not so much level distinction as confirm its importance for the establishment of reciprocities)—

> HAMLET (to Horatio)   blest are those
> Whose blood and judgment are so well co-meddled
> That they are not a pipe for Fortune's finger
> To sound what stop she please. (3.2.68-71, 1162)

Or it could be an incompetency, a failure to grasp and redeploy the figure, that affirmed the distinct places of speakers—

> HAMLET: Will you play upon this pipe?
> GUILDENSTERN: My lord, I cannot.
> . . . .
> HAMLET: . . . Look you, these are the stops.
> GUILDENSTERN: But these cannot I command to any utt'rance of harmony. I have not the skill.
> HAMLET: Why, look you now, how unworthy a thing you make of me! You would play upon me, you would seem to know my stops. . . . (3.2.350-52, 360-70, 1165)

As Castiglione's-Hoby's "M. Bernard Bibiena" advised, "meerie sayinges" are most felicitous "yf they be answered, and he that maketh answere continue in the self same metaphor spoken by the other" (173), if, that is, they become the intersubjective event of repartee, which functions not only to create reciprocity but perhaps more crucially to circumscribe and delimit the time and place of reciprocity. The sound of men in love could be refused, or another man's figure redirected to close off access to one's self and one's inwardness and to maintain the politic "secrecy" advised by Francis Bacon:[25]

> KING: But now, my cousin Hamlet, and my son—
> HAMLET: A little more than kin, and less than kind.
> KING: How is it that the clouds still hang on you?
> HAMLET: Not so, my lord, I am too much in the sun. (1.2.64-67, 1144)

The exchange of the figure was a performative transaction among speakers and between speakers and auditors, one particularly attuned to the making, appropriating, or respatializing of the available places for one's speaking. Key to the exercise of rhetoric, according to the treatises, was familiarity with the decorum of place, occasion, and the statuses and characters of one's interlocutors and the ability to opportune the moment, to reconfigure the time-space of an occasion through one's figures of speech. The attack on rhetorical figuration and wit in the later seventeenth and eighteenth centuries was not so much an attempt to purify thought of its linguistic distortions, to make writing the transparent vehicle of propositional content, as an attempt to seize speech and writing from the delimited and constraining places, occasions, and conventions of its former uses and to assign speech and writing instead a new spatialization, theoretically unleashed from the particular bodies of interlocutors and coeval with the emergent public sphere; the latter would be an ever-expanding, virtual domain of rational communicative exchange or critical publicity, in Jürgen Habermas's formulation, operating through a bracketing of status differences and emptied, in Neil Saccamano's paraphrase, of "any theatrical representation of speech."[26] Freed from its *habitus*, discourse could be mystified as a network of exchange, fraught with struggles and fragile compromises, between the privacy of inwardness (what cannot or would not be communicated) and the demand of representation (the demand to externalize oneself in the available technologies of communication).

We might see this claim to ground the self in the heroic negotiation of the publicness of private thought as a critique of actually existing procedures of deixis. For example, Johnson's famous letter to Lord Chesterfield, explaining his refusal to dedicate the *Dictionary* (1755) to the man who had assumed but failed to exercise the role of its patron, both appropriated the residual intimacies of handwriting, creating a proximity to Chesterfield otherwise denied to Johnson, and pointed toward the emergent contestatory power of print, both to the *Dictionary* that is the occasion of the letter and to the public interest in the private life of its compiler, Johnson, to whose authority to nationalize and therefore level English speaking Chesterfield himself had promised his own personal linguistic submission—"a total surrender of all [his] rights and privileges in the English language, as a freeborn British subject"—in a letter to *The World* published prior to the *Dictionary*'s appearance.[27] If Johnson did not, Chesterfield clearly did anticipate the print circulation of Johnson's letter and sought to derail its future public resignifications by relocating it within the compensatory deictic scenarios that James Boswell famously derided in the *Life*, that is, in print, "letting it [Johnson's letter] lay upon his table, where any body might see it," reading it to visitors and "point[ing] out the severest passages, and observ[ing] how well they were expressed" (*Life* 187).

The locutions of men in love, and the locations for speaking love, were consequences of the spatial and differential distribution of rhetorical education, based in the study of the Greek and Latin classics and under pressure from an expanding and heterogeneous vernacular. Let me now point to just four of the places of speaking within and against which the sound of men in love might have been heard. I will be construing each of the following places for speaking, not as the cause or origin of a certain mode of speaking, but as performatively constituted in a conventional mode of speaking. To speak "from" a given place is to have performed a deictic act. In the flow of their interactions, in the very heat and pride of their contention, speakers recreate and reuse deictic markers constituting and circumscribing place, occasion, and the positions of interlocutors, and they may also put those markers into play, relocating the boundaries of a speech convention or genre or appropriating a commonplace to give place to an otherwise illicit locution (for example, printing privileged speech, imitating the court masque on the commercial stage, as in *The Tempest*, or claiming the rhetoric of friendship for female-female intimate bonds, as in the poetry of Katherine Phillips).[28]

In the first place: In the male-bodied, homosocial grammar schools and universities, oral and written eloquence, achieved through the translation and imitation of classical texts, was the privileged vehicle of cultural production. Consider the interpolated Latin lesson in *The Merry Wives of Windsor* (1597?). Exercising young master William in his Latin numbers and cases, the parson Sir Hugh Evans urges the youth to display comeliness by holding up his head and addresses him, despite their differences of age and authority, formally, as "you" and "William" (4.1.7-85, 312). The vocatives "you" and "William" allow the boy to occupy an "I," inciting the boy to manhood; the youth derives the subject position "I," not from mere possession of a penis, but from the recognition conferred on his comely body by what Walter Ong called the male puberty or initiation rite of Latin education.[29] The vocative "William" is conferred on the youth by the parson only—his mother Mistress Page and Mistress Quickly, witnessing his oral examination, address him as "boy," "sirrah," and "child"—and the vocative can be taken away: when the boy forgets his cases, the parson chides him as "child" and threatens him with "breech[ing]," a whipping across the bare arse that, flipping the boy Will from front to back, from the public to the domestic, from the potentially autonomous to the materially dependent, returns the similitude of wills to the distinction of master and boy.

But the capacity of classical rhetoric to constitute what Johannes Fabian has memorably described as "allochronism," a universalizing time-space overlaying and erasing the differences of empirical spaces and historical time, was under pressure.[30] As Russ McDonald (among others) has observed, the encounter of the ideality of classical literary and rhetorical texts with the heterogeneity of the vernacular, and the attempt to reconcile the inventiveness and particularity of linguistic traffic in the sixteenth century with the stability and universality of grammar and diction represented by Latin, to create a language at once vernacular and literary, had opened up for Shakespeare and his contemporaries an unusually replete linguistic field.[31] Debating the uses of the vernacular could itself be a way for men to cite other men, whether to praise or bury them, even as it made space for the entrance into print rhetoric and public speaking of "exceptional" women (who generally wrote in the vernacular).[32] Hoby, in his dedicatory epistle, turned the long debate over literary diction in book one of *The Courtier* (57-74) to the question of the best language for advancing national knowledge: "where the Sciences are most tourned into the vulgar tunge, there are best learned men. . . ." (6). As St John's College, Cambridge fellow Sir John Cheke emphasized in his prefatory letter praising Hoby's *The Courtier*, Hoby had carefully purged his English translation of imported and Latinate words (10-11)—perhaps a response to Castiglione's own defense, in his introductory epistle to the Portuguese humanist Miguel de Sylva, of his choice to follow contemporary "use" in preferring "new" and "transport[ed]" words to those "that are not [or any longer] in commune speech" (15, see also 57-59).[33] Perfecting a grammar to stabilize and "refine" the vernacular was essential to the maturation of an English national culture, argued Richard Mulcaster in his *First Part of the Elementary which Entreateth Chefelie of the right writing of our Englifh tung* (1582); such a grammar would "fhew vs Englifhmē a verie great pleafur, if it help to the fining of our own Englifh tung, & thereby to make it to be of fuch account, as other tungs be, . . . whereby we our felues alfo fhall feme not to be barbarous, euē by mean of our tung, feing fair fpeche is fom parcell of praife, and a great argument of a well ciuilled peple" (50). Defending his choice to write in English rather than Latin, Mulcaster, like Hoby, observed that using the vernacular facilitated the production and circulation of knowledge: "For is it not in dede a meruellous bondage, to becom fervants to one tung for learning fake, [learning Latin requiring us to spend] the moft of our time, with loffe of moft time, whereas we maie haue the verie fame treafur in our own tung, with the gain of moft time? our own bearing the ioyfull title of our libertie and fredom, the Latin tung remembring vs, of our thraldom & bondage?" (254, see generally "The Peroration," 252-70).[34] (Chesterfield would repeat Mulcaster's terms over 150 years later.) The national advancement of knowledge required liberation from the enunciative field of Latin, from the intensive labor required to occupy a position in that field, and therefore from the terms of, and limitations posed by, Latin and the scholasticism it encoded. "I loue Rome," Mulcaster concluded, "but *London* better, I fauor *Italie*, but England more, I honor the *Latin*, but I worſhip the *Engliſh*".

Even as the vernacular replaced Latin by the early seventeenth century as the vehicle for the production and circulation of knowledge in print, Latin remained, according to McDonald, "the focus of a young man's education in the grammar schools."[35] Associated with the place and privilege of educated young men and, it follows, inhering in the sound of men in love, was (and is) a wastefulness, an excess to productivity and futurity heard within and against the emergence of a national culture as an echo of Englishmen's "thraldom" to the international and the "feudal." Distinguishing the education of those male-bodied persons able to attend grammar schools and universities from that of all other male- and female-bodied persons, the recitation of Latin was the vehicle and sign of an excess to the practical matters of everyday life: to the keeping of accounts and managing of the household, to the facilitating of trade across borders, to the advancement of the natural and physical sciences. Latin and Latinate expression performed, too, an excess to the speaker's intention to communicate facts, to refer to a verbally neutral world outside the situation of speech. Latin and Latinate expression located, problematized, and differentiated the (male) bodies of speakers and addressees—all the more so after 1660 when "the grammar schools diversified their curriculum," as Anthony Fletcher has noted, but the upper gentry continued to send their sons "to schools which preserved the classical regime, with its associated values of restraint on boyhood vigour and harsh discipline through corporal punishment."[36]

Heard as excess, Ciceronian rhetoric had opened male-bodied speakers to the charge of effeminacy. Aware of such criticism, William Guthrie differentiated Quintilian's eloquence from effeminate speech, specifying the latter in his preface to his 1755 translation of Quintilian's *Institutes* as that type of speaking required by men's subjugation to tyranny, for example, the "infantine diction" used at the court of Augustus and which Quintilian had set out to reform.[37] Effeminacy was thus a voluntary relinquishing of manly eloquence and a return to juvenility. As such, effeminate speaking was not the talk of women, except in the sense that women had been effectively excluded from rhetorical training and thus from the circuit of writing, reciting, and recording that provided access to the places and occasions of argumentative discourse and the critique of subjection, facilitating autonomy from dependence. If elite discourses construed the moral task of Ciceronian eloquence, in the words of Pat Parker, as "the dilation and control of a copiousness figured as female," the appropriation and containment of a specifically *female body* for the authority of manly speakers may have been only one tactic within a larger strategic response to the rhetorical power of corporealization, a more capacious strategy for opportuning, mobilizing, and negotiating its problems and possibilities for dominant speakers.[38] Viewed from the emergent perspective of a vernacular national culture claiming its own plain or "Attic" style, the choice of a residually copious or "Asiatic" Ciceronian style transformed male-bodied speakers into men who had turned their backs on futurity and freedom to occupy an anachronistic place, one, indeed, that Castiglione's-Hoby's "Syr Fridericke" had commended. Acknowledging the asymmetry of the courtier and his prince, an asymmetry that should make both love and conversation, in any properly Ciceronian sense, impossible, Syr Fridericke nevertheless exhorted his ideal male-bodied courtier to "turne al his thoughtes and force of minde to love, and (as it were) to reverence the Prince he serveth above al other thinges, and in his wil, maners, and facions, to be altogether pliable to please him" (120). The critique of classical rhetoric was already a theme within rhetoric itself, the "limit" and "outside" of rhetoric already "inside."[39]

Guthrie rehearsed Quintilian's alignment of eloquence and liberty, rhetoric and public virtue: "no man [could] be a complete orator," Quintilian had written, "unless he [was] a good man. . . ." (1:3) The study of oratory and the pursuit of virtue were one and the same; as Guthrie summarized the claim, Quintilian had meant his rhetorical education "to awaken the mind to sentiments of virtue and ideas of liberty; to raise, direct, and impel the great movements of the soul, to rouse the strong, and to inspire the tender passions; to fit the rules of eloquence to the arts of government, and to make the beauties of language the force of philosophy, and the fruits of experience subservient to the system of social happiness" ("Preface," i:ix-x).[40] Ciceronian rhetoric, in short, was the vehicle of the positive freedom of manliness—an enfranchisement and public orientation that the emergent modern state both made possible and harnessed. In this transitional period, the pursuit of eloquence contained the expansion of the modern state to manly bodies.

Elite female-bodied (and other) speakers did of course find means and opportunities to study and practice classical rhetoric, their achievements rehearsed by such advocates for "exceptional" women as Christine de Pizan, Boccaccio, and

Hoby's Lord Julian, the latter going so far as to locate an "exceptional" woman at the origin of revelation, philosophy, Latin letters, and the founding of Rome (238, see also 223, 240, 264). *The Courtier* staged both the celebration and containment of such exceptionality, however; forced to defend women against the misogyny of Unico Aretino, the Lady Emilia claims a capacity for logical argument and deploys such rhetorical figures as analogy, metaphor, simile, antithesis, and ellipsis, all the while stressing that she speaks only to "answere to that which you [Unico Aretino] lay to my charge" (274-75, quotation from 274). Such hegemonic exclusion of female-bodied persons from rhetorical speaking, as Parker has summarized, "had to do with the nature of rhetoric as specifically *public* speaking."[41] Richard Braithwaite would insist on this point in his *English Gentlewoman* (1631): "it suits not with her honour for a young woman to be prolocutor . . . especially when either men are in presence, or ancient matrons, to whom she owes a civil reverence." But, as Marguérite Corporaal has argued, Margaret Cavendish would respond to such claims through the persona of Lady Sanspareille in *Youth's Glory and Death's Banquet* (c. 1655), who argues, "And why may not women speak in publick and to publick assemblies, as well as in private visits, and particular entertainments, and to particular persons and acquaintance?"[42]

In the second place: At the mixed-gender courts, the rhetoric of heterosociality—say, the repartee of Beatrice and Benedict or the stricter protocols of Castiglione's competitive dialogues—spoke through and against patriarchal discourses of authority, alliance, property, and lineage and pederastic discourses of countenance and favor. Elite women also spoke, wrote, and read in this place, for example, through the "gendered reading formation" of court ladies, their women-in-waiting, and their female-bodied household servants studied by Louise Schleiner.[43] The speaking specific to courts, the speech that was the height of civility, would be criticized as morally ambivalent, not only in its privileging of linguistic artifice over clarity of thought and sincerity of intention, but in its inclusion of female-bodied speakers "encompassing two or three social classes," who, like the male-bodied speakers of various statuses housed at or visiting court, employed rhetorical skill to make themselves pleasing to their (current or potential) patrons at court.[44] Morally ambivalent, I offer, not only because these speakers were female-bodied but because their appropriation and opportuning of literacy and the rhetorical voice, in which they could be more skilled than the superiors to whom they read or for whom they wrote, entailed a crossing of places and a seizing of mobility. George [Richard] Puttenham prepared his *Arte of English Poesie*, he repeatedly noted, for "Ladies and young Gentlewomen, or idle Courtiers, desirous to become skilful in their owne mother tongue [reserving Latin and Greek to male-bodied scholars], and for their priuate recreation [reserving public speaking to more fit rhetors] to make now & then ditties of pleaſure, thinking for our parte none other ſcience ſo fit for them & the place [i.e., that they occupy, the court] as that which teacheth beau ſemblant, the chiefe profeſſiō aſwell of Courting as of poeſie. . . ."⁴⁵ Both the female-bodied, homosocial reading groups and the heterosocial conversational transactions, represented (and defended) by Puttenham as idle and ornamental, dedicated not to Ciceronian virtue but to private pleasure, could be distinguished as courtly, on the one hand, by their mode of address from the male homosocial schools and, on the other hand, by their delight in figures from the more utilitarian discourse of the mercantile classes.

In the third place: The lower gentry, mercantile, and professional classes constituted a largely literate (print) culture in Shakespearean England, according to Bruce R. Smith, but one in which linguistic heterogeneity, the appropriation of foreign terms, and an expanding vernacular had high value in facilitating scientific, technological, and commercial/colonial developments and transactions across borders.⁴⁶ At the same time, rhetorical skill, in Latin or in the vernacular, facilitated mobility of gender and status both; those male- and female-bodied individuals, ordinarily (or at least "officially") unskillful in "th[eir] cases and the numbers of the genders," as Master Evans puts it to Mistress Quickly in *The Merry Wives of Windsor*, could employ vernacular rhetorical handbooks, translations of the classics, and compendiums of famous passages. At the end of the Restoration, Aphra Behn, writing for the market, would likewise appropriate the Latin lesson, in translation, for a "[f]emale [p]en." By reciting "the Lives of the Romans and great men," that is, Sir Thomas North's Plutarch, Behn's narrative persona assimilates the eponymous hero of her novel *Oroonoko; or, The Royal Slave* (1688) to an aristocratic, and specifically Roman, aesthetics of virtue, even as she disclaims the efficacy of her pen, restricted to the vernacular and untrained in classical letters.⁴⁷ Reduced to anachronism by the mid-eighteenth century, the "Roman style" of Samuel Richardson's Robert Lovelace, designated "*Esq.*," and his "principal intimate and confidant" John Belford, likewise designated "*Esq.*," signals the friendly assent of each "to take in good part whatever freedoms they treated each other with," including some rather anxious *thou*-ing (Clarissa,1747-48):⁴⁸

> MR LOVELACE TO JOHN BELFORD, ESQ. But how I *excurse*!—Yet thou usedst to say, thou likest my excursions. If thou dost, thou'lt have enow of them. (420)

MR LOVELACE TO JOHN BELFORD, ESQ. THOU hast often reproached me, Jack, with my vanity, without distinguishing the humorous turn that accompanies it; and for which, at the same time that thou robbest me of the merit of it, thou admirest me highly. . . . But thou art too clumsy and too shortsighted a mortal to know how to account even for the impulses by which thou thyself art moved. (446)

Rehear(s)ing, here in this third place, nostalgic tropes of manly friendship, James Boswell would later exhort his friend and confidant John Johnston, Laird of Grange to indulge with him a melancholic and pastoral "antiquity," as in this letter from 1763:

I would beg my dear Johnston that you would sometimes on the Saturday forenoons if the day be good take a solitary walk to the King's Park, where we have so often strayed together and indulged warmth of heart and romantic feelings. . . . Then take some good Author out of your pocket and read and muse. . . . When you come to the Abbey of Holyroodhouse that most beloved object of all Think on James the fifth—Think on Queen Mary. Be much of an Antiquarian.[49]

Performing "antiquity" entailed sharing the same gestural relations to social, natural, and discursive spaces as one's absent friend, thereby making the absent other present in one's affective embodiment of oneself. By "antiquity" Boswell named that longing for (re)placement (often, as here, taking the form of Jacobitism) following on writing's (fictive) dislocation of the male-bodied subject from his particularized embodiment within residual pederasty. By investing ancient eloquence with sentimental melancholy, such humors perhaps provided Boswell, concerned as he was with the acquisition of status, the fiction of a more authentically embodied relation to the voice than had the scholarly Scots, trades, and professional men who, like Boswell himself, learned to speak from such elocutionists as John "Orator" Henley and Thomas Sheridan.[50]

If the long eighteenth century registered a general lowering of the threshold at which the sound of men in love became audible, due to the expansion of education in print forms of literacy, the leveling of the sound of men in love was limited by such claims to a residual orality or co-presence of speakers—a fictive presence that print, in a compensatory move, would try to emulate. Paradigmatic may be a scene in the *Life of Johnson* in which the labor of a young male rower, ferrying Johnson and Boswell from Temple-stairs to Greenwich, "furnish[ed] materials" for the "great mill" of Johnson's mind.[51] Boswell had asked Johnson "if he really thought a knowledge of the Greek and Latin languages an essential requisite to a good education."

> JOHNSON. 'Most certainly, Sir; for those who know them have a very great advantage over those who do not. . . .' 'And yet, (said I) people go through the world very well, and carry on the business of life to good advantage, without learning.' JOHNSON. 'Why, Sir, that may be true in cases where learning cannot possibly be of any use; for instance, this boy rows us as well without learning, as if he could sing the song of Orpheus to the Argonauts, who were the first sailors.' He then called to the boy, 'What would you give, my lad, to know about the Argonauts?' 'Sir, (said the boy,) I would give what I have.' Johnson was much pleased with his answer, and we gave him a double fare." (*Life* 323-34)

By the mid-eighteenth century, boys had become subjects—incipient men— whose necessary and organic autonomy from pederastic subjection (as I discussed in *The Gendering of Men*) had become a key concern of educational practice and had provided a central trope of political rhetoric. The boy whom Johnson here hails is no longer that boy—say, William in *Merry Wives*—for whom autonomy from subjection was not yet thinkable. Nevertheless, that Johnson's and Boswell's doubled fare—the gentleman's excess—could not have made a classical education possible for the boy might remind us that despite the expansion of print literacy the ability to cite classical commonplaces in a vernacular tuned by and to the Greek and Latin tongues still worked to secure a mostly elite and homogeneous circle of lettered men against exceptional instances of mobility.

Finally, in the fourth place[52]: Beneath the level of rhetorical hearing and of the printed texts that enabled appropriations of the rhetorical voice, were those lacking in print literacy, on whose material labors depended the everyday reproduction of the bodies and voices of men in love, including the agrarian laborers that, according to Smith, may have retained a primarily oral culture in early modern England.[53] Verbally complex and narrative rich, the orality of the laboring sorts flows into, and is filtered out of, the early modern printed texts that are the subject of the present study; omnivocal, they most likely are not heard in early modern printed texts except as recited by the rhetorical voice, transliterated, for example, into the voices of (aristocratic and gentle) shepherds, shepherdesses, and milkmaids, as well as the linguistically cunning clowns and gravediggers (university men in dirty disguises) heard providing places and occasions for the rhetorical voice.

The sound of men in love will be heard in the conflicts and contradictions among these places, as when Richard Puttenham's *Arte of English Poesie* (1589) recognized spatial and status differences as linguistic differences but nevertheless emphasized the court as the center of civility; or when Richard Mulcaster, considering the question of how best to select boys for learning in his *Elementary* (1582), recognized the possibility of merit distinct from birth but nevertheless chose a rank-specific "comeliness" of person and manner as the sign of the ideal boy student. Not only should the body be sufficiently sound to withstand the rigors of study, it should, wrote Mulcaster, be "perfonable withall, bycaufe perfonablenefe is an allurement to obedience, a gracious deliuerer of anie inward vertew, & fomtime was efteemed a thing moft worthie of the principal feat" (14). So far from being opposed to the ends of education, the schoolmaster's desire for the schoolboy's comely body distinguished the boy as the ideal subject of learning; Mulcaster cited Quintillian, who "bids[,] giue him that boy, which wilbe quikned with praife, which wilbe aloft with honor, which will wepe at a foill. This boy[,] faith he[,] muft be fed with braueries, him cherifhing will encourage, in him I fear no loytering" (15).[54]

Trained by the reading and imitation of printed rhetorical handbooks, the comely voice does not *precede* writing and print but comes into being as a mark of distinction from the heterogeneity of print; comeliness emerges as present only over and against the proliferation of positions promised by print. By (ostensibly) abjuring any particular mode of corporealization, including those situations of speech in which an "I" and a "you" had emerged in a specifiable relation of embodiment with each other, print promised a fully rationalized and ever expanding space enfolding deixis into itself, pointing, that is, only to its own operations rather than to any external grounding in time and space.[55] Print thereby provided, I would add, female-bodied as well as low-status male-bodied and other marginal speakers access to an "I" that seemed (illusively, or more precisely, ideally) to have no place, and therefore no body, outside of print writing, making the writing and reading subject coeval with the respatialization of sociality and publicity performed by print technologies but also, with the appropriation of those technologies by an expanding state machinery, increasingly subjecting bodies to the normalizing aims of citizenship.

The modern analysis of the freedom of English speakers rests on the disavowal of the sound of men in love, accelerating in the second half of the seventeenth century, following the rise of skepticism about rhetorical skill: from the displacement of the particular friend, and the particular relationship of embodiment shared with that friend, by a universalized civility, as in Locke, or universal benevolence, as in Kant (as Bray has shown); and from the displacement or subsuming of men's delight in speaking to an ostensibly objective and impersonal critical reason and scientific methodology "aligned with vision."[56] (This is not to say that the rhetorical voice did not have its visual and spatial qualities. Oratory and the arts of elocution and pronunciation, for example, correlated speaking with action, or gesture; manuscripts contained and appealed to both visual and aural pleasures; and the poetic line itself, as Mark Robson has observed, depends on and registers both aural and visual effects.[57]) From the sixteenth through the eighteenth centuries, the English elocutionary voice, as it encountered the other voices of female-bodied actors, speakers, writers, and readers and the heteroglossia of mercantile trade, colonialism, and tourism, reconstituted itself in print as the memory or echo, always already fading, of the sound of men in love.[58] To put this differently, the uncomely voices of others have appropriated for themselves new occasions for speaking, facilitated by the enormous expansion of print literacy.

If humanists appropriated Ciceronian discourses of friendship to negotiate their fraught placement within traditional hierarchies, their privatization of friendship, its dislocation from publicly affirmed and evaluable alliances, recalled the proximity of male-male love to sodomy. The solicitation of erotic pleasure could appropriate the topos of Ciceronian friendship, that is, the speech situation that had idealized itself (often in the melancholic voice of a lost and irreproducible past) as having transformed the coercive invasion of the other's body into the "secret" mutuality and intimacy, achieved through persuasive and pleasurable locutions, of the body of one's friend and one's self. As late as 1691, in a "Pastoral Dialogue" that an anonymous translator of Cicero appended to his *Laelius*, the shepherd Alcon argues that his love for his "sweet and gentle" Daphnis—we might hear, sweet because gentle, gentle because sweet—excels that of his friend and fellow shepherd Lycidas for Dorinda—that is, the love of a man for a woman. All the local shepherdesses had courted Daphnis, Alcon relates:

> Their Gifts He wou'd receive, their Mufick He wou'd hear,
>> Till weary'd with their Praifes He
>> Thank'd their Civility,
> Refus'd their Love, and haften'd home to Me.
>> There in a clasp'd embrace We lay,
> And with fweet Talk deceiv'd the live-long day,
> Pity'd the Wretches that in vain had woo'd,
> Smil'd at their Pafion and our own purfu'd.[59]

Through "ſweet Talk," Alcon and Daphnis had made themselves comely scholars for one another. The beloved now gone, his place is filled by the pastoral elegy, a singing contest in which two swains, Alcon and Lycidas, mourn their respective losses of Daphnis and Dorinda and debate the respective value of male-male and male-female loves.[60] As a singing contest between two male-bodied shepherds, the anonymous pastoral elegy is constructed as a competitive inventing, sharing, appropriating, and bettering of one man's figures and classical citations by another. Such sharing of tropes leads to only one place; persuaded that the "chaste fire" of friendship is superior to the corporeal passion of male-female love (17), Lycidas (like Orpheus) leaves behind Dorinda and all women and accepts Alcon's invitation to succeed Daphnis as his new friend—a highly suspicious ending in 1691, as the figure of the "molly," thanks to Edward Ward, had recently entered popular English discourses on male-male friendship, redefining the practice that had marked the limit of male-male friendship, sodomy, but an ending that nonetheless projected a residual and contested language of intimate, exclusive male-male love into the future.[61]

Dedicating his pastoral dialogue to the memory of one "F.T.," the anonymous poet at the same time withdrew his friendship with "F. T." into the (only recently) closed off space of privacy: "I hope the Reader is not curious to know" why he had published his translation and poem, the anonymous writer wrote in his preface, concluding, "I ſhall . . . wave all Evaſions, and boldly put my ſelf upon my Reader's mercy; for I don't underſtand why an Author may not have the liberty of keeping his Reaſons to himſelf, as well as his Name" (A4ᵛ). Both offering male-male love to, and withdrawing it from, a public hearing, the writer located his love and loss in the place opened up by Cicero's dialogue on friendship, itself a recitation of Cicero's teacher Scævola's rehearsal of Lælius's discourse recalling the death of his friend Scipio, as the anonymous singer took space in his own preface to remind us (A2ᵛ, see also 1-4, 68-69). The hooking up, across time and death, of male voices, one man's presence preserved by his song for the loss of his friend, institutes the genealogy of the pipes: a commonplace within men's (pastoral) speaking. But the anonymous pastoral elegy recites a sweet talking no longer available as such in 1691, suggesting a (new?) inability to possess male-male love within the common or public place and similitude of "I" and "you," as the Latinate, rhetorical voice gave way to the vernacular, the spatializing distinction of "thou"/"you" to the universalized "you" (a transformation possibly due to the agency of female-bodied speakers[62]), and was now only available as the trace, taken within the self (and returning as print orthography), of an array of imitative practices that had bound literate male speakers to citational places outside themselves. Condemning his confidant Belford for his attempts to intervene in his plot against Clarissa, Richardson's Lovelace addresses his male-bodied friend with the same polite, albeit menacing "you" he has otherwise reserved for Clarissa, denying him the playfulness of "thou": "And so you have actually delivered to the fair implacable [Clarissa] extracts of letters [Lovelace's to Belford] written in the confidence of friendship! Take care—take care, Belford—I do indeed love you better than I love any man in the world; but this is a very delicate point. The matter is grown very serious to me" (1184). The universalizing "you" both recognizes its addressee (male-bodied or female-bodied) as having an equal and autonomous relation to the circulation of speech and writing, an equal claim to the capacity to relocate writing from its authorizing source, and equates that autonomy with the threat of the removal of love.

In their Restoration adaptation of Shakespeare, *The Tempest, or the Enchanted Island* (1667), Sir William Davenant and John Dryden doubled the woman who had never seen a man (other than her father and her slave Caliban), Miranda, with a youth who had never seen a woman, Hippolito. Miranda is also given a younger, more forward, sister Dorinda, who is more coquettishly eager to view a man than is her elder sister. The baroque doubling allowed Davenant and Dryden to further the play's exploration of the problem of aurality and modernity by disposing it into three rhetorical places, proliferating the places of the text and thus opening up new spaces for speaking. In the first place, the male homosocial university: Davenant and Dryden followed Shakespeare in foregrounding Prospero's linguistically problematic relations with his good and his bad slaves, and students, Ariel and Caliban. In both versions, for example, Ariel and Caliban at first address Prospero, impudently, with the familiar "thou," just as he uses the condescending "thou" to them, but they switch to the formal "you" as Prospero threatens them. Here, in the Folio text, Prospero is the "you" of Caliban's curse—

> *Ca[liban]*: You taught me Language, and my profit on't
> Is, I know how to curfe :

which, as the colon indicates, he then demonstrates:

> *the red-plague rid you*
> For learning me your language. (*F* 5)

Prospero likewise retains his position as "you" in Davenant and Dryden's quotation of Ariel's "if you now beheld 'em, your affections / Would become tender."[63]

Within and between these iterations, the attention to an increasingly unstable distinction of "thou" and "you," which we might hear as the struggle to attend and give clarity to what was rapidly becoming noise, remarks a reestablishment of Caliban's and Ariel's subordination even as they resist and reword the master's speech acts.

In the second place, the heterosocial court: Davenant and Dryden relocated Miranda's and Ferdinand's courtship within the courtly, Petrarchan figure of the male-bodied lover killed by his mistress's cruel eyes, a figure which in fact provides the matter of Davenant's and Dryden's plotting as it informs both Hippolito's "natural" response to the first woman he sees and the emergence of the love-and-honor action through Hippolito's innocent rivalry with Ferdinand:

> *Hip[polito].* . . . I have still been kept a Prisoner
> For fear of Women.
> *Ferd[inand].* They indeed are dangerous,
> For since I came I have beheld one here,
> Whose Beauty pierc'd my heart.
> *Hip.* How did she pierce?
> You seem not hurt.
> *Ferd.* Alas! the wound was made by her bright Eyes,
> And festers by her absence.
> But to speak plain to you, Sir I love her.
> *Hip.* Now I suspect that Love's the very thing,
> That I feel too! (act 3, 63-64)

In this place, Prospero's lessons are derived not only from his schoolboy Latin texts but from the Italianate court: Prospero's attempt to promote Ciceronian friendship between Ferdinand and Hippolito—"I would have Friendship grow betwixt 'em. . . . Be earnest to unite their very Souls" (act 4, 66)—falters through his contradictory arousal of Ciceronian virtue and Petrarchan rivalries and jealousies.

In the third place, the heteroglossia of mercantile traffic: Davenant and Dryden displaced residual anxieties about courtly desire and pederastic pleasure and subordination onto the lowly mock court of Stephano, Trinculo, and two other sailors (more rhetorical doubling and antithesis), such that Caliban's planned assassination of Prospero, not representable in the early Restoration and so deleted, becomes instead a buffoonery civil war over possession of a cask, or butt, of wine, leading to a series of bad but telling puns on the multiple significations of "butt" current at the time—the lower end, terminal point or boundary mark; an object of scorn or ridicule; or a buttock, usually of meat (although "buttock" could be either a human's or an animal's hindquarters), with the connotation of a slab of flesh, or a strumpet (as when an "ill-fashioned" passerby in George Etherege's *The Man of Mode* [1676] refers to Belinda, proleptically, as an "oily _____ buttock").[64] So we hear this speech in which Stephano attempts to overthrow Trinculo's sovereignty, "I desire to be entertain'd, at your Butt, as becomes a Prince"; or this speech in which one sailor makes up to another: "Is it not better to pierce the Butt, than to quarrel and pierce one anothers bellies?" (act 4, 78); or Trinculo's underlining the sodomitical potential in Prospero's and Ariel's pederastic relationship when he drunkenly confesses to his own subordinate Stephano, "By Bottle, and by Butt I love thee" (act 4, 79). Here, a juvenile delight in punning—a copiousness that returns incessantly to male bodies, to sodomy as the basest or fundamental matter that a more mature rhetoric should reject—is consigned to the play's lowest and most easily circumscribed place. Here, one might hear the excesses and infelicities of Ciceronian eloquence aligned, retrospectively, with the ethical problematization of men's corporeal pleasures, with the re-citation of pederastic pleasures as sodomy.

In the Folio text, we never actually see Prospero drown his book or break his staff. Nor do we hear him do so; as George Wright has noted of the renunciation speech, Prospero's commitment to the pentameter, even as he promises to abjure his art, indicates that he has not yet done so:

> But this rough Magicke
> I heere abiure : and when I haue requir'd
> Some heauenly Muficke (which euen now I do)
> To worke mine end vpon their Sences, that
> This Ayrie-charme is for, I'le breake my ftaffe,
> Bury it certaine fadomes in the earth,
> And deeper then did euer Plummet found
> Ile drowne my booke. (*F* 16)

As Wright has written of this "highest achievement of [Shakespeare's] art," in the renunciation speech meter, syntax, "argumentative detail embodied in imagery," and the "accumulating rhetorical impact" of Prospero's periods all "proceed in time to achieve their collective design, which is complete only with the final word."[65] Wright did not make the point but that final word is "book": "And deeper then did euer Plummet found / Ile drowne my booke." In the act of renouncing classical rhetoric in order to emerge as the subject of Christian forgiveness, Prospero's thought disappears into, which is to say, resounds as a sequence of aural effects—

among them: **d**eeper, **did**, **d**rown; deep*er-ever*; pl**u**mmet, so**u**nd, dr**ow**n, b**oo**k—and Prospero emerges, not as the subject of an authentic moral action, the authenticity of which is to be grasped in its autonomy from any conventional place for speaking, but as a corporeality (re)fashioned by reciting a book. Montaigne's proverbial admonition to virtue rather than vengeance, heard in Florio's translation of "Of Cruelty" and resonating in Prospero's response to Ariel's call that he "become tender" (*F* 16), provided the framework within which Jacobean auditors might have heard Prospero's climactic Ovidian oration and evaluated his subsequent pledge to renounce his art. Reciting, Prospero ponders the value of his attempts to delimit the perlocutionary effects of sound, that force of speech resonating in the space of the other interlocutor and exceeding both the propositional content of my utterance and the conventions on which it draws and which authorize its illocutionary force. The perlocutionary field incites in the other interlocutor a responsiveness that, both by virtue of having already anticipated the illocutionary choices I will have made and by differing in her responsiveness from my purposes in making those choices, will make a claim on my own futurity, will require future speech of me. His illocutionary place as Duke having been usurped by his brother, Prospero has purposed to regain that place through a (theatrical or compensatory, compassionating) mastery of perlocutionary effects: "Some heauenly Muſicke . . . / To worke mine end vpon their Sences, that / This Ayrie-charme is for"; and "A ſolemne Ayre, and the beſt comforter / To an vnſetled fancie, Cure thy braines / (Now vſeleſ) boile within thy skull : " (*F* 16). But this is a control that one can neither have nor abjure; your perlocutionary response may be like or unlike, in unpredictable fashion, my illocutionary purpose. Here is Prospero, drawing Antonio's ear and receiving no response:

> For you (moſt wicked Sir) whom to call brother
> Would euen infect my mouth, I do forgiue
> Thy rankeſt fault ; all of them : and require
> My Dukedome of thee, which, perforce I know
> Thou muſt reſtore. (*F* 17)

In the space marked by Prospero's vesting, as "you," and divesting, as "thou," of his brother, silence registers the resistance and inscrutableness of the other. Thus the famous cruxes of the end of the play: Does Prospero's act of reconciliation conceal an actual expansion of his territorial powers? Does Antonio, who says nothing, consent to the notion of forgiveness (5.1.134, 195)? Can Caliban, who does consent to "seek for grace," in fact do so (5.1.295, 203)?

From its emergence at the end of the rhetorical voice, print writing (and we only have access to the Shakespearean *Tempest* as a printed text) already propelled verbal language into an asynchronicity of sender and receiver, of the "I" and the "you," that rendered the deictic conditions of moral personhood, and consequently the situations of friendship through which moral personhood could emerge, undecidable. Prospero's renunciation of elocution (if he has in fact done so) propels him into the historical temporality of print writing. Print proliferates the agency of spatialization that the common places of oral eloquence had at least partially circumscribed. Despite the mobilization and idealization of deixis as the enabling situation of Ciceronian male-male friendship, the likeness of "I" and "you" holds only as the recuperation, as re-placement, of the inevitable (re)spatialization of speaking. On the one hand, as Beneveniste showed, "I" has identity only in relation to a unique situation of speaking, that is, in relation to the concrete citational field that it summons and recites and which constitutes the illocutionary force of its utterances. On the other hand, because "I" cannot predict or contain the perlocutionary effects of "my" speech, the "you" that the citation of "I" brings into existence can never finally be known or identified. This holds "in reverse" as well: Because "I" am "you" for another, the "I" (my "I") that the other brings into existence for me (being a "you" to her) is necessarily unstable, not fully able to give (me) access to the fixed and individual substance it appears to name.[66] Deixis does not so much invest the subjectivity of the speakers marked "I" and "you" as attempt to circumscribe, through a kind of rehearing, or as a return to, the place of speaking. But deixis is always too late, that is to say, it cannot secure the past or present so much as make a demand for its continual restaging in the future. The spiraling of sound, emerging out of another's perlocutionary experience, generates future situations of discursive struggle; any "I" thus loses its place over and against the spiraling of "you," or, to put this differently, is mobilized for future speech acts that it had not predicted in advance, and for which it may not have a given competence.

Considering the problem of adjudicating between the structuralist's account, despairing or ecstatic, of linguistic performativity and the pragmatist's assumption of the normativity of ordinary language, Stanley Cavell has turned to the evidence of emotion in speech, reworking the late-seventeenth- and eighteenth-century acknowledgment of the materiality of speaking and listening bodies as spaces for and consequences of the exercising of the passions and trembling hope that the testimony of the senses would provide confirmation of sociality. Resituating strong feeling as the other of linguistic artifice, Cavell has attended to perlocutionary effects as vehicles of "passionate utterances," those domains of speaking "in which one person claims standing and singles out another for a response."[67] I have cited the asymmetry opened up by the gap between Prospero's illocutions and the unknowability of perlocutionary consequences, between Hamlet's drawing Horatio aside and Horatio's temerity in entering into that space, in order to attend to Cavell's proposal that passionate utterances may open an interpretative and ethical space in which the passions or inward movements of the souls of both speaker and addressee are at least potentially decipherable—a pragmatic investment of value in the belief that feeling can remark an ethical distance from the illocutionary conventions governing speech and thereby open an aural space of authenticity, as if Prospero, in drawing Antonio aside, or Hamlet, taking Horatio into his favor, had not in fact drawn them into a common place.

Noting that "while [J. L.] Austin [in his *How to Do Things with Words*] kept coming upon questions of passion . . . in speech, he invariably, quite consciously, turned away from pursuing those questions," Cavell has observed that Austin as a consequence failed to develop a list of perlocutionary verbs to parallel the list he provided of illocutionary verbs (say, a perlocutionary "alarming" parallel to an illocutionary "warning").[68] Cavell has proceeded to call attention to the difference of the perlocutionary field of speech effects: "To say 'I promise' [an illocutionary act] is (under accepted [that is, conventional] circumstances) to promise. Perlocutionary effects are not thus named: By saying 'I convince (or seduce, or astonish) you' I do not convince or seduce or astonish you. . . . Austin notices . . . that one cannot say (it is not English to say) 'I convince you,' just like that."[69] Recalling that the performative utterance (aligned by Cavell with the illocutionary) brings the "I" "essentially into the picture," while the passionate utterance (aligned with the perlocutionary) brings the "you" "essentially into the picture," Cavell has reminded us that the "I" instated by the illocutionary act is conventional.[70] By contrast, the perlocutionary ("you") is precisely not backed by any convention, that is to say, the field of perlocutionary forces and effects inhabited by you and filling out the empty deictic marker "you" are neither predicted nor delimited by the conventional procedures drawn on in the act of speaking. The perlocutionary (Cavell's "passionate utterance") will be precisely that field of responsiveness, to my speech-claim singling you out as the object of my passion, that is not fully predicted or governable by the conventional procedures in which I have grounded my speaking. For Cavell, the perlocutionary offers the possibility of a new sort of claim to life, one that does not yet have a conventional procedure for its articulation.[71] As Cavell has summarized it, "A performative utterance [that is, an illocutionary act] is an offer to participate in the order of law. A passionate utterance is an invitation to improvisation in the disorders of desire. . . ."[72]

Pushing Cavell's point, I would reject the analytical equation of the performative with the illocutionary, which narrows the performative to the isolable and testable, concerning itself with the question of how conventional procedures operate. This does not capture the complexity of social performance. The field of the performative, constituted in the mutual anticipation and responsiveness of interlocutors, is the recursivity of illocutionary acts and perlocutionary effects. Enfolding the pastness of the convention, the opportuning of the here-and-now, and the anticipation of future iterations and responses, this re-cycling of the illocutionary and perlocutionary constitutes the "flesh" of the voice, a flesh, it necessarily follows, not simply coeval with a body-space construed as the isolable origin, co-ordinate, or articulator of speech-acts.[73] Playing on Cavell, and emphasizing that the fraught togetherness of speaking—the making common of "communication," the talking alternately and together of "dialogue"—is always a rehearing, I might call the sound of men in love, always already residual and recuperative, "compassionating utterances." Given the asymmetry of the illocution and the perlocution, across the recursivity of speaking, the utterance consequently being irreducible to any bounded unit of speech, we might attend to the perlocutionary as that dynamism of the utterance that entails the respatialization or re-moving of already existing places for speaking. It is thus not so much not backed by any conventional (or rational) procedure as mobilizing against (if also invariably by means of) those procedures a heterogeneity and an irrationality that surrogates itself on the conventionality of the utterance, a heterogeneity and irrationality that, unpredicted by the conventional procedure, elicits the futurity of our speaking. The perlocutionary is not the consequence or expression of my being moved to speak (for "I" am not yet *there* prior to deixis) but the cause of my being *so moved*; that is, the "you" brought into being by an utterance must be moved to become the "I" of a future utterance, either giving or withholding speech or gesture.

This might suggest we have been asking the wrong question about the (linguistic) inwardness of the subject, about the relation of the subject to (or, in) language. Why, if we are seeking, say, Hamlet's inwardness, do we listen for it in his soliloquies (no less full of commonplaces) and look for it in his apartness rather than hear it in his intimacies, in the kinds of demands others make on him and which he, anticipating and responding to, must hear resounding within and as the space and time of his embodiment? Might we hear Hamlet's passionate, and passionating, utterances, not as his unpacking his heart with words like a very drab but as his compassionating of the present and future possibilities of his embodiment vis-à-vis another, say, Horatio?

Samuel Johnson would criticize Shakespeare's pleasure in the materiality of his language; in Johnson's often rehearsed words from the 1765 preface to his edition of Shakespeare,

> A quibble is to Shakespeare, what luminous vapours are to the traveller [sic]; he follows it at all adventures, it is sure to lead him out of his way, and sure to engulf him in the mire. It has some malignant power over his mind, and its fascinations are irresistible. . . . A quibble, poor and barren as it is, gave him such delight, that he was content to purchase it by the sacrifice of reason, propriety and truth. A quibble was to him the fatal Cleopatra for which he lost the world, and was content to lose it.[74]

Rhetorical pleasure had effeminated Shakespeare just as Cleopatra had effeminated Anthony. The contagion of rhetorical bodies: Shakespeare's fatal Cleopatra had been spoken by a boy, reminding us that the pursuit of manliness, because it required the exercise of rhetoric, could falter on the very comeliness of boyish bodies on which it depended for its reproduction. For Johnson, such dwelling with pleasure on one's metaphorical vehicles delayed the realization of their tenor.[75] But to dwell for a moment therein: even as we read Johnson's initial figure for the problem of Shakespeare's rhetorical pleasures, the *ignis fatuus*, a figure chosen to denounce the overuse of figures, we can hear Johnson reciting precisely Ariel's mimetic skill in *The Tempest*, his ability to "flam[e] amazement" and lead the Neapolitans out of their way, out of their senses, and into Prospero's magical circle (*F 3*). An echo of comeliness in the ear of monstrous Johnson, whose own unruly body had been marked by scrofula and made indecorous by convulsive tics, a bear whose barking intonation, ferocity of gesture, and mislocated attempts to destroy rhetorically his interlocutors undid the civility he also exemplified: the Caliban at the center of the English literary and critical traditions (see *Tempest* 4.1.188-89, 183).

Reconstrued as foppish, these residual sounds of men in love have summoned the central critical questions of the *Life*: Why should Johnson have made election of Boswell to write his biography? To what extent should our reading of Johnson be the critical exercise of disarticulating him from his embodiment by Boswell in the *Life*? We would do better to ask why it is that loving Dr. Johnson in the present time of our criticism so incessantly requires his dislocation from the specific situations of deixis through which, one might say, he more or less dictated the *Life* to his intimate friend Boswell.

The comeliness of the Quintilian boy-speaker could be appropriated, if residually, into the mid eighteenth century. Here it is repeated in Guthrie's 1755 translation of Quintilian's *Institutes*, exhorting the student to love his master: "This affectionate disposition is of infinite service to study; it makes students willing to hear, ready to believe, and ambitious to imitate their masters [just as Boswell would claim to be able "to recollect and record [Johnson's] conversation with its genuine vigour and vivacity" (*Life* 297)]; and to meet together with joy and chearfulness [sic] in the school of learning. When checked they will not be affronted, when commended they will be pleased, and each will vie with the other, who shall be the most dear to the master" (1:95-96). Boswell presented himself in the *Life* as deploying all his charms to entice Johnson to speech: "I introduced Aristotle's doctrine in his *Art of Poetry*, of '. . . the purging of the passions,' as the purpose of tragedy. 'But how are the passions to be purged by terrour and pity?' (said I, with an assumed air of ignorance, to incite him to talk, for which it was often necessary to employ some address)" (*Life* 744). What is often taken to be Boswell's foppishness here—putting himself at the origin or incitement of the Johnsonian voice, reintroducing theatricality and orality into the virtual public sphere of Johnson's printed writings—is rather his ostension of the commonplace, thus, the invitation to enter into the shared or common place and sociality which holds in check the ever present potential for desubjectification, the fall back into the monstrous or lunatic and outside the circle of intimacy. In turn, Johnson's willingness to initiate the young Boswell into manhood unfolded as a series of epistolary and conversational exchanges, all calculated to elicit Boswell's own scribal desire. Two years later, Boswell sent Johnson the *Thesis in Civil Law*, written in Latin and dedicated to his patron Lord Mountstuart, that he had published following his admission as an advocate at the Scottish bar. Johnson wrote back that he would punish Boswell for dedicating the thesis to a patron that he (Boswell) did not like as a man—that is, a man with whom he could be on reciprocal, or friendly, terms rather than in a situation of dependency and obligatory flattery: a failure to align eloquence and virtue—by correcting his Latin cases and numbers, after the fact of publication. Boswell's refutation of Johnson defended his Latin usage at length and cited the required classical authorities. Published in full in the *Life of Johnson*, the scene is one of those easily targeted as an instance of Boswellian foppery (*Life* 366-71).[76]

Reading the passage as a compassionating utterance, I would point out that Boswell both occluded the humiliating and disputed dedication and restored it sufficiently in his Latin grammar examples to republicize, through an ostentatious erasure, the absent origin of print textual exchange between men: literary patronage as the residual circulation of the sound of men in love within the modernity of print itself. As the locus of his desire for proximity to Johnson's body, the Latin grammar dispute deployed the economy of classical pederastic exchanges between men as an absent origin for modern male homosocial relations—the battle of the ancients and moderns played out as a debate, under erasure, over the morality of men's desire for proximity to the patron's body. The sound of men in love remains the tropical field that every act of male homosocial textual exchange must rewrite and, in the act of rewriting or writing over, (re)cover.

To what extent has literary criticism since Boswell's encounter with Johnson, and Johnson's with Shakespeare, entailed such a forgetting of the sound of men in love as the rhetorical place for the exercising of men's freedom? The subject at the end of the rhetorical voice lacks pleasure (these locutions insist), because he has rationalized his orality and because he has replaced *copia* (the amplification of places recited—or better, revisited) with the stance, vis-à-vis his speaking, that he has divested himself of, placement. If Prospero's act of abjuration has propelled us as readers into the historical time of print writing, understood as the confrontation with radical difference or discontinuity, it has simultaneously opened up a new enunciative field, one that can no longer have the sound of men in love as its legitimating condition and which overcodes the loss of that sound as the signifier of a new, as yet unrealized, futurity. "I shall miss thee, / But yet thou shalt have freedom":

Pleafe you draw neere.

Notes

1. William Shakespeare, *Mr. William Shakespeares Comedies, Histories, and Tragedies*. Published according to the True Original Copies [First Folio], eds. John Heminge and Henry Condell (London, 1623), 14, 17, Brandeis University, The Robert D. Farber University Archives and Special Collections Department, Waltham, MA, online, Perseus Digital Library, http://www.perseus.tufts.edu/cgibin/ptext?doc=Perseus%3Atext%3A1999.03.0018 (accessed 25 February 2006). Subsequent quotations from the Folio *Tempest* will be cited parenthetically as "*F.*"

2. I am indebted to a helpful online discussion of the second person singular by Andrew Brown, James E. Gill, Christine Jackson-Holzberg, Robert Lapides, Jack Lynch, Malinda Snow, and others, with the subject lines, "Second person singular," "Second person singular, or 'You, You, You'," and "You and Thou," C18-L: Resources for 18th-Century Studies across the Disciplines, http://www.personal.psu.edu/special/C18/c18-l.htm (June 28-30, 2008, July 6, 2008).

3. For the publicness of male-male friendship, see Alan Bray, *The Friend* (Chicago: University of Chicago Press, 2003), esp. 2, 6, 59, 217; and "Homosexuality and the Signs of Male Friendship in Elizabethan England," in *Queering the Renaissance*, ed. Jonathan Goldberg, Series Q (Durham, NC:

Duke University Press, 1994), 42-44; Jonathan Goldberg, *Sodometries: Renaissance Texts, Modern Sexualities* (Stanford, CA: Stanford University Press, 1992), 70-73. Jeffrey Masten has pointed to the "cycle of generative copying, gentlemanly reproduction, and the distinctly non-privatized property of words and identities" evident in male-male textual collaboration and in the exchange of the speaker-poet and patron-gentleman of Shakespeare's sonnets. See his *Textual Intercourse: Collaboration, Authorship, and Sexualities in Renaissance Drama* (Cambridge: Cambridge University Press, 1997), 3.

4. Bray, *The Friend*, passim, quotation from 158.

5. William Shakespeare, *The Tragedy of Hamlet, Prince of Denmark*, in *The Riverside Shakespeare*, eds. G. Blakemore Evans et al (Boston: Houghton Mifflin, 1974), 3.2.62-65, 1162. Subsequent citations will be given parenthetically.

6. Discourses of intimate and disinterested friendship, Bray argued, were fictions, "impossible space[s]" to occupy within the hierarchies and honor codes of early modern England. Bray, *The Friend*, 199-204, quotation from 199. The poetics of impossibility underlies the pervasive sense of loss, absence, and retrospection at stake in the works I examine here.

7. I aim to specify, as a spatialization of transactions among more and less powerfully placed bodies, such important accounts of rhetorical imitation and emulation as A. Bryson, "The Rhetoric of Status: Gesture, Demeanour and the Image of the Gentleman in Sixteenth and Seventeenth-Century England," in *Renaissance Bodies: The Human Figure in English Culture c. 1540-1660*, eds. Lucy Gent and Nigel Llewellyn (London: Reaktion Books, 1990), 136-53; Vernon Guy Dickson, "'Emulation Hath a Thousand Sons': Emulation, Rhetoric, and Social Decorum in Renaissance Drama" (PhD diss., Arizona State University, 2007); and Frank Whigham, "Interpretation at Court: Courtesy and the Performer-Audience Dialectic," *New Literary History* 14, no. 3, Renaissance Literature and Contemporary Theory (Spring 1983): 623-39.

8. Count Baldessare Castiglione, *The Book of the Courtier*, trans. Sir Thomas Hoby, ed. by Virginia Cox Everyman (London: J. M. Dent; and New York: E. P. Dutton, 1928. Reprint Rutland, VT: Charles E. Tuttle, 1994), 4; for the idealization of comeliness as the courtier's vehicle for drawing the prince toward virtue, see Castiglione, *The Book of the Courtier*, 39, 295, 299-300. Subsequent citations will be given parenthetically.

9. Jeffrey Kittay and Wlad Godzich, *The Emergence of Prose: An Essay in Prosaics* (Minneapolis: University of Minnesota Press, 1987), 19, see generally 18-22. Drawing on Emile Benveniste's important demonstration that the meanings of deictic words are specific to the speech situation in which they occur, and which they bring into being, "permit[ting] language to become discourse," Kittay and Godzich have observed that deictic vehicles "refer not to that which the utterance contains" but to "that which surrounds it and contains it" and "on which it depends"; through pointing, "discourse can make reference to its own eventfulness. . . ." See Kittay and Godzich, *Emergence of Prose*, 19, 234n6; Emile Benveniste, *Problems in General Linguistics*, trans. Mary Elizabeth Meek, Miami Linguistic Series 8 (Coral Gables, FL: University of Miami Press, 1971), 218. Giorgio Agamben, on whom Kittay and Godzich have drawn, has aligned deixis, as "the taking place of language," with "being" and has observed that "modern philosophy, from Descartes to Kant to Husserl, has been primarily a reflection on the status of the pronoun I." See Giorgio Agamben, *Language and Death: The Place of Negativity*, trans. Karen E. Pinkus with Michael Hardt, *Theory and History of Literature*, vol. 78 (Minneapolis: University of Minnesota Press, 1991), 26, 23. Agamben has

quoted Benveniste's terms "empty signs" and "full" signs on page 24; Benveniste, *Problems in General Linguistics*, 253.

10. Robert Burton, *The Anatomy of Melancholy*, eds. Thomas C. Faulkner, Nicolas K. Kiessling, and Rhonda L. Blair, 5 vols. (Oxford: Clarendon Press, 1989), 3:89. For Ficino's version, see Marsilio Ficino's *Commentary on Plato's Symposium*, trans. Sears Reynolds Jayne, (Columbia: University of Missouri, 1944), 223-24. This paragraph revisits and expands my earlier discussion of Burton's quotation of Ficino, in Thomas A. King, *The Gendering of Men 1600-1760, Volume 1, The English Phallus* (Madison: University of Wisconsin Press, 2004), 153; see 153-60 for a full discussion.

11. See for example Michèle Cohen, "Manliness, Effeminacy and the French: Gender and the Construction of National Character in Eighteenth-Century England," in *English Masculinities 1660-1800, Women and Men in History*, eds. Tim Hitchcock and Michèle Cohen (London and New York: Longman, 1999), 44-61; Dickson, "Emulation, Rhetoric, and Social Decorum;" Paul Goring, *The Rhetoric of Sensibility in Eighteenth-Century Culture* (Cambridge: Cambridge University Press, 2005); Thomas A. King, "The Subject at the End of the Voice," in *Considering Calamity*, eds. Tracy C. Davis and Linda Ben-Zvi. *Assaph, Section C, Studies in the Theatre* 21 (2007): 73-79; and Adam Potkay, *The Fate of Eloquence in the Age of Hume* (Ithaca, NY and London: Cornell University Press, 1994).

12. Michel de Montaigne and John Florio. *THE ESSAYES Or Morall, Politike and Millitairie Discourses of Lo: Michaell de Montaigne . . . new done into English* (London: Val. Sims for Edward Blount, 1603), 91. I have silently corrected this edition's "agreement of wits" to "agreement of wills"; compare Charles Cotton's nineteenth-century translation, "concordance of desires." For a full discussion see Masten, *Textual Intercourse*, 34-37, 178n17.

13. Masten, *Textual Intercourse*, 35; Montaigne and Florio, *Essayes*, 92, qtd. in Masten, *Textual Intercourse*, 34. For "residual pederasty," the publicizing, display, and corporealization, as pleasure, of relations of superordination and subordination, see King, *Gendering of Men, vol. 1: English Phallus*, esp. 5-6, 25-42, 50-53.

14. *Oxford English Dictionary*, 2nd ed. (Oxford: Clarendon Press, 1989), s.v. "will, n¹"; for the metonymic use of "will" as the male or female genitals, see Shakespeare's sonnets 135, 136, and 143.

15. William Shakespeare, *The Tempest*, ed. Stephen Orgel, Oxford World's Classics (Oxford and New York: Oxford University Press-World's Classics, 1998), 2.2.85-87, p. 147-48. Unless otherwise noted, subsequent references to *The Tempest* are from this edition and will be cited parenthetically.

16. Maurice Hunt, "The Backward Voice of Coriol-anus," in *Shakespeare Studies*, vol. 32 (Madison, NJ: Fairleigh Dickinson University Press 2004), 220-39. Hunt has taken the trope of "forward" (what I am calling "comely") and "backward" (excremental) voices from *The Tempest* but has found the figure throughout the Shakespearean canon.

17. King, "Subject at the End of the Voice," 56-57.

18. Samuel Johnson, "Preface to Abraham Cowley," in *The Lives of the English Poets* (1779)," Samuel Johnson's "Shakespeare" Preface, 1765," The Holloway Pages, Shakespeare Page, http://members.home.net/cjh5801/Shakespeare-johnson-preface.htm (accessed 7 September 2001). Bruce R. Smith has observed, "By Samuel Johnson's time, if not before, the rhetorical model of criticism had become a cerebral construct." See Bruce R. Smith, *The Acoustic World of Early Modern England: Attending to the O-Factor* (Chicago and London: University of Chicago Press, 1999), 24.

19. The following two paragraphs and a subsequent paragraph about Prospero's renunciation speech include material excerpted from King, "Subject at the End of the Voice," 55, 58-60. I am grateful for permission to reprint this material.

20. Shakespeare, *Tempest* 5.1.33-50, p. 189-90; Ovid, *The xv. Bookes of P. Ouidius Naso, entytuled Metamorphosis . . . .*, trans. Arthur Golding (1567), 7:197-209. For parallels with and quotations from Virgil's *Aeneid* and Ovid's *Metamorphoses* in *The Tempest*, see Orgel, "Introduction," in *Tempest*, ed. Orgel, 19-20, 39-42, 53. Russ McDonald has rehearsed the debate over the extent of Shakespeare's familiarity with the available rhetorical treatises in *Shakespeare and the Arts of Language*, Oxford Shakespeare Topics, gen. eds. Peter Holland and Stanley Wells (Oxford: Oxford University Press, 2001), 37; he has likewise summarized the evidence that Shakespeare knew Ovid's Metamorphoses both in Arthur Golding's translation (1567) and in the Latin original; see Russ McDonald, *The Bedford Companion to Shakespeare: An Introduction with Documents*, 2nd ed. (Boston and New York: Bedford-St. Martin's, 2001), 147-49.

21. Walter J. Ong, *Orality and Literacy: The Technologizing of the Word* (London and New York: Routledge, 2002), 109; see also Ong's *The Presence of the Word: Some Prolegomena for Cultural and Religious History, The Terry Lectures* (New Haven, CT and London: Yale University Press, 1967), 79-87; there, Ong describes collections of common places as "oral residue" and traces the impact of print on accelerating the collecting and categorizing of common places.

22. Ong, *Presence of the Word*, 63; Ong, *Orality and Literacy*, 9, 107-10; Smith, *Acoustic World of Early Modern England*, 127-8.

23. Michel de Certeau distinguished between the strategies that interpellate subjects into their proper places and the tactics by which agents make places habitable. Agents spatialize their world through their operations in the place of the other; space is practiced place. See Michel de Certeau, *The Practice of Everyday Life*, trans. Steven Rendall (Berkeley and Los Angeles: University of California Press, 1984), xix, 35-37, 106-7, 117.

24. *Oxford English Dictionary*, 2nd ed., s.v. "cite."

25. Francis Bacon, "Of Simulation and Dissimulation," *in Essays or Counsels Civil and Moral* (1597-1625), rpt. in *Selected Writings of Francis Bacon*, ed. Hugh G. Dick, The Modern Library (New York: Random House, 1955), 19; see also Bacon, "Of Discourse," *Selected Writings*, 87-89.

26. Jürgen Habermas, *The Structural Transformation of the Public Sphere: An Inquiry into a Category of Bourgeois Society*, trans. Thomas Burger with the assistance of Frederick Lawrence (Cambridge, MA: MIT, 1989), 7, 25-27; Neil Saccamano, "The Consolations of Ambivalence: Habermas and the Public Sphere," *MLN* 106, no. 3 (1991): 694-95.

27. James Boswell, *Life of Johnson*, World's Classics, ed. R. W. Chapman, intro. Pat Rogers (Oxford and New York: Oxford University Press, 1980), 183; hereafter cited parenthetically. Goring has called Johnson's *Dictionary of the English Language* "the most ambitious single project of language stabilisation in the eighteenth century"; see Goring, *Rhetoric of Sensibility*, 104; see also King, "Subject at the End of the Voice," 73-80. William C. Dowling has commented on the way the *Life* creates the illusion of an "inner world . . . in which social distinctions dissolve and a new order crystallizes around the figure of Johnson whenever he speaks." See William C. Dowling, *Language and Logos in Boswell's Life of Johnson* (Princeton, NJ: Princeton University Press, 1981), 154.

28. For an analysis of social and aesthetic performances as restored behavior, see Richard Schechner, *Between Theatre and Anthropology* (Philadelphia: University of Pennsylvania Press, 1985), 35-116.

29. Walter J. Ong, "Latin Language Study as a Renaissance Puberty Rite," *Studies in Philology* 56, no. 2 (1959): 103-24; see also Ong, *Presence of the Word*, 250-52. See also Anthony Fletcher, *Gender, Sex, and Subordination in England, 1500-1800* (New Haven, CT: Yale University Press, 1995), 300-5.

30. Johannes Fabian, *Time and the Other: How Anthropology Makes Its Object* (New York: Columbia University Press, 1983), 31-32, see also 146.

31. McDonald, *Shakespeare and the Arts of Language*, 28. For the early modern idealization of the fixity of Latin, see also Ong, *Presence of the Word*, 65, 76-79.

32. See Louise Schleiner, *Tudor and Stuart Women Writers*, Women of Letters Series (Bloomington and Indianapolis: Indiana University Press, 1994), 2. For the association of women, in everyday life and in education, with the vernacular, and the pressure women's education in the vernacular exerted on boy's and men's classical education, see also Ong, *Presence of the Word*, 241, 250-52.

33. For an account of Sir John Cheke's "linguistic purism," see Castiglione, *Courtier*, trans. Hoby, 377n14.

34. For a parallel discussion of Mulcaster, see McDonald, *Shakespeare and the Arts of Language*, 14.

35. Ibid., 11, 13.

36. Fletcher, *Gender, Sex, and Subordination*, 301. As Potkay has reminded us, "technical manuals of tropes and figures . . . continued to be included in school curricula and gentlemen's libraries" in eighteenth-century England, "and thus educated persons still experienced literature in terms of tropes and figures." Potkay, *Fate of Eloquence*, 64.

37. W[illiam]. Guthrie, "The Preface. With Some Account of the Life and Character of Quinctilian [sic]," in *Quinctilian's* [sic] Institutes of Eloquence, 2 vols. (London, 1805), 1:1x; subsequent references to Guthrie's preface will be given parenthetically.

38. Pat Parker, *Literary Fat Ladies: Rhetoric, Gender, Property* (London and New York: Methuen, 1987), 31, see also 14, 22.

39. For a discussion of "the alienation of figures within the analytical art of rhetoric itself," demonstrating the later-eighteenth-century identification of figurative excess with the "low language" of children, the savage other, and the laboring and serving classes, on the one hand, and "the equally untenable ornamentation of an outmoded aristocratic writing," on the other, see Potkay, *Fate of Eloquence*, 20-21, 67-73, 86-98; quotations from 20, 21. Potkay has provided an accessible review of Thomas Sprat's rejection of eloquence and advocacy of a "close, naked, natural way of speaking" in his *History of the Royal Society* (London, 1667); see Potkay, *Fate of Eloquence*, 4, 52-53. See also Potkay's account of John Locke's distrust of "wit and fancy," articulated in his *Essay concerning Human Understanding* (1689); see Potkay, *Fate of Eloquence*, 56-57.

40. For another discussion, see Parker, *Literary Fat Ladies*, 97, 115. Potkay has worked out in depth the party and class interests inherent in Georgian England's identification of eloquence with liberty, virtue, public spirit, and civic passions, particularly among writers in opposition to Robert Walpole; see Potkay, *Fate of Eloquence*, 2-4, 30-40.

41. Parker, *Literary Fat Ladies*, 104. For the normative Renaissance idealization of women's silence and restriction to the household, see Constance Jordan, *Renaissance Feminism: Literary Texts and*

Political Models (Ithaca, NY and London: Cornell University Press, 1990), 41-47, 116-19; see also Suzanne W. Hull, *Chaste, Silent and Obedient: English Books for Women 1475-1640* (San Marino, CA: Huntington Library, 1982).

42. Richard Braithwaite, *The English Gentlewoman* (1631), Tt1ᵛ, quoted in Marguérite Corporaal, "'Thy Speech eloquent, thy wit quick, thy expressions easy': Rhetoric and Gender in Plays by English Renaissance Women," *Renaissance Forum* 6, no. 2 (Winter 2003), http://www.hull.ac.uk/renforum/v6no2/corporaa.htm (accessed 18 February 2008), paragraph 1; Margaret Cavendish, *Youth's Glory and Death's Banquet* (c. 1655), quoted in Corporaal, paragraph 31.

43. Schleiner, *Tudor and Stuart Women Writers*, 1-29; and for the capacity of these groups to resist rigid patriarchal constraints on women's education and publicness, see esp. 4; see also Barbara Kiefer Lewalski, *Writing Women in Jacobean England* (Cambridge, MA: Harvard University Press, 1993), esp. 2, 4, 8.

44. Schleiner, *Tudor and Stuart Women Writers*, 3, see also 22, 29.

45. George Puttenham, [Richard Puttenham], *The Arte of English Poesie* (London, 1589), facsimile ed., The English Experience Series, 342 (Amsterdam: Theatrum Orbis Terrarum, 1971; New York: Da Capo Press, 1971), 132, see also 122, 129, 133-34; subsequent references will be cited parenthetically.

46. Smith has used data on literacy collected by David Cressy and Keith Thomas to suggest that the "oral/literate" mix of early modern England noted by Ong in fact had specific, rank-based contours; in Smith's account, "The 'residual' culture of agrarian labor may have been, by and large, an oral culture. The 'emergent' culture of merchant capitalism may have been, by and large, a literate culture. But the 'dominant' culture of aristocratic rule was, by most historians' accounts, mixed. . . . See Smith, *Acoustic World of Early Modern England*, 25. For education in the grammar schools and universities, see Fletcher, *Gender, Sex, and Subordination*, 297-321.

47. Aphra Behn, *Oroonoko; or, The Royal Slave*, ed. Catherine Gallagher with Simon Stern, Bedford Cultural Edition (Boston and New York: Bedford/St. Martin's, 2000), 74, 69, see also 100.

48. Samuel Richardson, *Clarissa, or, The History of a Young Lady*, ed. Angus Ross, Penguin Classics (London and Harmondsworth: Penguin, 2004), 37, 38, 142; subsequent quotations are from this edition and will be cited parenthetically.

49. Boswell to Grange, 22 February 1763, in Ralph S. Walker, ed. *The Correspondence of James Boswell and John Johnston of Grange*, The Yale Editions of the Private Papers of James Boswell, Research Edition, Boswell's Correspondence, vol. 1, gen. ed. Frederick W. Hilles (New York: McGraw-Hill, 1966), 49. My discussion here is partially quoted from Thomas A. King, *The Gendering of Men 1600-1760, Volume 2, Queer Articulations* (Madison: University of Wisconsin Press, 2008), 328.

50. Potkay: "The lectures delivered and published by the elocutionists were addressed largely to a rising class of small tradesmen, many of whom were not born in England and all of whom wished to become reputable members of the metropolitan language community." *Fate of Eloquence*, 95. See also Goring, *Rhetoric of Sensibility*, 11, 28, 60-70, 91-102.

51. James Boswell, *Boswell's Journal of a Tour to the Hebrides with Samuel Johnson, LL.D., 1773*, eds. Frederick A. Pottle and Charles H. Bennett, The Yale Edition of the Private Papers of James Boswell, new ed. (New York: McGraw-Hill, 1961), 231.

52. The timespaces of speaking can and should be multiplied, of course, to include, for example, legal, parliamentary, religious, and economic speech. There are as many timespaces of speaking as there are speech genres (and vice versa), and as many speaking subjects. My aim here is not to exhaust the times and places (the occasions) of speaking, or enumerate all the commonplaces of such speaking, but to suggest, through these few examples, that there is no single, generalizable, and necessary relationship of the subject and language.

53. See above, note 46.

54. Compare Puttenham's parallel praise of a comely and ornamental style, able to "delight and allure as well the mynde as the eare of the hearers" (114). Masten has unpacked at length the uses of "sweetness" in the Renaissance; see Jeffrey Masten, "Toward a Queer Address: The Taste of Letters and Early Modern Male Friendship," *GLQ* 10, no. 3 (2004): 367-84. See also my discussion in King, "The Canting Queen," chap. 3 of *Queer Articulations*.

55. Kittay and Godzich have assigned this capacity of a text to enfold deixis and other enunciative-scriptural functions within itself specifically to (fully developed) prose, and to the other genres after the full development of prose, rather than to the rationalization and expansion of print, as I do here. See Kittay and Godzich, *Emergence of Prose*, xviii-ix, 17, 55-56, 63-66, 109-11, 126, 198, 206-9. Kittay and Godzich have associated the abstraction of linguistic agency in and by prose narrative with the modern state; already in the early modern period, rhetoric, as in Machiavelli, facilitated the "reassignment of place" from "feudally determined [hierarchical] position[s]" to "a state form of organization" (Kittay and Godzich, *Emergence of Prose*, 207).

56. For the impact of Locke and Kant, see Bray, *The Friend*, 209-13, 258-59, 287, 304. For modern science as a transformation of aurality to visuality in the production of knowledge, and the quotations given here, see Ong, *Presence of the Word*, 219, 241-42. For "[t]he commitment of the commercial world to neutrally verbalized fact" utilizing the vernacular and its impact on "the Latin polemic tradition," see Ong, *Presence of the Word*, 242-49, quotations from 245.

57. Mark Robson, "Looking with Ears, Hearing with Eyes: Shakespeare and the Ear of the Early Modern," *Early Modern Literary Studies* 7, no. 1, Special Issue 8 (2001), at http://extra.shu.ac.uk/emls/07-1/robsears.htm (accessed October 4, 2012).

58. Potkay is noticing much the same thing, I suspect, when he opposes the polite heterosociality of eighteenth-century conversation, as advocated by Joseph Addison in the Spectator or David Hume in the Essays, to the "masculinism and attendant misogyny" of ancient eloquence: "The culture of eloquence, with its insistent force and rapture, its assertiveness and indeed its invasiveness, is a male culture, homosocial if not homosexual in nature." But the capacity to oppose heterosocial conversation to "homosocial if not homosexual" eloquence turns, as I have argued, on the overwriting of residual pederasty by the gendering of men and women and, in particular, by the appropriation and relocation of courtly heterosociality for the heteroerotic private and civic spaces of the polite classes. See Potkay, *Fate of Eloquence*, 74-86, quotations from 75; King, "Embodying Mr. Spectator," chap. 6 of *Gendering of Men*, vol. 1: *English Phallus*, 201-27.

59. [Anonymous,] *A Pastoral Dialogue concerning Friendship and Love. Occasion'd by the Death of the Honourable F. T.*, in [anonymous], Cicero's *Lælius*, 13; subsequent quotations from the "Pastoral Dialogue" will be cited parenthetically.

60. For surveys of this conventional debate, see Will Fisher, "Debates about Boys versus Women as Erotic Objects," paper given at the annual meeting of the Renaissance Society of America, Miami, FL: March 22, 2007; and Smith, *Homosexual Desire in Shakespeare's England*, 94-99.

61. For an analysis of the "molly," see chap. 2 of King, *Queer Articulations*.

62. Lynne Magnusson, "Interpreting Women's Sentences," paper given at the annual meeting of the Renaissance Society of America, Miami, FL: March 23, 2007.

63. John Dryden and William Davenant, *The Tempest; Or, The Enchanted Island* (1670), in *Shakespeare Adaptations*, ed. Montague Summers (New York: Benjamin Blom, 1966), act 1, 22; act 3, 48; subsequent references will be given parenthetically.

64. *Oxford English Dictionary Online* (June 2011), s.v. "butt, n.2," "butt, n.3," "butt, n.4"; *Oxford English Dictionary*, 2nd ed. (Oxford: Clarendon Press, 1989), online edition June 2011, s.v. "buttock, n.," http://www.oed.com.resources.library.brandeis.edu/view/Entry/25436 (accessed September 5, 2011). For the Shakespearean use of "butt" in the sense of "rump," and "buttock" as "whore," with the suggestion that "buttock" might have designated either a female- or male-bodied whore, see Gordon Williams, *Shakespeare's Sexual Language: A Glossary* (London: Continuum International Publishing, 2006), 60, online http://site.ebrary.com/lib/brandeis/Doc?id=10224687&ppg=69 (accessed July 29, 2011).

   George Etherege, "The Man of Mode; Or, Sir Fopling Flutter," in *The Broadview Anthology of Restoration & Early Eighteenth-Century Drama*, ed. J. Douglas Canfield, Broadview Anthologies of English Literature (Peterborough, ON and Orchard Park, NY: Broadview Press, 2001), 3.3.238, 559.

65. George T. Wright, *Shakespeare's Metrical Art* (Berkeley and Los Angeles: University of California Press, 1988), 226, 228. See also Kenneth Muir, "Shakespeare and the Metamorphosis of the Pentameter," in *Shakespeare Survey* 50 ("Shakespeare and Language"), ed. Stanley W. Wells (Cambridge: Cambridge University Press, 1997; reprint 2002), 150.

66. Kittay and Godzich, *Emergence of Prose*, 20.

67. Stanley Cavell, "The Incessant and the Absence of the Political," in *The Claim to Community: Essays on Stanley Cavell and Political Philosophy*, ed. Andrew Norris (Stanford, CA: Stanford University Press, 2006), 273.

68. Ibid., 270, 271.

69. Ibid., 271.

70. Ibid. Considering elsewhere Shoshana Felman's account of illocutionary force as the "excess of utterance over the statement it makes," an excess which is at the same time an "energizing residue," Stanley Cavell has called attention to J. L. Austin's distinction between the illocutionary act ("what is done in saying something") as an act which brings an "I" into being and the perlocutionary act ("what is done by saying something") as an act which brings a "you" into being. See Shoshana Felman, *The Scandal of the Speaking Body: Don Juan with J. L. Austin, or Seduction in Two Languages*, trans. Catherine Porter (Stanford, CA: Stanford University Press, 2003), 52; Stanley Cavell, foreword, in Felman, *Scandal of the Speaking Body*, xix-xx; see also Stanley Cavell, *Philosophy the Day after Tomorrow* (Cambridge, MA: Belknap Press of Harvard University Press, 2005), 169-81; J. L. Austin, *How to Do Things with Words*, ed. J. O. Urmson and Marina Sbisà, 2nd ed. (Cambridge,

MA: Harvard University Press, 1975), 61, 98-132. As Judith Butler has developed the point, if in the illocutionary act an utterance immediately does something, it does so on the basis of its conventional ("ritual") syntactical formulation, a conventionality secured (made felicitous) by what Austin called the "total speech situation," which as Butler has pointed out precisely locates the utterance in a temporality that is difficult to delimit. See Judith Butler, *Excitable Speech: A Politics of the Performative* (New York and London: Routledge, 1997), 2-4, 24-28; Austin, *How to Do Things*, 14-15, 18-19, 52, 148. The felicity of the illocutionary act, it follows, depends on securing the conventional authority of the speaker rather than on the quality, nature, or response of the addressee. A perlocutionary act by contrast is evaluated in terms of its consequences on another, the "you" that is brought into existence and who, as Cavell has pointed out, is the only one who can say precisely what those consequences have been.

71. Cavell, "The Incessance", 271-73. For Cavell, in the perlocutionary act (unlike the illocutionary act), "I am not invoking a [conventional] procedure but inviting an exchange"; see Cavell, *Philosophy the Day after Tomorrow*, 176.

72. Cavell, "The Incessance", 272, drawing on "Something out of the Ordinary," 30-31.

73. Mladen Dolar has called this "the object voice," an effect that has "emancipate[d] itself from its mechanical [or, here, physiological] origin, and start[ed] functioning as a surplus . .; as if there were an effect without a proper cause, an effect surpassing its explicable cause." See Dolar's *A Voice and Nothing More, Short Circuits* (Cambridge, MA: MIT Press, 2006), 8. The irrationalism of any utterance includes the trace, in my own speech, of the emotive/expressive activity of prior speakers, as well as the preparation for and opening up of the emergence, in my own speech, for another's emotional/expressive activity, what Jean-Luc Nancy has called "resonance." See Jean-Luc Nancy, *Listening*, trans. Charlotte Mandell (New York: Fordham University Press, 2007).

74. Samuel Johnson, "Preface," 1765." For a discussion, see McDonald, *Arts of Language*, 141.

75. McDonald, *Arts of Language*, 52.

76. Here is one such claim about Boswell's foppish investment in the Johnson he had constructed in the *Life*: "In making his portrait of Johnson, and playing himself off against this man invested with all Boswell's ideals, the biographer is trying to articulate himself, to make meaningful a life too often given to fictionalising and role-playing." See Greg Clingham, *James Boswell: The Life of Johnson*, Landmarks of World Literature Series (Cambridge: Cambridge University Press, 1992), 78. I will take occasion here only to note Bruce Redford's counter-argument: "Such pejorative views originate in Boswell's inability or unwillingness to do justice to his own designs. . . . [T]he biographer leads readers to devalue his achievement by attributing it to industry rather than art." See Bruce Redford, *Designing the* Life of Johnson, *The Lyell Lectures, 2001-2* (Oxford and New York: Oxford University Press, 2002), 115. For a fully developed critique of the notion of Boswell "as a mediating presence or consciousness" in the *Life*, one that attends instead to that in the biography which "refuses to be contained by Boswell's perspective," see Dowling, *Language and Logos*, esp. xi-xv, 26-34, quotations from 26, 32. Dowling has argued that readers should "view the world of Boswell's consciousness not as something identical with or containing the world of the *Life*, but as a limited world of discourse which now shrinks or dwindles to become only one among a plurality of worlds contained in the Life" (Dowling, *Language and Logos*, xiv-xv, see also 156).

I BEGIN WITH A STRIKING example of queer taxonomy, which appears in the introduction to an early nineteenth-century reprint of *A Narrative of the Life of Mrs. Charlotte Charke* (1755), that celebrated account of a cross-dressed life. The anonymous author of the introduction, which comes from the late 1820s, classifies Charke's autobiographical text as

> curious, as descriptive of the career of one of those reckless and anoma-
> lous individuals whose existence forms part of the romance of *real* life,
> which is often more wildly eccentric than that of the imagination. . . .
> [The] extreme singularity of [her] pursuits and tendencies render her a
> study to all those who take a pleasure in accounting for the *lusus naturae*
> of the moral world. In regard to these mental deviations, the critical
> anatomist is assisted by nearly the same sort of examination as his surgi-
> cal counterpart . . . and the acquirement of an extraordinary *subject* for
> dissection is equally valuable to both. Charlotte Charke was a something
> of this kind, and if no otherwise instructive, her Life will serve to shew
> what very strange creatures may exist, and the endless diversity of habits,
> tastes and inclinations which may spring up spontaneously, like weeds,
> in the hot-bed of corrupt civilization.[1]

The terms in which Charke and her *Narrative* are described here seem all too familiar: curious, reckless, anomalous, eccentric, singular, deviant, strange, diverse.
Individually, they might cover a multitude of sins; combined, they point to one,
which cannot be named—"a something of this kind". Charke's extreme singularity
marks her out as one of "the *lusus naturae* of the moral world", i.e. as a freak of

nature. As such, she is offered up as "an extraordinary subject for dissection" by "the critical anatomist", to be pinned down and taken apart.

In the late 1820s and early 1830s, however, dissecting the extraordinary cross-dressed subject was not just a rather lurid metaphor. This essay examines two cases of literal dissection, and the various ways in which the "extraordinary *subject[s]*" in question were represented. One was a woman who lived as James Allen, a manual labourer; the other, a man who lived as Eliza or Lavinia Edwards, variously employed as a tragedy actress, kept woman and part-time prostitute with numerous wealthy male clients. Both seem to have maintained their cross-sex disguise and identity against considerable odds: James Allen was married for twenty-one years to a woman who claimed she never knew her husband was really a woman, and Eliza or Lavinia Edwards lived at close quarters with a young woman, Maria, who said she was Edwards's sister and had no idea her supposed sister was really a man. In each case, despite an earlier medical examination, the cross-dresser's true sex seems to have been discovered only after death (Allen died following an industrial accident, Edwards from an inflammation of the lungs). Both cases attracted curious, hostile and sometimes disorderly crowds; the survivors of each relationship were implicated in the gender trouble created by cross-dressing; and there was extensive coverage of both cases in the newspapers and in other publications.[2]

The issue of dissection was one of pressing importance in the late 1820s and early 1830s, as Ruth Richardson's magisterial study, *Death, Dissection and the Destitute* (1987) shows.[3] James Allen died in 1829, Eliza/Lavinia Edwards in 1833, and the 1832 Anatomy Act lies like a faultline between the two cases. Before the Act, the only bodies legally available for medical and educational purposes were those of condemned and executed criminals, but the expansion of medical schools and changes in the law on capital offences meant that demand for cadavers increasingly outstripped supply. Public outcry had followed the revelations of the illegal trade in corpses carried out by "resurrection-men", who robbed graves to supply the medical schools, and the yet more spectacular murders committed by Burke and Hare in Edinburgh in 1828 and by the men known as the "London Burkers", active in the East End in 1831. The new Anatomy Act (2 and 3 Will. IV.c.75), devised by Jeremy Bentham, insisted on the licensing of anatomists by the Home Secretary and instituted Inspectors of Anatomy. The Act gave licensed anatomists legal access to corpses who were not claimed for burial by their relations, especially if the death took place in a prison or workhouse. Some relations chose to donate the corpse if they couldn't afford to pay for a funeral; burial would then take place at the expense of the anatomy school. As Richardson notes, the prospect of dying in poverty, or particularly in the workhouse, became an even more terrifying one, which persisted well into the twentieth century.[4]

Not surprisingly, questions of dissection featured largely in accounts of both Allen and Edwards. At Allen's funeral in January 1829, *The Times* reported, "a rumour was prevalent in the neighbourhood that several well-known 'resurrection men' were lurking about, in the hope of procuring the corpse of so remarkable a subject for dissection". To defeat this purpose, Allen's body was "deposited in a vault belonging to a private burial-ground" which was "well secured and guarded against the attacks of 'body-snatchers'".[5] In fact, Allen's body had already been dissected, as the 40-page pamphlet *Authentic Narrative of the Extraordinary Career of James Allen, the Female Husband*, revealed, promising (and delivering) details of "the 'Post Mortem' Examination of the Body".[6] Whereas Allen was dissected in an attempt to find some physical cause for her extraordinary imposture, however, the very reason Edwards's sex was discovered was that the corpse had been taken for dissection because nobody came forward to claim it for burial. The routine procedures laid down by the Act were followed: Edwards's body was brought to St. Margaret's Workhouse, duly accompanied by the correct printed form stating that this was a female. There was some debate at the inquest about whether the dissection should still have gone ahead once the discovery of Edwards's sex had been made.[7]

In both cases, reports of the post mortem examination insist on the body's conformity with accepted norms. Allen's body was discovered to be "a female, perfect in all respects";[8] we are told that "her body has been opened, and was found perfect in all its parts".[9] The *Times*'s account of the surgeon's report on Edwards states firmly that "The deceased was a perfect man".[10] These descriptions of sexual perfection contrast with other remarks about sexual and gender non-conformity in both cases: the reported speculation amongst Allen's workmates that their fellow labourer might be a hermaphrodite because of "his" weak voice and lack of facial hair; a report by a neighbour, Jane Daley, that Mrs. Allen said that her husband was "not a proper man", and Mrs. Daley's own description of James Allen as "a worthless, good-for-nothing thing, who was not a quarter of a man".[11] The *Times* says that Mrs. Allen had concluded from her husband's avoidance of sexual contact with her that James Allen must be "an imperfect person".[12] Reports on Edwards's body comment on its "very effeminate appearance; no appearance of a beard beyond that of a boy of 17 . . . The hair of the head was light brown, and upwards of two feet long behind, of a soft glossy texture, and the whole appearance of the countenance was that of a female."[13] Such was the incredulity of the coroner's jury at the sight of the dead man's long hair, the lack of facial hair, and the ears pierced for earrings, that they even questioned whether there could have been any substitution of Edwards's body (a suggestion flatly contradicted by the medical witnesses).[14]

What it means to describe a cross-dressed corpse as a perfect man or a perfect woman has a very specific meaning, as the pamphlet on Allen makes clear: "As the chief object of this examination was to observe whether there existed any impediment to the functions of nature, the most minute attention was paid to the organs of generation, which was found to be entire and perfect".[15] The only thing missing in Allen's case was the hymen, described in the pamphlet as "certain symbols of purity", an absence which caused some to speculate that "she had been ill-treated at an early period of life".[16] The beauty of Allen's body is remarked upon, exciting "very general admiration" for its "symmetrical proportions", and the description is characterized by superlatives: "As fine a formed woman was presented to their eyes as ever was looked upon"; the skin which had been swathed with bandages to disguise her sex is "of the purest white, intersected with veins of fine blue. The arms, legs, hips, &c. exhibiting the truest female proportions". In contrast to "the general beauty of the person", the record notes "the colour of the face and roughness of the hands, occasioned by the deceased's anti-feminine habits"—i.e., by Allen's life as a manual labourer working outdoors.[17] The repeated emphasis on Allen's hands—"large and the flesh extremely hard, owing to the work she was engaged in for so many years"—echoes oddly Mrs. Allen's reported statement that James Allen "could turn her hand to any thing".[18] It's a commonplace way of saying someone is versatile or multi-talented, a less pompous version of *The Times*'s statement that "deceased was of a most ingenious turn".[19] And yet that word "turn" begins to sound like an almost magical transformation, of which Allen's hand becomes the revealing synecdoche. This female husband narrative doesn't have a dildo in it; there's no hellish contrivance, as in Henry Fielding's account of Mary Hamilton, *The Female Husband* (1746), no rag-stuffed leather cylinder, as in Giovanni Bianchi's account of Catterina Vizzani (1751); instead of the fake phallus, the hand becomes the sign of Allen's masculinity.[20]

Accounts of the post-mortem on Edwards vary considerably in their scope and sexual precision, depending on the contexts in which they appear. Newspaper reports tend to confine themselves to the "perfect man" formulation, whilst medico-legal works may go into much greater detail. The contrast between the two kinds of report bears out H. G. Cocks's arguments about nineteenth-century public discourses on homosexual activity. In *Nameless Offences: Homosexual Desire in the Nineteenth Century*, Cocks suggests that the tension in such discourses between "liberal ideologies of public transparency and a more coercive desire to control obscenity in an age of mass print culture" is resolved in part by "separat[ing] knowledge of same-sex desire into authorised and unauthorised forms".[21] Cocks notes that newspaper reports

> began to develop a formulaic response to the coverage of indecent assaults, involving the liberal use of asterisks, ellipsis and euphemism. Homosexual offences were always referred to as an 'abominable crime', a 'nameless', 'infamous' or 'revolting' offence. The repetition of explicit testimony was avoided by the admission that 'the evidence was, of course, unfit for publication'. However, the accompanying detail and the remaining evidence which was published left little doubt as to what type of crime had been committed.[22]

Although Cocks is dealing with indecent assaults rather than with inquest reports, the "formulaic response" he identifies is also evident in press coverage of the Edwards case. *The Belfast News-Letter* for January 29, 1833, notes "On Thursday the investigation was resumed, when circumstances of an extraordinary character appeared, but totally unfit for publication"; *The Norwich Mercury* for February 2 notes that "Several other witnesses were examined, but their evidence related to circumstances which cannot, with propriety, be detailed"; *The Ipswich Journal* repeated the formula with a vengeance:

> The inquest terminated last night, after an examination of evidence unfit to meet the public eye. The body of the wretch had undergone a previous examination by the surgeons of Guy's Hospital, and proved its sex, and the disgusting habits of the deceased.[23]

Both the pamphlet and some newspaper reports mention the evidence of the chief surgeon who had performed the dissection, Alfred Swaine Taylor, who noted that Edwards's stomach was perfectly healthy (thus silencing speculations that Edwards had been poisoned) but that the liver showed significant signs of damage caused by excessive drinking, and that death had been caused by disease of the lungs. Taylor's autopsy report on Edwards in *The London Medical and Physical Journal* in February 1833, while providing more medical details about Edwards's internal organs, still requires some reading between the lines:

> It was the opinion of those who were present at the examination, that the deceased had been living for nine years in the lowest state of infamy, and

that he had probably assumed and maintained the disguise of a female, in order the more effectually to conceal his nefarious practices.[24]

Taylor's report is reprinted with slight variations in Michael Ryan's *A Manual of Medical Jurisprudence* (1836), which describes "the revolting case of Edwards" as "perhaps, one of the most extraordinary instances of imposture and vice in the annals of crime."[25] Safely contained in the decent obscurity of a specialist textbook, Ryan's account of Taylor's evidence at the inquest is less guarded than Taylor's own:

> Mr. Taylor . . . described to the Jury the organs of generation of the deceased, which he had minutely examined.–The penis was six inches and a quarter long, and the testicles of the usual size:–the rectum was unusually large, and a halfpenny might be dropped into it. There was not the slightest doubt in the minds of the Jury as to the horrible practices of the deceased.[26]

Taylor, who in later years became the foremost British authority on medical jurisprudence, returned several times in his writings over the next four decades to the case of Eliza Edwards. Initially, Edwards is mentioned as a singular case of concealed sex, as distinct from hermaphroditism:

> The features had a somewhat feminine character; the hair was very long, and parted in the centre; the beard had been plucked out, and the remains of this under the chin had been concealed by a peculiar style of dress. It was remarked during life that the voice was hoarse. The breasts were like those of a male, and the male sexual organs were perfectly developed. They had evidently been subjected to great traction, and appeared to have been drawn forward to the lower part of the abdomen. The state of the rectum left no doubt of the abominable practices to which this individual had been addicted.[27]

Taylor writes still more frankly about Edwards's body in the chapter on "Unnatural Offences" in his *Principles and Practices of Medical Jurisprudence* (1873), in which he discusses the chronic effects of sodomy on the passive partner:

> This person was found after death to be a man, although he had passed himself off in dress and habits during life as a woman. On an examination of the body there was strong evidence that he had been for many years addicted to unnatural habits. It was noticed by all present that

the aperture of the anus was much wider and larger than natural. There was a slight protrusion and thickening of the mucous membrane at the margin. The rugae or folds of skin which give the puckered appearance to the anal aperture had quite disappeared, so that this part resembled the labia of the female organs. The lining membrane was thickened at the verge of the anus and was in an ulcerated condition. The male organs had been drawn up and secured by a bandage bound round the lower part of the abdomen.[28]

Here, attention has shifted away from the "perfectly developed" male sexual organs, and from Edwards's imposture, to the physical signs of what this man has in common with others similarly "addicted to unnatural habits."

Yet what could be learned from the evidence of the corpse was only a part of the story. If Edwards's body left no doubt of "the horrible practices of the deceased", it nevertheless left unanswered crucial questions. In both the Allen and Edwards cases, the cross-dresser's true identity and motive for adopting such a disguise in the first place remained a mystery; more worryingly, so did the meaning of his/her most intimate relationships. How was it possible that Maria Edwards had never suspected her "sister" was really a man, or that Abigail Allen had been married to a woman for twenty-one years without realizing it? And what about Eliza/Lavinia's sexual partners, clients, lovers or protectors? Unlike Maria and Abigail, these men were not available for questioning: the casual pick-ups had disappeared back into the anonymity of the London streets, while the two longer-term protectors mentioned at the inquest had apparently left the country. Letters from one infatuated young man, Thomas Grimstead, who had supported Lavinia in a Surrey cottage, were read at the inquest, along with an oddly *Traviata*-ish exchange between the supplicating Lavinia and Thomas's irate father, who threatens to cast his son off forever if he doesn't give Lavinia up. (Thomas, the inquest learned, was now living in Italy, possibly as a result of his father's ultimatum.) Another letter, signed "Frederick", provides an indication of Edwards's cross-dressed prostitution: after an initial encounter with "Miss Edwards" in Jermyn Street (itself a suggestive location), "Frederick" has turned up as arranged to spend a few hours at "her" apartments but found no-one at home; he suggests another rendezvous at the corner of Regent Street and Conduit Street for 9 o'clock that evening.[29] But who or what do Thomas, Frederick and the rest think "Miss Edwards" is? And what possible language can be found in which to speak about these unspeakable relationships?

Though the newspapers could not report details of Edwards's cross-dressed prostitution, several state that both Edwards and Maria were assumed to be "kept women". The *Norwich Mercury* notes that

> This most extraordinary fact was . . . clearly proved– that the deceased had for some time led the life of a woman of the town, and even lived under what is called the protection of gentlemen. Letters from them, addressed to the deceased under the apparent impression that he was a female, were read to the jury. One of these epistles purported to be from a person who had met the deceased in Regent-street, and who was so fascinated by his feminine beauty and address, that he implored a second interview.[30]

This garbled and lightly ironic account of "Frederick"'s letter may be as close as the public press can get to the subject, though it's not clear how far readers are being cued by the mention of "Regent-street". Like Jermyn Street, Regent Street was already notorious for its associations with heterosexual prostitution, and was also a recognized part of London's emerging queer geography, an overlap which made Edwards's cross-dressed prostitution all the more difficult to interpret.[31] The jury's struggles to do so appear most clearly in Michael Ryan's report of *"The suppressed evidence given before the Coroner, but omitted in the daily press"*, and in particular the testimony of Maria Edwards:

> Maria Edwards, the supposed sister of the deceased, stated that her sister always supported her, and behaved to her in the most affectionate manner. Witness never went out in the streets herself, until her poor sister was taken ill, and unable to support herself: her sister would never let her go out. When she was taken ill, about two months ago, witness was compelled to go out and pick up men to support her sister.
>
> Juror.—Did she say any thing to you when you went out?—Oh, yes, sir; she could not bear the idea. It almost broke my poor sister's heart, she was so fond of me.
>
> Juror.—When your sister went out, where did she walk?——At different places—sometimes she walked in the Haymarket, Jermyn-street, and the Quadrant.
>
> Juror.—Did she often bring gentlemen home with her when she went out?—Very frequently.
>
> Juror.—What sort of persons did they appear to be?—Quite gentlemen, sir.

Juror.—When your sister brought a gentleman home, what did you do?—I always walked out of the room, and left them by themselves.

Juror.—How long did they remain together?—Sometimes a long time—perhaps an hour or two.

Juror.—Did you ever hear any noise or disturbance in the room?—did you ever hear any quarrelling?—Never, sir, that I remember.

Juror.—Did the gentlemen give your sister money?—Yes, sir.

Juror.—Did you know the names of any of the gentlemen?—I did not, sir,—only their christian [sic] names.

Juror.—Did any of the gentlemen ever come a second time to visit your sister?—Oh, yes, sir.

Juror.—And on your oath, you positively never knew that the person you call your sister was a man?—Oh dear, no sir!—I had no idea of it.[32]

Maria Edwards's evidence troublingly refuses to distinguish between the meaning of her own street-walking and that of her "sister"; in Maria's narrative, the only difference is the exchange of rôles caused by Edwards's illness, the supporter becoming the supported. The jurors' questions attempt to prise apart the two kinds of prostitution, to deny that apparent interchangeability: surely there must have been something unusual about Edwards's clients; surely there must have been abrupt departures, or scenes and "quarrelling" when Edwards's real sex was discovered; surely at least the men Edwards picked up wouldn't have come back a second time. None of these potentially reassuring assumptions is available, it seems. Either Edwards passed so superlatively as a woman that "she" remained undetected, or else at least some of "her" clients and keepers knew perfectly well what "she" was, even if "her" own sister didn't, or claimed not to.

Whereas in the Edwards case questions of intimate knowledge were diffused over Maria and the various men erotically or sexually associated with Eliza/Lavinia, in the Allen case such questions were concentrated in a solitary figure: the female husband's wife. Unlike Mary Hamilton's wives, however, Abigail as the widow of a female husband found herself with a different burden of proof—the uphill task of explaining how it was that she knew nothing when her husband couldn't be put in the dock, whipped at the cart's tail, or otherwise securely landed with the blame for sex between women. Accounts of the Allens' marriage repeatedly presented it as asexual: James had pleaded a stomach upset on the wedding night, and Abigail herself had been "suddenly and particularly indisposed"—a coded reference to menstruation—so that James's sickness came as a relief to her.[33]

After a short time in which James continued to plead illness, "he" had disappeared
for several months, possibly as a result of panic. On being reunited with Abigail,
James had exhibited "a remarkable aversion to coming into contact with her . . .
during the night", had seemed embarrassed and depressed about it, but would
become angry and even violent if Abigail referred to it.[34] Or so Abigail said; and
she was the only one left to tell the story. Many reports stressed her excellent moral
character and her entire ignorance of the deception, in line with the neighbour
Jane Daley's account of Abigail: " as innocent as my infant granddaughter . . . she
is a woman of ten thousand".[35] As Clayton points out, one reason for insisting on
Abigail's ignorance was that she needed the money from the benefit society James
Allen had subscribed to for funeral expenses, and so had to distance herself from
any notion of fraud or complicity. More unexpectedly, Abigail also had to assert
her own biological femaleness: as if in a bizarre attempt to restore the heterosexual balance, rumours were circulating that Abigail was really a man passing as
a woman, and she was accordingly besieged by crowds of the curious and hostile.
Throwing its weight behind the denial of the rumours, the Times insisted that "her
female friends [had] ascertained beyond all doubt that she and the deceased were
of the same sex."[36]

Abigail's status as woman and victim did not necessarily betoken sexual
innocence, however, as the unauthorized discourse of two contemporary ballads
suggests. For the anonymous ballad-writers, the marriage of two women represented an uproarious comedy of sexual frustration: "To hear about the wedding
night, / You'll laugh till all is blue", promised the more detailed of the two, *The
Female Husband*:

> The parties they were shown to bed,
> The bride sir, thought of that,
> But the bridegroom he was taken ill,
> Made every thing look flat,
> From his bride he turn'd and twisted,
> Then she to herself did say,
> My Husband is a Hermaphrodite,
> A wager I would lay.[37]

The ballad's language of innuendo ("thought of that", "Made every thing look
flat") is in keeping with its irreverent but practical advice to young women,
"Before you wed, your husbands try, / Or else you'll rue the day." In contrast
to any polite notions of female passionlessness, both ballads assume a degree of

sexual knowingness, expectation and appetite on the part of women. "The Female Husband's Nothing at all", subtitled "A celebrated Slang Consarn, as chaunted at various Lush Cribs", begins:

> Ye wives when you marry, of course you expect
> That your husbands with something in front will be deck'd;
> And should he be gifted with what's rather small,
> It's better than if he had nothing at all.

In this ballad, it's the wife rather than the husband who turns away—in disappointment, frustration or disgust—on the wedding night:

> The wife she did turn round her face to the wall,
> For she knew that her husband had—No-thing at all.

Here, however, sexual frustration is not confined to the wife: both women are imagined as longing for a good seeing-to from a properly equipped man:

> Then they laid all the night, and no doubt they both sigh'd,
> For a good strapping drayman their charms to divide;
> 'Twas very provoking it so did befall,
> That one for the other had—Nothing at all.[38]

"Their charms to *divide*" suggests a barely veiled hostility to the notion of the female couple, implicitly presenting these women as inseparables *faute de mieux*.[39] As Oram and Turnbull note, the ballads attempt to defuse through mockery the threat which the female husband poses not only to heterosexuality but also to the nation:

> Now for Twenty years they lived,
>   As man and wife so clever,
> Both eat and drank and slept,
>   And just these things together;
> If Women all could do the same,
>   And keep their virgin knot,
> Why the King and all his subjects,
>   Would quickly go to pot.[40]

In the absence of "a good strapping drayman", the forces of rhetoric and narrative must be marshalled to divide those whom marriage has (wrongly) joined together.

The pamphlet *Narrative*'s recognition of this task appears in its early comment about the importance of pronouns:

> As we have to treat of this singular personage during the period she assumed the character and habits of a man, we shall of course treat of her in that character, and apply the masculine term throughout this memoir, which we deem necessary, not only to render the story as intelligible as possible, but to avoid confounding the two associates together in the detail.[41]

For the *Narrative*, "confounding the two associates" risks not only losing intelligibility but also compromising Abigail, on whose account it is clearly and closely based. The suggestion of guilty knowledge threatened by "associate" must be pushed away by contrasts which separate the inseparables, making Abigail the injured party, victim both of James's deceptions and of "his" jealousy, anger and violence. A depressing feature of the Allen case is the normalizing effect of domestic violence: neighbours, workmates and acquaintances apparently see Allen as a man partly because "he" is abusive to "his" wife, or accuses her of being a spendthrift and a bad manager. Being an ill-tempered or violent husband functions as part of Allen's protective colouring, reinforcing gender difference within the relationship.

The language of violence and injury plays a significant part in the *Narrative*, particularly in relation to the Allens' sex life or lack of it. The legend under the frontispiece portrait of Abigail Allen insists that she "kept the secret of her injuries inviolable to the last"—but these injuries are not the everyday ones of domestic violence. Rather, they are the hidden injuries of the marital bed, and of the absence of consummation:

> But alas, soon was she miserably awakened to the deception practised upon her unsuspecting confidence: she arose from her bed on the following morning as unsullied a virgin as the hour she first laid down on it. . . . [James's "manifest embarrassment", "half smothered sighs" and sorrowful expression on the morning after their reunion] produced in her mind a compassion for him, which subdued all feelings of resentment for the injury which he too manifestly had inflicted upon her. Night after night but confirmed the revolting truth that she was condemned to the unnatural state of wedded widowhood.[42]

Abigail's uncertainty about what to do in "such trying and humiliating circumstances" costs her "many an hour of broken rest. She felt her wrongs, she but too keenly felt her degradation—her inevitable injuries", but suffers in silence rather than expose herself and her husband "to a slandering world".[43] The insistence on manifest and inevitable injuries, hours of broken rest, and the repetitiveness of "Night after night" forces the reader to think about what kind of injury and broken rest would usually characterize the night side of married life for a new bride. This simultaneous hyperawareness of and turning away from the body recalls the "remarkable aversion to coming into contact with [Abigail] which [James Allen] evinced during the night".[44]

Though the *Narrative* insists on Abigail's injuries, it is more reluctant to recognize the possibility of James's; discussing the post-mortem evidence and the absence of the hymen, it notes that "some of the gentlemen present declared their perfect conviction that [Allen] had been ill-treated at an early period of life",[45] which would explain why she had chosen to protect herself from further sexual assault by adopting male disguise. While acknowledging that this might be "the most feasible cause of the origin of the whole mystery", the *Narrative* sounds a note of caution: "Mr. Paul [the surgeon], whose experience and skill is unquestionable, expresses a doubt upon the positiveness of this proof, as innumerable instances are known of its [i.e., the hymen's] non-existence in infants".[46] Medical authority is invoked in order to keep the two injured females from blurring unhelpfully into one; the idea of James as a victim of rape or sexual assault in girlhood offers a non-threatening moral justification for his/her cross-dressed life, but the *Narrative* doesn't want that. Rather, it insists on the unknowable and mysterious nature of Allen's motives, and on what is extraordinary about him/her, as a way of normalizing Abigail:

> what led him in the first instance, so apparently unincumbered in body and mind, to conceal his sex; and, what is far worse, to link to his mysterious conduct another whom we presume could not have been interested, directly or indirectly, in the original cause which could have given rise to conduct so inexplicable? Was it an unconquerable affection for Abigail Allen, although of the same sex, and done to prevent a separation of their fortunes? or was it an act of revenge either to her or to any one likely to win her hand?—No one can tell. [Abigail] herself declares most solemnly that she has not the most remote idea of the original cause or motive by which this mysterious being was actuated.[47]

Despite the *Narrative*'s efforts to normalize her, Abigail constantly risks becoming extraordinary, not only because of the situation in which she finds herself and her failure to recognize that she has married another woman, but also because of her more-than-exemplary patience and silence, "[keeping] the secret of her injuries inviolable to the last . . . proving, incontestably, that a Woman can keep a Secret".[48] In this, of course, she becomes uncomfortably similar to her female husband, whose strength of mind the *Narrative* repeatedly marks as singular.[49] Allen's mind functions as the unknowable in the *Narrative*; even when the secrets of the body are uncovered (the corpse undressed, examined, opened), Allen remains a "mysterious being". There are tensions here between—and within—ideas of surface and depth; it's important for Abigail's story and justification that Allen remain a mystery, because if his/her secret can be known then the expectation is that it should have been, and most of all by Allen's wife. Despite the pamphlet's stated intention to "convey the facts of this singular case in somewhat of an intelligible shape,"[50] James Allen has to remain *un*intelligible. In a Postscript, the *Narrative* repudiates the inaccuracies of a rival account in an unspecified morning newspaper, including the false claim that Allen had borne "a child, now living, and upwards of twenty years of age"; the eminent surgeon Dr. Paul, it insists, "has assured us most positively, that not the slightest proof existed" to support such a belief.[51] Whereas the newspapers seize thankfully on any possible evidence of heterosexual activity in Allen's past, the *Narrative* rejects or belittles it—leaving tantalizingly (and perhaps unintentionally) open the nature of Allen's "unconquerable affection for Abigail Allen, although of the same sex."

Reproduction's normalizing force also figures in the bizarre epilogue to Eliza/Lavinia Edwards's story: some months after Edwards's death, the newspapers reported that Maria, "the supposed sister of Lavinia Edwards, the extraordinary man-monster", had given birth to "a fine female child". Although Maria herself had applied for an affiliation order against George Treherne, the man she said was her child's father, the *Times* reported that "the general impression upon every one is, that the deceased person, called Lavinia Edwards, is the real father."[52] Maria continued to maintain that Treherne, and not Edwards, was the father, and that she had never known Edwards was a man, though she had lived for years with him and they had usually shared a bed. What's particularly striking about the *Times*'s report is its excess: even without Maria's assertion that George Treherne is the father of her child, her known activities as a prostitute surely furnish numerous other possible candidates for paternity without the need to invoke Edwards. The desire to recuperate Edwards's narrative into some kind of heterosexual structure is painfully clear; if Edwards is really a man, then the apparently asexual bed-sharing of sisters must hide a guilty liaison, revealed in Maria's "fine female child". Yet this explanation raises as many questions as it answers. Despite some scepticism at the inquest about the sibling bond ("Juror.—How do you know that the deceased was your sister? Witness.—My mother told me so, and we lived together"[53]), the new family model of Edwards and Maria as sexual partners and co-parents is unavoidably shadowed by incest. In this narrative, excess persistently defeats itself: attempting to normalize Edwards as the father of Maria's child also puts pressure back on the meaning of his cross-dressed prostitution. The economic explanation which could make sense of James Allen's disguise will hardly do here; given the difference in available paid work for men and women, it seems an unnecessarily elaborate and risky way to support oneself and one's mistress.

It could be argued that the glaring disconnection between Edwards's cross-dressed prostitution and the *Times*'s normalizing hypothesis of fornication and bastardy tells us more about our own expectations than it does about anything else. Why, after all, should we expect sexual acts to "join up" into a consistent or coherent sexuality? Yet the language of addiction, or indeed of "horrible *practices*", suggests a nineteenth-century awareness of desires so strong, and habits so ingrained, that they begin to constitute an identity. The reports' sexualizing of Edwards's relation with Maria seems like a substitution necessitated by the absence of Edwards's male partners and clients—the only allowable, imaginable, speakable form of *knowing* sexual congress. To follow through the logic of Edwards's desires and imagine men having sex with Edwards in full knowledge of what he was is too threatening; so the burden of sexual knowledge must be displaced on to Maria. Yet even more than Maria's denial, the evidence of Edwards's body, which can't be spoken about in the public prints, resists this manoeuvre.

The logic of the body informs both these sharply contrasting examples of nineteenth-century cross-sex disguise. In the Allen case, the phallus is conspicuous by its absence, calling into question the nature and meaning of the Allens' apparently asexual marriage. Also largely absent from most accounts is the matter of James Allen's menstruation, though the *Narrative* offers a haunting little scene on the topic:

> his rising early was necessarily regulated by the tide, a material part of his duties being (while engaged in the dockyards) to wash away the mud from the "ship's way," . . . it is supposed that upon these occasions, being generally alone, he destroyed all proof of his feminine character, by consigning it to the deep.[54]

Abigail's menstruation, by contrast, becomes an additional, acceptable reason for the Allens' sexless wedding-night. The rumours that Abigail herself was a man passing as a woman may have aimed to restore heterosexual order by reinstating the phallus, but the idea of a double-drag marriage, like that of Edwards as the father of Maria's child, becomes a self-defeating piece of excess. In the Edwards case, the problem is not the phallus's absence, but its presence in the wrong place: Edwards's own genitals, with their evidence of having been subjected to great traction, and the apparently unmistakable signs of his chronic and frequent anal penetration by other men. Given how unspeakable and horrifying Edwards's "practices" are supposed to be, it's noticeable that everyone seems to understand at once what those signs mean. That paradox may have prompted the "indecent" behaviour of the rowdy medical students who thronged the Edwards inquest, interrupted the proceedings repeatedly, and accused the jurymen of being "a set of humbugs and jackasses".[55] The *Times* doesn't report the medical students' indecent remarks in more detail, but mentioning them at all adds another dimension to the newspapers' discourse on homosexual offences.

> In dealing with such offences, H.G. Cocks argues, the knowledge of the street and of a subculture which occasionally expressed itself through handbills, broadsides and songs was kept at arm's length from legitimate forms of public knowledge and the authorised, official discourse produced by the legal process.[56]

As we've seen, official medico-legal accounts can deal more forthrightly with the Edwards case than the newspapers can—though the rowdy indecency of the medical students suggests that an even franker discourse is being suppressed in both. The difficulty of keeping illegitimate and legitimate forms of knowledge separate is hinted at in the Allen pamphlet's address to the reader:

> It is perhaps necessary, and but fair, to inform you, that this *Narrative* is written by those who merely profess to give a plain, unvarnished, but faithful history of a most extraordinary Character; and to do that in a manner as free from any improper allusion as the subject will possibly admit of.[57]

The self-exculpatory stance here, like the *Narrative*'s declared reluctance to go into detail about the wedding-night,[58] may be a matter of form; Clayton suggests that accounts of the Allen case are frequently voyeuristic and consciously aimed at a predominantly male audience.[59] This is clearly true of the Female Husband ballads, even if what they insist is that there's nothing to see:

> But it happen'd one day, that this female did die,
> And the searchers were sent for, who quickly did spy,
> That instead of a three-square gimblet or awl,
> She'd a-a what-do'ye-call-it,– a nothing at all.[60]

Yet the more decent and legitimate discourses on the Allen case unintentionally create a something in the place of this nothing, whether in the repeated emphasis on Allen's hard and masculine hands, or in the *Narrative*'s metaphors of injury. Repeatedly, in both these cases, explanatory logics produce their own undoing.[61]

For their critical anatomists, dissecting Allen and Edwards aims to resolve the sexual and gender ambiguities created by their cross-dressing. Undressing the cross-dresser is not enough, it seems; you have to get inside his or her body as well, to reveal the underlying truth, and then attempt to penetrate still further into the unknowable space of the mind. Like Charlotte Charke, both Allen and Edwards could be seen as "*lusus naturae* of the moral world", though the moral meaning of the Female Husband and the extraordinary man-monster is clearly very different. Allen's transformation from female to male, understood as an upward progression, can be read through narratives of female and plebeian virtue, as an attempt to protect herself from (further) sexual outrage or to secure herself against the poverty she so clearly dreaded.[62] Edwards's (presumed downward) trajectory from male to female, a transformation which can be accepted as comic if it's staged and contained within figures such as the pantomime dame, becomes threatening if full illusion seems possible, whether the male performer is a tragedy actress, kept woman, or cross-dressed prostitute. In the absence of the phallus, the female husband seems easily containable, dismissible as no real threat to male heterosexual primacy or to gender hierarchy; the physical intimacy between two men poses a far more serious problem.

Yet the presence of the female husband's widow, like the absence of the cross-dressed male prostitute's clients, complicates any simple or straightforward analysis of Allen's or Edwards's behaviour. Critical anatomies of the cross-dresser inevitably raise awkward questions about his/her associates' motives and desires, questions crucially bound up with knowledge. Insisting on the cross-dresser's mysterious, incomprehensible and unknowable nature creates a possible safe space for the normality of those left behind, and indeed for the presumed normality of the society in which the cross-dresser passed for so long apparently undetected. It may be, paradoxically, in the interests of the normal that the contemporary discourses (authorized or unauthorized) on sex, gender and sexuality ultimately fail to account for the irreducibly queer lives of these extraordinary subjects.

Notes

1. Charlotte Charke, "Introduction," in *A Narrative of the Life of Mrs. Charlotte Charke, Youngest Daughter of Colley Cibber, Esq., Written by Herself, in Autobiography: A Collection of the most instructive and amusing Lives ever published, written by the parties themselves. With compendious sequels carrying on the course of events to the death of each writer*, vol. 7 (London: Hunt and Clarke, 1827), italics in original. This small family firm went bankrupt in April 1829 (possibly because they'd over-reached themselves in printing luxurious editions of Byron) and the unsold stock of the Autobiography series was bought up by the rising firm of Whittaker, Treacher and Arnot and reissued with new title pages. I am grateful to William St. Clair for his help in unravelling this piece of publishing history. As this essay suggests, Charke's *Narrative* and the publishers' introduction would have an added significance for readers when the volume was reprinted in 1829.

2. For a detailed account of James Allen, see Susan Clayton, "L'habit ferait-il le mari? L'exemple d'un female husband, James Allen (1787-1829)", *Clio: Histoire, femmes et sociétés*, 10 (1999), online at http://clio.revues.org/254. I'm grateful to Susan Clayton for introducing me to Allen's extraordinary story. Earlier twentieth-century accounts appear in C. J. S. Thompson, *Mysteries of Sex: Women Who Posed as Men and Men Who Impersonated Women* (London: Hutchinson, 1938); and Eric Dingwall, *Some Human Oddities: Studies in the Queer, the Uncanny and the Fanatical* (London: Home and Van Thal, 1947).

3. Ruth Richardson, *Death, Dissection and the Destitute* (London and New York: Routledge and Kegan Paul, 1987).

4. Ibid., xvi.

5. Anonymous,"The Female Husband," *The Times*, January 19, 1829, 6. On attempts to protect graves from body-snatchers, see R. Richardson, *Death, Dissection and the Destitute*, 75-99.

6. *An Authentic Narrative of the Extraordinary Career of James Allen, the Female Husband, who was married for the space of twenty-one years, without her real sex being discovered, even by her wedded associate: containing, also, the particulars of Her Singular Death: and the "Post Mortem" Examination of the Body: with a variety of other interesting and exclusive facts* (London: I.S. Thomas, 1829), title page. Hereafter abbreviated to *Narrative*.

7. "The Extraordinary Investigation," *The Times*, January 25, 1833, 3.

8. "Inquest", *The Times*, January 15, 1829, 3.

9. "The Female Husband", *The Times*, January 17, 1829, 3.

10. "The Extraordinary Investigation", *The Times*, January 25, 1833, 3. See also *The Extraordinary Investigation of the Jury on the body of a man called Eliza or Lavinia Edwards. With his portrait, Sketched as he lay in his Coffin, in St. Margaret's Workhouse* (n.p., January 30, 1833), [2]. This work,

which mostly reprints material from the newspaper accounts of Edwards's case, nevertheless notes on its title page "This pamphlet was intended for Sale; but on deliberation, it was deemed prudent to suppress it, the contents not being thought for general perusal; and only twelve copies were struck off." The British Library has a copy of this pamphlet.

11. "Inquest", *The Times*, Jan. 15, 1829, 3.

12. "The Female Husband", *The Times*, Jan. 17, 1829, 3.

13. "Extraordinary Investigation", *The Times*, Jan. 24, 1833, 5.

14. "Juror.–Has the head of the deceased been separated from the body? Witness.– It has not." ("Extraordinary Investigation", *The Times*, January 25, 1833, 3.)

15. *Narrative*, 37.

16. Ibid.

17. Ibid., 36.

18. "The Female Husband", *The Times*, January 17, 1829, 3.

19. "The Female Husband", *The Times*, January 19, 1829, 6; "The Female Husband", *The Times*, January 17, 1829, 3.

20. On Mary Hamilton, see Terry Castle, "Matters Not Fit to be Mentioned: Fielding's The Female Husband", *English Literary History*, 49, no. 3 (1982): 602-22; and Sally O'Driscol, "The Lesbian and the Passionless Woman: Femininity and Sexuality in Eighteenth-Century England", *The Eighteenth Century: Theory and Interpretation*, 44, nos. 2-3 (Summer-Fall 2003): 103-32. On Catterina Vizzani, see Clorinda Donato, "Public and Private Negotiations of Gender in Eighteenth-Century England and Italy: Lady Mary Wortley Montagu and the Case of Catterina Vizzani", *British Journal for Eighteenth-Century Studies*, 29, no. 2 (June 2006): 168-89. The English translation of Bianchi's work on Vizzani, attributed to John Cleland, is discussed by Emma Donoghue in *Passions Between Women: British Lesbian Culture 1668-1801* (London: Scarlet Press, 1993).

21. H. [Harry] G. Cocks, *Nameless Offences: Homosexual Desire in the Nineteenth Century* (London and New York: I.B. Tauris, 2003), 88.

22. Cocks, *Nameless Offences*, 81-2.

23. *The Ipswich Journal*, Jan. 26, 1833.

24. *The London Medical and Physical Journal*, 69 (February 1833): 168-70.

25. Michael Ryan, *A Manual of Medical Jurisprudence and State Medicine* (London: Sherwood, Gilbert and Piper, 1836), 229. Taylor's report is reprinted on 237-40. Amongst other changes, Ryan gives Edwards's age erroneously as thirty-four rather than as twenty-four.

26. Ryan, *Medical Jurisprudence*, 236.

27. Alfred Swaine Taylor, *Medical Jurisprudence*, ed. with additions by Edward Hartshorne, M.D. 5th American ed. from the 7th and revised London ed. (Philadelphia: Blanchard and Lee, 1861), 498.

28. Taylor, *The Principles and Practices of Medical Jurisprudence*, 2nd ed., vol. 2 (London: Churchill, 1873): 473.

29. The letters are reprinted in the pamphlet *Extraordinary Investigation*, as well as in *The Times*, January 24, 1833, 5.

30. "Extraordinary Inquest", *The Norwich Mercury*, February 2, 1833, 2.

31. On London's queer geography, see Cocks, *Nameless Offences*; Morris B. Kaplan, *Sodom on the Thames: Sex, Love and Scandal in Wilde Times* (Ithaca, NY: Cornell University Press, 2005); Rictor Norton, *Mother Clap's Molly House: The Gay Subculture in England 1700-1830* (London: Gay Men's Press, 1992); Mark W. Turner, *Backward Glances: Cruising the Queer Streets of New York and London* (London: Reaktion, 2003). This nineteenth-century geography is a male one for which there seems to be no contemporary female equivalent.

32. Ryan, *Medical Jurisprudence*, 235-6, italics in original.

33. *Narrative*, 12.

34. Ibid., 16.

35. "Inquest", *The Times*, January 15, 1829, 3. Susan Clayton attributes the remark about Abigail's innocence to a juror at the inquest, but in fact "By a juror" indicates that the witness is responding to a question by a juror.

36. "The Female Husband", *The Times*, January 19, 1829, 6.

37. *The Female Husband*, from Bodleian Catalogue, Johnson Ballads 18; Printed by T. Birt, no. 10, Great St. Andrew-Street, Seven Dials, n.d. Alison Oram and Annmarie Turnbull, eds. *The Lesbian History Sourcebook: Love and Sex Between Women in Britain from 1780 to 1970* (London: Routledge, 2001), 20-22, dates this ballad around 1838. Oram and Turnbull also reprint Michael Ryan's brief account of Allen (Ryan, *Medical Jurisprudence*, 227-9).

38. Anonymous. *The Rummy Cove's Delight; a Pretty Considerable Collection of Queer Staves* (London: Mitford, n.d. ca. 1833), paginated incorrectly as 118-19 (the pamphlet has only 48 pages).

39. On attitudes to inseparable female couples, see Christine Roulston, "Separating the Inseparables: Female Friendship and its Discontents in Eighteenth-Century France", *Eighteenth-Century Studies*, 32, no. 2 (1998-99): 215-31.

40. "The Female Husband", verse 8; Oram and Turnbull, *The Lesbian History Sourcebook*, 20. Susan Clayton, "L'habit ferait-il le mari?" notes the reporting of laughter at the Allen inquest as a form of control through mockery.

41. *Narrative*, 6. Further page references will appear parenthetically in the text.

42. Ibid., 16.

43. Ibid.

44. Ibid.

45. Ibid., 37.

46. Ibid.

47. Ibid., 14-15.

48. Ibid., frontispiece.

49. Ibid., 6, 10, 17, 18.

50. Ibid., "To The Reader."

51. Ibid., 40.

52. *The Times*, June 26, 1833, 6.

53. *The Times*, January 24, 1833, 5.

54. *Narrative*, 34.

55. *The Times*, January 25, 1833, 3.

56. Cocks, *Nameless Offences*, 8.

57. *Narrative*, 3.

58. Ibid., 11.

59. Clayton, "L'habit ferait-il le mari?"

60. *The Rummy Cove's Delight*.

61. On explanatory logics, see Valerie Traub, "The Present Future of Lesbian Historiography," in *A Companion to Lesbian, Gay, Bisexual, Transgender, and Queer Studies*, eds. George E. Haggerty and Molly McGarry (Madlen, MA and Oxford: Blackwell, 2007).

62. On the use of such narratives about cross-dressed women, see Fraser Easton, "Gender's Two Bodies: Women Warriors, Female Husbands and Plebeian Life," *Past & Present* 180, no. 1 (2003):131-74. Both the pamphlet *Narrative* and the newspaper reports stress Allen's dread of poverty and her "saving" disposition in making use of whatever scraps she could find.

Agamben, Giorgio. *Language and Death: The Place of Negativity*. Translated by Karen E. Pinkus with Michael Hardt. *Theory and History of Literature*, vol. 78. Minneapolis: University of Minnesota Press, 1991.

Albertazzi, Adolfo. "Il Romanzo." In *Storie dei generi letterari italiani*. Milano: Vallardi, 1902.

Algarotti, Francesco. *Newtonianismo per le dame*. Bologna, 1737.

An Authentic narrative of the extraordinary career of James Allen, the female husband, who was married for the space of twenty-one years, without her real sex being discovered, even by her wedded associate; containing, also, the particulars of her singular death, and the "post mortem" examination of the body. London: Thomas, 1829.

Andreadis, Harriette. *Sappho in Early Modern England: Female Same-Sex Literary Erotics, 1550-1714*. Chicago: University of Chicago Press, 2001.

Aristotle's master-piece compleated in two parts: the first containing the secrets of generation, in all the parts thereof . . . London: 1697.

Aspinall, Dana E. "The Play and the Critics." In *The Taming of the Shrew: Critical Essays*. Edited by Dana E. Aspinall, 3-38. New York and London: Routledge, 2002.

Austin, J. L. *How to Do Things with Words*. Edited by J. O. Urmson and Marina Sbisà. 2nd ed., Cambridge, MA: Harvard University Press, 1975.

Bach, Rebecca Ann. *Shakespeare and Renaissance Literature Before Heterosexuality*. New York: Palgrave Macmillan, 2007.

Bacon, Francis. *Selected Writings*. Introduction and notes by Hugh G. Dick, vol. 256. New York: Modern Library, 1955.

Baesi, Serena. "Italian Improwisatrici and their Influence on English Romantic Writers: Letizia Elizabeth Landon's Response." In *British Romanticism in Italian Literature: Translating, Reviewing, Rewriting*. Edited by Laura Bandiera and Dieco Saglia, 181-91. Amsterdam and Atlanta: Rodopi, 2005.

Bailey, Amanda. *Flaunting: Style and the Subversive Male Body in Renaissance England*. Toronto, Buffalo, NY, and London: University of Toronto Press, 2007.

Baldwin, Frances Elisabeth. *Sumptuary Legislation and Personal Regulation in England*. Baltimore, MD: Johns Hopkins University Press, 1926.

Barish, Jonas. *The Antitheatrical Prejudice*. Berkeley, Los Angeles and London: University of California Press, 1981.

Barker-Benfield, G. J. *The Culture of Sensibility: Sex and Society in Eighteenth-Century Britain.* Chicago: University of Chicago Press, 1992.

Baudrillard, Jean. *Simulacra and Simulation.* Translated by Sheila Faria Glaser. Ann Arbor: University of Michigan Press, 1994.

Behn, Aphra. *Oroonoko, or, The Royal Slave.* Edited by Catherine Gallagher with Simon Stern. Bedford Cultural Edition. Boston and New York: Bedford/St. Martin's, 2000.

Belsey, Catherine. "Disrupting Sexual Difference: Meaning and Gender in the Comedies." In *Alternative Shakespeares.* Edited by John Drakakis, 170-94. 2nd ed. New York and London: Routledge, 2002.

Benjamin, Walter. *Illuminations.* New York: Schocken, 1955, Reprint 1969.

Benserade, Isaac de. *Iphis et Iante.* 1634. Paris: Lampsaque, 2000.

———. *Poésie.* 1697. Genève: Slatkine Reprint, 1967.

Benveniste, Emile. *Problems in General Linguistics.* Translated by Mary Elizabeth Meek. Miami Linguistic Series 8. Coral Gables, FL: University of Miami Press, 1971.

Bersani, Leo. *Is the Rectum a Grave? And Other Essays.* Chicago: University of Chicago Press, 2010.

Biet, Christian. "A quoi rêvent les jeunes filles? Homosexualité féminine, travestissement et comédie: le cas d'Iphis et Iante d'Isaac de Benserade (1634)." In *La Femme au XVIIe siècle.* Edited by R. Hodgson, 54-81. Tübingen: Gunter Narr Verlag, 2002.

Binhammer, Katherine. "The Sex Panic of the 1790s." *Journal of the History of Sexuality* 6, no. 3 (1996): 409-34.

Bonnet, Marie-Jo. *Les Relations amoureuses entre les femmes du XVIe au XXe siècle.* Paris: Éditions Odile Jacob, 1995.

Bornstein, Kate. *Gender Outlaw.* New York: Routledge, 1994.

Borris, Kenneth, and George Rousseau, eds. *The Sciences of Homosexuality in Early Modern Europe.* New York and London: Routledge, 2008.

Boswell, James. *Life of Johnson, World's Classics.* Edited by R. W. Chapman. Oxford and New York: Oxford University Press, 1980.

———. *Boswell's Journal of a Tour to the Hebrides with Samuel Johnson, LL.D., 1773.* Edited by Frederick A. Pottle and Charles H. Bennett. The Yale Edition of the Private Papers of James Boswell, new edition. New York: McGraw-Hill, 1961.

Bradbrook, M. C. "The Elegant Eccentrics." *Modern Language Review* 44, no. 2 (1949): 184-198.

Brantôme, Messire Pierre de Bourdeille, seigneur de. *Le Dame galanti.* Translated by Alberto Savinio. Milan: Adelphi, 1994.

———. *Les Vies des Dames galantes.* 1666. Edited by Maurice Rat. Paris: Le Livre de Poche, 1962.

Braunmiller, A. R., ed. *Macbeth. By William Shakespeare. The New Cambridge Shakespeare.* 2nd ed. Cambridge: Cambridge University Press, 2008.

Braunschneider, Theresa. "Acting the Lover: Gender and Desire in Narratives of Passing Women." *The Eighteenth Century* 45, no. 3 (2004): 211- 29.

Bray, Alan. *The Friend.* Chicago: University of Chicago Press, 2003.

———. "Homosexuality and the Signs of Male Friendship in Elizabethan England." In *Queering the Renaissance.* Edited by Jonathan Goldberg, 42-44. Durham, NC: Duke University Press, 1994.

———. *Homosexuality in Renaissance England.* London: Gay Men's Press, 1982.

———. *Homosexuality in Renaissance England*. New York: Columbia University Press, 1995.

Bredbeck, Gregory. *Sodomy and Interpretation: Marlowe to Milton*. Ithaca, NY and London: Cornell University Press, 1991.

Breitenberg, Mark. *Anxious Masculinity in Early Modern England*. Cambridge: Cambridge University Press, 1996.

Bristow, Edward J. *Vice and Vigilance: Purity Movements in Britain since 1700*. Totowa, NJ: Rowman and Littlefield, 1977.

Brown, Pamela Allen, and Peter Parolin, eds. *Women Players in England, 1500-1660: Beyond the All-Male Stage*. Aldershot: Ashgate, 2005.

Bryson, A. "The Rhetoric of Status: Gesture, Demeanour and the Image of the Gentleman in Sixteenth and Seventeenth-Century England." In *Renaissance Bodies: The Human Figure in English Culture c. 1540-1660*. Edited by Lucy Gent and Nigel Llewellyn, 136-53. London: Reaktion Books, 1990.

Burton, Robert. *The Anatomy of Melancholy*. Edited by Thomas C. Faulkner, Nicolas K. Kiessling, and Rhonda L. Blair. 5 vols. Oxford: Clarendon Press, 1989.

Butler, Eleonor, and Eva Mary Bell. *The Hamwood Papers of the Ladies of Llangollen and Caroline Hamilton*. Editied by Mrs. G. H. Bell (John Travers). London: Macmillan, 1930.

Butler, Judith. *Excitable Speech: A Politics of the Performative*. New York and London: Routledge, 1997.

———. *Gender Trouble: Feminism and the Subversion of Identity*. New York and London: Routledge, 1990.

———. "Is Kinship Always Already Heterosexual?" *Differences* 13, no. 1 (2002): 14-44.

———. *Precarious Life: The Powers of Mourning and Violence*. London and New York: Verso, 2004.

———. "Sexual Politics, Torture, and Secular Time." *British Journal of Sociology* 59, no. 1 (2008): 1-23.

Caffiero, Marina, and Manola Ida Venzo, eds. *Scritture di donne: la memoria restituita*. atti del Convegno, Roma, 23-24 marzo 2004. Conference Publication. Roma: Viella, 2007.

Califia, Pat. "Identity Sedition and Pornography." In *PoMoSexuals: Challenging Assumptions about Gender and Sexuality*. Edited by Carole Queen and Lawrence Schimel, 87-106. San Francisco: Cleis Press, 1997.

Callaghan, Dympna. *Shakespeare Without Women: Representing Gender and Race on the Renaissance Stage*. New York and London: Routledge, 2000.

Castiglione, Count Baldessare. *The Book of the Courtier*. Translated by Sir Thomas Hoby, Edited by Virginia Cox Everyman. London: J. M. Dent; and New York: E. P. Dutton, 1928. Reprint Rutland, VT: Charles E. Tuttle, 1994.

Castle, Terry. *The Apparitional Lesbian: Female Homosexuality and Modern Culture*. New York: Columbia University Press, 1993.

———. "Matters Not Fit to be Mentioned: Fielding's The Female Husband." *English Literary History* 49, no. 3 (1982): 602-22.

Cavell, Stanley. "The Incessance and the Absence of the Political." In *The Claim to Community: Essays on Stanley Cavell and Political Philosophy*. Edited by Andrew John Norris, 199-226. Stanford, CA: Stanford University Press, 2006.

———. *Philosophy the Day after Tomorrow*. Cambridge, MA: Belknap Press of Harvard University Press, 2005.

Certeau, Michel de. *The Practice of Everyday Life*. Translated by Steven Rendall. Berkeley and Los Angeles: University of California Press, 1984.

Chaney, Joseph. "Turning to Men: Genres of Cross-Dressing in Charke's narrative and Shakespeare's The Merchant of Venice." In *Introducing Charlotte Charke: Actress, Author, Enigma*. Edited by Philip E. Baruth, 200-226. Urbana: University of Illinois Press, 1999.

Charke, Charlotte. *A Narrative of the Life of Mrs. Charlotte Charke*. Gainsville, FL: Scholars' Facsimiles & Reprints, 1969.

———. "Introduction." In *A Narrative of the Life of Mrs. Charlotte Charke, Youngest Daughter of Colley Cibber, Esq., Written by Herself, in Autobiography: A Collection of the most instructive and amusing Lives ever published, written by the parties themselves. With compendious sequels carrying on the course of events to the death of each writer*, Vol. 7. London: Hunt and Clarke, 1827.

Chauncey, George. *Gay New York: Gender, Urban Culture, and the Making of the Gay Male World, 1890-1940*. New York: Basic Books, 1994.

Cheng, Anne Anlin. *The Melancholy of Race: Psychoanalysis, Assimilation, and Hidden Grief*. New York: Oxford University Press, 2001.

Chessex, Pierre. "The Grand Tour." In *Encyclopaedia of the Enlightenment*. Edited by Michel Delon, 622-25. Chicago: Fitzroy Dearborn Publishers, 2001.

Cixous, Hélène. "The Laugh of the Medusa." In *New French Feminisms: An Anthology*. Edited by Elaine Marks and Isabelle de Courtivron, 245-64. New York: Schocken Books, 1981.

Clayton, Susan. "L'habit ferait-il le mari? L'exemple d'un female husband, James Allen (1787-1829)." *Clio: Histoire, femmes et sociétés* CLIO. [En ligne], 10 (1999), mis en ligne le 22 mai 2006. http://clio.revues.org/254, DOI: 10.4000/clio.254 (accessed September 20, 2012).

Cleland, John. *Memoirs of a Woman of Pleasure (1749)*. Edited by Peter Sabor. Oxford: Oxford University Press, 1985.

Clingham, Greg. *James Boswell: The Life of Johnson*. Landmarks of World Literature Series. Cambridge: Cambridge University Press, 1992.

Cloud, Christine. "The Chameleon, Cross-dressed Autobiography of Charlotte Charke." *Women's Studies* 38, no. 8 (2009): 857–71.

Cocks, H. G. [Harry]. *Nameless Offences: Homosexual Desire in the Nineteenth Century*. London and New York: I. B. Tauris, 2003.

Cohen, Michèle. "Manliness, Effeminacy and the French: Gender and the Construction of National Character in Eighteenth-Century England." In *English Masculinities 1660-1800*. Edited by Tim Hitchcock and Michèle Cohen, 44-61. London and New York: Longman, 1999.

Cook, Matt. *London and the Culture of Homosexuality, 1885-1914*. Cambridge and New York: Cambridge University Press, 2003.

Corporaal, Marguérite. "'Thy Speech eloquent, thy wit quick, thy expressions easy': Rhetoric and Gender in Plays by English Renaissance Women," *Renaissance Forum* 6, no. 2 (Winter 2003), http://www.hull.ac.uk/renforum/v6no2/corporaa.htm (accessed February 18, 2008).

Cortellessa, Andrea. "L'Antiquario fanatico e l'ombra di Vitruvio. Sincretismo estetico nelle *Notti romane*." 349n64, http://www.disp.let.uniroma1.it/fileservices/filesDISP/327-364_CORTELLESSA.pdf (accessed September 16, 2012).

Craciun, Adriana. *Fatal Women of Romanticism*. Cambridge and New York: Cambridge University Press, 2003.

Cristall, Ann Batten. *Poetical Sketches (1795), British Poetry 1780-1910: a Hypertext Archive of Scholarly Editions*, Edited by Jerome McGann and David Seaman, Charlottesville: University of Virginia Library, 1995. Electronic Text Center, http://etext.lib.virginia.edu/toc/modeng/public/CriSket.html.

Crivelli, Tatiana Speciale. "Sappho, ou le mythe de l'ancienne Grèce: L'Ecriture Romanesque entre orient et occident, antiquité et lumières." In *Les Lumières europénnes dans leurs relations avec les autres grandes cultures et religions*. Edited by Florence Lotterie and Darrin M. McMahon, 145-64. Paris: Honoré Champion Editeur, 2002.

Cromwell, Jason. "Passing Women and Female-bodied Men: (Re)claiming FTM History." In *Reclaiming Genders: Transsexual Grammars at the Fin de Siecle*, Edited by Kate More and Stephen Whittle, 34-61. New York: Cassell, 1999.

———. *Transmen and FTMs: Identities, Bodies, Genders, and Sexualities*. Urbana: University of Illinois Press, 1999.

Daileader, Celia R. "Back Door Sex: Renaissance Gynosodomy, Aretino, and the Exotic." *ELH* 69, no. 2 (2002): 303-34.

Danna, Bianca. "Saffo, l'"alter ego" al femminile." In *Metamorfosi dei Lumi. Esperienze dell'"io" e creazione letteraria tra Sette e Ottocento*. Edited by Simone Carpentari-Messina and Alessandria: Edizioni dell'Orso, 2000.

Danna, Daniela. *Amiche, Compagne, Amanti: Storia dell'amore tra donne*. Trento: UNI Service, 2003.

Darwin, Charles. *The Life and Letters of Charles Darwin, Including an Autobiographical Chapter*. Edited by Francis Darwin. 3 vols. London: J. Murray, 1887.

de Montaigne, Michel. "On Affectionate Relationships [On Friendship]." In *The Complete Essays*. Translated and edited by M. A. Screech. London: Penguin, 2003.

DeJean, Joan. *Fictions of Sappho, 1546-1937*. Chicago: University of Chicago Press, 1989.

Dekker, Rudolf M., and Lotte C. Van de Pol. *The Tradition of Female Transvestism in Early Modern Europe*. New York: St. Martin's Press, 1989.

Dickson, Vernon Guy. "'Emulation Hath a Thousand Sons': Emulation, Rhetoric, and Social Decorum in Renaissance Drama." PhD diss., Arizona State University, 2007.

Diderot, Denis. *Memoirs of a Nun. 1796*. Translated by Francis Birrell. London: David Campbell, 1992.

DiGangi, Mario. *The Homoerotics of Early Modern Drama*. Cambridge: Cambridge University Press, 1997.

———. "How Queer was the Renaissance?" In *Love, Sex, Intimacy, and Friendship between Men, 1550-1800*. Edited by Katherine O'Donnell and Michael O'Rourke, 128-47. Basingstoke and London: Palgrave, 2003.

Dingwall, Eric John. *Some Human Oddities: Studies in the Queer, the Uncanny and the Fanatical*. London: Home and Van Thal, 1947.

Dinshaw, Carolyn. *Getting Medieval: Sexualities and Communities, Pre- and Postmodern*. Durham, NC: Duke University Press, 1999.

Dinshaw, Carolyn, et al. "Theorizing Queer Temporalities: A Roundtable Discussion." *GLQ* 13, no. 2 (2007): 177-95.

Dixon, Susan M. *Between the Real and the Ideal: The Accademia degli Arcadi and Its Garden in Eighteenth-Century Rome*. Newark, DE: University of Delaware Press, 2006.

Dolan, Frances E. *Marriage and Violence: The Early Modern Legacy.* Philadelphia: University of Pennsylvania Press, 2008.

———, ed. *"The Taming of the Shrew:" Texts and Contexts.* Boston and New York: Bedford/St. Martin's, 1996.

Dolar, Mladen. *A Voice and Nothing More, Short Circuits.* Cambridge, MA: MIT Press, 2006.

Donato, Clorinda. "Public and Private Negotiations of Gender in Eighteenth-Century England and Italy: Lady Mary Wortley Montagu and the Case of Catterina Vizzani", *British Journal for Eighteenth-Century Studies* 29, no. 2 (2006): 169-89.

———. "Fresh Legacies: Giovanni Battista Piranesi's Enduring Style and Grand Tour Appeal." *Eighteenth-Century Studies* 43, no. 4 (2010): 508-11.

Donoghue, Emma. *Passions Between Women: British Lesbian Culture 1668-1801.* London: Scarlet Press, 1993.

Dowling, William C. *Language and Logos in Boswell's Life of Johnson.* Princeton, NJ: Princeton University Press, 1981.

Drouin, Jennifer. "Cross-Dressing, Drag, and Passing: Slippages in Shakespearean Comedy." In *Shakespeare Re-Dressed: Cross-Gender Casting in Contemporary Performance.* Edited by James C. Bulman, 23-56. Madison, NJ: Fairleigh Dickinson University Press, 2008.

Dryden, John. *All For Love.* Edited by David M. Vieth. Lincoln: University of Nebraska Press, 1972.

Dryden, John, and William Davenant. *The Tempest; Or, The Enchanted Island* (1670). In *Shakespeare Adaptations.* Edited by Montague Summers. New York: Benjamin Blom, 1966.

Dugaw, Dianne. *Warrior Women and Popular Balladry, 1650-1850.* New York: Cambridge University Press, 1989.

Dusinberre, Juliet. "The Taming of the Shrew: Women, Acting, and Power." *Studies in the Literary Imagination* 26, no. 1 (1993): 67-84.

Easton, Fraser. "Gender's Two Bodies: Women Warriors, Female Husbands and Plebeian Life." *Past & Present* 180, no. 1 (2003): 131-74.

Edelman, Lee. *Homographesis: Essays in Gay Literary and Cultural Theory.* New York: Routledge, 1994.

———. *No Future: Queer Theory and the Death Drive.* Durham, NC, and London: Duke University Press, 2004.

Edgeworth, Marie. *Belinda.* The Literature Network, http://www.online-literature.com/maria-edgeworth/belinda/19/ (accessed April 26, 2008).

Ekins, Richard, and Dave King, eds. *Blending Genders: Social Aspects of Cross-Dressing and Sex-Changing.* New York: Routledge, 1996.

Epstein, Julia, and Kristina Straub, eds. *Body Guards: The Cultural Politics of Gender Ambiguity.* New York: Routledge, 1991.

Estienne, Henri. *L'Introduction au traité de la conformité des merveilles anciennes avec les modernes ou Traité preparative à l'apologie pour Hèrodote.* Genève, 1566.

Etherege, George. "The Man of Mode; Or, Sir Fopling Flutter." In *The Broadview Anthology of Restoration & Early Eighteenth-Century Drama.* Edited by J. Douglas Canfield, 526-89. Peterborough, ON and Orchard Park, NY: Broadview Press, 2001.

Fabian, Johannes. *Time and the Other: How Anthropology Makes Its Object.* New York: Columbia University Press, 1983.

Faderman, Lillian. *Surpassing the Love of Men: Romantic Friendship and Love between Women from the Renaissance to the Present*. New York: William Morrow, 1981.

———. *Scotch Verdict: Miss Pirie and Miss Woods v. Dame Cumming Gordon*. New York: Columbia University Press, 1993.

Feinberg, Leslie. "Allow Me to Introduce Myself." In *Trans Liberation: Beyond Pink or Blue*, 14-35. Boston: Beacon Press, 1998.

———. *Transgender Warriors: Making History from Joan of Arc to Dennis Rodman*. Boston: Beacon Press, 1996.

Felman, Shoshana. *The Scandal of the Speaking Body: Don Juan with J. L. Austin, or Seduction in Two Languages*. Translated by Catherine Porter. Stanford, CA: Stanford University Press, 2003.

Ficino, Marsilio. *Commentary on Plato's Symposium*. Translated by Sears Reynolds Jayne. Columbia: University of Missouri, 1944.

Fielding, Henry. *The History of Tom Jones*. Edited by R. P. C. Mutter. New York: Penguin, 1989.

Fields, Polly S. "Charlotte Charke and the Liminality of her Bi-Genderings: A Study of Her Canonical Works." In *Pilgrimage for Love: Essays in Early Modern Literature in Honor of Josephine A. Roberts*. Edited by Sigrid King. Medieval & Renaissance Texts and Studies Series, Vol. 213, 221-48. Tempe, AZ: Arizona Center for Medieval and Renaissance Studies, 1999.

Findlen, Paula, Wendy Wassyng Roworth, and Catherine M. Sama, eds. *Italy's Eighteenth Century: Gender and Culture in the Age of the Grand Tour*. Stanford, CA: Stanford University Press, 2009.

Fisher, Will. *Materializing Gender in Early Modern English Literature and Culture*. Cambridge: Cambridge University Press, 2006.

———. "Debates about Boys versus Women as Erotic Objects." Paper given at the annual meeting of the Renaissance Society of America, Miami, FL: March 22, 2007.

Fletcher, Anthony. *Gender, Sex, and Subordination in England, 1500-1800*. New Haven, CT: Yale University Press, 1995.

Foscolo, Ugo. "'Life of Pius VI', Scritti vari di critica storica e letteraria (1817-1827)." In *Edizione nazionale delle Opere di Ugo Foscolo*. Edited by Uberto Limentani. Florence: Felice Le Monnier, 1978. First published *Edinburgh Review* 62 (1819): 271-95.

Foucault, Michel. *The History of Sexuality: An Introduction*. Translated by Robert Hurley. vol. 1. New York: Vintage Books, 1978.

Freccero, Carla. *Queer/Early/Modern*. Durham, NC: Duke University Press, 2005.

———. "Queer Spectrality: Haunting the Past." In *The Blackwell Companion to Lesbian, Gay, Bisexual, Transgender and Queer Studies*. Edited by George E. Haggerty and Molly McGarry, 194-213. Oxford: Blackwell, 2007.

Freeburg, Victor Oscar. *Disguise Plots in Elizabethan Drama: A Study in Stage Tradition*. New York: Columbia University Press, 1915. Reprint New York: Benjamin Blom, 1965.

Freeman, Elizabeth. "Introduction." *GLQ* 13, nos. 2-3 (2007): 159-76.

———. "Queer Temporalities." *GLQ* 13, nos. 2-3 (2007): 177-95.

———. "Still After." In *After Sex?: On Writing Since Queer Theory*. Special Issue of *South Atlantic Quarterly*. Edited by Janet Halley and Andrew Parker, 495-500. Durham, NC: Duke University Press, 2007.

———. "Time Binds, or, Erotohistoriography." *Social Text* 84-85, nos. 3-4 (October 2005): 57-68.

———. *Time Binds: Queer Temporalities, Queer Histories*. Chicago: University of Chicago Press, 2010.

———. "Turn the Beat Around: Sadomasochism, Temporality, History." *Differences* 19, no. 1 (2008): 32-70.

Freud, Sigmund, et al. *The Standard edition of the complete psychological works of Sigmund Freud (1920-1922), Beyond the pleasure principle, Group psychology and other works*. Translated by James Strachey, vol. 18. London: Hogarth Press, 1955.

———. "Mourning and Melancholia (1917)." In *General Psychological Theory: Papers on Metapsychology*. Translated by Joan Riviere and edited by Philip Rieff, 164-79. New York: Simon and Schuster, 1991. Reprinted 1997.

Friedli, Lynne. "Passing Women: A Study of Gender Boundaries in the Eighteenth Century." In *Sexual Underworlds of the Enlightenment*. Edited by G. S. Rousseau and Roy Porter, 234-60. Chapel Hill: University of North Carolina Press, 1988.

Friedman, Geraldine. "School for Scandal: Sexuality, Race, and National Vice and Virtue in *Miss Marianne Woods and Miss Jane Pirie Against Lady Helen Cumming Gordon*." *Nineteenth-Century Contexts* 27, no. 1 (March 2005): 53-76.

Friedman-Romell, Beth H. "Breaking the Code: Toward a Reception Theory of Theatrical Cross-Dressing in Eighteenth-Century London." *Theatre Journal* 47, no. 4 (1995): 459-79.

Fuss, Diana. *Essentially Speaking: Feminism, Nature & Difference*. New York: Routledge, 1989.

Garber, Marjorie B. *Dream in Shakespeare: From Metaphor to Metamorphosis*. New Haven, CT, and London: Yale University Press, 1974.

———. *Vested Interests: Cross-Dressing and Cultural Anxiety*. New York and London: Routledge, 1992.

Gaspari, Gianmarco. "La Prosa del Settecento, Dalla Negazione alla Rivolta." In *Il mito nella letteratura italiana, Vol. II: Dal Barocco all'illuminismo*. Edited by F. Cossutta, 265-84. Brescia: Morcelliana, 2006.

Gautier, Théophile. *Mademoiselle de Maupin*. Translated with an introduction by Joanna Richardson. Harmondsworth: Penguin, 1981.

Giese, Loreen L.. *Courtships, Marriage Customs, and Shakespeare's Comedies*. New York: Palgrave Macmillan, 2006.

Giuli, Paola. "Tracing a Sisterhood: Corilla Olimpica as Corinne's Unacknowledged Alter Ego." In *The Novel's Seductions: Staël's 'Corinne' in Critical Inquiry*. Edited by Karyna Szmurlo, 165-84. Lewisburg, PA, Bucknell University Press, 1999.

Goldberg, Jonathan. "The Anus in Coriolanus." In *Historicism, Psychoanalysis, and Early Modern Culture*. Edited by Carla Mazzio and Douglas Trevor, 260-71. New York and London: Routledge, 2000.

———. "The History that Will Be." In *Premodern Sexualities*. Edited by Louise Fradenburg and Carla Freccero, 3-21. New York: Routledge, 1996.

———. *Sodometries: Renaissance Texts, Modern Sexualities*. Stanford, CA: Stanford University Press, 1992.

Goldberg, Jonathan, and Madhavi Menon. "Queering History." *PMLA* 120, no. 5 (October 2005): 1608-17.

Gonda, Caroline. "The Odd Women: Charlotte Charke, Sarah Scott and the Metamorphoses of Sex." In *Lesbian Dames: Sapphism in the Long Eighteenth Century*. Edited by John C. Beynon and Caroline Gonda, 111-26. London and Burlington, VT: Ashgate, 2010.

Gonda, Caroline, and Chris Mounsey, eds. *Queer People: Negotiations and Expressions of Homosexuality, 1700-1800*. Lewisburg, PA: Bucknell University Press, 2007.

———, eds. "Friendship and Same-Sex Love." *SEL* 46, no. 3, Special Issue (2006).

González-Palacios, A., ed. *Fasto Romano: Dipinti, sculture, arredi dai palazzi di Roma*. Milano-Roma: Leonardo De Luca Editori, 1991.

Gordon, Mary. *Chase of the wild goose; the story of Lady Eleanor Butler and Miss Sarah Ponsonby, known as The Ladies of Llangollen*. Ruthin: John Jones, 1936.

Goring, Paul. *The Rhetoric of Sensibility in Eighteenth-Century Culture*. Cambridge: Cambridge University Press, 2005.

Gossett, Suzanne. "'Man-Maid, Begone!' Women in Masques." *ELR* 18, no. 1 (1988): 96-113.

Gosson, Stephen. *Playes confuted in fiue actions prouing that they are not to be suffred in a Christian common weale* . . . .London: Thomas Gosson, 1582.

Graziosi, Elizabeth. "Arcadia femminile: presenze e modelli," *Atti e memorie dell'Accademia degli Arcadi* 9, nos. 2-4 (1991-94).

Green, Jamison. *Becoming a Visible Man*. Nashville, TN: Vanderbilt University Press, 2004.

Greenblatt, Stephen, Walter Cohen, Jean E. Howard, and Katharine Eisaman Maus, eds. *The Norton Shakespeare: Based on the Oxford Edition*. 2nd ed. New York: W. W. Norton, 2008.

Greene, Ellen, ed. *Reading Sappho, Contemporary Approaches*, and *Re-Reading Sappho, Reception and Transmission*. 2 vols. Los Angeles: University of California Press, 1996.

Greene, John. *A refutation of the Apology for actors. Diuided into three briefe treatises. Wherein is confuted and opposed all the chiefe groundes and arguments alleaged in defence of playes: and withall in each treatise is deciphered actors*. . . . London: W. White, 1615.

Greppi, Emanuele, and Alessandro Giulini, eds. "Prefazione," in *Carteggio di Pietro e Alessandro Verri*, (Ottobre 1766-luglio 1767) vol. 1, pt. 1; and Milano: Cogliati, 1923.

Guthrie, W[illiam]. "The Preface. With Some Account of the Life and Character of Quinctilian [sic]." In *Quinctilian's* [sic] Institutes of Eloquence. 2 vols. London, 1805.

Habermas, Jürgen. *The Structural Transformation of the Public Sphere: An Inquiry into a Category of Bourgeois Society*. Translated by Thomas Burger with the assistance of Frederick Lawrence. Cambridge, MA: MIT Press, 1989.

Haggerty, George E. "Beckford's Paederasty." In *Illicit Sex: Identity Politics in Early Modern Culture*. Edited by Thomas DiPiero and Pat Gill, 123-42. Athens: University of Georgia Press, 1997.

———. *Horace Walpole's Letters: Masculinity and Friendship in the Eighteenth Century*. Lewisburg, PA: Bucknell University Press, 2011.

———. "Male Love and Friendship in the Eighteenth Century." In *Love, Sex, Intimacy, and Friendship between Men, 1550-1800*. Edited by Katherine O'Donnell and Michael O'Rourke, 70-81. Basingstoke and London: Palgrave Macmillan, 2003.

———. *Men in Love: Masculinity and Sexuality in the Eighteenth Century*. New York: Columbia University Press, 1999.

———. *Queer Gothic*. Urbana: Universtity of Illinois Press, 2006.

———. "Queering Horace Walpole." In "Friendship and Same Sex Love." Edited by Caroline Gonda and Chris Mounsey. *SEL* 46, no. 3, Special Issue (2006): 543–61.

Haggerty, George E., and Molly McGarry, eds. *The Blackwell Companion to Lesbian, Gay, Bisexual, Transgender and Queer Studies.* New York: Blackwell, 2007.

Halberstam, Judith. *Female Masculinities.* Durham, NC: Duke University Press, 1998.

———. *In a Queer Time and Place: Transgender Bodies, Subcultural Lives.* New York: New York University Press, 2005.

———. "Telling Tales: Brandon Teena, Billy Tipton, and Transgender Biography." In *Passing: Identity and Interpretation of Sexuality, Race and Religion.* Edited by Maria Carla Sanchez and Linda Schlossberg, 13-37. New York: New York University Press, 2001.

Halberstam, Judith, and C. Jacob Hale. "Butch/FTM Border Wars: A Note on Collaboration." *GLQ: A Journal of Lesbian and Gay Studies* 4, no. 2 (1998): 283-86.

Halperin, David M. *How to Do the History of Homosexuality.* Chicago: University of Chicago Press, 2002.

Halperin, David M., and Valerie Traub, eds. *Gay Shame.* Chicago: University of Chicago Press, 2009.

Hammill, Graham. *Sexuality and Form: Caravaggio, Marlowe, and Bacon.* Chicago: University of Chicago Press, 2000.

Harris, Joseph. "Disruptive Desires: Lesbian Sexuality in Isaac de Benserade's *Iphis et Iante (1634)*." *Seventeenth-Century French Studies* 24, no. 1 (2002): 151-63.

Hart, Lynda. *Fatal Women: Lesbian Sexuality and the Mark of Aggression.* Princeton, NJ: Princeton University Press, 1994.

Harte, Negley B. "State Control of Dress and Social Change in Pre-Industrial England." In *Trade, Government and Economy in Pre-Industrial England: Essays Presented to F .J. Fisher.* Edited by D.C. Coleman and A.H. John, 132-65. London: Weidenfeld and Nicolson, 1976.

Harvey, A. D. "Prosecutions for Sodomy in England at the Beginning of the Nineteenth Century." *Historical Journal* 21, no. 4 (1978): 939-48.

Hellman, Lillian. *Four Plays by Lillian Hellman. The Children's Hour. Days to Come. The Little Foxes. Watch on the Rhine.* New York: Modern Library, 1942.

Henke, Robert, and Eric Nicholson, eds. *Transnational Exchange in Early Modern Theater.* Aldershot and Burlington, VT: Ashgate, 2008.

Hillman, David. *Shakespeare's Entrails: Belief, Scepticism and the Interior of the Body.* New York: Palgrave Macmillan, 2007.

Hindley, Charles, ed. *The Old Book Collector's Miscellany: Or, a Collection of Readable Reprints of Literary Rarities . . .* , Vol. 4. London: Reeves and Turner, 1873.

Hocquenghem, Guy. *Homosexual Desire.* Translated by Daniella Dangoor. Durham, NC: Duke University Press, 1993.

Hodgdon, Barbara. *The Shakespeare Trade: Performances and Appropriations.* Philadelphia: University of Pennsylvania Press, 1998.

Hooper, Wilfrid. "The Tudor Sumptuary Laws." *English Historical Review* 30, no. 119 (1915): 433- 49.

Hopkins, Lisa. *The Shakespearean Marriage: Merry Wives and Heavy Husbands.* New York: St. Martin's Press, 1998.

Howard, Jean. *The Stage and Social Struggle in Early Modern England.* New York and London: Routledge, 1994.

Huchon, René Louis. *Mrs. Montagu and Her Friend, 1720-1800: A Sketch.* London, John Murray, 1907.

Hull, Suzanne W. *Chaste, Silent and Obedient: English Books for Women, 1475-1640.* San Marino, CA: Huntington Library, 1982.

Hunt, Alan. *Governance and the Consuming Passions: A History of Sumptuary Law.* New York: St. Martin's Press, 1996.

Hunt, Maurice. "The Backward Voice of Coriol-anus." In *Shakespeare Studies,* Vol. 32, 220-39. Madison, NJ: Fairleigh Dickinson University Press, 2004.

Husserl, Edmund. *Cartesian Meditations: An Introduction to Phenomenology.* Translated by Dorion Cairns, 12th ed. Dordrecht: Kluwer Academic Publishers, 1999.

Hyder, David Jalal. "Foucault, Cavailles, and Husserl on the Historical Epistemology of the Sciences." *Perspectives on Science* 11, no. 1 (2003): 107-29.

Irigaray, Luce. *Amante Marine: De Friedrich Nietzsche.* Paris: Minuit, 1980.

———. *Speculum of the Other Woman.* Translated by Gillian C. Gill. Ithaca, NY: Cornell University Press, 1985.

———. *This Sex Which is Not One.* Translated by Catherine Porter with Carolyn Burke. Ithaca, NY: Columbia University Press, 1985.

Jennings, Rebecca. *A Lesbian History of Britain: Love and Sex Between Women Since 1500.* Oxford and Westport, CT: Greenwood World Publishing, 2007.

Johnson, Claudia L. *Equivocal Beings: Gender and Sentimentality in the 1790s, Wollstonecraft, Radcliffe, Burney, Austen.* Chicago: Chicago University Press, 1995.

Johnson, Samuel. Preface to Abraham Cowley, In *The Lives of the English Poets* (1779). "Shakespeare Preface, 1765." The Holloway Pages, Shakespeare Page. http://members.home.net/cjh5801/ Shakespeare-johnson-preface.htm (accessed 7 September 2001).

Jones, Ann Rosalind, and Peter Stallybrass. *Renaissance Clothing and the Materials of Memory.* Cambridge: Cambridge University Press, 2000.

Jordan, Constance. *Renaissance Feminism: Literary Texts and Political Models.* Ithaca, NY and London: Cornell University Press, 1990.

Kaplan, Morris B.. *Sodom on the Thames: Sex, Love and Scandal in Wilde Times.* Ithaca, NY: Cornell University Press, 2005.

Keats, John. *Selected Letters.* Edited by Robert Gittings. Revised, with a new Introduction by Jon Mee. Oxford: Oxford University Press, 2002.

King, Thomas A. *The Gendering of Men 1600-1750: Volume 1, The English Phallus.* Madison: University of Wisconsin Press, 2004.

———. *The Gendering of Men 1600-1760: Volume 2, Queer Articulations.* Madison: University of Wisconsin Press, 2008.

———. "Performing 'Akimbo': Queer Pride and Epistemological Prejudice." In *The Politics and Poetics of Camp.* Edited by Moe Meyer, 23-50. New York: Routledge, 1994.

———. "The Subject at the End of the Voice." In *Considering Calamity.* Edited by Tracy C. Davis and Linda Ben-Zvi. *Assaph, Section C, Studies in the Theatre* 21 (2007): 55-95.

Kittay, Jeffrey, and Wlad Godzich. *The Emergence of Prose: An Essay in Prosaics.* Minneapolis: University of Minnesota Press, 1987.

Kopelson, Kevin. "Seeing Sodomy: Fanny Hill's Blinding Vision." *Journal of Homosexuality* 23 nos. 1-2 (1992): 173-84.

Kosofsky, Eve Sedgwick. "Epistemology of the Closet." In *The Gay and Lesbian Studies Reader*. Edited by Henry Abelove, Claudia Barale, and David Halperin, 45-61. New York: Routledge, 1993.

———. *Novel Gazing: Queer Readings in Fiction*. Durham, NC: Duke University Press, 1997.

———. "Shame, Theatricality, and Queer Performativity: Henry James's *The Art of the Novel*." In *Gay Shame*. Edited by David M. Halperin and Valerie Traub, 49-62. Chicago: University of Chicago Press, 2009.

———. *Touching Feeling*. Durham, NC: Duke University Press, 2003.

Kuchta, David. *The Three-Piece Suit and Modern Masculinity: England, 1550-1850*. Berkeley: University of California Press, 2002.

Lacan, Jacques. "The Mirror Stage as Formative of the Function of the I as revealed in Psychoanalytic Experience." In *Écrits: A Selection*. Translated by Alan Sheridan. London: Tavistock, 1977.

Lanser, Susan. "Put to the Blush': Romantic Irregularities and Sapphic Tropes." *Romantic Praxis* (2005). http://www.rc.umd.edu/praxis/sexuality/lanser/lanser.html (accessed September 20, 2012).

Laqueur, Thomas Walter. *Making Sex: Body and Gender from the Greeks to Freud*. Cambridge, MA, and London: Harvard University Press, 1990.

Lee, Nathaniel. *The rival queens; or, The death of Alexander the Great acted at the Theater-Royal by their majesties servants*. London : Printed for James Magnes and Richard Bentley, 1677.

Legault, Marianne. "Iphis & Iante: traumatisme de l'incomplétude lesbienne au Grand Siècle," *Dalhousie French Studies* (December 2007): 83-93.

Leibacher-Ouvrard, Lise. "Speculum de l'Autre Femme: Les Avatars d'*Iphis et Iante* (Ovide) au XVIIe Siècle." *Papers on French Seventeenth-Century Literature* MLA Convention 2002, 30, no. 59 (2003): 365-77.

Lethal Weapon. Directed by Richard Donner. 1987. Burbank, CA: Warner Home Video, 1997. DVD.

Levine, Laura. *Men in Women's Clothing: Anti-theatricality and Effeminization 1579-1642*. Cambridge: Cambridge University Press, 1994.

Lewalski, Barbara Kiefer. *Writing Women in Jacobean England*. Cambridge, MA: Harvard University Press, 1993.

Little, Arthur L., Jr. "'A Local Habitation and a Name': Presence, Witnessing, and Queer Marriage in Shakespeare's Romantic Comedies." In *Presentism, Gender, and Sexuality in Shakespeare*. Edited by Evelyn Gajowski, 207-36. New York: Palgrave Macmillan, 2009.

———. "The Rites of Queer Marriage in The Merchant of Venice." In *Shakesqueer: A Queer Companion to the Complete Works of Shakespeare*. Edited by Madhavi Menon, 215-24. Durham, NC and London: Duke University Press, 2011.

Lochrie, Karma. *Heterosyncrasies: Female Sexuality When Normal Wasn't*. Minneapolis and London: University of Minnesota Press, 2005.

Locke, John. *Essay concerning Human Understanding*. 2 vols. in folio. 1689.

Love, Heather. *Feeling Backward: Loss and the Politics of Queer History*. Cambridge, MA: Harvard University Press, 2007.

Luzzi, Joseph. *Romantic Italy and the Ghost of Italy*. New Haven, CT: Yale University Press, 2008.

Mackie, Erin. "Desperate Measures: The Narratives of the Life of Mrs. Charlotte Charke." *ELH* 58, no. 4 (1991): 841-65.

MacKinnon, Catherine A. "Does Sexuality Have a History?" In *Discourses of Sexuality from Aristotle to AIDS.* Edited by Domna C. Stanton, 117-36. Ann Arbor: University of Michigan Press, 1992.

Magnusson, Lynne. "Interpreting Women's Sentence." Paper given at the annual meeting of the Renaissance Society of America, Miami, FL: March 23, 2007.

Marcus, Leah S. *Unediting the Renaissance: Shakespeare, Marlowe, Milton.* New York and London: Routledge, 1996.

Marks, Elaine. "Lesbian Intertextuality." In *Homosexuality and French Literature: Cultural Contexts, Critical Texts.* Edited by George Stambolian and Elaine Marks, 353-77. Ithaca, NY: Cornell University Press, 1979.

Masten, Jeffrey. "Is the Fundament a Grave?" In *The Body in Parts: Fantasies of Corporeality in Early Modern Europe.* Edited by David Hillman and Carla Mazzio, 129-45. New York and London: Routledge, 1997.

——. *Textual Intercourse: Collaboration, Authorship, and Sexualities in Renaissance Drama.* Cambridge: Cambridge University Press, 1997.

——. "Toward a Queer Address: The Taste of Letters and Early Modern Male Friendship." *GLQ* 10, no. 3 (2004): 367-84.

McClintock, Anne. *Imperial Leather: Race, Gender and Sexuality in the Colonial Context.* New York and London: Routledge, 1995.

McDonald, Russ. *The Bedford Companion to Shakespeare: An Introduction with Documents.* 2nd ed. Boston and New York: Bedford-St. Martin's, 2001.

——. *Shakespeare and the Arts of Language,* Oxford Shakespeare Topics, Edited by Peter Holland and Stanley Wells. Oxford: Oxford University Press, 2001.

McFarlane, Cameron. *The Sodomite in Fiction and Satire, 1660-1750.* New York: Columbia University Press, 1997.

McGann, Jerome J. *The Poetics of Sensibility: A Revolution in Literary Style.* New York: Oxford University Press, 1996.

McManus, Clare. *Women on the Renaissance Stage: Anne of Denmark and Female Masquing in the Stuart Court, 1590-1619.* Manchester: Manchester University Press, 2002; New York: Palgrave Macmillan, 2002.

McNeil, Peter. "That Doubtful Gender: Macaroni Dress and Male Sexualities." *Fashion Theory: Journal of Dress, Body & Culture* 3, no. 4 (1999): 411-47.

Michasiw, Kim. "Camp, Masculinity, Masquerade." In *Feminism Meets Queer Theory.* Edited by Elizabeth Weed and Naomi Schor, 157-86. Bloomington, IN: Indiana University Press, 1997.

Moe, Nelson. *The View from Vesuvius.* Berkeley: University of California Press, 2002.

Moncrief, Kathryn M. "'Show me a child begotten of thy body that I am father to': Pregnancy, Paternity, and the Problem of Evidence in All's Well That Ends Well." In *Performing Maternity in Early Modern England.* Edited by Kathryn M. Moncrief and Kathryn Read McPherson, 29-43. Aldershot and Burlington, VT: Ashgate, 2007.

Montaigne, Michel de, and John Florio. *THE ESSAYES Or Morall, Politike and Millitairie Discourses of Lo: Michaell de Montaigne . . . new done into English.* London: Val. Sims for Edward Blount, 1603.

Moore, Lisa. *Dangerous Intimacies: Toward a Sapphic History of the British Novel.* Durham, NC: Duke University Press, 1997.

Morris, Brian, ed. *The Taming of the Shrew, by William Shakespeare. The Arden Shakespeare,* 3rd series. Walton-on-Thames: Thomas Nelson and Sons, 1981.

Morris, Marilyn. "Transgendered Perspectives on Premodern Sexualities." In "Friendship and Same Sex Love." Edited by Caroline Gonda and Chris Mounsey. *SEL* 46, no. 3, Special Issue (2006): 585-600.

Most, Glenn W. "Reflecting Sappho." In *Rereading Sappho: Reception and Transmission,* ed. Ellen Greene, 11-35. Los Angeles: University of California Press, 1996.

Muir, Kenneth. "Shakespeare and the Metamorphosis of the Pentameter." In *Shakespeare Survey* 50. Edited by Stanley W. Wells. Cambridge and New York: Cambridge University Press, 1997. Reprinted 2002.

Mullaney, Steven. *The Place of the Stage: License, Play, and Power in Renaissance England.* Chicago and London: University of Chicago Press, 1988.

Nagle, Christopher C. *Sexuality and the Culture of Sensibility in the British Romantic Era.* Basingstoke and New York: Palgrave Macmillan, 2007.

Nancy, Jean-Luc. *Listening.* Translated by Charlotte Mandell. New York: Fordham University Press, 2007.

Nardi, Peter. "Friendship." In *Gay Histories and Cultures: An Encyclopedia.* Edited by George E. Haggerty, John Beynon, and Douglas Eisner, vol. 2. New York: Garland, 2000.

Neely, Carol Thomas. *Broken Nuptials in Shakespeare's Plays.* New Haven, CT, and London: Yale University Press, 1985.

Nestle, Joan. *Persistent Desire: A Femme-Butch Reader.* Boston: Alyson Publications, 1992.

Newman, Karen. *Fashioning Femininity and English Renaissance Drama.* Chicago and London: University of Chicago Press, 1991.

Norton, Rictor. *Mother Clap's Molly House: The Gay Subculture in England, 1700-1830.* London: Gay Men's Press, 1992.

O'Donnell, Katherine, and Michael O'Rourke, eds. *Love, Sex, Intimacy, and Friendship between Men, 1550-1800.* Basingstoke and New York: Palgrave Macmillan, 2003.

O'Driscoll, Sally. "A Crisis of Femininity: Re-Making Gender in Popular Discourse." In *Lesbian Dames: Sapphism in the Long Eighteenth Century.* Edited by John C. Beynon and Caroline Gonda, 45-60. London and Burlington, VT: Ashgate Press, 2010.

———. "The Lesbian and the Passionless Woman: Femininity and Sexuality in Eighteenth-Century England", *The Eighteenth Century: Theory and Interpretation,* 44, nos. 2-3 (Summer-Fall 2003): 103-32.

Oliver, H. J., ed. *The Taming of the Shrew. By William Shakespeare. Oxford World's Classics.* Oxford: Oxford University Press, 1998.

Ong, Walter J. "Latin Language Study as a Renaissance Puberty Rite." *Studies in Philology* 56, no. 2 (1959): 103-24.

———. *Orality and Literacy: The Technologizing of the Word.* London and New York: Routledge, 2002.

———. *The Presence of the Word: Some Prolegomena for Cultural and Religious History, The Terry Lectures.* New Haven, CT and London: Yale University Press, 1967.

Oram, Alison, and Annmarie Turnbull, eds. *The Lesbian History Sourcebook: Love and Sex Between Women in Britain from 1780 to 1970*. London: Routledge, 2001.

Orgel, Stephen. *Impersonations: The Performance of Gender in Shakespeare's England*. Cambridge: Cambridge University Press, 1996.

Ovid. *Heroides*. Translated by Harold C. Cannon. New York: Dutton, 1971.

———. *Metamorphoses Book IX-XII*. Translated by D. E. Hill. Warminster: Aris & Philips, 1999.

Oxford English Dictionary, 20 vols. 2nd ed. Oxford: Clarendon Press, 1989. Online edition, http://www.oed.com.resources.library.brandeis.edu/view/Entry/25436 (June 2011).

Park, Katherine, and Robert A. Nye. "Destiny in Anatomy." *New Republic*, February 13, 1991, 53-57.

Parker, Patricia. *Literary Fat Ladies: Rhetoric, Gender, Property.* London and New York: Methuen, 1987.

———. "Preposterous Reversals: Love's Labor's Lost." *Modern Language Quarterly* 54, no. 4 (1993): 435-82.

Paster, Gail Kern. *The Body Embarrassed: Drama and the Disciplines of Shame in Early Modern England*. Ithaca, NY: Cornell University Press, 1993.

Patterson, Craig. "The Rage of Caliban: Eighteenth-Century Molly Houses and the Twentieth-Century Search for Sexual Identity." In *Illicit Sex: Identity Politics in Early Modern Culture*. Edited by Thomas DiPiero and Pat Gill, 256–69. Athens: University of Georgia Press, 1997.

Patridge, Eric. *Shakespeare's Bawdy*, 3rd ed. New York and London: Routledge, 1968.

Peters Bowron, Edgar. *Pompeo Batoni-Prince of Painters in Eighteenth-Century Rome*. New Haven, CT: Yale University Press, 2007.

Pieretti, Marina. "Margherita Sparapani Gentili Boccapaduli. Ritratto di una gentildonna romana (1735-1820)." *Rivista Storica del Lazio* 8-9 (2000-2001): 13-14.

———. "*Il Viaggio d'Italia* di Margherita Sparapani Gentili Boccapaduli." In *Scritture di donne: La memoria resituita*, eds. Marina Caffiero and Manola Ida Venzo, 61-78. Roma: Viella, 2007.

Pizzamiglio, Gilberto. "Le fortune del romanzo e della letteratura e della letteratura d'intrattenimento." In *Storia della cultura veneta. Dalla Controforma alla fine della repubblica. Il Settecento* 5, no. 1 (Venice: N. Pozza, 1986): 171-96.

Plain Reasons for the Growth of Sodomy in England, to which is added, The Petit Maitre, an odd sort of unpoetical Poem, in the trolly-lolly stile. London, 1728.

A pleasant conceited historie, called The taming of a shrew As it was sundry times acted by the Right honorable the Earle of Pembrook his seruants. London: Peter Short, 1594.

Polachek, Dora E.. "A la recherche du spirituel: L'Italie et les *Dames Gallantes* de Brantôme." *Romanic Review* 94, nos. 1-2 (2003): 227-43.

Pompeati-Lucchini, Arturo. *Vincenzo Monti*. Bologna: N. Zanicchelli, 1928.

Potkay, Adam. *The Fate of Eloquence in the Age of Hume*. Ithaca, NY and London: Cornell University Press, 1994.

Pritchard, Rev. John. *An Account of the Ladies of Llangollen*. Llangollen: Printed and Published by H. Jones at the Atmospheric Gas Printing Works, 1884.

Prosser, Jay. "Queer theory's embrace of the transsexual 'No Place Like Home: The Transgendered Narrative of Leslie Feinberg's *Stone Butch Blues*.'" *Modern Fiction Studies* 41, nos. 3-4 (1995): 483-514.

Prynne, William. *Histrio-mastix The players scourge, or, actors tragaedie* . . . . London: Edward Allde, Augustine Mathewes, Thomas Cotes and William Jones, 1633.

Puttenham, George [Richard]. *The Arte of English Poesie* (London, 1589), facsimile ed., The English Experience Series, 342. Amsterdam: Theatrum Orbis Terrarum, 1971; New York: Da Capo Press, 1971.

Rackin, Phyllis. "Androgyny, Mimesis, and the Marriage of the Boy Heroine on the English Renaissance Stage." *PMLA* 102, no. 1 (1987): 29-41.

Radel, Nicholas F. "Can the Sodomite Speak? Sodomy, Satire, and the Castlehaven Case." In *Love, Sex, Intimacy and Friendship between Men, 1550-1800.* Edited by Katherine O'Donnell and Michael O'Rourke, 148-67. New York: Palgrave Macmillan, 2003.

Rainoldes, John. *Th'overthrow of stage-playes, by the way of controversie betwixt D. Gager and D. Rainoldes* . . . . Middelburg: Richard Schilders, 1599.

Redford, Bruce. *Designing the Life of Johnson, The Lyell Lectures, 2001-2.* Oxford and New York: Oxford University Press, 2002. Reprint 2005.

Reynolds, Margaret. *The Sappho Companion.* Basingstoke and New York: Palgrave Macmillan, 2000.

Rich, Adrienne. "Compulsory Heterosexuality and Lesbian Existence." In *The Lesbian and Gay Studies Reader.* Edited by Henry Abelove, Michèle Aina Barale, and David M. Halperin, 227-54. New York: Routledge, 1993.

Rich, Jennifer A. "'(W)right in the Faultlines': The Problematic of Identity in William Wyler's *The Children's Hour.*" In *The Queer Sixties.* Edited by Patricia Juliana Smith, 187-200. New York: Routledge, 1999.

Richardson, Ruth. *Death, Dissection and the Destitute.* London and New York: Routledge and Kegan Paul, 1987.

Richardson, Samuel. *Clarissa, or, The History of a Young Lady.* Edited by Angus Ross. Penguin Classiscs. London and Harmondsworth: Penguin, 2004.

Robson, Mark. "Looking with Ears, Hearing with Eyes: Shakespeare and the Ear of the Early Modern." *Early Modern Literary Studies* 7, no. 1, Special Issue 8 (2001). http://extra.shu.ac.uk/emls/07-1/robsears.htm (accessed October 4, 2012).

Rogers, Pat. "The Breeches Part." In *Sexuality in Eighteenth-Century Britain.* Edited by Paul-Gabriel Boucé, 244-58. Totawa, NJ: Manchester University Press, 1982.

Roughead, William. "Closed Doors; Or, the Great Drumsheugh Case." In *Bad Companions.* Edinburgh: W. Green, 1930.

Roulston, Christine. "Separating the Inseparables: Female Friendship and its Discontents in Eighteenth-Century France." *Eighteenth-Century Studies* 32, no. 2 (1998-99): 215-31.

Rousseau, G. S. "The Pursuit of Homosexuality in the Eighteenth Century: 'Utterly Confused Category and/or Rich Repository?'" *Eighteenth-Century Life* 9 (May 1985): 132-68.

Roussel, Roy. *The Conversation of the Sexes: Seduction and Equality in Selected Seventeenth- and Eighteenth-Century Texts.* Oxford and New York: Oxford University Press, 1986.

Routledge International Encyclopedia of Queer Culture. Edited by David A. Gerstner. New York: Routledge, 2007.

The Rummy Cove's Delight; a Pretty Considerable Collection of Queer Staves. London: Mitford, n.d. ca.1833.

Rutter, Carol Chillington, ed. *Documents of the Rose Playhouse*. Manchester and New York: Manchester University Press, 1999.

Ryan, Michael. *A Manual of Medical Jurisprudence and State Medicine*. London: Sherwood, Gilbert and Piper, 1836.

Saccamano, Neil. "The Consolations of Ambivalence: Habermas and the Public Sphere." *MLN* 106, no. 3 (1991): 685-98.

Sade, Donatien Alphonse François, comte de. *Augustine de Villeblanche ou le stratagème de l'amour*. 1788. *Œuvres complètes du Marquis de Sade*. Tome treizième. Paris: Au cercle du livre précieux, 1962.

Sappho. *Sapphus, poetriae Lesbiae: fragmenta et elogia, quotquot in auctoribus antiquis graecis et latinis reperiuntur, cum virorum doctorum notis integris / cura et studio Jo. Christiani Wolfii ... qui vitam Sapphonis & indices adjecit*. Hamburgi: apud Abrahamum Vandenhoeck, 1733.

Schafer, Elizabeth, ed. *The Taming of the Shrew. By William Shakespeare. Shakespeare in Production*. Cambridge: Cambridge University Press, 2003.

Schechner, Richard. *Between Theatre and Anthropology*. Philadelphia: University of Pennsylvania Press, 1985.

Schleiner, Louise. *Tudor and Stuart Women Writers*: Women of Letters Series. Bloomington and Indianapolis: Indiana University Press, 1994.

Schnapp, Jeffrey Thompson. *Anno X. La Mostra della Rivoluzione fascista del 1932: genesi - sviluppo - contesto culturale-storico – ricezione*. Afterword by Claudio Fogu. Rome-Pisa: Istituti editoriali e poligrafici internazionali, 2003.

Sedgwick, Eve Kosofsky. *see* Kosofsky, Eve Sedgwick.

Senelick, Laurence. *The Changing Room: Sex, Drag and Theatre*. London and New York: Routledge, 2000.

——. "Mollies or Men of Mode? Sodomy and the Eighteenth-Century London Stage." *Journal of the History of Sexuality* 1, no. 1 (1990), 33-67.

Shakespeare, William. *Mr. VVilliam Shakespeares Comedies, Histories, & Tragedies* . . . . London: Isaac Iaggard, and Ed. Blount, 1623. Published according to the True Original Copies [First Folio], eds. John Heminge and Henry Condell (London, 1623). Brandeis University, The Robert D. Farber University Archives and Special Collections Department, Waltham, MA, online, Perseus Digital Library. http://www.perseus.tufts.edu/cgibin/ptext?doc=Perseus%3Ate xt%3A1999.03.0018 (accessed 25 February 2006).

——. *The Tempest*. Edited by Stephen Orgel. Oxford World's Classics. Oxford and New York: Oxford University Press-World's Classics, 1998.

——. *The Tragedy of Hamlet, Prince of Denmark, in The Riverside Shakespeare*. Edited by G. Blakemore Evans et al. Boston: Houghton Mifflin, 1974.

Shapiro, Michael. "Framing the Taming: Metatheatrical Awareness of Female Impersonation in The Taming of the Shrew." *Yearbook of English Studies* 23 (1993): 143-66.

——. *Gender in Play on the Shakespearean Stage: Boy Heroines and Female Pages*. Ann Arbor: University of Michigan Press, 1994.

Shapiro, Stephen. "Of Mollies: Class and Same-Sex Sexualities in the Eighteenth Century." In *In a Queer Place: Sexuality and Belonging in British and European Contexts*. Edited by Kate Chedgzoy, Emma Francis, and Murray Pratt, 154-76. Aldershot and Burlington, VT: Ashgate, 2002.

Shapiro, Susan C. "'Yon Plumed Dandebrat': Male 'Effeminacy' in English Satire and Criticism", *Review of English Studies*, New Series 39, no. 155 (1988): 400-412.

Silverman, Kaja. *Male Subjectivity at the Margins*. New York: Routledge, 1992.

Singh, Frances B. "Recovering Jane." *Notes and Queries*, January 22, 2011, 1-2.

———. "Digging for Jane and Finding Yorrick." *Nineteenth-Century Contexts* 33, no. 1 (2011): 53-78.

Smith, Amy L. "Performing Marriage with a Difference: Wooing, Wedding, and Bedding in The Taming of the Shrew." *Comparative Drama* 36, no. 3 (2002): 289-320.

Smith, Bruce R. *The Acoustic World of Early Modern England: Attending to the O-Factor*. Chicago and London: University of Chicago Press, 1999.

———. *Homosexual Desire in Shakespeare's England: A Cultural Poetics*. Chicago and London: University of Chicago Press, 1991.

Smollett, Tobias. *The Adventures of Roderick Random 1748*. Edited by Paul-Gabriel Boucé. Oxford: Oxford University Press, 1979.

Sokol, B. J., and Mary Sokol. *Shakespeare, Law, and Marriage*. Cambridge and New York: Cambridge University Press, 2003.

Spacks, Patricia Meyer. "Introduction." In *Augustan Poetry*. New York: Irvington, 1979.

Sprat, Thomas. *History of the Royal Society*. London, 1667.

Staves, Susan. "A Few Kind Words for the Fop," *Studies in English Literature, 1500-1900* 22, no. 3 (1982): 413-28.

Stockton, Will. *Playing Dirty: Sexuality and Waste in Early Modern Comedy*. Minneapolis and London: University of Minnesota Press, 2011.

Straub, Kristina. "The Guilty Pleasures of Female Theatrical Cross-Dressing and the Autobiography of Charlotte Charke." In *Introducing Charlotte Charke: Actress, Author, Enigma*. Edited by Philip E. Baruth 107-36. Urbana: University of Illinois Press, 1999.

———. *Sexual Suspects: Eighteenth-Century Players and Sexual Ideology*. Princeton, NJ: Princeton University Press, 1992.

Stubbes, Philip. *The anatomie of abuses . . . .* London: John Kingston, 1583.

Swetnam, Joseph. *The araignment of leuud, idle, froward, and vnconstant women . . .* London: George Purslowe, 1615.

Taylor, Alfred Swaine. *Medical Jurisprudence*. Edited, with additions, by Edward Hartshorne, M.D. 5th American ed. from the 7th and revised London ed. Philadelphia: Blanchard and Lee, 1861.

———. *The Principles and Practices of Medical Jurisprudence*, 2nd ed., 2 vols. London: Churchill, 1873.

Ten Plagues of England: Plague III, Effeminacy (London, 1757).

Thompson, Ann, ed. *The Taming of the Shrew. By William Shakespeare*. The New Cambridge Shakespeare Series. Cambridge: Cambridge University Press, 1984.

Thompson, C. J. S. *Mysteries of Sex: Women Who Posed as Men and Men Who Impersonated Women*. London: Hutchinson, 1938.

Thompson, Mark, ed. *Leatherfolk: Radical Sex, People, Politics & Practice*. Los Angeles: Alyson Books, 1991.

The Times. "Extraordinary Investigation", *The Times*, January 24, 1833, 5. Reprint "Extraordinary Inquest," *The Norwich Mercury*, February 2, 1833.

———. "The Extraordinary Investigation," January 25, 1833, 3.

———. "The Female Husband," January 17, 1829, 3.

———. "The Female Husband," January 19, 1829, 6.

———. "Inquest", January 15, 1829, 3.

Titus, Mary. "Murdering the Lesbian: Lillian Hellman's *The Children's Hour.*" *Tulsa Studies in Women's Literature* 10, no. 2 (Autumn 1991): 215-32.

Toppan, Bruno. *Du "Caffè" aux "Nuits romaines:" Alessandro Verri romancier.* Nancy: Presses universitaires de Nancy, 1984.

Traub, Valerie. "Friendship's Loss: Alan Bray's Making of History." *GLQ* 10, no. 3 (2004): 339–54.

———. "The Present Future of Lesbian Historiography," In *A Companion to Lesbian, Gay, Bisexual, Transgender, and Queer Studies.* Edited by George E. Haggerty and Molly McGarry. Madlen, MA and Oxford: Blackwell, 2007.

———. *The Renaissance of Lesbianism in Early Modern England.* Cambridge and New York: Cambridge University Press, 2002.

Trench, Melesina. "The Recollections of Melesina Trench with extracts from her Diary and Correspondence", unpublished manuscript, ref. MS 23M93, Hampshire Record Office, n.d. 19th century, 90.

———. *Laura's Dream; or the Moonlanders.* Southampton: J. Hatcher, 1815.

Trumbach, Randolph. "London's Sapphists: from three sexes to four genders in the making of modern culture," in *Body Guards: the Cultural Politics of Gender Ambiguity.* Edited by Julia Epstein and Kristina Straub. London: Routledge, 1991.

——— "London's Sodomites: Homosexual behavior and Western Culture in the 18th Century." *Journal of Social History* 11, no. 1 (1977): 1-33.

———. *Sex and the Gender Revolution.* Vol. 1, Chicago Series on Sexuality, History and Society. Chicago: University of Chicago Press, 1998.

Tuhkanen, Mikko. "Breeding (and) Reading: Lesbian Knowledge, Eugenic Discipline, and *The Children's Hour.*" *Modern Fiction Studies* 48, no. 4 (Winter 2002): 1001-40.

Turley, Hans. *Rum, Sodomy, and the Lash: Piracy, Sexuality, and Masculine Identity.* New York: New York University Press, 2001.

Turner, Mark W. *Backward Glances: Cruising the Queer Streets of New York and London.* London: Reaktion, 2003.

d'Urfey, Thomas. *The Old Mode and the New, or, Country Miss with her Furbeloe.* London, 1703.

Valentine, David. *Imagining Transgender: An Ethnography of a Category.* Durham, NC: Duke University Press, 2007.

Verri, Alessandro. *Le Avventure di Saffo Poetesse di Mitilene a cura di A. Cottignoli.* Roma: Salerno Editrice, 1991.

———. *The adventures of Sappho, poetess of Mitylene.* Translation from the Greek original, newly discovered ... London, 1789.

Vicinus, Martha. *Intimate Friends: Women Who Loved Women 1778-1928.* Chicago: University of Chicago Press, 2004.

Voisine, Jacques. Review of *Metamorfosi dei Lumi. Esperienze dell'"io" e creazione letteraria tra Sette e Ottocento* by ed. Simone Carpentari. Messina and Alessandria: Edizioni dell'Orso, 2000.

Waelti-Walters, Jennifer. *Damned Women: Lesbians in French Novels, 1796-1996.* Montreal: McGill-Queens University Press, 2000.

Wahl, Elizabeth Susan. *Invisible Relations: Representations of Female Intimacy in the Age of Enlightenment.* Stanford, CA: Stanford University Press, 1999.

Walker, Ralph S., ed. *The Correspondence of James Boswell and John Johnston of Grange.* The Yale Editions of the Private Papers of James Boswell. Research Edition. Boswell's Correspondence, Vol. 1. General Editor Frederick W. Hilles. New York: McGraw-Hill, 1966.

Waquet, Françoise. *Le Modèle français et l'Italie savante: Conscience de soi et perception de l'autre dans la république des lettres (1660-1750).* Rome: Ecole francaise de Rome, 1989.

Ward, Edward [Ned]. *The Secret History of Clubs: Particularly the Kit-Cat, Beef-Stake, Vertuosos, Quacks, Knights of the Golden-Fleece, Florists, Beaus, &c. with their original.* 2 parts. London: 1709.

Warner, Michael. "Pleasures and Dangers of Shame." In *Gay Shame.* Edited by David M. Halperin and Valerie Traub, 49-62. Chicago: University of Chicago Press, 2009.

Wiesen Cook, Blanche. "'Women Alone Stir My Imagination': Lesbianism and the Cultural Tradition." *Signs* 4, no. 4 (1979): 718-39.

Wells, Stanley W., and Gary Taylor, "No Shrew, A Shrew, and The Shrew: Internal Revision in The Taming of the Shrew." In *Shakespeare: Text, Language, Criticism: Essays in Honour of Marvin Spevack.* Edited by Bernhard Fabian and Kurt Tetzeli von Rosador, 351-70. Hildesheim, Zurich, and New York: Olms-Weidman, 1987.

Wheelwright, Julie. *Amazons and Military Maids: Women Who Dressed as Men in the Pursuit of Life, Liberty and Happiness.* Boston and London: Pandora, 1989.

Whigham, Frank. "Interpretation at Court: Courtesy and the Performer-Audience Dialectic." *New Literary History* 14, no. 3, Renaissance Literature and Contemporary Theory (Spring 1983): 623-39.

Williams, Gordon. *A Glossary of Shakespeare's Sexual Language.* Atlantic Highlands, NJ: Athlone Press, 1997.

———. *Shakespeare's Sexual Language: A Glossary.* London: Continuum International Publishing, 2006. http://site.ebrary.com/lib/brandeis/Doc?id=10224687&ppg=69

Wilson, Elizabeth. *Adorned in Dreams: Fashion and Modernity.* Berkeley: University of California Press, 1985.

Wolf, Johann Christoph. *Muliervm Græcarum quae Oratione Prosa Usae Sunt Fragmenta et Elogia Graece et Latine cvm Viorvm Doctorvm Notis et Indicibvs.* Göttingen: Abrahamvm Vandenhoeck, 1739.

Wolfthal, Diane. *In and Out of the Marital Bed: Seeing Sex in Renaissance Europe.* New Haven, CT, and London: Yale University Press, 2010.

Woods, Marianne, Jane Pirie, and Helen Cumming Gordon. *Miss Marianne Woods and Miss Jane Pirie against Dame Helen Cumming Gordon.* New York: Arno Press, 1975.

Wordsworth, William. *Lyrical Ballads with other poems.* London: Longman and Rees, 1800.

Wright, George T. *Shakespeare's Metrical Art.* Berkeley and Los Angeles: University of California Press, 1988.

Wroth, Lady Mary. *The Countesse of Mountgomeries Urania . . . .* London: John Marriott and John Grismand, 1621.

Young, Michael B. *King James and the History of Homosexuality.* New York: New York University Press, 2000.

Young, Robert J. C. *Colonial Desire: Hybridity in Theory, Culture and Race.* London: Routledge, 1996.

Zimmerman, Susan, ed. "Disruptive Desire: Artifice and Indeterminacy in Jacobean Comedy." In *Erotic Politics: Desire on the Renaissance Stage*, 39-61. New York and London: Routledge, 1992.

Zirpolo, Lilian H. "Christina of Sweden's Patronage of Bernini: The Mirror of Truth Revealed by Time." *Women's Art Journal* 26, no. 1 (2005): 38-43.

Chris Mounsey worked for several years in theatre before an accident and four months' immobility, in which reading was the only possible occupation, led to an academic career. Degrees in Philosophy, Comparative Literature and English from the University of Warwick followed, and a doctorate on Blake founded an interest in the literature of the eighteenth century. Dr. Mounsey, who now teaches at the University of Winchester, is author of *Christopher Smart: Clown of God* and editor of *Presenting Gender* and *Queer People* (for Bucknell University Press). He is also author of *Understanding the Poetry of William Blake through a Dialectic of Contraries* (Lewiston, 2011) and *Being the Body of Christ* (Sheffield, 2012).

Clorinda Donato is Professor of French and Italian at California State University, Long Beach. She has published extensively on eighteenth-century encyclopedism, including the co-edited volumes *The Encyclopédie in an Age of Revolution* with Robert Maniquis, and *Une Encyclopédie à vocation européene: le Dictionnaire universel raisonné des connaissances humaines de F.-B. De Felice (1770 – 1780)*. Her articles cover a wide range of eighteenth-century topics. Recently she has been working on figures of the Italian enlightenment including Giovanni Bianchi, the Prince of San Severo, Gaetano Filangieri, and Alessandro Verri. This article is part of a much larger project on Italian eighteenth-century sapphism.

Caroline Gonda is a Fellow and Director of Studies in English at St. Catharine's College, Cambridge. Her essays have appeared in *Romanticism: The Journal of Romantic Culture and Criticism, Women's Writing, The British Journal of Eighteenth-Century Studies*, and *SEL: Studies in English Literature*. Her book, *Reading Daughters' Fictions, 1709-1834: Novels and Society from Manley to Edgeworth*, was published in 1996.

George E. Haggerty is Professor of English at the University of California at Riverside. He served as editor of *The Encyclopedia of Gay Histories and Cultures* (2000), and his books include *Unnatural Affections: Women and Fiction in the Later Eighteenth Century* (1998), *Men in Love: Masculinity and Sexuality* (Columbia, 1999) and *Queer Gothic* (2006).

Thomas A King is Associate Professor of Restoration and Eighteenth-Century Studies, and Gender Studies at Brandeis University and author of *The Gendering of Men, 1600-1750, Volume 1: the English Phallus* and *The Gendering of Men, 1600-1750, vol. 2: Queer Articulations* (2004 and 2008).

Katharine Kittredge is Associate Professor of English at Ithaca College. She is the editor of *Lewd and Notorious: Female Transgression in the Eighteenth Century*, (2003) and also of *Power and Poverty: Old Age in the Pre-Industrial Past* (2002).

Dr. Marianne Legault was born and raised in Montreal, Canada. She completed her PhD in Vancouver at the University of British Columbia in 2003. She currently teaches seventeenth- and eighteenth-century French literature in the Department of Critical Studies. Her research areas include women's literary production in seventeenth- and eighteenth-century France—with special emphasis on novels, fairy tales, and drama—and queer studies. She has written on the representations of female friendships in seventeenth-century French literature. She has recently published *Narrations déviantes : L'intimité entre femmes dans l'imaginaire français du dix-septième siècle* (2008).

Chris Mounsey worked for several years in theatre before an accident and four months' immobility, in which reading was the only possible occupation, led to an academic career. Degrees in Philosophy, Comparative Literature and English from the University of Warwick followed, and a doctorate on Blake founded an interest in the literature of the eighteenth century. Dr. Mounsey, who now teaches at the University of Winchester, is author of *Christopher Smart: Clown of God* and editor of *Presenting Gender* and *Queer People*. He is also author of *Understanding the Poetry of William Blake through a Dialectic of Contraries* (2011) and *Being the Body of Christ* (2012).

Christopher Nagle is Associate Professor of English at Western Michigan University where he specializes in women's writing of the long eighteenth century, British and Irish Romanticism, gender studies, and critical theory. He has been a visiting summer fellow at the University of California, Berkeley and at the University of Notre Dame's Keough-Naughton Institute for Irish Studies. His previous work has appeared in *English Literary History, Comparative Drama*, and *Persuasions: The Jane Austen Journal*. He is the author of *Sexuality and the Culture of Sensibility in the British Romantic Era* (2008).

Sally O'Driscoll is Associate Professor of English and Women's Studies at Fairfield University. She has published widely in the field of sexuality studies.

David L. Orvis gained his doctorate in English literature at the University of Arizona, and now works at Appalachian State University. His teaching and research interests include early modern English literature, especially the drama of Shakespeare and his contemporaries, and LGBT Studies and Queer Theory. His dissertation, tentatively titled "[E]Strange[d] Bedfellows in Early Modern England," centers on representations of bedfellowship in early modern English texts, including playtexts, prose works, poems, translations of classical texts, sermons, trial proceedings, medical treatises, and theatrical polemics. Exploring the larger social/cultural contexts in which bedfellowship circulates (sexuality, gender, class), he analyzes the importance of bedfellowship as both a widely recognized, highly publicized cultural institution and a private, intimate space. With Linda Phillips Austern and Kari Boyd McBride, he edited *Psalms in the Early Modern World* (2011).

Chris Roulston is Associate Professor of French and Women's Studies at the University of Western Ontario, Canada. She has published articles on Rousseau, women's epistolary writing, women's friendship, marriage and the visual arts in the eighteenth century. She has recently published *Narrating Marriage in Eighteenth-Century England and France* (2010).